Who's Who
OF THE
BIBLE

Who's Who
OF THE
BIBLE

Martin H. Manser
& Debra K. Reid

LION

The authors assert the moral right
to be identified as the authors of this work

A Lion Book
an imprint of
Lion Hudson plc
Wilkinson House, Jordan Hill Road,
Oxford OX2 8DR, England
www.lionhudson.com
ISBN 978 0 7459 5518 6

Distributed by:
UK: Marston Book Services, PO Box 269, Abingdon, Oxon,
OX14 4YN
USA: Trafalgar Square Publishing, 814 N. Franklin Street, Chicago,
IL 60610
USA Christian Market: Kregel Publications, PO Box 2607,
Grand Rapids, Michigan 49501

First edition 2012
10 9 8 7 6 5 4 3 2 1 0

Acknowledgments
Scripture quotations taken from the Holy Bible, New International
Version, copyright © 1979, 1984, 2011 by Biblica (formerly International
Bible Society). Used by permission of Hodder & Stoughton Publishers, an
Hachette UK company. All rights reserved. 'NIV' is a registered trademark
of Biblica (International Bible Society). UK trademark number 1448790.

The text paper used in this book has been made from wood
independently certified as having come from sustainable forests.

A catalogue record for this book is available
from the British Library

Typeset in 9/11 ITC Stone Serif
Printed and bound by MPG Books

Author websites
http://www.martinmanser.com
http://www.spurgeons.ac.uk

The authors would like to thank Nicola Bull, Alison Hull, Richard Johnson, Lawrence Osborn, and Jessica Tinker for their editorial work on this book.

Contents

Special Features and Articles

Books of the Bible in Alphabetical Order

Books of the Apocrypha in Alphabetical Order

Introduction

The Bible includes the names of over 3,000 different individuals. *Who's Who of the Bible* is an exhaustive listing of every named person in the 66 books of the Bible, together with a concise description of their life and significance. You will find this book helpful to answer such questions as *Why is Abraham important? Who were Hophni, Jezebel, Eliphaz, or Phoebe? Who were Ananias and Sapphira? What did Epaphroditus do?*

Alphabetical listing of names

An alphabetical list of every personal name with page numbers can be found at the end of the book. Look up the name you want in this list and then turn to the page number given:

Aaron	43
Abaddon	252
Abagtha	196

In the alphabetical listing many people (where there are multiple entries [1], [2], etc. – see below) are given a brief description to help you locate which Ananias, Joseph, Simon, etc., you are looking for:

Ananias   Sapphira's husband [1] 235; Christian in Damascus [2] 236; high priest [3] 241

Dates

Dates have been added after each name to show when the person lived. In many instances it is not possible to give exact dates, so many dates are shown with c. (circa. = 'about'), for example:

Joshua
(c. 1480–1370 BC)

Rahab
(late C15th BC)

For additional notes on dates, see pages 13, 20, 57 and 121.[1]

Arrangement of entries

Entries are arranged by the first Bible book in which the person is mentioned.

This has the advantage that individuals in family groups or people in the same part of the Bible appear together:

Luke

Simeon[2]
(C1st BC)
A righteous and devout man on whom the Holy Spirit rested. He was in the temple courts in Jerusalem when Jesus' parents presented him there to fulfil the requirements of the Law. He recognized Jesus as the promised Messiah and blessed him and his family and praised God.

📖 (2:25–35)

Anna
(C1st BC)
Daughter of Phanuel, from the tribe of Asher. She was very old and had been a widow for many years when Mary[1] and Joseph[6] brought Jesus to the temple. She worshipped continuously in the temple and when she saw Jesus she praised God and spoke about the redemption he would bring.

📖 (2:36–38)

Where more than one person has the same name, the different individuals are given the numbers [1], [2], etc., generally in the order in which they appear in the Bible text.

At the end of each entry the most important Bible references to that person are listed, preceded by the symbol 📖. Where the name of the Bible book is omitted, it is the one in which the entry is included.

---

1 The main sources of reference for these dates are:

McFall, Leslie, 'The Chronology of Saul and David', Journal of the Evangelical Theological Society, 53:3 (September 2010), pages 475-533

Oswalt, J.N., 'Chronology of the Old Testament', International Standard Bible Encyclopedia: Volume 1 Eerdmans, 1979, pages 673-685

Thiele, Edwin R. The Mysterious Numbers of the Hebrew Kings Kregel, revised edition, 1994

Variants and alternative names

The spellings of most names is definitive; however, a few names have variants. We have used the New International Version of the Bible (2011 edition) as a basis to give guidance on spellings; variant spellings are shown in brackets:

Abimelek[1] (Abimelech)
(reigned mid C19th BC)
King of Gerar who was deceived by Abraham...

Alternative names are also included:

Sarai/Sarah
(1942–1815 BC)
Wife of Abram who accompanied him...

Hananiah[15], Mishael[3], Azariah[25]
(born late C7th BC)
Also known respectively by the Babylonian names Shadrach, Meshach and Abednego...

Grouped entries

To save space, sometimes names of people are grouped together:

Euodia, Syntyche
(mid C1st AD)
Two Christian women in the church at Philippi...

From the tribe of Issachar

Uzzi[2], Rephaiah[3], Jeriel, Jahmai, Ibsam
(mid C17th BC)
Sons of Tola[1]. Grandsons of Issachar[1]...

Izrahiah
(late C17th BC)
Son of Uzzi[2]. Grandson of Tola[1]...

Michael[5], Obadiah[3], Joel[6], Ishiah[1] (Isshiah)
(early C16th BC)
Sons of Izrahiah. Grandsons of Uzzi[2]...

Additional features

In-depth feature articles and family trees provide additional information, e.g. on the names and titles of God, Jesus Christ and the Holy Spirit, and the genealogies of individuals such as Abraham and David. See list of special features on p. 7.

Cross-references

Certain entries direct you to a different location:

Nathanael
(C1st AD)
See **Bartholomew** *in Matthew, p. 224.*
📖 (1:45–51)

Appendix

Selected entries from the books of the Apocrypha (deuterocanonical books) are included in an appendix to give the main personal names in those books.

Note that in the Appendix numbers are not added after names of individuals whose names have already been included in the main part of the book, although the names are included in the Index and are marked by [Ap].

Abbreviations

AD	anno Domini; after Christ
AM	anno Mundi; from the creation of the earth: see note on page 14
Ap	(in index) entry in the Apocrypha
BC	before Christ
C	century
c	(in family trees) concubine
c.	circa; about
m	(in family trees) married

Martin H. Manser
Debra K. Reid

1 The Pentateuch

The Pentateuch is the name given to the first five books of the Old Testament of the Bible (Genesis, Exodus, Leviticus, Numbers and Deuteronomy). These books are collectively called 'The books of the Law' or 'The Torah' or 'The Books of Moses'. They begin with the act of creation and then trace the earliest beginnings of the Israelite nation until the death of Moses. Abraham and his descendants are introduced as the fathers of this nation. The Israelite people face oppression in Egypt, and Moses leads them from Egypt, into the wilderness, travelling towards the Promised Land of Canaan. First, however, the God of Abraham appears to Moses and reveals his love and purposes for the Israelite people – expressed in terms of a covenant commitment (a binding agreement) to them. The people are called to respond with love and loyalty to God. In the uncertain years before entering Canaan, God's people begin to regulate their community and religious life in the light of this covenant.

Because of the impossibility of establishing precise dates for Genesis 1–11, the dates from Adam to Terah have been given in years AM (Anno Mundi: from the creation of the earth). The ages that are given in Genesis have been taken at face value.

Genesis

Adam
(0–930 AM)

The first man in the Bible, created by God, made in the image of God and described as 'the son of God'. His name sounds like the Hebrew word for 'ground' and points to the origin of man whom God forms 'from the dust of the ground' (2:7). Adam lived in the Garden of Eden where Eve became his 'helper'. He was the father of Cain, Abel and Seth and other unnamed sons and daughters. He lived for 930 years. Adam is also a generic term for the human race. In the light of Adam's involvement in the first sin of human beings against God (the Fall, Genesis 3), his name is used in the New Testament to refer to human rebellion against God, so contrasting with Jesus Christ, 'the new Adam'. Luke's genealogy of Jesus begins with Adam. Paul explains the different roles of men and women in the church by referring back to Adam and Eve.

(2:20; 3:17, 20–21; 4:1, 25; 5:3–5; 1 Chronicles 1:1; Hosea 6:7; Luke 3:38; Romans 5:12–14; 1 Corinthians 11:8–9; 15:22, 45; 1 Timothy 2:13–14; Jude 14)

Eve
(0–? AM)

The first woman in the Bible – the helper and then wife of Adam, formed from Adam's rib. Mother of Cain, Abel and Seth and other sons and daughters. Her name means 'living' and the Bible describes her as 'mother of all the living'. In Genesis 3, Eve succumbs first to the serpent's temptation and then encourages her husband to succumb to temptation too.

📖 (2:20–25; 3:1–21; 4:1–2, 25; 2 Corinthians 11:3; 1 Timothy 2:13–14)

Cain
(?C1st AM)

Eldest son of Adam and Eve. Father of Enoch[1]. Grandfather of Irad. A farmer. He was the first murderer (he killed his brother Abel) and following this his life was unsettled although God protected him.

📖 (4:1–17, 24–25; Hebrews 11:4; 1 John 3:12; Jude 11)

Abel
(?C1st AM)

Second son of Adam and Eve. A shepherd who brought the best of his flocks to God as an offering. Murdered by his brother but in Hebrews he is commended for his righteousness and faith.

📖 (4:2–10, 25; Matthew 23:35; Luke 11:51; Hebrews 11:4; 12:24)

God

The existence of God is assumed, not argued, in the Bible. God is the Creator and Redeemer of the world. He reveals himself to people in Scripture and supremely in Jesus Christ. The Bible emphasizes that God is personal and that he is completely trustworthy. He is the Father of Jesus Christ and of all believers. Christianity sees God as Trinity: only one God in three persons: Father, Son and Holy Spirit. Each person of the Trinity is distinct from, but also interrelated with, the others. All three persons are divine. See also **Jesus Christ**, p. 219; **Holy Spirit**, p. 234.

The titles and names of God

Although there are many names for God in the Bible, one name is particularly significant: YHWH, which is God's personal name and is pronounced something like 'Yahweh'. When reading their Scriptures, the Jews considered God's name to be too holy to be spoken and so replaced that name by the title 'the Lord', which is also the common term for God in the New Testament. The name *Yahweh* was explained to Moses as 'I am who I am' (Exodus 3:13–14). It suggests that God is eternal, unique, unchangeable. He is actively present with his people as their Redeemer and committed to them as their covenant Lord. In English Bibles, the name Yahweh is usually printed as 'the Lord'.

Names based on Yahweh (Hebrew YHWH) ('The Lord')

Yahweh-sabaoth	The Lord of Hosts (Lord Almighty)	1 Samuel 17:45
Yahweh-shalom	The Lord is peace	Judges 6:24
Yahweh-shamma	The Lord is there	Ezekiel 48:35
Yahweh-tsidkenu	The Lord is our righteousness	Jeremiah 23:6
Yahweh-yireh	The Lord provides	Genesis 22:8, 14

Names with El ('God')

El Elyon	God Most High	Genesis 14:18–20
El Olam	God Eternal	Genesis 21:33
El Shaddai	God Almighty	Genesis 17:1

1 The Pentateuch

Other common names and descriptions

Ancient of Days	Daniel 7:9, 13, 22
Creator	Isaiah 40:28
Father	Psalm 68:5–6; Mark 14:36; John 10:27–30
First and Last	Isaiah 44:6
Fortress	Psalm 18:2
God of peace	Romans 15:33
God of your fathers	Exodus 3:13
Holy One of Israel	Isaiah 12:6
Hope of Israel	Jeremiah 17:13
Husband	Hosea 2:16
Judge	Psalm 94:2
King	Isaiah 6:5; 1 Timothy 6:15
Living God	Psalm 84:2
Mighty One	Luke 1:49
Name	1 Kings 8:29
Redeemer	Isaiah 43:14
Refuge	Psalms 46:1; 91:2
Rock	Psalm 144:1
Saviour	Titus 1:3
Shepherd	Psalm 23:1
Shield	Genesis 15:1
Stronghold	Psalm 18:2

Enoch[1]
(?C2nd AM)

Son of Cain. Grandson of Adam. Father of Irad. Grandfather of Mehujael.

📖 (4:17–18)

Irad
(?C3rd AM)

Son of Enoch. Father of Mehujael. Grandfather of Methushael.

📖 (4:18)

Mehujael
(?C4th AM)

Son of Irad. Grandson of Enoch. Father of Methushael. Grandfather of Lamech[1].

📖 (4:18)

Methushael
(?C5th AM)

Son of Mehujael. Grandson of Irad. Father of Lamech[1].

📖 (4:18)

Lamech[1]
(?C6th AM)

Son of Methushael. Grandson of Mehujael. Father of Jabal and Jubal, Tubal-Cain and Naamah. First man to have more than one wife. He murdered someone who had injured him, so taking vengeance that exceeded what was legitimate for the crime.

📖 (4:18–19, 23–24)

Adah[1]
(?C6th AM)

Wife of Lamech[1]. Mother of Jabal and Jubal.

📖 (4:19-20, 23)

Zillah
(?C6th AM)

Wife of Lamech[1]. Mother of Tubal-Cain and Naamah.

📖 (4:19, 22-23)

Jabal
(?C7th AM)

Son of Lamech[1] and Adah[1]. A tent dweller and keeper of livestock.

📖 (4:20)

Jubal
(?C7th AM)

Son of Lamech[1] and Adah[1]. A musician (stringed instruments and pipes).

📖 (4:21)

Tubal-Cain
(?C7th AM)

Son of Lamech[1] and Zillah. Brother of Naamah[1]. Maker of bronze and iron tools.

📖 (4:22)

Naamah[1]
(?C7th AM)

Daughter of Lamech[1] and Zillah. Sister of Tubal-Cain.

📖 (4:22)

Seth
(130-1042 AM)

Third son of Adam and Eve, born after Abel's death. Father of Enosh. Lived 912 years. His descendants were mainly upright and followed God's ways (in contrast to those of his brother Cain). Mentioned in the genealogy of Jesus.

📖 (4:25-26; 5:4, 6-8; 1 Chronicles 1:1; Luke 3:38)

Enosh
(235-1140 AM)

Son of Seth. Grandson of Adam. Father of Kenan (and other sons and daughters). Lived 905 years. Mentioned in the genealogy of Jesus.

📖 (4:26; 5:6-7, 9-11; 1 Chronicles 1:1; Luke 3:38)

Kenan
(325-1235 AM)

Son of Enosh. Father of Mahalalel[1] (and other sons and daughters). Lived 910 years. Mentioned in the genealogy of Jesus.

📖 (5:9-14; Luke 3:37)

Mahalalel[1]
(395-1290 AM)

Son of Kenan. Father of Jared (and other sons and daughters). Lived 895 years. Mentioned in the genealogy of Jesus.

📖 (5:12-17; Luke 3:37)

Jared
(460-1422 AM)

Son of Mahalalel[1]. Father of Enoch[2] (and other sons and daughters). Lived 962 years. Mentioned in the genealogy of Jesus.

📖 (5:15-20; Luke 3:37)

Enoch[2]
(622-987 AM)

Son of Jared. Father of Methuselah (and other sons and daughters). Lived 365 years. He 'walked faithfully with God' and then he did not die but 'God took him away'. Mentioned in the genealogy of Jesus. Commended in Hebrews as a man of faith.

📖 (5:18-24; Luke 3:37; Hebrews 11:5; Jude 14-15)

Methuselah
(687-1656 AM)

Son of Enoch[2]. Father of Lamech[2] (and other sons and daughters). Grandfather of Noah. Oldest man in the Bible: lived for 969 years. Mentioned in the genealogy of Jesus.

📖 (5:21–27; Luke 3:37)

Lamech[2]
(874–1651 AM)

Son of Methuselah. Father of Noah[1] (and other sons and daughters). Lived for 777 years.

📖 (5:25–31)

Noah[1]
(1056–2006 AM)

Son of Lamech[2]. Grandson of Methuselah. Father of Shem, Ham and Japheth. His name sounds like the Hebrew word meaning 'comfort'. Noah was 'a righteous man, blameless' who 'walked faithfully with God' at a time when humanity had become evil and corrupt. Following God's instructions, Noah built an ark so he, his family and animals were saved from the flood of judgment that God sent. He stayed in the ark for one year and upon leaving it God blessed Noah and made a promise that his descendants would be numerous. God also promised Noah that he would not destroy the earth again by a flood. The rainbow was given as a sign of that promise. Noah lived 950 years. In the New Testament, the flood is a reminder of the unexpected nature of divine acts of judgment. In Hebrews, Noah is commended as a man of faith.

📖 (5:28–32; 6:1 – 9:29; 1 Chronicles 1:3–4; Matthew 24:37–39; Luke 17:26–27; Hebrews 11:7; 1 Peter 3:20–21)

Shem
(1558–2158 AM)

Son of Noah[1]. Grandson of Lamech[2]. Entered the ark with his wife. After the flood, he received Noah's blessing because he preserved Noah's dignity. He became father of Arphaxad (and other sons and daughters) and the Semite clans from whom Abram descended. Lived for 600 years. Mentioned in the genealogy of Jesus.

📖 (5:32; 6:10; 7:13; 9:18–29; 10:21–31; 11:10–11; 1 Chronicles 1:4, 17; Luke 3:36)

Ham
(c.1560–? AM)

Youngest son of Noah[1]. Grandson of Lamech[2]. Entered the ark with his wife. After the flood he disgraced Noah who then cursed him. He became father of Cush, Egypt, Put and Canaan, from whom the Canaanite clans descended.

📖 (5:32; 6:10; 7:13; 9:18–29; 10:6–20; 1 Chronicles 1:4, 8)

Japheth
(1556–? AM)

Son of Noah[1]. Grandson of Lamech[2]. Entered the ark. After the flood he was blessed by Noah because he preserved Noah's dignity. He became father to seven sons.

📖 (5:32; 6:10; 7:13; 9:18–29; 10:2–4; 1 Chronicles 1:4–5)

Canaan
(?late C17th AM)

Son of Ham. Grandson of Noah[1]. His firstborn son was Sidon from whom the Canaanite clans descended. Noah cursed Canaan's descendants.

📖 (9:18, 22, 25–27; 10:6, 15–19)

Gomer[1], Magog, Madai, Javan, Tubal, Meshek[1] (Meshech), Tiras
(?late C17th AM)

Sons of Japheth. Grandsons of Noah[1].

📖 (10:2–3; 1 Chronicles 1:5)

Ashkenaz, Riphath, Togarmah
(?early C18th AM)

Sons of Gomer[1]. Grandsons of Japheth.

📖 (10:3; 1 Chronicles 1:6)

Elishah, Tarshish[1]
(?early C18th AM)

Sons of Javan. Grandsons of Japheth. Tarshish was the ancestor of sea traders.

(10:4–5; 1 Chronicles 1:7)

Cush[1], Egypt (Mizraim), Put
(?late C17th AM)

Sons of Ham. Grandsons of Noah[1]. Cush was the father of Nimrod.

(10:6–8; 1 Chronicles 1:8–9)

Seba, Havilah[1], Sabtah/Sabta, Raamah, Sabteka
(?early C18th AM)

Sons of Cush[1]. Grandsons of Ham.

(10:7; 1 Chronicles 1:9)

Sheba[1], Dedan[1]
(?mid C18th AM)

Sons of Raamah. Grandsons of Cush[1].

(10:7; 1 Chronicles 1:9)

Nimrod
(?early C18th AM)

Son of Cush[1]. Grandson of Ham. Known as 'a mighty warrior/hunter'. He made Babylon, Uruk, Akkad and Kalneh important centres in Shinar and then built Nineveh, Rehoboth Ir, Calah and Resen.

(10:8–12; 1 Chronicles 1:10)

Sidon
(?early C18th AM)

Firstborn son of Canaan. Grandson of Ham.

(10:15; 1 Chronicles 1:13)

Eber[1]
(1723–2187 AM)

Descendant of Shem. Son of Shelah[1]. Grandson of Arphaxad. Father of Peleg and Joktan (and other sons and daughters). Lived 464 years. Mentioned in the genealogy of Jesus.

(10:21, 25; 11:14–17; 1 Chronicles 1:18–19; Luke 3:35)

Elam[1], Ashur (Asshur)
(?late C17th AM)

Sons of Shem. Grandsons of Noah[1].

(10:22; 1 Chronicles 1:17)

Arphaxad
(1658–2096 AM)

Son of Shem. Grandson of Noah[1]. Father of Shelah[1] (and other sons and daughters). Lived 438 years. Mentioned in the genealogy of Jesus.

(10:22, 24; 11:10–13; 1 Chronicles 1:17–18, 24; Luke 3:36)

Lud/Lydia[1], Aram[1]
(?late C17th AM)

Sons of Shem. Grandsons of Noah[1].

(10:22; 1 Chronicles 1:17)

Uz[1], Hul, Gether, Meshek[2] (Meshech)
(?early C18th AM)

Sons of Aram[1]. Grandsons of Shem.

(10:23; 1 Chronicles 1:17)

Shelah[1]
(1693–2126 AM)

Son of Arphaxad. Grandson of Shem. Father of Eber[1] (and other sons and daughters). Lived 403 years. Mentioned in the genealogy of Jesus.

(10:24; 11:14–15; 1 Chronicles 1:18; Luke 3:35)

Peleg
(1757–1996 AM)

Son of Eber[1]. Grandson of Shelah[1]. His name means 'divide' and symbolized that the earth was divided in his lifetime. Father of Reu (and other sons and daughters). Lived 239 years. Mentioned in the genealogy of Jesus.

(10:25; 11:16–19; 1 Chronicles 1:19; Luke 3:35)

Joktan
(?late C18th AM)

Son of Eber[1]. Grandson of Shelah[1]. Father of 13 sons.

(10:25–29; 1 Chronicles 1:19–23)

Almodad, Sheleph, Hazarmaveth, Jerah, Hadoram[1], Uzal, Diklah, Obal, Abimael, Sheba[2], Ophir, Havilah[2], Jobab[1]
(?early C19th AM)

Sons of Joktan. Grandsons of Eber[1].

📖 (10:26–29; 1 Chronicles 1:20–23)

Reu
(1787–2026 AM)

Son of Peleg. Grandson of Eber[1]. Father of Serug (and other sons and daughters). Lived 239 years. Mentioned in the genealogy of Jesus.

📖 (11:18–21; 1 Chronicles 1:25; Luke 3:35)

Serug
(1819–2049 AM)

Son of Reu. Grandson of Peleg. Father of Nahor[1] (and other sons and daughters). Great-grandfather of Abraham. Lived 230 years. Mentioned in the genealogy of Jesus.

📖 (11:20–23; 1 Chronicles 1:26; Luke 3:35)

Nahor[1]
(1849–1997 AM)

Son of Serug. Grandson of Reu. Father of Terah (and other sons and daughters). Grandfather of Abraham. Lived 148 years. Mentioned in the genealogy of Jesus.

📖 (11:22–26; 1 Chronicles 1:26; Luke 3:34)

Terah
(1878–2083 AM/2082–1877 BC)

Son of Nahor[1]. Grandson of Serug. Father of Abram, Nahor[2] and Haran. He left Ur of the Chaldeans with his family and set out for Canaan. They settled in Harran where Terah died. Lived 205 years. Mentioned in the genealogy of Jesus.

📖 (11:24–32; 1 Chronicles 1:26; Luke 3:34)

For the period from Abraham to David, there is much controversy about the chronology, which depends entirely on when the Israelites entered and then left Egypt. Major chronological problems remain whichever dates are assumed. Without wishing to be dogmatic on the issue, for the sake of the dates in this dictionary we have worked within the framework of an entry into Egypt in 1662 BC, with the exodus occurring in 1447 and the entry into Canaan in 1407. Appropriate adjustments will have to be made if the dates are earlier or later than these; but in any case all dates prior to the monarchy should be treated with extreme caution.

Abram/Abraham
(1952–1777 BC)

Son of Terah. Grandson of Nahor[1]. Brother of Nahor[2] and Haran[1], and uncle of Lot. God called him to leave Harran and he set out for Canaan having received God's promise that he would become a great nation and would be blessed and bring blessing to 'all peoples on earth'. He separated from his nephew Lot and settled near the trees of Mamre at Hebron. God's 'everlasting covenant' with Abraham included the promise of protection, land and many descendants. He became the father of Ishmael by his servant Hagar and of Isaac by his wife Sarai/Sarah in her old age. God tested Abraham by commanding him to offer his son Isaac as a sacrifice: his willingness to do so is commended in the New Testament as an example of faith. On his journey with God, Abraham experienced moments of revelation and worship. As a sign of his devotion to God, Abraham and all the males in his household were circumcised. Abraham pleaded with God for the righteous few in the wicked cities of Sodom and Gomorrah. He was not

Abraham Family Tree

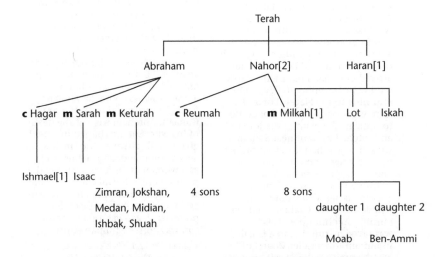

without fault: he deceived people about the identity of his wife and doubted God's promise and fathered an heir through his servant. After Sarah's death he took another wife (Keturah) and had five more sons. Isaac's sons Jacob and Esau were his grandsons. Abraham lived for 175 years. He was buried in a cave near Mamre with Sarah, in a field he had bought from the Hittites. Jews today view Abraham as 'the father of the faith'. They consider that their faith began with Abraham's call and obedience, and the subsequent history of the Jewish people is seen as the ongoing fulfilment of God's promises to Abraham. In the Bible, God is often described as 'the God of Abraham', and Abraham as 'friend' of God. The significance of Abraham to Christian belief is particularly evident in John's Gospel and in the writings of Paul. In the New Testament he is the father of all followers of Christ. His faith is celebrated in Hebrews 11.

📖 (11:26 – 25:11, 19; 48:15–16; 49:30–31; Exodus 3:6, 15–16;

Nehemiah 9:7; Isaiah 41:8; 51:2; Ezekiel 33:24; Matthew 1:1–2, 17; 3:9; Luke 3:8, 34; 16:22–30; 19:9; 20:37; John 8:33, 37, 39–40, 52–58; Acts 3:13; 7:2–8; 13:26; Romans 4:1–25; 11:1; 2 Corinthians 11:22; Galatians 3:6–18, 29; 4:22–23; Hebrews 6:13–15; 7:1–10; 11:8–12, 17–19; James 2:21–23)

Nahor[2]
(C20th BC)

Son of Terah; brother of Abraham. Grandson of Nahor[1]. He had eight sons with his wife Milkah and four more sons through a concubine (Reumah). There are indications that Nahor, like Abraham, was a man of faith.

📖 (11:26–29; 22:23)

Haran[1]
(born late C21st BC)

Son of Terah. Grandson of Nahor[1]. Father of Lot, Milkah[1] and Iskah. Died in Ur before his family started out for Canaan.

📖 (11:26–29)

Lot
(born late C20th BC)

Son of Haran[1]. Grandson of Terah.
Father of two unnamed daughters.
After the death of his father, Lot
was taken by Terah, with Abram
and Sarai, from Ur to Harran. After
Terah's death, responding to the call
of God, Abram and Lot left Harran,
arrived in Canaan but then escaped
famine by travelling to Egypt. On
returning to the Negev, Lot and
Abram parted company. Lot chose
to settle in the plain of the Jordan
and pitched his tent near Sodom, a
wicked city. When it was ransacked
by four kings who carried off Lot
and all his possessions, Abram came
to his nephew's rescue. Finally
Sodom (along with Gomorrah)
was destroyed as God rained down
burning sulphur upon it. Lot
was saved by running to a small
mountain town called Zoar, but his
wife became a pillar of salt because
she looked back to Sodom. Lot and
his daughters lived in a cave, but
his daughters got him drunk and
took turns to sleep with him and
they both became pregnant by
their father. Lot's inner torment is
mentioned in 2 Peter because of the
evil that surrounded him.

📖 (11:27, 31; 12:4–5; 13:1–13; 14:8–16;
19:1–38; Luke 17:32; 2 Peter 2:7–9)

Sarai/Sarah
(1942–1815 BC)

Wife of Abram who accompanied
him on his journeys. She was
beautiful, but originally unable to
conceive. Abram tried to pass her
off as his sister (in Egypt and then
in Gerar) in order to protect his own
life. At Sarai's instigation, Hagar (her
servant) slept with Abram and gave
birth to Ishmael through whom
Sarai hoped to build her family
line. However, God's covenant with
Abram included the promise of a
son through Sarai who was then 90
years old. Both Abraham and Sarah
laughed at the prospect but within
a year Isaac was born. Sarah lived
for 127 years and died in Hebron in
Canaan. Abraham wept at the death
of his wife. She was buried in a field
given to Abraham by the Hittites.
She is commended in Hebrews 11
as a woman of faith who trusted the
promise of God. Paul contrasts Sarah
with Hagar: Sarah was a free woman
and recipient of a son by divine
promise; Hagar was a slave whose
son was born by human effort.

📖 (11:29; 12:5, 10–20; 16:1–16;
17:15–22; 18:1–15; 20:1–18;
21:1–13; 23:1–20; Romans 4:19;
Galatians 4:21–31; Hebrews 11:11)

Milkah[1] (Milcah)
(born mid C20th BC)

Daughter of Haran and wife of
Nahor[2] with whom she had
eight sons. Abraham's niece and
grandmother of Rebekah.

📖 (11:29; 22:23; 24:15, 24, 47)

Iskah (Iscah)
(born mid C20th BC)

Daughter of Haran. Abraham's niece.

📖 (11:29)

Pharaohs

The word *Pharaoh* is an Egyptian one meaning 'great house'. In the Bible it is a title used for the king of Egypt and is applied to different individuals without their specific identity being made clear. Archaeological finds have enabled scholars to suggest proper names for some of the Pharaohs referred to in the Bible.

- The Pharaoh who discovered Abraham's deception that Sarah was his sister (Genesis 12:15–20).
- The Pharaoh at the time of Joseph[1] (Genesis 37–50; Acts 7:10, 13).
- The Pharaoh(s) who oppressed the Israelites (Exodus 1–2).
- The stubborn Pharaoh of the exodus, possibly Rameses II (Exodus 5–12; Romans 9:14–18).
- The Pharaoh who was the father of Bithiah, wife of Mered in Judah (1 Chronicles 4:18).
- The Pharaoh who captured Gezer and then gave it as a wedding gift to his daughter on her marriage to Solomon (1 Kings 3:1; 9:16).
- The Pharaoh who provided refuge for Hadad[4] of Edom and gave him in marriage to his sister-in-law (1 Kings 11:14–22).
- Pharaoh Shishak (= Sheshonq I) who attacked Jerusalem in Rehoboam's reign (1 Kings 11:40; 14:25–26).
- Pharaoh So, possibly referring to Shabaka or Osorkon IV, to whom Hoshea[2] had sent envoys (2 Kings 17:4).
- Pharaoh Tirhakah, king of Cush (Ethiopia) (2 Kings 19:9; Isaiah 37:9).
- Pharaoh Necho (Neco) who killed Josiah, deposed and took Josiah's son Jehoahaz[2] off to Egypt and made another of Josiah's sons, Jehoiakim, vassal king, but was himself defeated by Nebuchadnezzar at Carchemish (2 Kings 23:29 – 24:7; Jeremiah 46:2).
- Pharaoh Hophra, whose downfall was prophesied (Jeremiah 44:30; Ezekiel 29:1–16).

Amraphel, Arioch[1], Kedorlaomer, Tidal
(reigned mid C19th BC)

Mesopotamian kings (of Shinar [Babylonia], Ellasar, Elam and Goyim [Goiim] respectively) who formed an alliance and took part in various successful military campaigns against the Amalekites and Amorites. They also ransacked Sodom and Gomorrah but were defeated by Abraham who acted to defend Lot.

📖 (14:1–17)

Bera, Birsha, Shinab, Shemeber
(reigned mid C19th BC)

Four kings (of Sodom, Gomorrah, Admah, Zeboyim respectively) who formed an alliance with the king of Bela (Zoar) in the Dead Sea Valley. They rebelled against Kedorlaomer, having been his subjects for 12 years.

📖 (14:1–24)

Mamre, Eshkol (Eshcol), Aner
(mid C19th BC)

Three Amorite brothers who became Abraham's allies and helped him rescue Lot.

📖 (14:13, 24)

Melchizedek
(mid C19th BC)

This Canaanite 'king of Salem' (i.e. Jerusalem) blessed Abram when he returned from defeating the kings who had raided Sodom. His name means 'king of righteousness' and he is also described as 'priest of God Most High'. Psalm 110 explains that Melchizedek is both priest and king and therefore is of a higher order than the priests of the tribe of Levi[1]. Jesus refers to this psalm when he talks about the Messiah's identity (Matthew 22:41–46).

Hebrews understands Christ's role as priest as being similar but superior to that of Melchizedek: Christ's priesthood is unique because it endures for ever, it combines kingly and priestly duties and Christ too is king of righteousness (*zedek*) and peace (*salem*).

📖 (14:18–19; Psalm 110:4; Hebrews 5:6–10; 6:20 – 7:22)

Eliezer[1]
(mid C19th BC)

Abraham's servant from Damascus who would inherit Abraham's estate if Abraham had no children of his own. It is possible that this servant was the senior household servant whom Abraham sent to find a wife for Isaac.

📖 (15:2–4; 24:2–67)

Hagar
(born early C19th BC)

Sarah's servant who slept with Abraham and gave birth to his son Ishmael[1]. Twice fearing the wrath of Sarah, she left for desert places and at wells encountered God and was promised that her son would become a great nation. Paul contrasts Sarah with Hagar: Sarah was a free woman and recipient of a son by divine promise; Hagar was a slave whose son was born by human effort.

📖 (16:1–16; 21:8–21; Galatians 4:21–31)

Ishmael[1]
(1866–1729 BC)

Son of Abraham and Hagar, given his name (meaning 'God hears') by the angel of the Lord in recognition that the Lord heard about Hagar's misery. God promised that Ishmael's descendants would become a great nation even though his covenant people would be established through Isaac. Ishmael was circumcised aged 13 on the same day as his father and all the other males in Abraham's household. His 12 sons became tribal rulers. Lived 137 years. His descendants became known as the Ishmaelites (Midianites) – the travellers to whom Joseph[1] was sold by his brothers. Paul refers to Ishmael's birth by a slave woman.

📖 (16:15–16; 17:20–27; 21:8–21; 25:12–18; 37:25–28; 39:1; Judges 8:24; Galatians 4:21–31)

Isaac
(1852–1672 BC)

Son of Abraham and Sarah, born in their old age. His name means 'he laughs' and served as a reminder that his parents laughed in disbelief when God promised them a son. He was circumcised at eight days old. Abraham was prepared to sacrifice Isaac as a burnt offering but God provided a ram instead and reaffirmed his promise that Isaac's descendants would be blessed and a blessing to other nations. At 40 years old Isaac married Rebekah who comforted him when his mother died. They became parents of twins (Esau and Jacob[1]). In Gerar, Isaac (like Abraham before him) lied about his wife's identity to protect himself. He also opened up the wells Abraham had dug. The Lord appeared to him at Beersheba. With the help of Rebekah, his younger son Jacob deceived him and Isaac gave to Jacob the blessing and birthright of Esau. Isaac was 180 years old when he died in Hebron. When God revealed himself to Moses he identified himself as the

God of Abraham and Isaac and Jacob, so establishing Isaac's place as one of the fathers of the Israelite faith. In the New Testament, Isaac is compared to all Christian people who are likewise 'children of promise'. He is commended in Hebrews 11 for the faith he exercised when he blessed his children.

📖 (17:19; 21:1–8; 22:1–18; 24:1–67; 25:19–34; 26:1–33; 27:1 – 28:9; 35:27–29; Exodus 3:6; Matthew 8:11; Luke 13:28; Galatians 4:28; Hebrews 11:20)

Moab
(born mid C19th BC)

Son of Lot. His mother was Lot's eldest daughter.

📖 (19:37)

Ben-Ammi
(born mid C19th BC)

Son of Lot. His mother was Lot's youngest daughter. His name means 'son of my people' and his descendants were the Ammonites.

📖 (19:38)

Abimelek[1] (Abimelech)
(reigned mid C19th BC)

King of Gerar who was deceived by Abraham into thinking Sarah was his sister and not his wife. God intervened to stop Abimelek from sleeping with Sarah, possibly by making him impotent. Despite Abraham's deceit, Abimelek treated Abraham kindly. Abraham prayed for him and his wife and they became able to have children. Abimelek and Abraham made an agreement together at Beersheba following Abraham's objection to the seizing of a well his servants had dug.

📖 (20:1–18; 21:22–33)

Phicol[1]
(mid C19th BC)

Commander of the forces of Abimelek[1], king of the Philistines. With Abimelek[1] he made a treaty with Abraham at Beersheba. (Possibly a title rather than a proper name.)

📖 (21:22, 32)

Uz[2], Buz[1], Kemuel[1], Kesed, Hazo, Pildash, Jidlaph
(born late C20th BC)

Sons of Nahor[2] and Milkah[1]. Nephews of Abraham.

📖 (22:21–22)

Aram[2]
(born early C19th BC)

Son of Kemuel[1]. Grandson of Nahor[2].

📖 (22:21)

Bethuel
(born early C19th BC)

Son of Nahor[2] and Milkah[1]. Nephew of Abraham. Father of Rebekah. An Aramean from Paddan Aram.

📖 (22:22–23; 25:20)

Rebekah
(c.1830–1710? BC)

Daughter of Bethuel. Granddaughter of Nahor[2] and Milkah[1]. Sister of Laban. Wife of Isaac. Mother of Jacob[1] and Esau. From Paddan Aram. In his old age Abraham told his servant to find Isaac a non-Canaanite wife. The servant met Rebekah at a well and she was taken to Isaac. They married when Isaac was 40 years old: their marriage was based on love and comfort. Twenty years later she gave birth to twin boys but Rebekah always favoured the younger twin Jacob. Under her direction, Jacob tricked his father to give him the blessing reserved for the firstborn son. Rebekah then persuaded Jacob to flee to her brother Laban in Harran for his own safety. It seems that Rebekah never saw Jacob again. She was buried in the family burial place acquired by Abraham with Abraham, Sarah, Isaac, Jacob and Leah.

📖 (22:23; 24:15–67; 25:20–26; 26:7–9; 27:5–17, 42–46; 28:5; 49:31)

Reumah
(born mid C20th BC)

Concubine of Nahor[2]. Brother of Abraham. Mother of Tebah, Gaham, Tahash and Maakah[1].

📖 (22:24)

Tebah, Gaham, Tahash, Maakah[1] (Maacah)
(born late C20th BC)

Sons of Nahor[2] and Reumah.

📖 (22:24)

Ephron
(late C19th BC)

Son of Zohar[1]. He sold his field in Machpelah near Mamre to Abraham so he could use the cave there as a family burial site.

📖 (23:7–20)

Zohar[1]
(mid C19th BC)

Father of Ephron. A Hittite man.

📖 (23:8)

Laban
(born late C19th BC)

Son of Bethuel. Brother of Rebekah. Grandson of Nahor[2]. Father of Rachel and Leah. Uncle and father-in-law of Jacob[1]. An Aramean. Along with his father Bethuel, Laban recognized that the Lord himself had directed Abraham's servant to choose Rebekah as Isaac's wife. Laban opened his home to Jacob when he fled there at his mother's instruction to escape the wrath of Esau. Jacob worked for Laban for seven years in order to marry Rachel but Laban tricked Jacob and gave him first Leah as a wife. He worked another seven years for Rachel. Eventually Jacob fled from Laban who had become wary of his growing prosperity. Laban pursued Jacob but he was reassured that Jacob would look after his daughters and grandchildren and they made a memorial at Gilead to mark their promises to each other before Laban returned home.

📖 (24:28–33, 50–51, 53–60; 25:20; 27:43 – 28:5; 29:10–29; 30:25 – 31:55)

Deborah[1]
(mid C19th–late C18th BC)

Rebekah's nurse who left Laban's house with her when Abraham's servant took Rebekah back to Isaac. She died in old age sometime after Rebekah's own grandchildren were grown up but before Isaac died. She was buried under an oak tree near Bethel which was named Allon Bakuth ('Oak of Weeping'), signifying the affection there was towards her.

📖 (24:59; 35:8)

Keturah
(born mid C19th BC)

Second wife of Abraham. Mother of Zimran, Jokshan, Medan, Midian, Ishbak and Shuah. Also called Abraham's concubine.

📖 (25:1, 4; 1 Chronicles 1:32–33)

Zimran, Medan, Ishbak, Shuah
(born late C19th BC)

Sons of Abraham and Keturah.

📖 (25:2; 1 Chronicles 1:32)

Jokshan
(born late C19th BC)

Son of Abraham and Keturah. Father of Sheba[3] and Dedan[2].

📖 (25:2–3; 1 Chronicles 1:32)

Midian
(born late C19th BC)

Son of Abraham and Keturah. Father of Ephah[1], Epher[1], Hanok[1], Abida and Eldaah. His descendants were the Midianites.

📖 (25:2, 4; 1 Chronicles 1:32–33)

Sheba[3], Dedan[2]
(born early C18th BC)

Sons of Jokshan. Grandsons of Abraham and Keturah. The Ashurites, Letushites and Leummites descended from Dedan.

📖 (25:3; 1 Chronicles 1:32)

Ephah[1], Epher[1], Hanok[1] (Hanoch), Abida, Eldaah
(born early C18th BC)
Sons of Midian. Grandsons of Abraham and Keturah.

(25:4; 1 Chronicles 1:33; Isaiah 60:6)

Nebaioth
(born late C19th BC)
First son of Ishmael[1]. Grandson of Abraham and Hagar. Brother of Mahalath[1]/Basemath[2] who married Esau.

(25:13; 28:9; 36:3; 1 Chronicles 1:29; Isaiah 60:7)

Kedar, Adbeel, Mibsam[1], Mishma[1], Dumah, Massa, Hadad[1], Tema, Jetur, Naphish, Kedemah
(born late C19th BC)
Sons of Ishmael. Grandsons of Abraham and Hagar.

(25:13–15; 1 Chronicles 1:29–31; 5:19; Isaiah 60:7)

Esau/Edom
(1792–after 1672 BC)
Firstborn of twin boys born to Isaac and Rebekah. Grandson of Abraham and Sarah and Bethuel. Nephew of Laban. Father of Eliphaz[1], Reuel[1], Jeush[1], Jalam and Korah[1]. His name means 'hairy' and Esau is described as hairy, red (he is also called Edom, meaning 'red'), a skilful hunter with a preference for the outdoor life. He was his father's favourite son but he sold his birthright as the firstborn in return for some stew when he was hungry. He married Judith and Basemath[1], both Hittite women, and an Israelite woman called Basemath[2] (also called Mahalath[1]), Ishmael's daughter, before taking other Canaanite wives (Adah[2] and Oholibamah[1]). When his brother tricked their father, Isaac gave the blessing reserved for Esau as the firstborn son to the younger Jacob[1]. This caused friction between the brothers and they were separated for

many years. Esau took up residence in Seir and it was from here that he went up to Peniel in order to meet Jacob who had left Laban's home and had sent ahead many gifts to pacify Esau. But Esau was just happy to see his long lost brother again. Eventually they parted company again on account of their many possessions, livestock and people, and Esau settled in the hill country of Seir. He became the father of the Edomites. The New Testament uses the example of Esau to warn God's people about the long-term results of impetuous decisions to reject God's blessings.

(25:24–34; 26:34 – 28:9; 32:3–21; 33:1–16; 35:1; 36; Deuteronomy 2:4–8, 12, 22, 29; Joshua 24:4; 1 Chronicles 1:34–35; Jeremiah 49:8, 10; Obadiah 6, 9, 18–19, 21; Malachi 1:2–3; Romans 9:10–13; Hebrews 11:20; 12:16–17)

Jacob[1]/Israel
(1792–1645 BC)
The younger twin born to Isaac and Rebekah. Grandson of Abraham and Sarah and Bethuel. Nephew of Laban. Father of sons Reuben, Simeon[1], Levi[1], Judah[1], Dan, Naphtali, Gad[1], Asher, Issachar[1], Zebulun, Joseph[1] and Benjamin[1] (the patriarchs of the 12 tribes of Israel) and daughter Dinah. His name means 'he grasps the heel', which is indicative of the way he grasped Esau's heel at birth and figurative of his deceitful nature. He became known as 'Israel' after his wrestling encounter with God at Peniel. He was his mother's favourite son and she helped him deceive his father in order to gain the blessing usually reserved for the firstborn son. Jacob left for Paddam Aram to flee his brother's anger and to satisfy his parents' desire that he should not marry a Canaanite woman. He worked for Laban for seven years for each of his daughters, marrying both Leah and Rachel. He also had sons by Rachel's servant Bilhah and Leah's servant Zilpah. He was welcomed home by his brother Esau despite

his earlier act of deception. On his travels he encountered God, and named and renamed certain places accordingly (e.g., Bethel meaning 'house of God' [formerly Luz]; Mahanaim meaning 'camp of God'; Peniel meaning 'face of God'). On his return from Laban's home, Jacob settled in Mamre near Hebron in the land of Canaan. Jacob's favourite son was Joseph and this caused friction in his family. His other sons plotted against Joseph and convinced Jacob that Joseph was dead and this caused Jacob to mourn deeply. However, in his old age Jacob saw his son Joseph again when he finally came to Egypt with his family (now 75 in number). Jacob blessed Joseph's sons and his own sons before he died. He was embalmed for 40 days by Egyptian physicians who mourned him for 70 days. Joseph observed a further seven-day period of mourning for him near the Jordan. He was buried in the cave in the field of Machpelah near Mamre where Abraham, Sarah, Isaac, Rebekah and Leah were buried. Jacob is mentioned in Matthew's and Luke's genealogy of Jesus. Throughout the Bible, Jacob is mentioned along with Abraham and Isaac as one of the three fathers of faith.

📖 (25:24–34; 27:6 – 28:7; 28:10 – 35:29; 37:1–11, 31–35; 42:1–5, 29–38; 43: 1–14; 45:25 – 46:8; 46:25–30; 47:7–10, 28–31; 48:1–22; 49:1–33; 50:12–14; Exodus 1:1–5; 3:6; Leviticus 26:42; Deuteronomy 9:27; Joshua 24:4, 32; 1 Samuel 12:8; 1 Chronicles 16:13; Psalms 77:15; 105:6; Isaiah 2:3, 5–6; 58:14; Jeremiah 2:4; 30:10; 51:19; Ezekiel 20:5; 28:25; Hosea 12:12; Amos 8:7; 9:8; Obadiah 10, 17–18; Micah 3:8–9; 5:7–8; Malachi 1:2; Matthew 1:2; 8:11; 22:32; Mark 12:26; Luke 1:33; 3:34; 13:28; 20:37; John 4:5–6, 12; Acts 3:13; 7:8, 12, 14–16, 32; Romans 9:13; 11:26; Hebrews 11:9, 20–21)

Abimelek[2] (Abimelech)
(early C18th BC)

King of the Philistines in Gerar who was misled by Isaac about the identity of Rebekah. He recognized God's presence with Isaac and made a peace agreement with him at Beersheba.

📖 (26:1, 8, 11, 16, 26–31)

Ahuzzath
(early C18th BC)

Personal advisor of Abimelek[2]. Accompanied Abimelek and Phicol[2] when they visited Isaac at Beersheba and made a peace agreement with him.

📖 (26:26)

Phicol[2]
(early C18th BC)

Commander of the forces of Abimelek[2]. Accompanied Abimelek[2] and Ahuzzath when they visited Isaac at Beersheba and made a peace agreement with him.

📖 (26:26)

Judith
(born early C18th BC)

Daughter of Beeri[1]. Wife of Esau.

📖 (26:34)

Beeri[1]
(late C19th BC)

Father of Judith. A Hittite.

📖 (26:34)

Basemath[1]
(born early/mid C18th BC)

Daughter of Elon[1]. Wife of Esau. Possibly sister of Adah[2].

📖 (26:34; 36:2)

Elon[1]
(late C19th BC)

Father of Basemath[1]. A Hittite.

📖 (26:34)

Mahalath[1]
(born mid C18th BC)

Daughter of Ishmael. Sister of
Nebaioth. Granddaughter of
Abraham. Wife of Esau. Also called
Basemath[2] and identified as the
mother of Reuel[1].

📖 (28:9; 36:3–4, 10, 13, 17)

Rachel
(c.1730–c.1690 BC)

Daughter of Laban described as
being beautiful with a lovely figure.
She cared for her father's sheep
and was leading them to a well for
water when she first met her cousin
Jacob[1] who became her husband.
Jacob worked for Laban for a total of
14 years so he could marry Rachel.
Rachel was loved more than Jacob's
first wife, Leah, her older sister.
When Jacob fled from Laban's home,
Rachel took her father's household
gods with her. Although she was
originally unable to conceive,
she gave birth to Joseph[1] and
Benjamin[1], the youngest two
sons of Jacob. She died giving birth
to Benjamin[1] and was buried on
the way to Bethlehem (Ephrath).
Jacob set up a pillar to mark the
place of her tomb. Rachel and Leah
are mentioned in words of blessing
given to Ruth upon her marriage to
Boaz.

📖 (29:6, 9–12, 16–31; 30:1–8, 14–15,
   22–25; 31:4, 14, 19, 32–35; 33:1–2, 7;
   35:16–20, 24–25; 46: 19, 22, 25; 48:7;
   Ruth 4:11; Jeremiah 31:15; Matthew
   2:18)

Leah
(born mid C18th BC)

Eldest daughter of Laban. First
wife of Jacob[1] though by her
father's planning rather than by
her husband's desire. Mother
of Reuben, Simeon[1], Levi[1],
Judah[1], Issachar[1] and Zebulun
(who became the patriarchs of the
tribes of Israel named after them)
and a daughter called Dinah. She
is described as having 'weak' (or

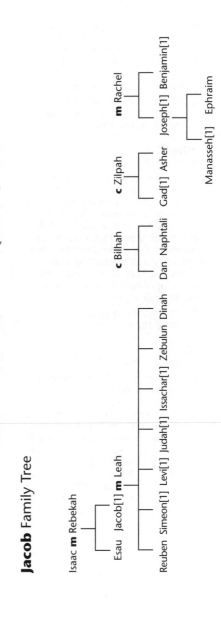

Jacob Family Tree

Isaac **m** Rebekah

Esau   Jacob[1] **m** Leah

m Rachel — Joseph[1] Benjamin[1]
            └ Manasseh[1] Ephraim

c Zilpah — Gad[1] Asher

c Bilhah — Dan Naphtali

Reuben Simeon[1] Levi[1] Judah[1] Issachar[1] Zebulun Dinah

'delicate') eyes with the implication that she was not as beautiful as her younger sister Rachel. Leah was buried by Jacob in the cave in the field of Machpelah, near Mamre, where Abraham, Sarah, Isaac, Rebekah and, later, Jacob were buried. Rachel and Leah are mentioned in words of blessing given to Ruth upon her marriage to Boaz.

📖 (29:16–17, 23–35; 30:9–21; 31:4, 14, 33; 33:1–2, 7; 34:1; 35:23, 26; 46:15, 18; 49:31; Ruth 4:11)

Zilpah
(born mid C18th BC)

Female servant of Leah given to her by Laban as an attendant on the occasion of her marriage to Jacob[1]. By Jacob she became mother of Gad[1] and Asher, patriarchs of the two tribes of Israel named after them. Although Zilpah was Leah's servant and was given to Jacob by Leah to provide Leah herself with more offspring, Zilpah is referred to as Jacob's wife.

📖 (29:24; 30:9–12; 35:26; 37:2; 46:16–18)

Bilhah
(born mid C18th BC)

Female servant of Rachel given to her by Laban as an attendant on her marriage to Jacob[1]. By Jacob she became mother of Dan and Naphtali, patriarchs of the two tribes of Israel named after them. Although Bilhah was Rachel's servant and was given to Jacob by Rachel to provide Rachel herself with offspring when Rachel was childless, Bilhah is referred to as Jacob's wife as well as his concubine. Bilhah also slept with Jacob's eldest son Reuben.

📖 (29:29; 30:3–8; 35:22, 25; 37:2; 46:23–25)

Reuben
(born late C18th BC)

Eldest son of Jacob[1] and Leah. Father of Hanok[2] (Hanoch), Pallu, Hezron[1] and Karmi[1] (Carmi). His name means 'see a son' and Leah hoped that his arrival marked the end of her second place in Jacob's affections. He slept with his father's wife Bilhah, which was his downfall, as Jacob's final words to his son recognize. He was instrumental in his brothers' decision not to kill Joseph[1] but instead throw him into a cistern. It seems that Reuben wanted to return Joseph safely to his father and was distraught when his brothers sold him to the Midianite (Ishmaelite) traders. He put his own sons up as security against the safe return of Benjamin[1] when Joseph[1] required Benjamin[1] to go to Egypt. One of the 12 patriarchs of the Israelites, his name is used to refer to the tribe of Israel that bears his name.

📖 (29:32; 35:22–23; 37:21–22, 29–30; 42:22, 37; 46:8–9; 49:3–4; Exodus 1:2; 6:14; Numbers 1:5, 20; 26:5; Deuteronomy 27:13; 33:6; 1 Chronicles 2:1; 5:1, 3; Ezekiel 48:31; Revelation 7:5)

Simeon[1]
(born late C18th BC)

Second son of Jacob[1] and Leah. Father of Jemuel/Nemuel[2], Jamin[1], Ohad, Jakin[1]/Jarib, Zohar[2]/Zerah and Shaul[2]. His name means 'he hears'. With Levi[1], Simeon took revenge on the house of Hamor the Hivite because his son Shechem[1] raped their sister Dinah. Simeon was taken prisoner by Joseph[1] in Egypt as surety that the brothers would return with Benjamin[1]. Before Jacob died, he addressed Simeon and Levi as men of fierce anger and violence. One of the 12 patriarchs of the Israelites, Simeon's name is used to refer to the tribe of Israel that bears his name.

📖 (29:33; 34:25–31; 35:23; 42:24; 36; 43:23; 46:10; 49:5–7; Exodus 1:2; 6:15; Numbers 1:6, 22–23; 26:12–14; Deuteronomy 27:12; 1 Chronicles 2:1; 4:24; Ezekiel 48:33; Revelation 7:7)

Levi Family Tree

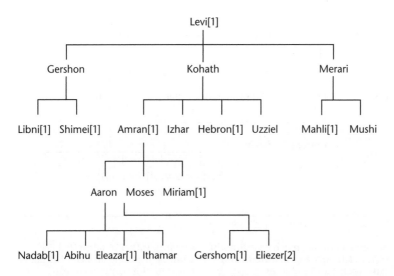

Levi[1]
(c.1705–1568 BC)

Third son of Jacob[1] and Leah. Father of Gershon (Gershom), Kohath and Merari. His name is associated with a word meaning 'attached'. With Simeon[1], Levi took revenge on the house of Hamor the Hivite because his son Shechem[1] raped their sister Dinah. Before Jacob died, he addressed Simeon and Levi as men of fierce anger and violence. Levi lived for 137 years. One of the 12 patriarchs of the Israelites, his name is used to refer to the tribe of Israel that bears his name and was responsible for the tabernacle.

📖 (29:34; 34:25–31; 35:23; 46:11; 49:5–7; Exodus 1:2; 6:16; Numbers 1:47–53; 26:57–61; Deuteronomy 27:12; 1 Chronicles 2:1; 6:1, 16; Ezekiel 48:13; Revelation 7:7)

Judah[1]
(born late C18th BC)

Fourth son of Jacob[1] and Leah. Father of Er[1], Onan, Shelah[2], Perez and Zerah[3]. His name is associated with 'praise'. He persuaded his brothers to sell Joseph[1] rather than kill him. Judah parted company with his brothers and stayed with Hirah in Adullam. There he married the daughter of a Canaanite man called Shua[1]. Tamar[1], his daughter-in-law, acted like a prostitute and Judah slept with her producing two more sons, Perez and Zerah[3]. In negotiations with Joseph in Egypt, Judah took the lead, as he did when negotiating with his father. Before Jacob died, he blessed Judah, suggesting he would rule over his brothers and other nations. One of the 12 patriarchs of the Israelites, his name is used to refer to the tribe of Israel that bears his name and also the kingdom which received the Lord's favour and blessing. King David was a

Judah Family Tree

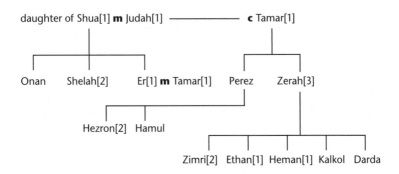

descendant of Judah, which assures in turn Judah's place in Matthew's and Luke's genealogies of Jesus.

📖 (29:35; 35:23; 37:26; 38:1–30; 43:3–10; 44:16–34; 46:12; 49:8–13; Exodus 1:2; Numbers 1:7, 26–27; 26:19–22; Deuteronomy 27:12; 33:7; 1 Chronicles 2:1; 5:2; Ezekiel 48:31; Matthew 1:2–3; Luke 3:33; Revelation 7:5)

Dan
(born late C18th BC)

Son of Jacob[1] and Bilhah (Rachel's servant). Father of Hushim[1]/ Shuham. His name, given to him by Rachel, means 'he judges/vindicates'. Before Jacob died, he named Dan as the one who will bring justice for his people. One of the 12 patriarchs of the Israelites, his name is used to refer to the tribe of Israel that bears his name. The tribe of Dan is missing from the list of tribes in Revelation 7:5–8.

📖 (30:6; 35:25; 46:23; 49:16–17; Exodus 1:4; Numbers 1:12, 38–39; 26:42–43; Deuteronomy 27:13; 33:22; 1 Chronicles 2:2; Ezekiel 48:32)

Naphtali
(born late C18th BC)

Son of Jacob[1] and Bilhah (Rachel's servant). Father of Jahziel/Jahzeel, Guni[1], Jezer and Shillem. His name, given to him by Rachel, means 'my struggle'. Before Jacob died, he compared Naphtali to a doe. One of the 12 patriarchs of the Israelites, his name is used to refer to the tribe of Israel that bears his name.

📖 (30:8; 35:25; 46:24; 49:21; Exodus 1:4; Numbers 1:15, 42–43; 26:48–50; Deuteronomy 27:13; 33:23; Isaiah 9:1; Ezekiel 48:34; Matthew 4:13, 15; Revelation 7:6)

Gad[1]
(born late C18th BC)

Son of Jacob[1] and Zilpah (Leah's servant). Father of Zephon, Haggi, Shuni, Ezbon[1]/Ozni, Eri, Arodi and Areli. His name, given to him by Leah, means 'good fortune' or 'a troop'. Before Jacob died, he predicted that Gad would attack those who raided him. One of the 12 patriarchs of the Israelites, his name is used to refer to the tribe of Israel that bears his name.

📖 (30:11; 35:26; 46:16; 49:19; Exodus 1:4; Numbers 1:14, 24–25; 26:15–18; Deuteronomy 27:13; 33:20; 1 Chronicles 2:2; Ezekiel 48:34; Revelation 7:5)

Asher
(born late C18th BC)

Son of Jacob[1] and Zilpah (Leah's servant). Father of Imnah[1], Ishvah, Ishvi, Beriah and a daughter Serah. His name, given to him by Leah, means 'happy'. Before Jacob died, he described Asher as a man of great food and delicacies. One of the 12 patriarchs of the Israelites, his name is used to refer to the tribe of Israel that bears his name. The prophet Anna based in Jerusalem in Jesus' lifetime was a descendant of the tribe of Asher.

(30:13; 35:26; 46:17; 49:20; Exodus 1:4; Numbers 1:13, 40–41; 26:44–47; Deuteronomy 27:13; 33:24–25; 1 Chronicles 2:2; Ezekiel 48:34; Luke 2:36; Revelation 7:6)

Issachar[1]
(born late C18th BC)

Son of Jacob[1] and Leah. Father of Tola[1], Puah[1], Jashub[1] and Shimron. His name means 'reward'. Before Jacob died, he described Issachar as someone prepared for hard work. One of the 12 patriarchs of the Israelites, his name is used to refer to the tribe of Israel that bears his name.

(30:18; 35:23; 46:13; 49:14–15; Exodus 1:3; Numbers 1:8, 28–29; 26:23–25; Deuteronomy 27:12; 33:18–19; 1 Chronicles 2:1; Ezekiel 48:33; Revelation 7:7)

Zebulun
(born late C18th BC)

Son of Jacob[1] and Leah. Father of Sered, Elon[2] and Jahleel. His name means 'honour'. Before Jacob died, he described Zebulun as a man of the sea. One of the 12 patriarchs of the Israelites, his name is used to refer to the tribe of Israel that bears his name.

(30:20; 35:23; 46:14; 49:13; Exodus 1:3; Numbers 1:9, 30–31; 26:26–27; Deuteronomy 27:13; 33:18–19; 1 Chronicles 2:1; Isaiah 9:1; Ezekiel 48:33; Matthew 4:13, 15; Revelation 7:8)

Dinah
(born late C18th BC)

Daughter of Jacob[1] and Leah. She was raped by Shechem who loved her and wanted her for his wife. Jacob and his sons insisted that the men of Shechem be circumcised before allowing Dinah to marry Shechem, but after they were circumcised Levi and Simeon took revenge for their sister's rape and killed every man in the city and looted their property.

(30:21; 34:1–31; 46:15)

Joseph[1]/Zaphenath-Paneah
(c.1701–1591 BC)

Son of Jacob[1] and Rachel. Father of Manasseh[1] and Ephraim. Husband of Asenath. His name means 'may he add' and expresses Rachel's desire that her first son would not be her last. After Joseph's birth, Jacob left Laban's home in Paddan-Aram and returned to Canaan. Joseph had a special place in his father's affections, which was demonstrated by his gift of a special robe for him. This, and Joseph's dreams about his superiority over them, provoked jealousy from his brothers and they sold him aged 17 to Midianite (Ishmaelite) traders who took him to Egypt. As the result of a false accusation from the wife of Potiphar, Joseph was imprisoned but interpreted dreams for two of Pharaoh's discredited officials, a cupbearer and baker. Later, Pharaoh had his own dreams and Joseph was summoned from prison to interpret them. He did so, interpreting that a severe famine would come in Egypt. Pharaoh recognized God's Spirit was in Joseph and appointed him, aged 30, as his second-in-command. As the famine spread, people from throughout the world (including his own brothers) came to Egypt to buy food from Joseph. Once Joseph revealed his identity to his brothers, his whole family including his aged father Jacob relocated to Egypt. Before Jacob died, he blessed his sons but his blessing on Joseph was the greatest. He was described as fruitful, strong in battle, prince among his brothers, with God's blessing on him. Joseph wept over his father and instructed Egyptian physicians to embalm him. Joseph buried his father in the cave in the field of Machpelah near Mamre which Abraham had acquired. On Jacob's death, Joseph reassured his brothers that he held no grudge against them because what they had meant for harm God intended for good and the saving of many lives. Joseph lived for 110 years and saw his grandchildren and great grandchildren, before dying in Egypt. As one of the 12 patriarchs of the Israelites, his name is used to refer to the tribe of Israel that is preserved through the two half-tribes named after his sons Ephraim and Manasseh. In the New Testament Stephen mentions Joseph in his account of the history of salvation to the Sanhedrin (i.e. the Jewish Council). Joseph is also celebrated as a man of faith in Hebrews 11.

📖 (30:24–25; 33:7; 35:24; 37:2–36; 39:1 – 48:4; 48:8–22; 49:22–26; 50:1–10, 15–26; Exodus 1:5–8; 13:19; Numbers 1:10; 24:32–33; 26:28–37; 27:1; 32:33; Deuteronomy 27:12; 33:13–17; Joshua 14:4; 16:4; 1 Chronicles 2:2; 5:1–2; Psalms 77:15; 105:17–22; Ezekiel 48:32; John 4:5; Acts 7:9–18; Hebrews 11:22; Revelation 7:8)

Hamor
(mid C18th BC)

Father of Shechem[1]. A Hivite based in the city of Shechem. Jacob[1] bought a field from Hamor's son so he could pitch his tent and build an altar. Hamor tried to secure Dinah as his son's wife but her brothers Simeon[1] and Levi[1] killed him and his family by the sword.

📖 (33:19; 34:2, 4, 6–10, 18–26; Joshua 24:32; Judges 9:28; Acts 7:16)

Shechem[1]
(born late C18th BC)

Son of Hamor. He raped Dinah, daughter of Jacob[1], but he also loved her and wanted her as his wife. The men of his city agreed to be circumcised to make this possible but Dinah's brothers Simeon[1] and Levi[1] killed Shechem and his family and all the men of the city, and looted the city of Shechem in revenge for her rape.

📖 (33:19; 34:2–26; Joshua 24:32; Judges 9:28)

Benjamin[1] (Ben-Oni)
(c.1690–? BC)

Son of Rachel and Jacob[1]. Father of Bela[2], Beker[1], Ashbel, Ehi/Ahiram/Aher/Aharah, Rosh, Muppim/Shupham/Shephuphan, Huppim/Hupham/Huram[1] and Ard (and possibly also Gera[1] and Naaman[1]). Rachel died giving birth to this her second son and she named him Ben-Oni ('son of my trouble') but his father called him Benjamin ('son of my right hand'). When his brothers went down to Egypt to obtain food, Benjamin was at first left behind but Joseph[1] insisted he return with them. Joseph was overcome by seeing Benjamin and bestowed special favours on him (including more food, clothing and money than his brothers received). When Joseph revealed his identity, he embraced Benjamin first. Before Jacob died, he blessed Benjamin whom he described as a ravenous wolf that devours his prey and takes plunder. One of the 12 patriarchs of the Israelites, his name refers to the tribe of Israel that was particularly known for its skill in battle. King Saul and the apostle Paul had connections with this tribe.

📖 (35:18, 24; 42:36; 43:15–16, 29–30, 34; 45:12, 22; 46:19, 21; 49:27; Exodus 1:3; Numbers 1:11, 36–37; 26:38–41; Deuteronomy 27:12; 33:12; 1 Samuel 9:21; 1 Chronicles 2:2; 7:6; 8:1, 40; 12:2; Ezekiel 48:32; Zechariah 14:10; Romans 11:1; Philippians 3:5; Revelation 7:8)

Adah[2]
(born early C18th BC)
Wife of Esau. Daughter of Elon[1].
Mother of Eliphaz[1]. Possibly sister
of Basemath[1].

(36:2, 4, 10, 12, 16)

Oholibamah[1]
(born early C18th BC)
Daughter of Anah[1] and wife of
Esau. Granddaughter of Zibeon[1]
the Hivite. Mother of Jeush[1], Jalam
and Korah[1].

(36:2, 5, 14, 18, 25)

Anah[1]
(late C19th BC)
Father of Oholibamah[1] and
Dishon[2]. Son of Zibeon[1] the
Hivite.

(36:2, 14; 1 Chronicles 1:41)

Zibeon[1]
(mid C19th BC)
Father of Anah[1]. Grandfather of
Oholibamah[1] and Dishon[2]. A
Hivite.

(36:2, 14)

Basemath[2]
(born mid C18th BC)
Daughter of Ishmael and sister of
Nebaioth. Wife of Esau. Also called
Mahalath[1] (28:9). Mother of
Reuel[1].

(36:3–4, 10, 13, 17)

Eliphaz[1]
(mid C18th BC)
Son of Esau and Adah[2]. Born in
Canaan. Father of Teman, Omar,
Zepho, Gatam and Kenaz[1].

(36:4, 10–12, 15–16; 1 Chronicles
1:35–36)

Reuel[1]
(late C18th BC)
Son of Esau and Basemath[2]. Born
in Canaan. Father of Nahath[1],

Zerah[1], Shammah[1] and Mizzah.

(36:4, 10, 13, 17; 1 Chronicles 1:35, 37)

Jeush[1], Jalam, Korah[1]
(mid C18th BC)
Sons of Esau and Oholibamah[1].
Born in Canaan.

(36:5, 14, 18; 1 Chronicles 1:35)

**Teman, Omar, Zepho, Gatam,
Kenaz[1]**
(late C18th BC)
Sons of Eliphaz[1]. Grandsons
of Esau and Adah[2]. Chiefs in
Edom.

(36:11, 15; 1 Chronicles 1:36, 53)

Timna[1]
(mid C18th BC)
Concubine of Eliphaz[1]. Mother of
Amalek. Sister of Lotan. Daughter
of Seir.

(36:12, 22; 1 Chronicles 1:36, 39)

Amalek
(late C18th BC)
Son of Eliphaz[1] and Timna[1].
Grandson of Esau and Adah[2].

(36:12, 16; 1 Chronicles 1:36)

**Nahath[1], Zerah[1],
Shammah[1], Mizzah**
(early C17th BC)
Sons of Reuel[1]. Grandsons of Esau
and Basemath[2]. Chiefs in Edom.

(36:13, 17; 1 Chronicles 1:37)

Zibeon[2]
(mid C19th BC)
Son of Seir. A Horite chief. Father of
Aiah[1] and Anah[3].

(36:24; 1 Chronicles 1:40)

Korah[2]
(late C18th BC)
Son of Eliphaz[1]. Grandson of Esau
and Adah[2].

(36:16)

Seir
(early C19th BC)
A Horite. Father of Lotan, Shobal[1],
Zibeon[2], Anah[2], Dishon[1], Ezer
and Dishan.

📖 (36:20–21; 1 Chronicles 1:38)

**Lotan, Shobal[1], Anah[2],
Dishon[1], Ezer[1], Dishan**
(mid C19th BC)
Sons of Seir. Horite chiefs.

📖 (36:20–30; 1 Chronicles 1:38)

Hori[1], Homam (Hemam)
(late C19th BC)
Sons of Lotan. Grandsons of Seir.
Nephews of Timna[1]. Homam was
Eliphaz[1]'s concubine.

📖 (36:22; 1 Chronicles 1:39)

**Alvan, Manahath, Ebal, Shepho,
Onam[1]**
(late C19th BC)
Sons of Shobal[1]. Grandsons of Seir
the Horite.

📖 (36:23; 1 Chronicles 1:40)

Aiah[1], Anah[3]
(late C19th BC)
Sons of Zibeon[2]. Grandsons of Seir.
Anah discovered hot springs in the
desert.

📖 (36:24; 1 Chronicles 1:40)

Dishon[2]
(early C18th BC)
Son of Anah[2]. Grandson of Seir.

📖 (36:25; 1 Chronicles 1:41)

**Hemdan, Eshban, Ithran[1],
Keran**
(mid C18th BC)
Sons of Dishon[1]. Grandsons of Seir.

📖 (36:26; 1 Chronicles 1:41)

Bilhan[1], Zaavan, Akan
(late C19th BC)
Sons of Ezer. Grandsons of Seir.

📖 (36:27; 1 Chronicles 1:42)

Uz[3], Aran
(late C19th BC)
Sons of Dishan. Grandsons of Seir.

📖 (36:28; 1 Chronicles 1:42)

Bela[1]
(unknown)
First king of Edom. Son of Beor[1].
His city was Dinhabah.

📖 (36:32–33; 1 Chronicles 1:43–44)

Beor[1]
(unknown)
Father of Bela[1].

📖 (36:32; 1 Chronicles 1:43)

Jobab[2]
(unknown)
King of Edom. Son of Zerah[2]. From
Bozrah. Succeeded Bela[1]. His city
was Dinhabah.

📖 (36:33–34; 1 Chronicles 1:44–45)

Zerah[2]
(unknown)
Father of Jobab[2].

📖 (36:33; 1 Chronicles 1:44)

Husham
(unknown)
King of Edom. From the land of the
Temanites. Succeeded Jobab[2].

📖 (36:34–35; 1 Chronicles 1:45–46)

Hadad[2]
(unknown)
King of Edom. Son of Bedad.
Succeeded Husham. His city was
Avith.

📖 (36:35–36; 1 Chronicles 1:46–47)

Bedad
(unknown)
Father of Hadad[2].

📖 (36:35; 1 Chronicles 1:46)

Samlah
(unknown)

King of Edom. From Masrekah.
Succeeded Hadad[2].

📖 (36:36–37; 1 Chronicles 1:47–48)

Shaul[1]
(unknown)

King of Edom. From Rehoboth.
Succeeded Samlah.

📖 (36:37–38; 1 Chronicles 1:48–49)

Baal-Hanan[1]
(unknown)

King of Edom. Son of Akbor[1].
Succeeded Shaul[1].

📖 (36:38–39; 1 Chronicles 1:49–50)

Akbor[1] (Acbor)
(unknown)

Father of Baal-Hanan[1].

📖 (36:38; 1 Chronicles 1:49)

Hadad[3]
(unknown)

King of Edom. Succeeded Baal-
Hanan[1]. His city was Pau. Husband
of Mehetabel[1].

📖 (36:39; 1 Chronicles 1:50–51)

Mehetabel[1]
(unknown)

Wife of Hadad[3], king of Edom.
Daughter of Matred. Granddaughter
of Me-Zahab.

📖 (36:39; 1 Chronicles 1:50)

Matred
(unknown)

Mother of Mehetabel[1]. Daughter of
Me-Zahab.

📖 (36:39; 1 Chronicles 1:50)

Me-Zahab
(unknown)

Probably father of Matred
(alternatively a place name).

📖 (36:39; 1 Chronicles 1:50)

**Timna[2], Alvah, Jetheth,
Oholibamah[2], Elah[1], Pinon,
Kenaz[2], Mibzar, Magdiel, Iram**
(? C18th BC)

Clan chiefs of Edom. Descendants
of Esau.

📖 (36:40–43; 1 Chronicles 1:51–54)

Potiphar
(late C18th BC)

An official of Pharaoh and captain
of the guard who bought Joseph[1]
from Midianite (Ishmaelite)
merchants and took him to Egypt.
Joseph lived in his house, and
Potiphar's household prospered
because God was with Joseph and
blessed him. Joseph was put in
charge of all Potiphar's house until
his wife falsely accused Joseph of
molesting her. Potiphar put Joseph
in prison.

📖 (37:36; 39:1–20)

Hirah
(early C17th BC)

Resident of Adullam with whom
Judah[1] stayed when he met and
married Shua[1]. He accompanied
Judah to Timnah where he met
Tamar[1] disguised as a prostitute.
Later he tried to get back the seal,
cord and staff which Judah had given
Tamar as a pledge.

📖 (38:1, 12, 20–23)

Shua[1]
(late C18th BC)

A Canaanite man whose unnamed
daughter became the wife of Judah[1]
and mother of Er[1], Onan and
Shelah[2].

📖 (38:2; 1 Chronicles 2:3)

Er[1]
(born early C17th BC)

First son of Judah[1]. Grandson of
Jacob[1]. Husband of Tamar[1], but
the Lord put him to death for his
wickedness before they had children.

📖 (38:3; 46:12; 1 Chronicles 2:3)

Onan
(born early C17th BC)

Second son of Judah[1]. Grandson of Jacob[1]. Refused to fulfil his responsibilities to Tamar[1] and provide children for her and so perpetuate the family line. Instead he spilled his semen on the ground when he slept with Tamar. For his refusal to fulfil his responsibility to his deceased brother, God put him to death.

(38:4, 8–10; 46:12; 1 Chronicles 2:3)

Shelah[2]
(born early C17th BC)

Third son of Judah[1]. Grandson of Jacob[1]. Born at Kezib. Shelah was too young to be given to Tamar[1] as a husband when Onan died but Judah promised Tamar that Shelah would be given to her, although he broke this promise. Shelah went to Egypt with Jacob and his family.

(38:5, 11–14, 26; 46:12; Numbers 26:20; 1 Chronicles 2:3)

Tamar[1]
(born early C17th BC)

Wife of Judah's first son Er[1]. She disguised herself as a prostitute in order to become pregnant by her father-in-law. Mother of twin boys: Perez and Zerah[3]. Judah recognized that his own mistreatment of Tamar outweighed Tamar's own deception. Mentioned in the genealogy of Jesus.

(38:6–30; Ruth 4:12; 1 Chronicles 2:4; Matthew 1:3)

Perez
(born mid C17th BC)

Son of Tamar[1] and Judah[1]. Twin to Zerah[3]. Father of Hezron[2] and Hamul. His name means 'breaking out' in recognition of his surprise arrival before his younger brother whose hand appeared first. Perez's family line is mentioned in Ruth as a form of blessing on the family of Ruth and Boaz, probably because it was through Perez that Judah's family line was preserved. Mentioned in the genealogy of Jesus.

(38:27–30; 46:12; Numbers 26:20–21; Ruth 4:12, 18; 1 Chronicles 2:4–5; 4:1; 9:4; 27:3; Nehemiah 11:4, 6; Matthew 1:3; Luke 3:33)

Zerah[3]
(born mid C17th BC)

Son of Tamar[1] and Judah[1]. Younger twin brother of Perez. His name means 'scarlet'. Zerah's hand appeared before Perez was born and the midwife tied a scarlet thread on his wrist. Mentioned in the genealogy of Jesus but only as Perez's brother. His sons were: Zimri[2], Ethan[1], Heman[1], Kalkol, and Darda.

(38:27–30; 46:12; Numbers 26:20; 1 Chronicles 2:4, 6; Matthew 1:3)

Zaphenath-Paneah
(c.1701–1591 BC)

See **Joseph[1]** *in Genesis, p. 33.*

(41:45)

Asenath
(early C17th BC)

Daughter of Potiphera, priest of On. Given by Pharaoh to Joseph[1] as his wife. Mother of Manasseh[1] and Ephraim.

(41:45, 50–52)

Potiphera
(late C18th BC)

Father of Asenath. Priest of On (Heliopolis).

(41:45, 50; 46:20)

Manasseh[1]
(born c.1670 BC)

Firstborn son of Joseph[1] and Asenath. Father of Makir[1]. His name is associated with the word meaning 'forget', signifying Joseph had moved on from the trouble he had found in his own home life. Jacob[1] blessed Manasseh[1] before he died, but his blessing was inferior to that received by Ephraim. When Moses blessed the tribes before his death, he referred to the tens of thousands of Ephraim and the thousands of Manasseh, so recognizing the proliferation of Ephraim's descendants above those of Manasseh.

📖 (41:51; 46:20; 48:1, 5, 10–20; 50:23; Numbers 1:10, 34–35; 26:28–34; 27:1; 32:39–41; Deuteronomy 33:17)

Ephraim
(born c.1668 BC)

Second son of Joseph[1] and Asenath. His name sounds like 'twice fruitful', reflecting Joseph's prosperity in Egypt. When Jacob[1] blessed Joseph's sons before he died, Ephraim was placed ahead of Manasseh[1] and received the blessing normally expected on the eldest son. The descendants of Ephraim dominated the northern kingdom, which was often referred to as 'Ephraim' in recognition of this.

📖 (41:52; 46:20; 48:1, 5, 10–20; Numbers 1:10, 32–33; 26:35–37; 34:24; Deuteronomy 33:17)

Hanok[2] (Hanoch), Pallu, Hezron[1], Karmi[1] (Carmi)
(born early C17th BC)

Sons of Reuben. Grandsons of Jacob[1]. Their families went to Egypt with Jacob and left under Moses.

📖 (46:9; Exodus 6:14; Numbers 26:5; 1 Chronicles 5:3)

Jemuel/Nemuel[2], Jamin[1], Ohad, Jakin[1]/Jarib, Zohar[2]/ Zerah
(born early C17th BC)

Sons of Simeon[1]. Grandsons of Jacob[1]. Their families went to Egypt with Jacob and left under Moses.

📖 (46:10; Exodus 6:15; Numbers 26:12; 1 Chronicles 4:24)

Shaul[2]
(born early C17th BC)

Son of Simeon[1] and a Canaanite woman. Grandson of Jacob[1]. His family went to Egypt with Jacob and left under Moses.

📖 (46:10; Exodus 6:15; Numbers 26:13; 1 Chronicles 4:24–25)

Gershon
(born mid C17th BC)

Firstborn son of Levi[1]. Grandson of Jacob[1]. His family went to Egypt with Jacob and left under Moses.

📖 (46:11; Exodus 6:16; Numbers 3:17–18; 26:57; 1 Chronicles 6:1, 16–17, 20)

Kohath
(mid C17th–late C16th BC)

Son of Levi[1]. Grandson of Jacob[1]. Father of Amram[1], Izhar, Hebron[1], and Uzziel[1]. Head of the Kohathite clans, including the Hebronites. His family went to Egypt with Jacob and left under Moses.

📖 (46:11; Exodus 6:16; Numbers 3:17, 19; 26:57; 1 Chronicles 6:1–2, 16, 18, 22)

Merari
(born mid C17th BC)

Son of Levi[1]. Grandson of Jacob[1]. Father of Mahli[1] and Mushi. Head of the Merarite clan. His family went to Egypt with Jacob and left under Moses.

📖 (46:11; Exodus 6:16; Numbers 3:17, 20; 26:57; 1 Chronicles 6:1, 16, 19, 29)

Hezron[2]
(born late C17th BC)

Son of Perez. Grandson of Judah[1]. Husband of Abijah[5]. Father of Jerahmeel[1], Ram[1], Caleb[2], Segub[2] and Ashhur. Head of the Hezronite clan. Mentioned in the genealogies of King David in Ruth and Jesus in Matthew and Luke.

📖 (46:12; Numbers 26:21; Ruth 4:18–19; 1 Chronicles 2:5, 9, 18, 21–25; 4:1; Matthew 1:3; Luke 3:33)

Hamul
(born late C17th BC)

Son of Perez. Grandson of Judah[1]. Head of the Hamulite clan.

📖 (46:12; Numbers 26:21; 1 Chronicles 2:5)

Tola[1], Puah[1], Jashub[1], Shimron
(born early C17th BC)
Sons of Issachar. Grandsons of Jacob[1]. Their families went to Egypt with Jacob and left under Moses.
📖 (46:13; Numbers 26:23–24; 1 Chronicles 7:1–2)

Sered, Elon[2], Jahleel
(born early C17th BC)
Sons of Zebulun. Grandsons of Jacob[1]. Their families went to Egypt with Jacob and left under Moses.
📖 (46:14; Numbers 26:26)

Zephon, Haggi, Shuni, Ezbon[1]/Ozni, Eri, Arodi, Areli
(born early C17th BC)
Sons of Gad[1]. Grandsons of Jacob[1]. Their families went to Egypt with Jacob and left under Moses.
📖 (46:16; Numbers 26:15–17)

Imnah[1], Ishvah, Ishvi, Beriah[1]
(born early C17th BC)
Sons of Asher. Grandsons of Jacob[1]. Their families went to Egypt with Jacob and left under Moses.
📖 (46:17; Numbers 26:44–45; 1 Chronicles 7:30–31)

Serah
(born early C17th BC)
Daughter of Asher. Granddaughter of Jacob[1]. Her family went to Egypt with Jacob and left under Moses.
📖 (46:17; Numbers 26:46; 1 Chronicles 7:30)

Heber[1]
(born mid C17th BC)
Son of Beriah[1]. Grandson of Asher. Father of Japhlet, Shomer, Hotham and a daughter Shua[2]. His family went to Egypt with Jacob[1] and left under Moses. Went to Egypt with his family.
📖 (46:17; Numbers 26:45; 1 Chronicles 7:31–32)

Malkiel
(born mid C17th BC)
Son of Beriah[1]. Grandson of Asher. Father of Birzaith. His family went to Egypt with Jacob[1] and left under Moses.
📖 (46:17; Numbers 26:45; 1 Chronicles 7:31)

Bela[2], Beker[1], Ashbel, Ehi/ Ahiram/Aher/Aharah, Rosh, Huppim/Hupham/Huram[1], Ard
(born early–mid C17th BC)
Sons of Benjamin[1]. Grandsons of Jacob[1]. Their families went to Egypt with Jacob and left under Moses.
📖 (46:21; Numbers 26:38–40; 1 Chronicles 7:6–8; 8:1–5)

Gera[1], Muppim/Shupham/ Shephuphan[1]
(born early C17th BC)
Sons of Benjamin[1]. Grandsons of Jacob[1]. (Or sons of Bela[2] and grandsons of Benjamin[1].) Their families went to Egypt with Jacob and left under Moses.
📖 (46:21; 1 Chronicles 8:3, 5)

Naaman[1]
(born early C17th BC)
Son of Benjamin[1]. Grandson of Jacob[1]. (Or son of Bela[2] and grandson of Benjamin[1].) His family went to Egypt with Jacob and left under Moses.
📖 (46:21; Numbers 26:40; 1 Chronicles 8:4)

Hushim[1]/Shuham
(born early C17th BC)
Son of Dan. Grandson of Jacob[1]. His family went to Egypt with Jacob and left under Moses. Became leader of the Shuhamite clan.
📖 (46:23; Numbers 26:42)

Jahziel/Jahzeel, Guni[1], Jezer, Shillem
(born early C17th BC)

Sons of Naphtali. Grandsons of Jacob[1]. Their families went to Egypt with Jacob and left under Moses.

📖 (46:24; Numbers 26:48–49; 1 Chronicles 7:13)

Makir[1]
(born mid C17th BC)

Son of Manasseh[1], through his Aramean concubine. Grandson of Joseph[1]. Father of Gilead[1], Peresh and Sheresh. Married Maakah[6] from the Huppites and Shuppites. His children were presented to Joseph towards the end of Joseph's life. His descendants drove out the Amorites from Gilead and the Makirite clan settled there. They also occupied Bashan.

📖 (50:23; Numbers 26:29; 27:1; 32:39–40; 36:1; Deuteronomy 3:15; Joshua 13:31; 17:1, 3; Judges 5:14; 1 Chronicles 2:21, 23; 7:14–17)

Exodus

Shiphrah, Puah[2]
(late C16th BC)

Hebrew midwives who disobeyed Pharaoh's command to kill Hebrew male babies, because they feared God.

📖 (1:15)

Moses
(1527–1407 BC)

Son of Amran[1] and Jochebed (Levites). Brother of Aaron and Miriam[1]. Moses was hidden at three months old in the reeds along the bank of the Nile in order to escape being killed at the command of Pharaoh. He was found, given the name Moses (related to the Hebrew verb 'to draw out', in recognition of being lifted out of the Nile reeds) and then brought up as an Egyptian by Pharaoh's own daughter. He received an Egyptian education but never forgot his Hebrew roots. He killed an Egyptian and fled to Midian where he married Zipporah. Father of Gershom[1] and Eliezer[2]. He worked as a shepherd for Jethro and on Mount Horeb encountered God in a burning bush (Exodus 3). Hesitantly, Moses accepted God's call, and he and his brother Aaron pleaded with Pharaoh on behalf of the Hebrew people. After God's judgment had fallen on Egypt in the form of plagues, Pharaoh allowed Moses to lead them out of Egypt. They experienced God's miraculous deliverance at the Red Sea. Moses led the people into the desert of Sin where God continued to provide for them during 40 years of wandering. Moses judged disputes between the people and led their campaigns against other peoples they encountered. At Mount Sinai, God revealed himself again to Moses, this time in fire and smoke, and the mountain itself trembled. Here Moses received the covenant promises of God and the instructions for living as the people of God, including the Ten Commandments, and these regulated the life of the Hebrew people. In meeting with God, Moses encountered God's glory and his face is described as radiant (e.g. Exodus 34:30). Moses gave the people God's instructions for building the tabernacle and the ark. The days of desert wandering ended when God commanded Moses to lead the people towards Canaan. Deuteronomy 4–30 (Moses' 'farewell speech') contains Moses' words to the people as they are about to enter Canaan. But Moses' death was imminent and it was Joshua who led the people into the Promised Land. Moses died in the plains of Moab aged 120 years. Moses' legacy is recorded at the end of Deuteronomy: 'no prophet has risen in Israel like Moses, whom the Lord knew face to face' (Deuteronomy 34:10–11). His story dominates Exodus to Deuteronomy. He is celebrated throughout the Bible as the father of the Hebrew faith. He combined the roles of prophet, priest and king/judge. God spoke to him as a 'friend' (Exodus 33:11) but he was also known for his great humility (Numbers 12:3). Hebrews 3 records Moses' faithfulness as a servant of God. Although Moses played a key role in the exodus from Egypt, the Bible celebrates God's providence in the creating of a new nation: Moses was only an agent. In the New Testament he is referred to when Jesus is questioned about the Law and he appears at the transfiguration of Jesus (Matthew 17; Luke 9). He is remembered by Stephen in his speech to the Sanhedrin (Acts 7) and, along with his parents, is commended for his faith in Hebrews 11. In the New Testament (particularly in Hebrews) Moses' ministry is viewed as one that anticipates the ministry of Christ: Christ is the mediator of a new covenant, an eternal priest, the one who shares the glory of God and acts as an intercessor for God's people. In this way, Moses' involvement in the deliverance of the Israelites and the formation of a nation is only a shadow of Christ's work of salvation for all nations.

(2:10 – 40:38; Leviticus 1:1 – 27:34; Numbers 1:1 – 36:13; Deuteronomy 1:1 – 34:12; Joshua 1:1–7; 11:15; 12:6; 14:5–11; 24:5; Judges 1:20; 18:30; 1 Kings 8:9; 1 Chronicles 6:3; 23:13–15; 26:24; 2 Chronicles 5:10; Nehemiah 8:14; Psalms 77:20; 99:6; 105:26; 106:16, 23, 32–33; Isaiah 63:11–12; Jeremiah 15:1; Daniel 9:11; Micah 6:4; Malachi 4:4; Matthew 8:4; 17:3–4; 19:7–8; 22:24; 23:2; Mark 1:44; 7:10; 9:4–5; 10:3–5; 12:19, 26; Luke 2:22; 5:14; 9:30–33; 16:29, 31; 20:28, 37; 24:27, 44; John 1:17, 45; 3:14; 5:45–46; 6:32; 7:19–23; 8:5; 9:28–29; Acts 3:22; 6:11, 14; 7:20–38, 40, 44; 13:39; 15:1, 5, 21; 21:21; 26:22; 28:23; Romans 5:14; 9:15; 10:5, 19; 1 Corinthians 9:9; 10:2; 2 Corinthians 3:7, 13, 15; 2 Timothy 3:8; Hebrews 3:1–5, 16; 7:14; 8:5; 9:19; 10:28; 11:23–28; 12:21; Jude 9; Revelation 15:3)

Zipporah
(born late C16th BC)

Daughter of Jethro. Wife of Moses. Mother of Gershom[1] and Eliezer[2]. Exodus 4:24–26 suggests she demonstrated her own commitment to God by performing circumcision on her son in order to save Moses from judgment. Separated from Moses when he returned to Egypt, she was received back into Jethro's home. Later Jethro brought Zipporah to Moses when he was encamped with the Israelites near Mount Sinai.

(2:21–22; 4:24–26; 18:2)

Gershom[1]
(born early C15th BC)

First son of Moses and Zipporah. Grandson of Jethro. Father of Jonathan[1]. Moses chose his name as it resembled the Hebrew word for 'foreigner' – Moses recognized that was his status in Midian. It was presumably Gershom who was circumcised by his mother.

(2:22; 4:24–26; 18:3; Judges 18:30; 1 Chronicles 23:15–16; 26:24)

Jethro/Reuel[2]
(late C16th BC)

Priest in Midian. Father of Zipporah and Hobab. Father-in-law of Moses. Moses stayed with Jethro for about 40 years before returning to Egypt with Jethro's blessing. Jethro took Zipporah to visit Moses near Mount Sinai and there he rejoiced in what God had done for the Israelites. Jethro himself acted as priest, offering sacrifices to God in the company of Aaron and other elders. Jethro advised Moses to appoint leaders to delegate and share the responsibility of judging the people's disputes. He was a supportive father-in-law and a man of faith and wisdom.

(2:18, 21; 3:1; 4:18; 18:1–27; Numbers 10:29)

Aaron
(c.1530–1407 BC)

Son of Amram[1] and Jochebed (Levites). Brother of Moses and Miriam[1]. Husband of Elisheba. Father of Nadab[1], Abihu, Eleazar[1] and Ithamar. When Moses received God's call to lead his people, he was reluctant, because his speech lacked eloquence. Moses was reminded that Aaron, his elder brother, was a gifted speaker. Aaron became Moses' helper and together they confronted Pharaoh. Aaron was able to work miracles. His staff became a snake when he threw it down before Pharaoh and it was used to bring the plague of gnats to Egypt. God appointed Aaron and his sons to serve as priests. Their priestly garments were designed to reflect the honour and dignity of this role and their consecration ceremony culminated in anointing with oil. Aaron was encouraged by the people to make gods of gold and he acquiesced. Moses confronted Aaron and the people about the sin of making a golden calf and God struck them with a plague. Leviticus records detailed instructions about the way Aaron and his sons should fulfil the role of priests. Numbers shows how Moses and Aaron took a census of the Israelites and organized their religious life on their journey. There were moments of tension between the people and Aaron and Moses. Aaron died on Mount Hor near the border of Edom, which led to 30 days of mourning in Israel. In the New Testament, Aaron is mentioned when Elizabeth (mother of John the Baptist) is introduced and the story of the golden calf is retold in Stephen's speech. In Hebrews, Aaron's role as high priest is compared to that of Jesus Christ.

📖 (4:14; 6:23; 7:1–12; 8:16–17; 28:1–14; 29:1 – 30:33; 32:1 – 33:6; 34:30–31; 35:19; 38:21; 39:1, 27, 41; 40:12–15, 31; Leviticus 1–27; Numbers 1:3, 17; 3:1–51; 8:1–26; 12:1–12; 16:3, 11, 16–22, 40–50; 20:22–29; Deuteronomy 9:15–21; 10:6; Joshua 21:4; 1 Samuel 12:6–8; 1 Chronicles 6:3, 50–60; 23:13; 24:1; Ezra 7:5; Psalms 77:20; 99:6; 105:26; 106:16; 115:10, 12; Luke 1:5; Acts 7:40–41; Hebrews 5:4; 7:11)

Libni[1]
(born early C16th BC)

Son of Gershon. Grandson of Levi[1]. Father of Jahath[2].

📖 (6:17; Numbers 3:18, 21; 26:58; 1 Chronicles 6:17, 20)

Shimei[1]
(born early C16th BC)

Son of Gershon. Grandson of Levi[1].

📖 (6:17; Numbers 3:18, 21; 1 Chronicles 6:17; 23:7)

Amram[1]
(c.1590–1453 BC)

Son of Kohath. Grandson of Levi[1]. Husband of Jochebed. Father of Aaron, Moses and Miriam[1]. Lived 137 years.

📖 (6:18, 20; Numbers 3:19; 26:58–59; 1 Chronicles 6:2–3, 18; 23:12–13; 24:20)

Izhar
(born early C16th BC)

Son of Kohath. Grandson of Levi[1]. Father of Krah[3], Nepheg and Zikri[1] (and according to 1 Chronicles 23:18, Shelomith[3]). Uncle of Moses.

📖 (6:18, 21; Numbers 3:19; 16:1; 1 Chronicles 6:2, 18, 38; 23:12, 18; 24:22)

Hebron[1]
(born early C16th BC)

Son of Kohath. Grandson of Levi[1]. According to 1 Chronicles 23:19, father of Jeriah, Amariah[3], Jahaziel[3] and Jekameam. Uncle of Moses.

📖 (6:18; Numbers 3:19; 1 Chronicles 6:2, 18; 15:9; 23:12, 19; 24:23)

Uzziel[1]
(born early C16th BC)

Son of Kohath. Grandson of Levi[1]. Father of Mishael[1], Elzaphan/Elizaphan[1], Sithri (and according to 1 Chronicles 23:20, Micah[4], although this may be a variant of Mishael[1], and Ishiah[3]). Uncle of Moses and Aaron. His descendants took responsibility for the ark.

📖 (6:18, 22; Leviticus 10:4; Numbers 3:19, 27–30; 1 Chronicles 6:2, 18; 15:10; 23:12, 20; 24:24)

Mahli[1]
(born early C16th BC)

Son of Merari. Grandson of Levi[1]. Father of Libni[2], Eleazar[4] and Kish[3]. Along with other Merarite families, his family worked at the tent of meeting.

📖 (6:19; Numbers 3:20, 33–37; 4:29–33; 26:58; 1 Chronicles 6:19, 29; 23:21)

Mushi
(born early C16th BC)

Son of Merari. Grandson of Levi[1]. Father of Mahli[2], Eder[2] and Jerimoth[3]. Along with other Merarite families, his family worked at the tent of meeting.

📖 (6:19; Numbers 3:20, 33–37; 4:29–33; 26:58; 1 Chronicles 6:19, 47; 23:21, 23)

Jochebed
(born early C16th BC)

Wife of Amram[1]. Sister of Kohath. Mother of Moses, Aaron and Miriam[1]. A Levite. She gave birth to Moses when the lives of Hebrew boys were under threat so she hid him in a papyrus basket in the Nile. At Pharaoh's daughter's request she nursed her own son.

📖 (2:1–3, 8–9; 6:20)

Korah[3]
(born late C16th BC)

Son of Izhar. Grandson of Kohath. Father of Assir[1], Elkanah[1] and Abiasaph. Korah and his companions led a revolt against

Moses and Aaron, questioning their authority as leaders and priests. Because of this sin, the earth swallowed up Korah, although his family line was not completely wiped out. His family were gatekeepers at the tent of meeting and also musicians. His rebellion became notorious and is mentioned in the New Testament letter of Jude.

📖 (6:21, 24; Numbers 16:1–17; 26:9–11; 1 Chronicles 6:37; 9:19; 26:19; Jude 11)

Nepheg[1], Zikri[1] (Zicri)
(born late C16th BC)

Sons of Izhar. Grandsons of Kohath.

📖 (6:21)

Mishael[1], Sithri
(born late C16th BC)

Sons of Uzziel[1]. Grandsons of Kohath.

📖 (6:22; Leviticus 10:4–5)

Elzaphan/Elizaphan[1]
(born late C16th BC)

Son of Uzziel[1]. Grandson of Kohath. Leader of the Kohathites who were responsible for the care of the ark.

📖 (6:22; Leviticus 10:4–5; Numbers 3:30; 1 Chronicles 15:8; 2 Chronicles 29:13)

Elisheba
(born late C16th BC)

Daughter of Amminadab[1]. Sister of Nahshon. Wife of Aaron. Mother of Nadab[1], Abihu, Eleazar[1] and Ithamar.

📖 (6:23)

Amminadab[1]
(born mid C16th BC)

Father of Elisheba and Nahshon. As an ancestor of David he is mentioned in Matthew's and Luke's genealogies of Jesus.

📖 (6:23; Numbers 1:7; 2:3; 7:12, 17; 10:14; Ruth 4:19–20; 1 Chronicles 2:10; Matthew 1:4; Luke 3:33)

Nahshon
(born late C16th BC)

Son of Amminadab[1]. Brother
of Elisheba. Father of Salmon.
Grandfather of Boaz. Leader of the
tribe of Judah. He helped Moses and
Aaron with the census in the Desert
of Sinai. When the tabernacle was
dedicated, Nahshon was the first
tribal leader to bring his offering. As
an ancestor of David he is mentioned
in Matthew's and Luke's genealogies
of Jesus.

📖 (6:23; Numbers 1:7; 2:3; 7:12, 17;
10:14; Ruth 4:20; 1 Chronicles 2:10–11;
Matthew 1:4; Luke 3:32)

Nadab[1], Abihu
(born early C15th BC)

Sons of Aaron and Elisheba.
Appointed as priests and went up
Mount Sinai with Moses and Aaron
and 70 elders where they 'saw the
God of Israel'. They died (consumed
by fire from the presence of the Lord)
in the Desert of Sinai after they made
an offering using 'unauthorized fire',
contrary to the command of God.

📖 (6:23; 24:1, 9–11; 28:1; Leviticus
10:1–3; Numbers 3:2–4; 26:60–61;
1 Chronicles 6:3; 24:1–2)

Eleazar[1]
(born early C15th BC)

Son of Aaron and Elisheba. Father of
Phinehas[1]. Appointed as priest and
with Ithamar was allowed to eat a
share of the sacrifices. Eleazar became
leader of the Levites, in charge of
the tabernacle and everything in it.
On Aaron's death, Eleazar succeeded
him as high priest and Moses put
Aaron's priestly robes on him. He
worked alongside Moses offering
guidance and support. Eleazar
witnessed the commissioning of
Joshua[1] as Moses' successor. He
worked alongside Joshua as judge
and advisor, especially regarding
the division of the land of Canaan
between the tribes. His death is
recorded at the end of the book of
Joshua and he was buried at Gibeah

in Ephraim, which had been allotted
to his son.

📖 (6:23; 28:1; Leviticus 10:6–20; Numbers
3:2–4, 32; 4:16; 16:37, 39; 19:3–4;
20:25–28; 25:7, 11; 26:1, 3, 60, 63;
27:18–23; 31:6, 12–13, 21, 26, 29,
31, 41, 51–54; 34:17; Deuteronomy
10:6; Joshua 14:1; 17:4; 19:51; 21:1;
22:13, 31–32; 24:33; Judges 20:28;
1 Chronicles 6:3–4; 24:1–6)

Ithamar
(born early C15th BC)

Son of Aaron and Elisheba.
Appointed as priest during Aaron's
lifetime and allowed to eat a share
of the sacrifices. He took a leading
role among the Levites in the
construction of the tabernacle and
the supervision of those working
in it.

📖 (6:23; 28:1; 38:21; Leviticus 10:6–20;
Numbers 3:2–4; 4:28, 33; 7:8; 26:60;
1 Chronicles 6:3; 24:1–6; Ezra 8:2)

**Assir[1], Elkanah[1], Abiasaph/
Ebiasaph**
(born early C15th BC)

Descendants of Korah[3] or possibly
Korah[5].

📖 (6:24; 1 Chronicles 6:22–23, 37; 9:19)

Putiel
(late C16th BC)

Father of Eleazar[1]'s wife and other
daughters.

📖 (6:25)

Phinehas[1]
(mid C15th BC)

Son of Eleazar[1] through Putiel's
daughter. Grandson of Aaron. Father
of Abishua[1]. Ancestor of Ezra[1].
Phinehas supervised the gatekeepers
at the tent of meeting and 'the
Lord was with him'. At Shittim,
God's people angered God by their
immorality but Phinehas killed
an Israelite man and a Midianite
woman caught in the act of adultery
by driving his spear through them.
This averted God's anger, and God's

plague of judgment that had killed 24,000 people ended. The Lord commended Phinehas because he was zealous for the honour of God. He led a delegation to question the tribes of Reuben, Gad[1] and Manasseh[1] about an altar they had built. Phinehas's faith is evident: he declared that the episode reaffirmed the Lord's presence with them.

📖 (6:25; Numbers 25:6–13; 31:6; Joshua 22:13, 30–32; 24:33; Judges 20:28; 1 Chronicles 6:4, 50; 9:20; Ezra 7:5; 8:2, 33; Psalm 106:30)

Miriam[1]
(born late C16th BC)

Daughter of Amram[1] and Jochebed. Sister of Moses and Aaron. She is unnamed in Exodus 2 but she played a significant role in watching Moses, her brother, who was hidden in the Nile's bulrushes and then in negotiating with Pharaoh's daughter. Miriam was called a prophet and she led the people in song and dance when they escaped from Egypt. Along with Aaron, Miriam opposed Moses and questioned his authority over them. For this she was punished by God and her skin became leprous. Moses pleaded to the Lord for her and after seven days she was allowed to return to the camp, but her role was diminished. She died and was buried at Kadesh in the Desert of Zin.

📖 (2:1–9; 15:20–21; Numbers 12:1–15; 20:1; 26:59; Deuteronomy 24:9; 1 Chronicles 6:3; Micah 6:4)

Joshua[1]/Hoshea[1]
(c.1480–1370 BC)

Son of Nun. Leader of the tribe of Ephraim. Moses changed his name from Hoshea to Joshua (meaning 'the Lord saves'). Joshua was among those sent out from the Desert of Paran to explore the land of Canaan. Along with Caleb[1], Joshua encouraged the Israelites to trust God and enter Canaan. He became Moses' aide. When the

Amalekites attacked the Israelites at Rephidim, Moses sent Joshua to fight them and he overcame the Amalekite army. Before Moses died, he identified Joshua as his natural successor. God promised Joshua, 'I myself will be with you' and encouraged him to be 'strong and courageous'. Joshua became the military leader of the Israelites, leading them across the Jordan into Canaan. He also led their religious life (e.g. performing circumcision, celebrating the Passover, leading covenant renewal ceremonies, writing down the Law). His military achievements dominate the book of Joshua and included the destruction of Ai (chapter 8), the defeat of the five Amorite kings who attacked his allies in Gibeon (chapter 10) and the defeat of the northern kings at the Waters of Merom (chapter 11). In all these accounts Joshua's faith in God is emphasized: praise for victories is given to the Lord. At the end of his life he addressed the people and led them in a covenant renewal ceremony (i.e. a ceremony providing the opportunity to renew vows of commitment to God) at Shechem. He died at the age of 110 and was buried in Ephraim.

📖 (17:9–14; 24:13; 32:17; 33:11; Numbers 11:28; 13:8, 16; 14:6–9, 30, 38; 26:65; 27:18, 22; 32:12, 28; 34:17; Deuteronomy 1:38; 3:21, 28; 31:3, 7–8, 14, 23; 32:44; 34:9; Joshua 1–24; Judges 1:1; 2:6–8, 21, 23; 1 Kings 16:34; 1 Chronicles 7:27; Nehemiah 8:17; Acts 7:45; Hebrews 4:8)

Hur[1]
(born mid C16th BC)

Son of Caleb[2] and Ephrath. Father of Uri[1]. From the tribe of Judah. Along with Aaron, Hur held up Moses' hands when Joshua was fighting the Amalekites in order to ensure victory. This symbolic act was significant in that it recognized the people's dependence on God. Hur often worked alongside Aaron, and when Moses went up Mount Sinai to confirm the covenant he left Hur in joint charge with Aaron.

(17:10, 12; 24:14; 31:2; 35:30; 38:22; 1 Chronicles 2:19–20, 50; 4:1, 4; 2 Chronicles 1:5)

Eliezer[2]
(born early C15th BC)

Son of Moses and Zipporah. Father of only one son, Rehabiah, but through him he had many grandsons. Name means 'my God is helper'.

(18:4; 1 Chronicles 23:15, 17; 26:25)

Bezalel[1]
(born early C15th BC)

Son of Uri[1]. Grandson of Hur[1]. In charge of those involved in the artistic design of the tabernacle and its contents, including the ark. In addition to his artistic skills, he was a man 'filled with the Spirit of God, with wisdom and understanding, with knowledge and with all kinds of skills'.

(31:2; 35:30; 36:1–2; 37:1–9; 38:22; 1 Chronicles 2:20; 2 Chronicles 1:5)

Uri[1]
(late C16th BC)

Son of Hur[1]. Father of Bezalel[1].

(31:2; 35:30; 38:22; 1 Chronicles 2:20; 2 Chronicles 1:5)

Oholiab
(born early C15th BC)

Son of Ahisamak. He helped Bezalel[1] with the artistic design of the tabernacle and its contents. He was an engraver, designer and embroiderer.

(31:6; 35:34; 36:1–2; 38:23)

Ahisamak (Ahisamach)
(late C16th BC)

Father of Oholiab. From the tribe of Dan.

(31:6; 35:34; 38:23)

Nun
(late C16th BC)

Father of Joshua[1] and only mentioned in connection with his son.

(33:11; Numbers 11:28; Joshua 1:1; 2:1, 17:4; 24:29; Judges 2:8; 1 Kings 16:34; 1 Chronicles 7:27; Nehemiah 8:17)

Leviticus

Shelomith[1]
(late C16th BC)

Daughter of Dibri. Married an Egyptian. Mother of an unnamed Israelite man who cursed the name of the Lord and was stoned to death outside the Israelite camp.

(24:10–11, 23)

Dibri
(mid C16th BC)

Father of Shelomith[1]. From the tribe of Dan.

(24:11)

Numbers

Elizur
(born late C16th BC)

Son of Shedeur. Head of the tribe of Reuben. He helped Moses and Aaron with the first census of the Israelites in the Desert of Sinai. At the dedication of the tabernacle he brought his offering on the fourth day. He led his tribe when the people set out from Sinai.

(1:5; 2:10; 7:30, 35; 10:18)

Shedeur
(mid C16th BC)

Father of Elizur.

(1:5; 2:10; 7:30, 35; 10:18)

Shelumiel
(born late C16th BC)

Son of Zurishaddai. Head of the tribe of Simeon[1]. He helped Moses and Aaron with the first census of the Israelites in the Desert of Sinai. At the dedication of the tabernacle he brought his offering on the fifth day. He led his tribe when the people set out from Sinai.

📖 (1:6; 2:12; 7:36, 41; 10:19)

Zurishaddai
(mid C16th BC)

Father of Shelumiel.

📖 (1:6; 2:12; 7:36, 41; 10:19)

Nethanel[1]
(born late C16th BC)

Son of Zuar. Head of the tribe of Issachar[1]. He helped Moses and Aaron with the first census of the Israelites in the Desert of Sinai. At the dedication of the tabernacle he brought his offering on the second day. He led his tribe when the people set out from Sinai.

📖 (1:8; 2:5; 7:18, 23; 10:15)

Zuar
(mid C16th BC)

Father of Nethanel[1].

📖 (1:8; 2:5; 7:18, 23; 10:15)

Eliab[1]
(born late C16th BC)

Son of Helon. Head of the tribe of Zebulun. He helped Moses and Aaron with the first census of the Israelites in the Desert of Sinai. At the dedication of the tabernacle he brought his offering on the third day. He led his tribe when the people set out from Sinai.

📖 (1:9; 2:7; 7:24, 29; 10:16)

Helon
(mid C16th BC)

Father of Eliab[1].

📖 (1:9; 2:7; 7:24, 29; 10:16)

Elishama[1]
(born late C16th BC)

Son of Ammihud[1]. Head of the tribe of Ephraim. He helped Moses and Aaron with the first census of the Israelites in the Desert of Sinai. At the dedication of the tabernacle he brought his offering on the seventh day. He led his tribe when the people set out from Sinai.

📖 (1:10; 2:18; 7:48, 53; 10:22; 1 Chronicles 7:26)

Ammihud[1]
(mid C16th BC)

Son of Ladan[1]. Grandson of Tahan[1]. Father of Elishama[1].

📖 (1:10; 2:18; 7:48, 53; 10:22; 1 Chronicles 7:26)

Gamaliel[1]
(born late C16th BC)

Son of Pedahzur. Head of the tribe of Manasseh[1]. He helped Moses and Aaron with the first census of the Israelites in the Desert of Sinai. At the dedication of the tabernacle he brought his offering on the eighth day. He led his tribe when the people set out from Sinai.

📖 (1:10; 2:20; 7:54, 59; 10:23)

Pedahzur
(mid C16th BC)

Father of Gamaliel[1].

📖 (1:10; 2:20; 7:54, 59; 10:23)

Abidan
(born late C16th BC)

Son of Gideoni. Head of the tribe of Benjamin[1]. He helped Moses and Aaron with the first census of the Israelites in the Desert of Sinai. At the dedication of the tabernacle he brought his offering on the ninth day. He led his tribe when the people set out from Sinai.

📖 (1:11; 2:22; 7:60, 65; 10:24)

Gideoni
(mid C16th BC)
Father of Abidan.
📖 (1:11; 2:22; 7:60, 65; 10:24)

Ahiezer[1]
(born late C16th BC)
Son of Ammishaddai. Head of the tribe of Dan. He helped Moses and Aaron with the first census of the Israelites in the Desert of Sinai. At the dedication of the tabernacle he brought his offering on the tenth day. He led his tribe when the people set out from Sinai.
📖 (1:12; 2:25; 7:66, 71; 10:25)

Ammishaddai
(mid C16th BC)
Father of Ahiezer[1].
📖 (1:12; 2:25; 7:66, 71; 10:25)

Pagiel
(born late C16th BC)
Son of Okran. Head of the tribe of Asher. He helped Moses and Aaron with the first census of the Israelites in the Desert of Sinai. At the dedication of the tabernacle he brought his offering on the eleventh day. He led his tribe when the people set out from Sinai.
📖 (1:13; 2:27; 7:72, 77; 10:26)

Okran (Ocran)
(mid C16th BC)
Father of Pagiel.
📖 (1:13; 2:27; 7:72, 77; 10:26)

Eliasaph[1]
(born late C16th BC)
Son of Deuel. Head of the tribe of Gad[1]. He helped Moses and Aaron with the first census of the Israelites in the Desert of Sinai. At the dedication of the tabernacle he brought his offering on the sixth day. He led his tribe when the people set out from Sinai.
📖 (1:14; 2:14; 7:42, 47; 10:20)

Deuel
(mid C16th BC)
Father of Eliasaph[1].
📖 (1:14; 2:14; 7:42, 47; 10:20)

Ahira
(born late C16th BC)
Son of Enan. Head of the tribe of Naphtali. He helped Moses and Aaron with the first census of the Israelites in the Desert of Sinai. At the dedication of the tabernacle he brought his offering on the twelfth day. He led his tribe when the people set out from Sinai.
📖 (1:15; 2:29; 7:78, 83; 10:27)

Enan
(mid C16th BC)
Father of Ahira.
📖 (1:15; 2:29; 7:78, 83; 10:27)

Eliasaph[2]
(born late C16th BC)
Son of Lael. From the tribe of Levi[1]. Leader of the Gershonites, who were responsible for the care of the tabernacle furnishings.
📖 (3:24)

Lael
(mid C16th BC)
Father of Eliasaph[2].
📖 (3:24)

Elizaphan[1]/Elzaphan
(born late C16th BC)
See **Elzaphan** in Exodus, p. 44.
📖 (3:30)

Zuriel
(born late C16th BC)
Son of Abihail[1]. From the tribe of Levi[1]. Leader of the Merarites, who were responsible for the care of the structure of the tabernacle.
📖 (3:35)

Abihail[1]
(mid C16th BC)

Father of Zuriel.

📖 (3:35)

Hobab
(born early C15th BC)

Son of Reuel[2]/Jethro. A relative of Moses (possibly his brother-in-law). He was either a Kenite or a Moabite. Moses persuaded him to travel with the Israelites when they began their wandering days in the desert because he knew the desert area well.

📖 (10:29; Judges 4:11)

Reuel[2]/Jethro
(born late C16th BC)

See **Jethro** in Exodus, p. 42.

📖 (10:29)

Eldad, Medad
(born late C16th BC)

Two Israelite elders who stayed in the camp when 70 elders went to the tent of meeting with Moses to receive the Spirit of God. The Spirit came upon them in the camp and they prophesied there.

📖 (11:26)

Shammua[1], Shaphat[1], Igal[1], Palti, Gaddiel, Gaddi, Ammiel[1], Sethur, Nahbi, Geuel
(born early C15th BC)

The 10 leaders of the tribes who were sent by Moses with Caleb[1] and Hoshea/Joshua to explore Canaan. When they reported back to Moses their report was negative, expressing fearfulness, because of the greatness of the people already occupying the land.

📖 (13:1–16, 26–29)

Zakkur[1] (Zaccur)
(born late C16th BC)

Father of Shammua[1].

📖 (13:4)

Hori[2]
(born late C16th BC)

Father of Shaphat[1].

📖 (13:5)

Caleb[1]
(c.1490–after 1405 BC)

Son of Jephunneh[1]. Brother of Kenaz[3]. Father of Iru, Elah[4] and Naam and a daughter called Aksah[1] (Acsah) who married Caleb's nephew Othniel. Caleb was one of 12 men who were sent from the Desert of Paran to explore Canaan. He was leader of the tribe of Judah and also called a Kenizzite. Although the others who returned from Canaan with him brought back and circulated negative reports that exposed their fearfulness, Caleb told Moses and the people that they should take possession of the land because the Lord was with them. Joshua[1] joined forces with Caleb and the Lord promised that only these two men of all the people in the Desert of Paran would enter the land of Canaan. Caleb led the attack against the Anakites in Hebron and when the land was divided up, the villages and fields around Hebron were given to Caleb. He assumed responsibility along with nine other tribal leaders for the distribution of the land for the tribes under the direction of Joshua[1] and Eleazar[1]. The Old Testament refers to Caleb as someone who 'followed the Lord wholeheartedly'.

📖 (13:6, 30; 14:6–9, 24, 30, 38; 26:65; 32:12; 34:19; Deuteronomy 1:36; Joshua 14:6, 13–14; 15:13–19; 21:12; Judges 1:12–20; 3:9; 1 Samuel 30:14; 1 Chronicles 4:15; 6:56)

Jephunneh[1]
(born late C16th BC)

Father of Caleb[1]. Grandfather of Iru, Elah[4] and Naam. He is called a Kenizzite.

📖 (13:6; 14:6, 30, 38; 26:65; 32:12; 34:19; Deuteronomy 1:36; Joshua 14:6, 13–14; 15:13; 21:12; 1 Chronicles 4:15; 6:56)

Joseph[2]
(late C16th BC)

Father of Igal[1].

📖 (13:7)

Hoshea
(c.1480–1370 BC)

See **Joshua[1]** in Exodus p. 46.

📖 (13:8)

Raphu
(born late C16th BC)

Father of Palti.

📖 (13:9)

Sodi
(born late C16th BC)

Father of Gaddiel.

📖 (13:10)

Susi
(born late C16th BC)

Father of Gaddi.

📖 (13:11)

Gemalli
(born late C16th BC)

Father of Ammiel[1].

📖 (13:12)

Michael[1]
(born late C16th BC)

Father of Sethur.

📖 (13:13)

Vophsi
(born late C16th BC)

Father of Nahbi.

📖 (13:14)

Maki
(born late C16th BC)

Father of Geuel.

📖 (13:15)

Ahiman[1], Sheshai, Talmai[1]
(mid C15th BC)

The three sons of Anak who were living in Hebron when the 12 leaders of tribes were sent to inspect the land of Canaan. The Anak people, descendants of the Nephilim, were feared by the Israelites on account of their great size. When the Israelites advanced on Canaan, Caleb[1] defeated the Anakites.

📖 (13:22; Joshua 15:14; Judges 1:10)

Anak
(early C15th BC)

Father of Ahiman[1], Sheshai and Talmai[1]. Descendant of Arba. He gave his name to the Anakites who lived in Canaan before the Israelites and who were feared by the Israelites on account of their great size.

📖 (13:22, 28, 33; Joshua 15:13–14; 21:11; Judges 1:20)

Dathan, Abiram[1]
(born early C15th BC)

Sons of Eliab[2]. Brothers of Nemuel[1]. These Reubenites joined Korah[3] and On and another 250 Israelite men to oppose Moses' leadership. The result was that the earth swallowed up them and their companions and all their families and possessions.

📖 (16:1, 12–15, 24–35; 26:9–10; Deuteronomy 11:6; Psalm 106:17–18)

Eliab[2]
(born late C16th BC)

Son of Pallu. Father of Nemuel[1], Dathan and Abiram[1]. A Reubenite.

📖 (16:1, 12; 26:8–9; Deuteronomy 11:6)

On
(born early C15th BC)

Son of Peleth[1]. He joined Korah[3], Dathan, Abiram[1] and another 250 Israelite men to oppose Moses' leadership. The result was that the earth swallowed up On and his companions and all their families and possessions.

📖 (16:1)

Peleth[1]
(late C16th BC)
Father of On.
📖 (16:1)

Sihon
(reigned late C15th BC)
Amorite king of Heshbon. His
territory included half of Gilead
and the eastern Arabah area. He
would not allow the Israelites to
pass through his land. The Israelites
therefore attacked Sihon's army and
defeated them in battle at Jahaz.
They took all his towns from Aroer
to Gilead. His land was given to the
Reubenites, Gadites and half-tribe of
Manasseh[1].

📖 (21:21, 23–31, 34; 32:33; Deuteronomy
1:4; 2:24–37; 3:2, 6; 4:46; 29:7–8; 31:4;
Joshua 2:10; 9:10; 12:2–3, 5; 13:10,
21, 27; Judges 11:19–21; 1 Kings 4:19;
Nehemiah 9:22; Psalms 135:11; 136:19;
Jeremiah 48:45)

Og
(reigned late C15th BC)
Amorite king of Bashan. He would
not allow the Israelites to pass
through his territory. The Israelites
attacked Og's army and defeated
them in battle at Edrei. There were
no survivors in Og's army and the
Israelites took control of Bashan
in Ashtaroth and the 60 fortified
cities of Og in the region of Argob.
Og is described as 'the last of the
Rephaites' (a tall ancient people
who resided in the land east of the
Jordan). His land was given to the
Reubenites, Gadites and half-tribe of
Manasseh[1].

📖 (21:33–35; 32:33; Deuteronomy 1:4;
3:1–4, 10–11, 13; 4:47–48; 29:7–8;
31:4; Joshua 2:10; 9:10; 12:4–5; 13:12,
30–31; 1 Kings 4:19; Nehemiah 9:22;
Psalms 135:11; 136:20)

Balak
(reigned late C15th BC)
King of Moab. Son of Zippor. He
tried to persuade Balaam to curse the
Israelites, whose exploits against the

Amorite kings had become known
– Balak was afraid of their growing
power. Balak took Balaam to three
separate places to see the Israelites
with the aim of encouraging Balaam
to curse them. But instead of cursing
the Israelites, Balaam blessed them
three times and then spoke further
messages declaring their power over
other nations. Balak was angry and
did not give Balaam the financial
rewards he had promised. He was
silenced by Balaam's determination
to speak God's words and not his
own.

📖 (22:2–18, 35–40; 23:1–30; 24:10–14,
25; Joshua 24:9; Judges 11:25; Micah
6:5; Revelation 2:14)

Zippor
(mid C15th BC)
Father of Balak.
📖 (22:2, 4, 10, 16; Joshua 24:9; Judges
11:25)

Balaam
(late C15th BC)
Son of Beor[2]. A prophet who
practised divination and lived in
Pethor near the River Euphrates in
north-west Mesopotamia. When
Balaam is first mentioned, he appears
to be serving the interests of God's
people. Balak tried to persuade
Balaam to curse the Israelites. Balak
sent his officials to bring Balaam
to Moab to comply with his wishes
on the promise of financial reward.
At first Balaam resisted Balak's
demands and refused to go, but
finally he agreed. On the way, the
Lord sent an angel who spoke to
Balaam through the mouth of his
own donkey. It is clear that God
was angry with Balaam. The Lord
reminded Balaam that he should
only speak as the Lord directed
him. On arrival in Moab, despite
all Balak's efforts, Balaam delivered
messages of blessing on the Israelites
and declared that other nations
would come to ruin on account of
them. On another occasion Balaam's
duplicity was exposed more clearly.

Balaam worked with the Midianites, suggesting their only option was to lure the Israelites into sexual sin. This resulted in Balaam's death along with the Midianite kings. The New Testament references to Balaam suggest that Balaam was really a deceiver, a lover of money, whose evil intent masqueraded itself in religious activity.

📖 (22:5 – 24:25; 31:8, 16; Deuteronomy 23:4–5; Joshua 13:22; 24:9–10; Nehemiah 13:2; Micah 6:5; 2 Peter 2:15–16; Jude 11; Revelation 2:14)

Beor[2]/Bezer[1]
(mid C15th BC)

Father of Balaam.

📖 (22:5; 24:3, 15; 31:8; Deuteronomy 23:4; Joshua 13:22; 24:9; Micah 6:5; 2 Peter 2:15)

Agag[1]
(unknown)

Either an unknown man or a prophetic reference to Agag[2].

📖 (24:7)

Zimri[1]
(late C15th BC)

Son of Salu. He was killed by Phinehas[1] when he brought a Midianite woman, Kozbi, into his tent to have sex with her. Phinehas's spear was driven through them both and resulted in the end of the plague which had already killed 24,000 Israelites.

📖 (25:14)

Salu
(mid C15th BC)

Father of Zimri[1]. Leader of a Simeonite family.

📖 (25:14)

Kozbi (Cozbi)
(late C15th BC)

Daughter of a tribal chief called Zur[1]. This Midianite woman was brought into the Israelite camp by Zimri[1] and was killed with him

by Phinehas[1]'s spear. As a result of this incident, the Lord instructed the Israelites to treat the Midianites as enemies.

📖 (25:15, 18)

Zur[1]
(mid C15th BC)

Father of Kozbi, who was brought into the Israelite camp in order to have sex with Zimri[1], an Israelite man. One of the five kings of Midian who had become allies of Sihon and were killed by the Israelites in the same offensive in which Balaam was killed (see **Mahlah[1]** etc., 26:33).

📖 (25:15; 31:8; Joshua 13:21)

Nemuel[1]
(early C15th BC)

Son of Eliab[2]. Grandson of Pallu and great-grandson of Reuben. Brother of Dathan and Abiram[1].

📖 (26:9)

Nemuel[2]/Jemuel
(born early C17th BC)

Descendant of Simeon[1] and founder of the Nemuelite clan. See **Jemuel** in Genesis p. 39.

📖 (26:12; 1 Chronicles 4:24)

Gilead[1]
(late C17th BC)

Son of Makir[1]. Grandson of Manasseh[1]. His name was given to land east of the Jordan.

📖 (26:29–30; 27:1; 36:1; Joshua 17:1, 3; Judges 5:17; 11:1–2; 1 Chronicles 2:21, 23; 7:14, 17)

Iezer/Abiezer[1]
(early C16th BC)

Son of Gilead[1]. Leader of the Iezerite clan. See **Abiezer[1]** in Joshua, p. 59.

📖 (26:30; Judges 6:34; 8:2)

Helek
(early C16th BC)
Son of Gilead[1]. Leader of the
Helekite clan.
📖 (26:30; Joshua 17:2)

Asriel
(early C16th BC)
Son of Gilead[1]. Leader of the
Asrielite clan.
📖 (26:31; Joshua 17:2; 1 Chronicles 7:14)

Shechem[2]
(early C16th BC)
Son of Gilead[1]. Leader of the
Shechemite clan.
📖 (26:31; Joshua 17:2)

Shemida
(early C16th BC)
Son of Gilead[1]. Leader of the
Shemidaite clan. Father of Ahian,
Shechem[3], Likhi and Aniam.
📖 (26:32; Joshua 17:2; 1 Chronicles 7:19)

Hepher[1]
(early C16th BC)
Son of Gilead[1]. Leader of the
Hepherite clan. Ancestor of
Zelophehad.
📖 (26:32-33; 27:1; Joshua 17:2-3)

Zelophehad
(early C15th BC)
Descendant of Hepher[1]. Father
of five daughters: Mahlah[1],
Noah[2], Hoglah, Milkah[2] (Milcah)
and Tirzah. He had no sons but
his daughters were given his
inheritance.
📖 (26:33; 27:1-7; Joshua 17:3-6;
    1 Chronicles 7:15)

**Mahlah[1], Noah[2], Hoglah,
Milkah[2] (Milcah), Tirzah**
(late C15th BC)
The five daughters of Zelophehad,
who brought a test case before
Moses, by asking if they could be
given their father's inheritance

because they had no brothers. Moses
in turn brought the case before
the Lord, who adjudicated in their
favour. In turn the daughters married
within the tribe of Manasseh[1] to
comply with a further divine ruling
that their inheritance should not
pass to another tribe.
📖 (26:33; 27:1-11; 36:1-12; Joshua 17:3)

**Shuthelah[1], Beker[2],
Tahan[1]**
(mid C17th BC)
Sons of Ephraim. Leaders of the
Shuthelahite, Bekerite and Tahanite
clans.
📖 (26:35-36; 1 Chronicles 7:20)

Eran
(late C17th BC)
Son of Shuthelah[1]. Leader of the
Eranite clan.
📖 (26:36)

Ahiram
(early C17th BC)
See **Ehi/Ahiram/Aher/Aharah** in
Genesis, p. 40.
📖 (26:38)

Shupham
(born early C17th BC)
Descendant of Benjamin[1]. Leader
of the Shuphamite clan.
📖 (26:39)

Shuham
(born early C17th BC)
See **Hushim** in *Genesis p. 40.*
📖 (26:42)

Jahzeel
(born early C17th BC)
See **Jahziel/Jahzeel** in *Genesis,
p. 41.*
📖 (26:48)

Evi, Rekem[1], Hur[2], Reba
(late C15th BC)
Four of the five kings of Midian who

had become allies of Sihon and were killed by the Israelites in the same offensive in which Balaam was killed (see also **Zur[1]**, 25:15).

📖 (31:8; Joshua 13:21)

Jair[1]
(late C15th BC)

A descendant of Manasseh[1] through Makir[1]. He captured the settlements of Gilead in the region of Argob in Bashan, which was at that time populated by the Rephaites, and he renamed them Havvoth Jair ('the settlements of Jair').

📖 (32:41; Deuteronomy 3:14; Joshua 13:30; 1 Kings 4:13)

Nobah
(late C15th BC)

Probably a descendant of Manasseh[1] through Makir[1]. Captured Kenath and its settlements and renamed it Nobah after himself.

📖 (32:42)

Shemuel
(born mid C15th BC)

Son of Ammihud[2]. Leader of the tribe of Simeon[1]. He was appointed to assist Eleazar[1] and Joshua[1] in the distribution of land among the Israelite tribes.

📖 (34:20)

Ammihud[2]
(born early C15th BC)

Father of Shemuel. A Simeonite.

📖 (34:20)

Elidad
(born mid C15th BC)

Son of Kislon. Leader of the tribe of Benjamin. He was appointed to assist Eleazar[1] and Joshua[1] in the distribution of land among the Israelite tribes.

📖 (34:21)

Kislon
(born early C15th BC)

Father of Elidad. A Benjamite.

📖 (34:21)

Bukki[1]
(born mid C15th BC)

Son of Jogli. Leader of the tribe of Dan. He was appointed to assist Eleazar[1] and Joshua[1] in the distribution of land among the Israelite tribes.

📖 (34:22)

Jogli
(born early C15th BC)

Father of Bukki[1]. A Danite.

📖 (34:22)

Hanniel[1]
(born mid C15th BC)

Son of Ephod. Leader of the tribe of Manasseh[1]. He was appointed to assist Eleazar[1] and Joshua[1] in the distribution of land among the Israelite tribes.

📖 (34:23)

Ephod
(born early C15th BC)

Father of Hanniel[1]. From the tribe of Manasseh[1].

📖 (34:23)

Kemuel[2]
(born mid C15th BC)

Son of Shiphtan. Leader of the tribe of Ephraim. He was appointed to assist Eleazar[1] and Joshua[1] in the distribution of land among the Israelite tribes.

📖 (34:24)

Shiphtan
(born early C15th BC)

Father of Kemuel[2]. From the tribe of Ephraim.

📖 (34:24)

Elizaphan[2]
(born mid C15th BC)

Son of Parnak (Parnach). Leader of the tribe of Zebulun. He was appointed to assist Eleazar[1] and Joshua[1] in the distribution of land among the Israelite tribes.

📖 (34:25)

Parnak (Parnach)
(born early C15th BC)

Father of Elizaphan[2]. From the tribe of Zebulun.

📖 (34:25)

Paltiel[1]
(born mid C15th BC)

Son of Azzan. Leader of the tribe of Issachar[1]. He was appointed to assist Eleazar[1] and Joshua[1] in the distribution of land among the Israelite tribes.

📖 (34:26)

Azzan
(born early C15th BC)

Father of Paltiel[1]. From the tribe of Issachar[1].

📖 (34:26)

Ahihud[1]
(born mid C15th BC)

Son of Shelomi. Leader of the tribe of Asher. He was appointed to assist Eleazar[1] and Joshua[1] in the distribution of land among the Israelite tribes.

📖 (34:27)

Shelomi
(born early C15th BC)

Father of Ahihud[1]. From the tribe of Asher.

📖 (34:27)

Pedahel
(born mid C15th BC)

Son of Ammihud[3]. Leader of the tribe of Naphtali. He was appointed to assist Eleazar[1] and Joshua[1] in the distribution of land among the Israelite tribes.

📖 (34:28)

Ammihud[3]
(born early C15th BC)

Father of Pedahel. From the tribe of Naphtali.

📖 (34:28)

Deuteronomy

Moses
(1527–1407 BC)
See **Moses** in Exodus, p. 41.

Aaron
(c.1530–1407 BC)
See **Aaron** in Exodus, p. 43.

Joshua
(c.1480–1370 BC)
See **Joshua[1]** in Exodus, p. 46.

Caleb
(c.1490–after 1405 BC)
See **Caleb[1]** in Numbers, p. 50.

2 The History Books

The books of Joshua to Esther are known as the 'history books' of the Old Testament. They record the events from the time Joshua leads the Israelites into Canaan until they return to Jerusalem and the city walls are rebuilt under Ezra and Nehemiah. During this period Israel becomes a nation with its own king. Then the nation divides and they war with other nations. The people are exiled and at the point of despair, but a remnant returns and future hope is re-established. Spiritually, the nation has its ups and downs but covenant renewal (i.e. the opportunity to begin again with God and renew vows of commitment) is an ever-present possibility. The nation's political fortunes are linked with their spiritual commitment. The history books are not a continuous narrative and many events are recorded more than once, with different emphases added by different authors. However, as a whole they bear witness to a deep conviction that the records of history give evidence of God's promises being fulfilled among his chosen people.

For the period from Joshua to David, there is much controversy about chronology. This controversy is centred on the date when the Israelites entered Canaan. Whatever date is assumed, chronological problems remain. Without wanting to be dogmatic on the issue, this book has adopted 1407 BC as the date for the conquest. Appropriate adjustments will have to be made if the conquest occurred in the mid thirteenth century BC; but in any case all dates prior to David should be treated with caution.

Joshua

Joshua
(c.1480–1370 BC)

See **Joshua[1]** in Exodus, p. 46.

📖 (1:1)

Rahab
(late C15th BC)

A prostitute who lived in a house in the city wall of Jericho. She hid in her home two spies whom Joshua[1] sent from Shittim. She told messengers sent from the king of Jericho that the spies had already left her home. When it was safe, she let the spies leave by means of a scarlet cord, which she lowered through her window. In return she asked the spies to save her family from death when the Israelites came to take control of the land. She delivered a powerful confession of faith, which revealed her understanding of God's purposes and recognition of his sovereignty. The spies assured Rahab that she and her family would be protected if she tied the scarlet cord to her window when the Israelites advanced. When Joshua entered Jericho, he burnt down the whole city but spared Rahab. Rahab appears in the list of the people of faith in Hebrews 11, which is noteworthy as she was a non-Israelite and a prostitute. James celebrates Rahab as someone whose faith was supported by her deeds. It seems likely that the reference to Rahab in the genealogy of Jesus in Matthew 1 is a reference to this same Rahab, which in turn indicates she became the mother of Boaz and the great-great-grandmother of King David.

📖 (2:1–21; 6:17, 23, 25; Matthew 1:5; Hebrews 11:31; James 2:25)

Achan/Achar
(late C15th BC)

Son of Karmi[2] (Carmi). Grandson of Zimri[2]. From the tribe of Judah. When Joshua[1]'s army tried to take over Ai, they were surprisingly defeated. The Lord revealed to Joshua that the defeat was inflicted because Israel had sinned by taking some of the possessions of those they had defeated rather than destroying them as they had been commanded to do. Achan was identified as the perpetrator of this crime as he had hidden in his tent a beautiful robe along with some silver and gold. In the Valley of Achor (meaning 'trouble') the people stoned Achan and his family to death and burnt all his possessions. They marked the site with a heap of rocks, and God's anger turned from the people. Achan's fate is a reminder to Israel of the community consequences of one person's sin.

📖 (7:1, 16–26; 22:20; 1 Chronicles 2:7)

Karmi[2] (Carmi)
(mid C15th BC)

Father of Achan. Son of Zimri[2]. Descendant of Zerah[3]. From the tribe of Judah[1].

📖 (7:1, 18; 1 Chronicles 2:7; 4:1)

Zimri[2]
(early C15th BC)

Father of Karmi[2]. Grandfather of Achan. Descendant of Zerah[3], Judah[1] and Tamar[1].

📖 (7:1, 17–18; 1 Chronicles 2:6)

Adoni-Zedek
(late C15th BC)

King of Jerusalem when Joshua[1] defeated Ai and made a treaty with the city of Gibeon. Fearful of the Israelites' growing power, he joined forces with the four other Amorite kings to attack Gibeon but Joshua's armies came to Gibeon's aid and the Amorite kings were defeated. As a result of Joshua's victory, the sun stopped still for a day over Gibeon. The five kings fled to a cave at Makkedah but Joshua pursued them and put them to death. Their bodies were returned to the cave in which they had hidden.

📖 (10:1, 3, 5, 16–27; 12:10)

Hoham, Piram, Japhia[1], Debir
(late C15th BC)

Amorite kings of Hebron, Jarmuth, Lachish and Eglon who joined forces with Adoni-Zedek and three other Amorite kings against Joshua (see **Adoni-Zedek**).

📖 (10:3–5, 16–27; 12:10–12)

Jashar
(unknown)

Possibly the writer of an ancient history book known by Old Testament writers. We know nothing else about the book or its writer.

📖 (10:13; 2 Samuel 1:18)

Horam
(late C15th BC)

King of Gezer who unsuccessfully tried to help Lachish stand against Joshua[1]'s advances in the south of Canaan. There were no survivors from Gezer's army.

📖 (10:33; 12:12)

Jabin[1]
(late C15th BC)

King of Hazor who summoned the kings of Madon, Shimron and Akshaph, and all the northern kings, to the Waters of Merom, to fight against Israel. The Israelites defeated them and there were no survivors. The Israelites obeyed the Lord's instruction and hamstrung their horses and burnt their chariots.

📖 (11:1; 12:19)

Jobab[3]
(late C15th BC)

King of Madon. Summoned by Jabin[1] to fight against the Israelites.

📖 (11:1; 12:19)

Arba
(unknown)

A great Anakite leader. Hebron was at one time called Kiriath Arba in his honour.

📖 (14:15; 15:13; 21:11)

Bohan
(unknown)

Son (or descendant) of Reuben. A landmark called the stone of Bohan was named after him.

📖 (15:6; 18:17)

Aksah[1] (Acsah)
(mid C14th BC)

Daughter of Caleb[1]. Granddaughter of Jephunnah[1]. She became Othniel's wife because Caleb promised to give her to the man who captured Kiriath Sepher (Debir). Caleb gave her land in the Negev and water springs.

📖 (15:16–19; Judges 1:12–13)

Othniel
(mid C14th BC)

Son of Kenaz[3]. Father of Hathath and Meonothai. Caleb[1]'s nephew. Grandson of Jephunnah[1]. Husband of Aksah[1]. After Israel settled in Canaan and warfare had ended, the Israelites compromised their faith by adopting the practices of other nations and by intermarrying with them. The Lord was angry with them for their apostasy and he allowed the king of Aram Naharaim to oppress them for an eight-year period. The people cried out to the Lord and he gave them Othniel as their warrior and judge. He was empowered by the Spirit of the Lord. Under his leadership the Israelites defeated their oppressors. The result was a 40-year period of peace until Othniel died.

📖 (15:17–18; Judges 1:13–14; 3:7–11; 1 Chronicles 4:13; 27:15)

Kenaz[3]
(early C14th BC)

Father of Othniel and Seraiah[4]. Younger brother of Caleb[1].

📖 (15:17; Judges 1:13; 3:9, 11; 1 Chronicles 4:13)

Abiezer[1]
(early C16th BC)

See **Iezer/Abiezer[1]** in *Numbers p. 53.*

📖 (17:2)

Judges

Adoni-Bezek
(early C14th BC)

Canaanite king of Bezek. When the Israelites attacked the Canaanites and Perizzites, Adoni-Bezek fled. The Israelites chased him and cut off his big toes and thumbs: the same punishment he had inflicted on others. Adoni-Bezek acknowledged that God was paying him back. He was taken to Jerusalem and died there.

📖 (1:5–7)

Cushan-Rishathaim
(mid C14th BC)

King of Aram Naharaim (Northwest Mesopotamia). He ruled the Israelites for eight years until they were delivered by Othniel.

📖 (3:8–11)

Eglon
(late C14th BC)

King of Moab. He ruled the Israelites in Canaan for 18 years. He is described as 'a very fat man'. Israel's deliverer Ehud[1] killed him with his sword at a private audience with him. This marked the end of Moab's power over the Israelites.

📖 (3:12–15, 17–25)

Ehud[1]
(late C14th BC)

Son of Gera[2]. He was appointed as a judge and leader who would deliver the Israelites from subjection to the Moabites. Having first sent tribute to Eglon, he killed him in the upper room of his palace by plunging a sword into the king's stomach. He then summoned the Israelites to war against the Moabites and struck down 10,000 powerful Moabites. The result was peace for the Israelites for 80 years. Ehud is described as 'a left-handed man', possibly indicating his right hand had restricted use in some way.

📖 (3:15–28)

Gera[2]
(mid C14th BC)

Father of Ehud[1] (or possibly a more distant ancestor). A Benjamite.

📖 (3:15)

Shamgar
(mid C13th BC)

Son of Anath. The judge who followed Ehud[1] as leader of the Israelites. He delivered Israel by using an ox goad to kill 600 Philistines.

📖 (3:31; 5:6)

Anath
(early C13th BC)

Father of Shamgar.

📖 (3:31; 5:6)

Jabin[2]
(late C13th BC)

After the death of Ehud[1], the Israelites were cruelly oppressed by this Canaanite king who ruled from Hazor for 20 years. The judge Deborah[2] led the Israelite uprising against him, destroying his armies.

📖 (4:2, 7, 17, 23–24; Psalm 83:9)

Sisera[1]
(late C13th BC)

Commander of Jabin[2]'s army based in Harosheth Haggoyim. He had 900 chariots of iron but when the Israelites attacked under Barak's leadership, Sisera fled from his defeated army and sought refuge in the tent of Jael the wife of Heber[2] the Kenite. But Jael killed him by hammering a tent peg through his forehead.

📖 (4:2, 7, 9, 12–18, 22; 5:20, 26, 30; 1 Samuel 12:9; Psalm 83:9)

Deborah[2]
(late C13th BC)

A prophet and judge, also called 'the wife of Lappidoth', though this may simply mean 'woman of fire' (i.e. a spirited woman). She undertook legal, political and military tasks and settled disputes by holding court under a palm tree in Ephraim. She brought God's word to the people and particularly to Barak, whom she directed to advance against the armies of Sisera[1]. This successful battle brought Israel peace for 40 years. The success is celebrated in Barak's and Deborah[2]'s song (Judges 5) in which Deborah identifies herself as 'a mother in Israel'.

📖 (4:4–5, 9–10, 14; 5:1–31)

Lappidoth
(late C13th BC)

Possibly the name of Deborah[2]'s husband.

📖 (4:4)

Barak
(late C13th BC)

Son of Abinoam. From Kadesh in
Naphtali. Following Deborah[2]'s
instructions he took 1,000 men to
attack the army of Sisera[1]. The
Lord gave him success and Israel
experienced peace for 40 years. The
victory is celebrated in the song of
Deborah and Barak (Judges 5) and
mentioned by Samuel. The writer
of Hebrews mentions Barak among
those who conquered nations,
administered justice and gained what
was promised by his faith.

(4:6–24; 5:1–31; 1 Samuel 12:11;
Hebrews 11:32)

Abinoam
(mid C13th BC)

Father of Barak.

(4:6, 12; 5:1, 12)

Heber[2]
(late C13th BC)

A Kenite man, husband of Jael,
who lived in a tent by a great tree
in Zaanannim near Kadesh. When
Sisera[1] fled under attack from
Deborah[2] and Barak, he went to
Heber's tent because the king of
Hazor's family had an alliance with
Heber's family.

(4:11, 17, 21)

Jael
(late C13th BC)

Wife of Heber[2]. She killed Sisera[1]
by driving a tent peg through his
head when he came to take refuge
in her tent following his army's
defeat at the hand of Deborah[2]
and Barak.

(4:17–22)

Joash[1]
(early C12th BC)

Father of Gideon. An Abiezrite. After
Gideon tore down the altar to Baal (a
pagan god), Joash defended his son
and saved his life by challenging the
crowd who wanted to kill Gideon

to leave it to Baal to contend with
Gideon.

(6:11, 29–31)

Gideon/Jerub-Baal/Jerub-Besheth
(mid C12th BC)

Son of Joash[1]. He had many
wives and 70 sons, including his
eldest son Jether[1], the youngest
Jotham[1], and Abimelek[3], son
of his concubine in Shechem. The
angel of the Lord appeared to Gideon
and called him to deliver his people
from the Midianites. Despite initial
protests about his own weakness, he
responded to God's call. He built an
altar at Ophrah named 'The Lord is
peace' because the Lord promised he
would not die despite this encounter
with the Lord. He destroyed the altar
to Baal (a pagan god) and from its
wood built an altar to the Lord. The
Midianites meanwhile joined forces
with the Amalekites and others to
attack Israel but Gideon summoned
his own army. He asked God to
assure him of his saving presence
and laid out a fleece. As Gideon
requested, on the first day the fleece
was wet and the ground dry; on the
second day the fleece was dry and
the ground was wet with dew. By
watching how his men drank water
from the spring at Harod, Gideon
reduced his army to 300 men, and
they overcame the Midianite army
and the inhabitants of Sukkoth
and Peniel. Gideon restored peace
to Israel for 40 years. However, his
decision to make a gold ephod from
the gold earrings of the plunder
was a snare to his family, and after
Gideon's death the people returned
to pagan worship. He died in old age
and was buried in his father's tomb
in Ophrah. The writer of Hebrews
mentions him among those who
conquered nations, administered
justice and gained what was
promised by his faith.

(6:11 – 8:35; 1 Samuel 12:11; 2 Samuel
11:21; Hebrews 11:32)

Purah
(mid C12th BC)

Servant of Gideon who went with him at night-time to listen to what the Midianites were saying about Gideon and his army. They heard a Midianite man retell his dream, which was interpreted to mean that God had given the Midianites into the hands of the Israelites. On the basis of this encouragement, Gideon went ahead and attacked the Midianite camp.

📖 (7:10–11)

Oreb, Zeeb
(mid C12th BC)

Midianite leaders captured and killed by Gideon at the place known as 'the rock of Oreb'.

📖 (7:25; 8:3; Psalm 83:11; Isaiah 10:26)

Zebah, Zalmunna
(mid C12th BC)

Kings of Midian. They killed Gideon's brothers at Tabor. Gideon himself killed them following Jether[1]'s reluctance to do so.

📖 (8:5–7, 10–12, 15–21)

Jether[1]
(mid C12th BC)

Eldest son of Gideon but still only a boy when Gideon asked him to kill Zebah and Zalmunna. It appears that he was afraid to use his sword, so his father killed the two kings instead.

📖 (8:20)

Abimelek[3] (Abimelech)
(late C12th BC)

Son of Gideon by his concubine from Shechem. After Gideon's death, Abimelek persuaded the people of Shechem to appoint him as their ruler. He acquired money from them and hired some reckless men. He went to his father's home in Ophrah and murdered his 70 brothers, with the exception of the youngest, Jotham[1], who escaped. The people of Shechem crowned Abimelek king but they were challenged by Jotham about their lack of loyalty to Gideon. After three years the people of Shechem rebelled against Abimelek under Gaal's leadership. Although Abimelek survived this uprising, it led to the destruction of Shechem, as Abimelek killed its entire people. Next, Abimelek tried to capture Thebez, but all the people had fled to a strong tower in the city. When Abimelek approached the tower, a woman dropped a millstone on his head. As he died, Abimelek asked his sword-bearer to kill him by the sword so it would not be said that a woman had killed him. The writer of Judges comments that in this way God repaid Abimelek for the evil he had done by killing his brothers.

📖 (8:31; 9:1–6, 16–57; 2 Samuel 11:21)

Jotham[1]
(late C12th BC)

Youngest son of Gideon. By telling a parable from the top of Mount Gerizim, he challenged the people of Shechem about their decision to make Abimelek[3] king. He issued a curse that fire would consume them for disloyalty to Gideon. Out of fear of Abimelek, Jotham fled to Beer. After a few years Abimelek wiped out the city of Shechem and its people. The writer of Judges comments that God repaid the people for all their wickedness and 'the curse of Jotham son of Jerub-Baal came on them'.

📖 (9:5–21, 57)

Gaal
(late C12th BC)

Son of Ebed[1]. Moved into Shechem while Abimelek[3] was ruling over the city. He led the people in an unsuccessful revolt against Abimelek. Gaal and his relatives were driven out of Shechem.

📖 (9:26–41)

Ebed[1]
(mid C12th BC)

Father of Gaal.

📖 (9:26, 28, 30–31, 35)

Zebul
(late C12th BC)

Governor of the city of Shechem. Second in command to Abimelek[3]. He warned Abimelek of Gaal's uprising and advised him to attack Gaal during the night. While Abimelek stayed in Artumah, Zebul drove out Gaal and his relatives from Shechem.

📖 (9:28, 30, 36–38, 41)

Tola[2]
(late C12th BC)

Son of Puah[3]. Grandson of Dodo[1]. He lived in Shamir in the hills of Ephraim. He led Israel for 23 years after Abimelek[3]'s time.

📖 (10:1–2)

Puah[3]
(mid C12th BC)

Father of Tola[2]. Son of Dodo[1]. From the tribe of Issachar[1].

📖 (10:1)

Dodo[1]
(early C12th BC)

Father of Puah[3].

📖 (10:1)

Jair[2]
(late C12th BC)

Followed Tola[2] and led Israel for 22 years. With his 30 sons, each of whom rode his own donkey, he ruled the towns of Gilead, which were named Havvoth Jair ('the settlements/villages of Jair') in his honour. He was buried at Kamon.

📖 (10:3–5)

Jephthah
(early C11th BC)

Son of Gilead[2]. His mother was a prostitute. Father of only one daughter. He is called 'a mighty warrior' but his father's other sons (by Gilead's wife) drove him away and he settled in Tob. When the Ammonites attacked the Israelites, his brothers asked Jephthah to help. He agreed only on the condition that should he be successful against the Ammonites he would become their head. Jephthah tried unsuccessfully to negotiate peace with the Ammonites. The Spirit of the Lord came on him (a phrase signifying the gift of God's special presence and strength), and he advanced against the Ammonites. He promised the Lord that if he was given the victory he would sacrifice as a thank-offering whatever first came out of his house when he returned home. He subdued the Ammonites, destroying 20 towns. When his daughter greeted him as he returned to his home in Mizpah, he gave her a two-month reprieve but then sacrificed her to the Lord as he had vowed. Enmity arose between the Gileadites and the Ephraimites. Jephthah's men captured the fords leading down to Ephraim and in total 42,000 Ephraimites were killed. After leading the Israelites for six years, he died and was buried at Gilead. The writer of Hebrews mentions Jephthah among those who conquered nations, administered justice and gained what was promised by his faith.

📖 (11:1 – 12:7; 1 Samuel 12:11; Hebrews 11:32)

Gilead[2]
(late C12th BC)

Father of Jephthah (by a prostitute) and other sons (by his wife).

📖 (11:1)

Ibzan
(mid C11th BC)

Followed Jephthah and led Israel for seven years. He had 30 sons and 30 daughters, all of whom married people outside their own clan. He was from Bethlehem and was buried there.

📖 (12:8–10)

Elon[3]
(mid C11th BC)

Followed Ibzan and led Israel for 10 years. He was from Zebulun and was buried in Aijalon (Zebulun).

📖 (12:11–12)

Abdon[1]
(mid C11th BC)

Son of Hillel. He had 40 sons and 30 grandsons, each of whom rode their own donkey. He followed Eglon[3] and led Israel for eight years. He was buried in Pirathon (Ephraim) in the hill country of the Amalekites.

📖 (12:13–15)

Hillel
(early C11th BC)

Father of Abdon[1], from Pirathon.

📖 (12:13, 15)

Manoah
(early C11th BC)

Father of Samson. A Danite from Zorah. Manoah and his wife were childless when the angel of the Lord appeared to them and promised that they would have a son who would be a Nazirite (i.e. undertake special vows of service to God) and would secure Israel's deliverance from the Philistines. The angel instructed Manoah to prepare a burnt offering to the Lord and as the flame rose from the altar the angel of the Lord ascended in the flame. Manoah feared that they would die because they had seen God but his wife reassured him that the Lord had shown them favour. Manoah was buried between Zorah and Eshtaol.

📖 (13:2–23; 16:31)

Samson
(mid C11th BC)

Son of Manoah. A Nazirite who was dedicated to God from birth. An angel of the Lord visited his parents and promised them a son. As Samson grew up, 'the Lord blessed him and the Spirit of the Lord began to stir him'. As a consequence he became known for his amazing strength. On his way to Timnah to get a Philistine wife, the Spirit of the Lord enabled him to tear apart a lion which came roaring towards him. Later, bees made honey in the carcass and he posed a riddle to the 30 men who were accompanying him at a seven-day wedding feast. His wife persuaded him to explain the riddle to her and she in turn told the men. Samson returned to his father's house and his wife was given to one of his Philistine companions. When he was refused access to his wife, Samson destroyed all the Philistine supplies of food by sending foxes with burning torches attached to them through their fields, vineyards and olive groves. The Philistines blamed his wife and her father and burnt them to death. Samson swore he would get revenge on them. He demonstrated physical power over his enemies and led Israel for 20 years. He fell in love with Delilah, to whom the Philistines promised great sums of money if she could find out the secret of Samson's strength. Samson fooled her three times into believing a lie about the source of his strength but eventually he told her that his strength lay in his hair, which had never been cut by a razor. This was connected with his Nazirite vow. His hair was cut off as he slept on Delilah's lap and his strength left him. The Philistines gouged out his eyes and shackled and imprisoned him, but his hair began to grow back. Having prayed to God for strength one more time, Samson pushed the central pillars of the temple of the pagan god Dagon and it fell and he died with all the Philistines there. He was buried at his father's tomb between Zorah and Eshtaol. The writer of Hebrews mentions Samson among those commended for their faith by which they conquered nations and administered justice.

📖 (13:24–25; 14:1 – 16:31; 1 Samuel 12:11fn; Hebrews 11:32)

Caleb
(c.1490–after 1405 BC)
See **Caleb[1]** in Numbers, p. 50.

📖 (14:6)

Delilah
(mid C11th BC)
Samson's lover, from the Valley of Sorek. She caused Samson to lose his strength, as she persuaded him by her continuing questioning and emotional blackmail to reveal the secret of his strength. She was motivated by money to betray the man who loved her. As Samson slept in her arms, the Philistines cut Samson's hair. She woke him up by crying out, 'Samson, the Philistines are upon you' and witnessed the Philistine men seizing and imprisoning him.

📖 (16:4–20)

Micah[1]
(mid C11th BC)
A man from the hill country of Ephraim who stole silver from his own mother. When he returned the money, she used some of it to make a silver image for Micah's house where he had a shrine and had installed one of his sons as priest. When a young Levite from Bethlehem, Jonathan[1], came to his house, Micah installed him as his priest believing this would bring blessing from the Lord.

📖 (17:1–13; 18:2–4, 13–31)

Jonathan[1]
(mid C11th BC)
Descendant of Gershom[1] and Moses. A young Levite whom Micah[1] installed as his priest and treated as one of his own sons. However, when the Danites passed through Micah's home in order to find themselves new territory they persuaded Jonathan to go with them. They took him and Micah's idol and household gods to Laish, which they conquered and renamed Dan. Jonathan and his sons served the Danites as priests for many years and they continued to worship Micah's idol.

📖 (17:7 – 18:31)

Ruth

Elimelek (Elimelech)
(early C12th BC)
Husband of Naomi. Father of Mahlon and Kilion. An Ephrathite. Lived in Bethlehem during the time of the judges but took his family to Moab to escape a famine. Died before his sons married Orpah and Ruth.

📖 (1:2–3; 2:1, 3; 4:3, 9)

Naomi
(early C12th BC)
Wife of Elimelek. Mother of Mahlon and Kilion. Mother-in-law of Orpah and Ruth. Relative of Boaz. Lived in Bethlehem during the time of the judges but went to Moab to escape a famine. Her husband died there and she became a widow. When her two sons also died in Moab, and the famine had ended, Naomi decided to return to Bethlehem. En route she pleaded with her two daughters-in-law to return to their homeland in Moab but Ruth insisted on going to Bethlehem with Naomi. When they arrived, Naomi announced that her name was changed from Naomi (meaning 'pleasant') to Mara (meaning 'bitter'), signifying her bitter life experiences. However, Naomi did not wallow in her grief, but directed Ruth to work in the field of Boaz until harvest time ended. Naomi then set about securing Boaz as Ruth's husband. When this was accomplished and Ruth and Boaz's son Obed[1] was born, the women of Bethlehem blessed Naomi. They

acknowledged Ruth's love for her and rejoiced that Ruth's son would be like a son to her. Naomi took Obed in her arms and cared for him.

📖 (1:2 – 4:17)

Mahlon, Kilion
(mid C12th BC)

Sons of Elimelek and Naomi. Husbands of Ruth and Orpah. They left Bethlehem with their families to escape famine and died in Moab 10 years later.

📖 (1:2–5; 4:9–10)

Orpah
(mid C12th BC)

Moabite wife of Kilion. Daughter-in-law of Naomi. Within 10 years of marriage she became a widow. Once the famine in Judah had ended, Orpah set out with Ruth and Naomi to return to Bethlehem but Naomi urged both her daughters-in-law to return to their home in Moab. After an emotional farewell to Naomi, Orpah returned to Moab.

📖 (1:4, 6–14)

Ruth
(mid C12th BC)

Moabite wife of Mahlon and then Boaz. Daughter-in-law of Naomi. Mother of Obed[1], grandmother of Jesse and great-grandmother of David. Within 10 years of her marriage to Mahlon, she became a widow. Once the famine in Judah had ended, Ruth set out with Orpah and Naomi to return to Bethlehem. Despite Naomi urging her to return to her home in Moab, Ruth delivered a remarkable statement of faith and commitment to Naomi and to the God of Israel, and then accompanied Naomi to Bethlehem. She embarked on the task of providing food for Naomi and herself, and found herself working in the field of one of Naomi's relatives called Boaz. She worked diligently, gleaning in the fields by day and threshing the barley in the evening. Following

Naomi's advice, she stayed in Boaz's field until the end of harvest time and benefited from his generosity. Again following Naomi's advice, Ruth approached Boaz by lying down next to him at night on the threshing floor. Boaz clearly understood her actions as some kind of marriage proposal. In the morning Boaz secured his right to marry Ruth by obtaining the agreement of a closer relative who had the first right of refusal. Those who witnessed this agreement blessed Ruth and Boaz. Ruth became Boaz's wife and then the mother of Obed[1]. At this point Naomi's friends commended Ruth: she was worth more than seven sons to Naomi. This superlative recognizes the integrity, loyalty and affection that Ruth exemplified. Her son Obed became the father of Jesse, who was the father of King David, and thus this Moabite woman became the great-grandmother of Israel's greatest king. Ruth is mentioned in Matthew's genealogy of Jesus.

📖 (2:1 – 4:13; Matthew 1:5)

Boaz
(mid C12th BC)

Descendant of Salmon. Relative of Naomi and second husband of Ruth. Father of Obed[1], grandfather of Jesse and great-grandfather of King David. From the clan of Naomi's husband Elimelek and therefore an Ephrathite. He is described as 'a man of standing', indicating his social position as well as the respect in which he was held. He owned a field in which some women worked during harvest time. He also worked hard himself and was found winnowing barley on the threshing floor at night-time. He was a man of faith and integrity, greeting his workers by blessing them in the name of the Lord. He commended Ruth for her commitment to Naomi and was extremely kind to her, ensuring that his men left plenty of stalks of barley for her. When Ruth presented herself during the night on the threshing floor, he was delighted and vowed to 'redeem' Ruth if a closer relative did not wish to do so. It appeared that Boaz desired to fulfil the role of a kinsman redeemer in respect of Ruth, although this was normally undertaken by the brother of the deceased husband. Boaz ensured he dealt with the matter carefully. Appropriate witnesses were put in place before he reached agreement with the closer relative that he would buy the property Naomi's family once owned, acquiring Ruth as wife in the process and ensuring the survival of Elimelek's name in his hometown. Boaz married Ruth, and Obed[1] was born. Boaz is mentioned in the genealogies of Jesus in Matthew's Gospel (which suggests Rahab was Boaz's mother) and in Luke's Gospel.

📖 (2:1 – 4:13, 21; 1 Chronicles 2:11–12; Matthew 1:5; Luke 3:32)

Obed[1]
(late C12th BC)

Son of Ruth and Boaz. Grandson of Salmon and, by marriage, Naomi who cared for him. Father of Jesse. Grandfather of King David. Mentioned in Matthew's and Luke's genealogies of Jesus.

📖 (4:13–17, 21–22; 1 Chronicles 2:12; Matthew 1:5; Luke 3:32)

Ram[1]
(early C16th BC)

Son of Hezron[2]. Father of Amminadab[1]. Mentioned in the genealogy of King David and in Matthew's and Luke's genealogies of Jesus.

📖 (4:19; 1 Chronicles 2:9–10; Matthew 1:3–4; Luke 3:33)

Salmon
(early C15th BC)

Son of Nahshon. Ancestor of Boaz. Mentioned in the genealogy of King David and in Matthew's and Luke's genealogies of Jesus.

📖 (4:20–21; 1 Chronicles 2:11; Matthew 1:4–5; Luke 3:32)

Jesse
(early C11th BC)

See **1 Samuel**, *p. 72.*

📖 (4:17, 22)

David
(1040–970 BC)

See **1 Samuel**, *p. 73.*

📖 (4:17, 22)

1 Samuel

Elkanah[2]
(late C12th BC)

Son of Jeroham[1]. Grandson of Elihu[1]. Husband of Hannah and Peninnah. Father of Samuel and three other sons and two daughters. An Ephraimite from Ramathaim who went up to Shiloh every year to worship the Lord.

📖 (1:1–8, 19, 21–23; 2:11, 20; 1 Chronicles 6:27, 34)

Jeroham[1]
(mid C12th BC)

Son of Elihu[1]. Father of Elkanah[2]. Grandfather of Samuel.

📖 (1:1; 1 Chronicles 6:27, 34)

Elihu[1]/Eliel[2]
(early C12th BC)

Son of Tohu. Father of Jeroham[1]. Grandfather of Elkanah[2]. Possibly the same person as Eliab[4], 1 Chronicles 6:27.

📖 (1:1; 1 Chronicles 6:34)

Tohu/Toah
(late C13th BC)

Son of Zuph. Father of Elihu[1]. Grandfather of Jeroham[1]. Possibly the same person as Nahath, 1 Chronicles 6:26.

📖 (1:1; 1 Chronicles 6:34)

Zuph
(mid C13th BC)

Father of Tohu. Grandfather of

Elihu[1]. An Ephraimite also identified with the Kohathite Levites.

📖 (1:1; 1 Chronicles 6:35)

Hannah
(late C12th BC)

Beloved wife of Elkanah[2], who was for many years barren. Peninnah taunted her on account of her barrenness. Weeping bitterly, she cried out to the Lord and he heard her cry. She gave birth to Samuel, whom she presented to Eli at Shiloh for service in the temple, in fulfilment of her earlier vow. She offered a prayer of thankfulness to the Lord. She continued to make the annual journey with Elkanah to Shiloh to offer sacrifice and took with her a robe for Samuel. Eli prayed for them and they had three other sons and two daughters as signs of God's blessing on them.

📖 (1:2, 4–28; 2:1–10, 18–21)

Peninnah
(late C12th BC)

A second wife of Elkanah[2] who had children with him and taunted Hannah on account of her barrenness.

📖 (1:2–7)

Hophni, Phinehas[2]
(mid C11th BC)

Sons of Eli. They served as priests in Shiloh but treated the offerings to the Lord with contempt and they slept with the women who served at the entrance to the tent of meeting. They ignored their father's warnings about their behaviour and brought the Lord's judgment on their father's house. They were killed by the Philistines on the day when the ark of God (the symbol of God's presence with his people) was captured. Eli died when he heard news of their deaths, as did Phinehas's wife, who gave birth to a son Ichabod on her deathbed.

📖 (1:3; 2:12–17, 22–25, 27–36; 4:1–22; 14:3)

Eli
(early C11th BC)

Father of Hophni and Phinehas[2]. He led Israel for 40 years. He was priest at Shiloh when Elkanah[2] and his family came to worship the Lord. He saw Hannah weeping and prayed that God would give her what she desired. When Samuel was born, he was presented to Eli and served the Lord under Eli. Eli guided Samuel to respond to the call of the Lord. Eli confronted his sons about their wicked ways but they did not listen to him. When Eli learnt about God's judgment on his family, he accepted the Lord's purposes. At the age of 98 he learnt of the death of his two sons and the capture of the ark of God. He fell off his chair by the gate and broke his neck and died.

📖 (1:3, 9–18, 24–27; 2:11 – 3:18; 4:4, 11–22; 14:3; 1 Kings 2:27)

Samuel
(c.1100–c.1015 BC)

Son of Elkanah[2] and Hannah. Father of Joel[1] and Abijah[1]. He was presented to Eli to fulfil his mother's promise that if God gave her a son she would dedicate him to the Lord's service. Samuel grew up serving Eli and the Lord faithfully. He wore priestly garments and grew in stature and favour before God and all the people. One night the Lord called to Samuel in the temple and Eli guided Samuel to recognize the voice of the Lord. The Lord revealed to Samuel his intention to destroy the house of Eli. People began to recognize Samuel's calling as a prophet and the Lord continued to speak with Samuel. After the death of Eli and his sons, Samuel became leader of Israel. At Mizpah he cried out to the Lord and God delivered the Israelites from the Philistines. Until old age he moved around Bethel, Gilgal, Mizpah and his home in Ramah, holding court, judging Israel and leading the people in acts of worship. He appointed his sons as leaders in Israel, but the people did not accept them because they did not act faithfully. Responding to the people's demand for a king like other nations, Samuel anointed Saul[1] with oil and the Spirit of God came upon him in Zuph. Samuel gathered the Israelites at Mizpah and declared Saul as God's chosen king over Israel. He explained the duties of kingship. Samuel reaffirmed Saul's kingship at Gilgal and the people celebrated. Until his death Samuel kept a watchful eye on Saul and rebuked him when he disobeyed the Lord, prophesying that Saul's kingdom would not endure. When Saul disobeyed God in respect of the livestock belonging to the defeated Amalekites, Samuel left Saul and returned home. He did not see Saul again but mourned that the Lord had rejected him. Samuel's final act was to anoint David as king in Bethlehem. When Saul tried to kill David, David was saved by going to Samuel's house in Ramah where the Spirit of God descended and fell on Saul and his men. All Israel mourned at Samuel's death. After Samuel's death, Saul consulted him through a medium at Endor and Saul learnt that the Israelites would be defeated by the Philistines the next day and that he and his sons would die.

📖 (1:11, 20–28; 2:11–26; 3:1 – 4:1; 7:3 – 10:25; 11:7, 12–15; 12:1–25; 13:1–15; 15:1–3, 10–35; 16:1–13; 19:18–24; 25:1; 28:3, 11–16; 1 Chronicles 6:28, 33; 9:22; 11:3; 26:28; 29:29; 2 Chronicles 35:18; Psalm 99:6; Acts 3:24; 13:20; Hebrews 11:32)

Ichabod
(mid C11th BC)

Son of Phinehas[2]. Brother of Ahitub[1]. Born after his father's death and on his mother's deathbed. As she died, his mother announced his name, which means 'no glory', in recognition that glory had left Israel because the ark of God had been captured.

📖 (4:19–22; 14:3)

Joshua[2]
(mid C11th BC)

The owner of the field in Beth Shemesh where the ark of God stopped when it was returned on a cart by the Philistines. The Levites set the ark on a large rock in Joshua's field.

📖 (6:14, 18)

Abinadab[1]
(early C11th BC)

Father of Eleazar[2], Uzzah[1] and Ahio[1], he was the owner of the house on the hill where the ark of God was taken when it left Beth Shemesh and went to Kiriath Jearim. He consecrated Eleazar[2] to guard the ark and it stayed there for 20 years.

📖 (7:1; 2 Samuel 6:3; 1 Chronicles 13:7)

Eleazar[2]
(mid C11th BC)

Son of Abinadab[1]. He was consecrated by his father to guard the ark of God.

📖 (7:1)

Joel[1], Abijah[1]
(mid C11th BC)

Sons of Samuel. Although Samuel appointed them to lead the Israelites, the Israelites rejected them because they did not follow in Samuel's footsteps. Joel was the father of Heman[2].

📖 (8:1; 1 Chronicles 6:28, 33; 15:17)

Kish[1]
(late C12th BC)

Son of Abiel[1] (or Ner[2], see 1 Chronicles 8:33). Father of Saul[1]. Grandfather of Jonathan[2]. A Benjamite of Matri's clan. He sent Saul to look for his lost donkeys and that led to Saul's encounter with Samuel and his anointing as king. Buried in Zela in a tomb later shared with his son Saul and grandson Jonathan.

📖 (9:1–5; 10:11, 21; 14:51; 2 Samuel 21:14; 1 Chronicles 8:33; 9:39; 12:1; 26:28; Acts 13:21)

Abiel[1]
(early C11th BC)

Son of Zeror. Father of Kish[1].
Grandfather of Saul[1] and Abner[1].

📖 (9:1; 14:51)

Zeror
(late C12th BC)

Son of Bekorath. Father of Abiel[1].
Grandfather of Kish[1].

📖 (9:1)

Bekorath (Becorath)
(mid C12th BC)

Son of Aphiah. Father of Zeror.
Grandfather of Abiel[1].

📖 (9:1)

Aphiah
(early C12th BC)

Father of Bekorath. Grandfather of
Zeror.

📖 (9:1)

Saul[1]
(c.1080–1010 BC)

Son of Kish[1]. Father of Jonathan[2],
Ishvi[2] and Malki-Shua (also
Abinadab[3] and Esh-Baal [Ish-
Bosheth] according to 1 Chronicles
8:33; 9:39) and two daughters
(Merab and Michal). Husband of
Ahinoam[1]. A physically impressive
man, he was anointed by Samuel
as the first king of Israel at 30
years old, reigning for 42 years.
Originally he did not believe that
God would choose someone from
the smallest tribe of Benjamin and
the insignificant clan of Matri to
lead Israel. But, at Mizpah, Samuel
reassured the people that God
had appointed Saul. Saul quickly
assumed a military role. He was
instrumental in the deliverance
of the people of Jabesh from the
hand of the Ammonites. A further
kingship ceremony was held at
Gilgal. The Spirit of the Lord came
upon Saul in power and it is to this
that his military successes, and his
ability to prophesy, were credited.

He led bitter military campaigns
against the Philistines, the Moabites,
the Ammonites, Edom, the kings
of Zobah and the Amalekites. Saul
recognized his need of God's help
and sought the Lord in prayer and
by listening to advice from Samuel.
But he was not wholeheartedly
committed to the Lord, so he
preserved some of the livestock of
the Amalekites that Samuel had
instructed should be destroyed.
Samuel announced that the Lord
had rejected Saul as king and he
anointed David. David entered Saul's
service as a lyre player to soothe
Saul because the Lord's Spirit had
departed from him and he was now
tormented by an evil spirit. When
David defeated Goliath, Saul became
jealous of David's popularity and
plotted to kill him. Saul's own son
Jonathan[2] protected David. The
rest of Saul's life was driven by this
murderous intent. But when David
had opportunities to kill Saul, he did
not take them and Saul expressed
some degree of repentance. After
Samuel died, Saul sought the advice
of Samuel by utilizing the services of
a medium at Endor. Samuel rebuked
Saul for this and confirmed that the
Israelites would be defeated by the
Philistines. Saul took his own life
when he was critically wounded by
the Philistine army who had already
killed his three sons. The Philistines
displayed the bodies of Saul and
his sons on a wall at Beth Shan,
although the people of Jabesh Gilead
retrieved their bodies, burnt them
and buried their bones under a tree
in Jabesh (in the tomb of Kish[1]).
David wept bitterly for Saul and
Jonathan[2] and wrote a lament in
their memory. After Saul's death, the
house of David and the house of Saul
continued to war against each other
for seven and a half years.

📖 (9–11; 13–31; 2 Samuel 1; 2:1 – 5:5;
6:16–23; 7:15; 9:1–9; 12:7; 16:8;
21:1–14; 1 Chronicles 8:33; 9:39; 10:1
– 11:2; 12:1–2, 19; 13:3; 15:29; 26:28;
titles of Psalms 18, 52, 54, 57, 59; Isaiah
10:29)

Matri
(unknown)

The head of the Benjamite family clan of Saul[1].

📖 (10:21)

Nahash[1]
(late C11th BC)

Father of Hanun[1]. An Ammonite king who besieged Jabesh Gilead. His provocative action led to the intervention of Saul[1], the defeat of the Ammonites and the subsequent confirmation of Saul's kingship. On Nahash's death, David sent some messengers to extend his sympathy to his son Hanun. But instead of welcoming this, Hanun humiliated David's men by removing their beards and clothing. David responded by declaring war on the Ammonites, who were defeated by his armies.

📖 (11:1–2; 12:12; 2 Samuel 10:1–19; 1 Chronicles 19:1–19)

Jonathan[2]
(c.1058–1010 BC)

Son of Saul[1]. Father of Merib-Baal (Mephibosheth[1]). Grandfather of Micah[2]. With his father Saul[1] he led military campaigns against the Philistines, including one in which, with the help of his armour-bearer, he killed about 20 men. He was a devoted friend of David and made a covenant commitment to him (i.e. he took special vows of loyalty). When he became aware of Saul's plans to kill David, he tried to reason with his father and devised a plan to secure David's safety. This concern for David aroused Saul's anger and Saul hurled his spear at Jonathan. When David was on the run from Saul, Jonathan visited him at Horesh and encouraged him to remain strong in God (presumably reminding David that God was with him so he need not be afraid of Saul's hostility). Jonathan died at the hands of the Philistines in the same battle in which Saul was critically

wounded. The Philistines displayed Jonathan's body, along with those of his father and brothers, on a wall at Beth Shan, although the people of Jabesh Gilead retrieved their bodies, burnt them and buried their bones in the tomb of Kish[1]. David wept bitterly for Saul and Jonathan[2] and wrote a lament in their memory.

📖 (13:2 – 14:49; 18:1–4; 19:1–7; 20:1–42; 23:16–18; 31:2–13; 2 Samuel 1:4–5, 12, 17–27; 9:1–7; 21:7, 12–14; 1 Chronicles 8:33–34; 9:39–40; 10:2)

Ahijah[1]
(late C11th BC)

Son of Ahitub[1]. Grandson of Phinehas[2]. One of 600 men who stayed with Saul[1] on the outskirts of Gibeah. He wore an ephod and undertook the role of priest.

📖 (14:3, 18)

Ahitub[1]
(mid C11th BC)

Son of Phinehas[2]. Father of Ahijah[1] and Ahimelek[1] (Ahimelech). Grandfather of Abiathar. Grandson of Eli.

📖 (14:3; 22:9, 11, 12, 20)

Ishvi[2], Malki-Shua
(late C11th BC; Malki-Shua died 1010 BC)

Sons of Saul[1].

📖 (14:49; 31:2; 1 Chronicles 8:33; 9:39; 10:2)

Merab
(late C11th BC)

Oldest daughter of Saul[1]. Saul offered Merab to David as a wife but he refused her and she married Adriel. David appeased the Gibeonites' anger against the house of Saul by handing over to them Merab's five sons, whom they killed.

📖 (14:49; 18:17–19; 2 Samuel 21:8–9)

Michal
(late C11th BC)

Youngest daughter of Saul[1]. Childless wife of David. Michal fell in love with David. Saul said David could marry her only if he first brought to Saul 100 Philistine foreskins. Saul had hoped David would die in achieving this, but he did not and Michal became his wife. On another occasion when Saul tried to kill David, Michal helped David escape through a window. Later, Saul gave Michal to Paltiel[2] as a wife, although David secured her return to his house. When David accompanied the ark of God on its return to Jerusalem, Michal despised him because she thought he was undignified in leaping and dancing before the Lord. David defended his actions and reprimanded Michal.

(14:49; 18:20–28; 19:11–17; 25:44; 2 Samuel 3:13–16; 6:16–23; 1 Chronicles 15:29)

Ahinoam[1]
(late C11th BC)

Wife of Saul[1]. Daughter of Ahimaaz[1].

(14:50)

Ahimaaz[1]
(mid C11th BC)

Father of Ahinoam[1]. Father-in-law of Saul[1].

(14:50)

Abner[1]
(died 1003 BC)

Son of Ner[1]. Grandson of Abiel[1]. Father of Jaasiel[2]. Cousin of Saul[1]. Commander of Saul's army. He brought David before Saul after he had killed Goliath. He set up Saul's son Ish-Bosheth as king over Israel in opposition to David's kingship over the house of Judah. He arranged a contest between Ish-Bosheth's men and David's men at the pool of Gibeon. The battle was fierce and Abner and the Israelites were defeated. He was pursued by Asahel[1] and then, after Abner killed Asahel, Zeruiah's two other sons (Joab[1] and Abishai) pursued him. The ensuing battle led to a long

period of war between the house of Saul and the house of David. Later, Abner sought peace with David but Joab avenged his brother's blood by killing Abner. David mourned Abner's death and demonstrated that he was innocent of Abner's murder. Abner was buried at Hebron.

(14:50–51; 17:55–57; 20:25; 26:5, 7, 14; 2 Samuel 2:8 – 3:1; 3:6 – 4:1; 1 Kings 2:5, 32; 1 Chronicles 26:28; 27:21)

Ner[1]
(mid C11th BC)

Son of Abiel[1]. Brother of Kish[1]. Father of Abner[1].

(14:50–51; 26:5, 14; 2 Samuel 2:8, 12; 3:23, 25, 28, 37; 1 Kings 2:5, 32; 1 Chronicles 26:28)

Agag[2]
(late C11th BC)

King of the Amalekites (the enemies of the Israelites since their days in Egypt). When the Amalekites were defeated by Saul[1], he took Agag alive. Having received Samuel's rebuke for disobeying the Lord by not destroying all the livestock of the Amalekites, Saul presented Agag in chains before Samuel, who put Agag to death at Gilgal to avenge the innocent deaths for which he had been responsible.

(15:7–9, 20–33)

Jesse
(mid C11th BC)

Son of Obed[1]. Grandson of Boaz. Father of David and seven other sons and two daughters, Zeruiah and Abigail[2]. An Ephrathite from Bethlehem, in Judah. Samuel went to Bethlehem to offer a sacrifice to the Lord and asked Jesse to present his sons to him. Last of all, Jesse presented David, whom Samuel anointed. When David was summoned by Saul[1] to play his lyre, Jesse sent David to Saul on a donkey with bread and wine and a young goat. He allowed David to remain in Saul's service and David combined his service to Saul with tending his father's sheep. Jesse sent David with provisions for his brothers, who were fighting the Philistines under Saul in the Valley of Elah. This led to David's encounter with Goliath. Jesse is mentioned in Matthew's and Luke's genealogies of Jesus.

(Ruth 4:17, 22; 1 Samuel 16:1–22; 17:12–20; 20:27–31; 2 Samuel 23:1; 1 Kings 12:16; 1 Chronicles 2:12–13; 2 Chronicles 11:18; Psalm 72:20; Isaiah 11:1, 10; Matthew 1:5–6; Luke 3:32; Acts 13:22; Romans 15:12)

Eliab[3]
(late C11th BC)

Firstborn son of Jesse. Brother of David. Father of Abihail[4], who was the mother of Mahalath[2] who married Rehoboam. He was presented by his father to Samuel. Served in Saul[1]'s army when it fought the Philistines in the Valley of Elah and showed some animosity towards David when he arrived there.

(16:6; 17:13, 28; 1 Chronicles 2:13; 2 Chronicles 11:18)

Abinadab[2]
(late C11th BC)

Second son of Jesse. Brother of David. Presented by his father to Samuel but not chosen to be anointed. Served in Saul[1]'s army when it fought against the Philistines in the Valley of Elah.

(16:8; 17:13; 1 Chronicles 2:13)

Shammah[2]/Shimeah[1]/ Shimea[1]/Shimei[2]
(late C11th BC)

Third son of Jesse. Father of Jonadab[1] and Jonathan[4]. Brother of David. He was presented by his father to Samuel. Served in Saul[1]'s army when it fought against the Philistines in the Valley of Elah.

(16:9; 17:13; 2 Samuel 13:3, 32; 21:21; 1 Chronicles 2:13; 20:7)

David
(1040–970 BC)

Youngest son of Jesse. Married a number of wives, including Michal, Abigail[1], Ahinoam[2] and Bathsheba. Father of Solomon and numerous other children. He reigned in Hebron for seven years and in Jerusalem for 33 years. He was anointed by Samuel at his home in Bethlehem and 'the Spirit of the Lord came upon David in power'. He assumed a role in Saul[1]'s service playing the lyre. In the Valley of Elah he confronted the giant Goliath while still a handsome young lad. He killed the Philistine giant with five stones and a sling. He aroused the jealousy of Saul, who tried to kill him. When David had the opportunity to kill Saul in the Desert of En (and later again in the Desert of Ziph), he refused to do so in recognition of the fact that the Lord had appointed Saul as king. Thanks to his friendship with Saul's son Jonathan[2], he survived the threat from Saul. He led campaigns against the Philistines. To escape Saul he took up residence in Gath in Philistine territory for 16 months and allied himself with Achish, king of Gath. He returned to Ziklag to find that the Amalekites had attacked the city, capturing the wives and children of David and his men. David attacked the celebrating Amalekites and reclaimed their families and possessions. On hearing of Saul and Jonathan's deaths, David wept, mourned and fasted and sang a lament in their honour, and then returned to Judah and settled in Hebron. A long period of war between the house of Saul and the house of David ensued. After Abner[1] and Ish-Bosheth were murdered, David became king over all Israel. David captured Jerusalem from the Jebusites. Hiram built a palace for David in Jerusalem which became his headquarters. Along with Three mighty warriors David resumed campaigns against the Philistines. He ensured the safe return of the ark to Jerusalem and led the celebrations of this symbolic event. Through Nathan[2] God promised David that his kingdom would endure for ever. He led successful campaigns against the Moabites, the Arameans, and the Ammonites. However, he committed adultery with Bathsheba and then ensured her husband Uriah[1] was killed in battle. Nathan rebuked him and the child they had conceived died. Absalom[1], David's son, led a conspiracy against David which caused David to leave Jerusalem for a while but Absalom's men were finally defeated and Absalom himself was killed. David mourned bitterly for his son before returning to Jerusalem. In his old age his son Adonijah[1] planned to take his throne but David made Solomon king. He gave some final instructions to Solomon before his death. He was buried in Jerusalem. David is remembered for his contribution to the book of Psalms. Many of these relate to incidents in his life and his commitment to lead God's people in worship. In the prophetic books, the messianic expectation is connected to the family line of David. In the Gospels, David's name appears in the genealogies of Jesus and in the title 'Son of David' used to address Jesus, establishing his messianic status. Later New Testament literature uses this title to emphasize Jesus' authority. In Acts, David is described as 'a man after my [God's] own heart'.

(Ruth 4:17, 22; 1 Samuel 16:10–23; 17:12 – 30:31; 2 Samuel 1:1 – 3:35; 4:8 – 13:37; 15:13 – 17:4; 17:16 – 24:25; 1 Kings 1:1–37, 47; 2:1–12; 3:1–6; 5:1–7; 8:15–26; 11:12–15, 32–38; 15:3–11, 24; 22:50; 1 Chronicles 3:1–9; 11:1 – 29:30; 2 Chronicles 1:1–10; 2:3–7; titles of many psalms, e.g. 3–9; 11–41; 51–70; 108–110; 131–145; Psalms 72:20; 78:70–72; 89:3, 20, 35, 49; Isaiah 7:2, 13; Jeremiah 33:15–26; Ezekiel 34:23–24; 37:24–25; Amos 9:11; Zechariah 12:7–12; Matthew 1:1, 6, 17, 20; 9:27; 12:3, 23; 15:22; 20:30–31;

21:9, 15; 22:42–45; Mark 2:25; 10:47–48; 11:10; 12:35–37; Luke 1:27, 32, 69; 2:4, 11; 3:31; 6:3; 18:38–39; 20:41–44; John 7:42; Acts 1:16; 2:25, 29, 34; 4:25; 7:45; 13:22, 34, 36; 15:16; Romans 1:3; 4:6; 11:9; 2 Timothy 2:8; Hebrews 4:7; 11:32; Revelation 3:7; 5:5; 22:16)

Goliath
(died c.1020 BC)

Brother of Lahmi. A Philistine giant, nearly three metres tall, from Gath. He wore heavy armour and carried a bronze javelin. He intimidated the Israelites in the Valley of Elah before David killed him with a slingshot that sunk a stone into his forehead. David cut off his head and brought it to Jerusalem. When Abner[1] brought David before Saul[1], David was still carrying Goliath's head.

(17:1–57; 21:9; 22:10; 2 Samuel 21:19; 1 Chronicles 20:5)

Adriel
(late C11th BC)

Son of Barzillai. Husband of Saul[1]'s eldest daughter Merab. From Meholah. His five sons were handed over to the Gibeonites by David and were killed in revenge for Saul's action against them.

(18:19; 2 Samuel 21:8)

Ahimelek[1] (Ahimelech)
(late C11th BC)

Son of Ahitub[1]. Grandson of Phinehas[2]. Father of Abiathar. Priest in Nob, when David arrived fleeing from Saul[1]. He fed David with the consecrated bread and gave him the sword of Goliath. His actions infuriated Saul[1], who ordered Doeg, an Edomite, one of his officials, to put Ahimelek and all the priests of Nob to death. Only Abiathar escaped. (Note: It is likely that the order of names is reversed in 2 Samuel 8:17 and 1 Chronicles 18:16 and that these verses refer to the same Ahimelek, father of Abiathar.)

(21:1–9; 22:9–20; 23:6; Psalm 52 title)

David Family Tree

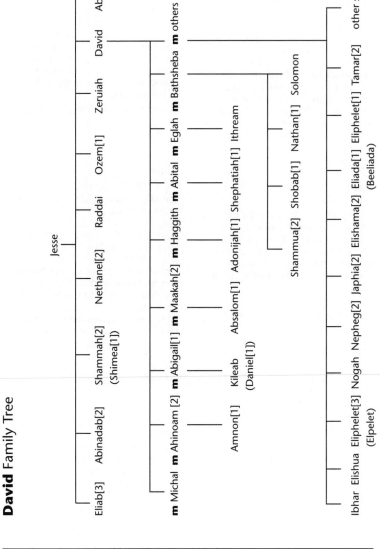

Achish

(late C11th–early C10th BC)

Son of Maok (Maoch). When fleeing from Saul[1], David went to Achish, king of Gath. David suspected that Achish was wary of him, so David pretended to be insane before escaping to the cave of Adullam. David returned to Gath (this time with 600 men) and lived there for 16 months. He conducted campaigns against the Geshurites, Girzites and Amalekites, although Achish thought he was attacking Judah. Achish trusted David and wanted him to accompany the Philistines against the army of Saul, but Achish's commanders would not allow it.

📖 (21:10–14; 27:2 – 28:3; 29:2–9; 1 Kings 2:39–40)

Gad[2]

(late C11th BC)

A prophet who brought the word of the Lord to David, advising him on military matters. He also instructed David to make an altar to the Lord at the threshing floor of Araunah. He organized music for worship in the temple.

📖 (22:5; 2 Samuel 24:11–13, 18–19; 1 Chronicles 21:9–19; 2 Chronicles 29:25)

Doeg

(late C11th BC)

An Edomite. One of Saul[1]'s officials. He witnessed Ahimelek[1] giving provisions to David and persuaded Saul of the treachery of Ahimelek and the priests of Nob. Doeg struck down 85 priests and everything else in the town, including men, women, children, babies and livestock.

📖 (22:9–22; Psalm 52 title)

Abiathar

(late C11th–early C10th BC)

Son of Ahimelek[1] (see note under Ahimelek[1]). Grandson of Ahitub[1]. Father of Jonathan[2]. A priest of Nob, only he escaped when Doeg wiped out the town of Nob. David invited Abiathar to stay with him and assured him he would be safe. He sought the Lord on David's behalf to determine Saul[1]'s next move. He worked alongside Zadok[1] and together they returned the ark of God to Jerusalem. At the end of David's life, he turned against David's house and supported Adonijah[1]'s attempt to become king. Solomon said that Abiathar deserved to die for his actions but he showed him mercy because of his former service to David. However, he stripped Abiathar of his priesthood.

📖 (22:20–23; 23:6–12; 30:7–8; 2 Samuel 8:17; 15:24–36; 17:15; 19:11; 20:25; 1 Kings 1:7, 25, 42; 2:22, 26–27, 35; 1 Chronicles 18:16; 24:6; Mark 2:26)

Nabal

(late C11th BC)

A wealthy man in Maon who had property in Carmel. Husband of Abigail[1]. A Calebite. He rejected David's greeting and refused his request for supplies for his men and instead insulted them. David gathered 400 men to attack Nabal and his household, but Abigail intervened, without her husband's knowledge, and won David over. When Abigail told Nabal what she had done the following morning, his heart failed and he died 10 days later. David praised God that he had brought Nabal's wrongdoing on his own head.

📖 (25:2–39; 27:3; 30:5; 2 Samuel 2:2; 3:3)

Abigail[1]

(late C11th BC)

The beautiful and intelligent wife of Nabal and then David. Mother of Kileab (called Daniel[1] in 1 Chronicles 3:1), who was born to David in Hebron. When Nabal incurred David's anger by refusing to offer him supplies, Abigail intervened and took David food, gifts and wine. She made a passionate and wise speech reminding David that the Lord God would deliver him from his enemies. David responded by praising

God for Abigail's good judgment. On return to Nabal's house she found her husband drunk and waited until the morning to tell him what she had done. Upon Nabal's death, David asked Abigail to become his wife. She agreed and along with five female attendants she entered his house. She was captured with Ahinoam[2] by the Amalekites when they took the city of Ziklag but David rescued both his wives and everything the Philistines had taken. David then settled with his wives in Hebron.

📖 (25:3, 14–42; 27:3; 30:5, 18; 2 Samuel 2:2; 3:3; 1 Chronicles 3:1)

Ahinoam[2]
(late C11th BC)

One of David's wives, from Jezreel. Mother of Amnon[1]. She was captured with Abigail[1] by the Amalekites when they took the city of Ziklag but David rescued both his wives and everything the Philistines had taken. David then settled with his wives in Hebron.

📖 (25:43; 27:3; 30:5, 18; 2 Samuel 2:2; 3:2; 1 Chronicles 3:1)

Paltiel[2]
(late C11th BC)

Second husband of Michal. Saul[1] took his daughter away from David but Ish-Bosheth removed her from Paltiel following David's agreement with Abner[1]. Paltiel obviously loved Michal and, weeping, followed her all the way to Bahurim until Abner commanded him to return home.

📖 (25:44; 2 Samuel 3:15)

Laish
(mid C11th BC)

Father of Paltiel[2]. From Gallim.

📖 (25:44; 2 Samuel 3:15)

Ahimelek[2] (Ahimelech)
(late C11th BC)

A Hittite man who served alongside David.

📖 (26:6)

Abishai
(late C11th–early C10th BC)

Son of Zeruiah. Brother of Joab[1] and Asahel[1]. He accompanied David into Saul[1]'s camp at night and asked David to allow him to kill Saul while he was asleep. But David would not allow it. With Joab[1] he pursued and killed Abner[1] in revenge for the murder of their brother Asahel. He was chief of David's Three mighty warriors. He saved David from the murderous intentions of the Philistine strong man Ishbi-Benob but did not always understand God's ways.

📖 (26:6–11; 2 Samuel 2:18, 24; 3:30; 10:10, 14; 16:9, 11; 18:2, 5, 12; 19:21; 20:6; 21:17; 23:18; 1 Chronicles 2:16; 11:20; 18:12; 19:11, 15)

Zeruiah
(mid C11th BC)

Mother of Abishai, Joab[1] and Asahel[1]. Her family had a tomb in Bethlehem. Possibly sister or half-sister of King David.

📖 (26:6; 2 Samuel 2:13, 18; 3:39; 8:16; 14:1; 16:9–10; 17:25; 18:2; 19:21–22; 21:17; 23:18, 37; 1 Kings 1:7; 2:5, 22; 1 Chronicles 2:16; 11:6, 39; 18:12, 15; 26:28; 27:24)

Joab[1]
(late C11th–early C10th BC)

Son of Zeruiah. Brother of Abishai and Asahel[1]. His armour-bearer was Naharai, the Berothite. He led David's men in battle and at the pool of Gibeon they fought against Abner[1] and Ish-Bosheth. With Abishai he pursued and killed Abner in revenge for the murder of their brother Asahel. He led David's army's successful campaign against the Ammonites. In a later battle against the Ammonites, Joab followed David's command and put Uriah[1] at the front of the battle line to ensure his death. Joab brought Absalom[1] back to Jerusalem. When Absalom continued to conspire against him, David permitted Joab to pursue him. When Absalom got stuck in an oak tree, Joab took three javelins and plunged them into Absalom's heart and killed him. This led to conflict between Joab and David, who appointed Amasa[1] as his commander in place of Joab. However, Joab took an early opportunity to kill Amasa. Joab gave his support to Adonijah[1], who tried to succeed David. He became the commander of Adonijah's army. On his deathbed David charged Solomon to deal with Joab for the way he had killed Abner and Amasa. At Solomon's command Benaiah[1] killed Joab.

(26:6; 2 Samuel 2:13–32; 3:22–37; 8:16; 10:7–14; 11:1, 6–18, 22, 25; 12:26–27; 14:1–33; 18:2–29; 19:1, 5, 13; 20:7–23; 23:18, 24, 37; 24:2–4, 9; 1 Kings 1:7, 19, 41; 2:5, 22–35; 11:16, 21; 1 Chronicles 2:16; 11:6, 8, 20, 26, 39; 18:15; 19:8–15; 21:1–6; 26:28; 27:7, 24, 34)

Maok (Maoch)/Maakah[3] (Maacah)
(mid C11th BC)

Father of Achish.

(27:2; 1 Kings 2:39)

Abinadab[3]
(died 1010 BC)

Son of Saul[1]. Killed by the Philistines along with his brothers Jonathan[2] and Malki-Shua before Saul, critically wounded, took his own life.

(31:2; 1 Chronicles 8:33; 9:39; 10:2)

2 Samuel

Ish-Bosheth/Esh-Baal
(1050–1003 BC)

Son of Saul[1]. After Saul's death, Abner[1] appointed him king over Gilead, Ashuri, Jezreel, Ephraim, Benjamin and all Israel. He was 40 years old and reigned for two years. This resulted in a period of conflict between the house of Judah (led by David) and the house of Israel (Saul's house led by Ish-Bosheth). Ish-Bosheth was really just a puppet king under Abner's control. Ish-Bosheth gave the order for David's wife to be returned to him from Paltiel[2]. Following Abner's death, the house of Saul lost courage and in an attempt to impress David two of the leaders of Ish-Bosheth's raiding parties (Baanah[1] and Rekab[1]) killed Ish-Bosheth and brought his head to David. David, however, condemned them to death, describing Ish-Bosheth as an innocent man.

(2:8–15; 3:7–15; 4:1, 5, 8, 12; 1 Chronicles 8:33; 9:39)

Asahel[1]
(died c.1004 BC)

Son of Zeruiah. Father of Zebadiah[5]. Brother of Joab[1] and Abishai. He heads the list of David's Thirty mighty men. After a battle at the pool of Gibeon, Asahel ('as fleet-footed as a wild gazelle') pursued Abner[1], until Abner[1] speared him through his stomach and killed him. He was buried in his father's tomb in Bethlehem. Despite the fact that Abner later turned to support David, Joab and Abishai murdered him to avenge Asahel's death.

(2:18–23, 30–32; 3:27, 30; 23:24; 1 Chronicles 2:16; 11:26; 27:7)

Amnon[1]
(died c 987 BC)

Son of David and Ahinoam[2]. He fell in love with his half-sister Tamar[2]. Following the advice of his cousin and advisor Jonadab[1], Amnon tricked Tamar into entering his bedroom and then raped her. His love for Tamar then turned to anger and Tamar left weeping. When Absalom[1] found out what had happened, he took Tamar into his house and he was full of hatred towards Amnon. David likewise was furious. Two years later at Baal Hazor, Amnon was killed by Absalom[1]'s men and David and his brothers mourned his death.

📖 (3:2; 13:1–33; 1 Chronicles 3:1)

Kileab/Daniel[1]
(born late C11th BC)

Son of David and Abigail[1]. Born in Hebron.

📖 (3:3; 1 Chronicles 3:1)

Absalom[1]
(c.1006–982 BC)

Son of David and Maakah[2]. Grandson of Talmai[2]. When Tamar[2] was raped by Amnon[1], Absalom took her into his own house. He took revenge on Amnon by arranging his death. He fled to his grandfather's house in Geshur and stayed with Talmai for three years. During this time his father David longed for him and following the intervention of Joab[1], David brought Absalom back to Jerusalem, although David would not see Absalom. Everyone recognized Absalom as being handsome. He had three sons and a daughter called Tamar[3], who was beautiful. After two years he was allowed to see David, who kissed him, showing his affection for his son. However, Absalom conspired against David and tried to secure political advantage. He surrounded himself with 200 men in Hebron and also one of David's counsellors Ahithophel. As Absalom entered Jerusalem, David fled, leaving behind Abiathar and Zadok[1] and their sons, looking after the ark of God, and Hushai[1], David's confidant, as a spy. Absalom's army pursued David but David, sending three troops of men out from Mahanaim, asked them to be gentle with Absalom. The battle took place in the forest of Ephraim and Absalom's men were routed. Absalom himself died when his hair got stuck on a branch when he was riding his mule and he was left hanging in the air. Joab plunged three javelins into Absalom's heart and he was killed. They put Absalom's body in a pit in the forest. David wept bitterly when he received news of Absalom's death.

📖 (3:3; 13:1, 4, 20–39; 14:1, 21–33; 15:1–19, 31, 34, 37; 16:8, 15–23; 17:1–26; 18:5–18, 29–33; 19:1–10; 20:6; 1 Kings 1:6; 2:7, 28; 1 Chronicles 3:2; 2 Chronicles 11:20–21; Psalm 3 title)

Maakah[2] (Maacah)
(late C11th BC)

Wife of David. Mother of Absalom[1]. Daughter of Talmai[2].

📖 (3:3; 1 Chronicles 3:2)

Talmai[2]
(mid C11th BC)

Son of Ammihud[4]. Father of Maakah[2]. King of Geshur. After Absalom[1] killed Amnon, he fled to Geshur and stayed with Talmai for three years.

📖 (3:3; 13:37; 1 Chronicles 3:2)

Adonijah[1]
(c.1006–970 BC)

Son of David and Haggith. A handsome man whom David never challenged about his unacceptable behaviour. When David became old, Adonijah conspired against him and set himself up as king. Bathsheba made David aware of Adonijah's actions in order to safeguard the succession of her son Solomon. David quickly declared Solomon king, and Adonijah pleaded for mercy from Solomon. When Adonijah tried to secure Abishag, David's nurse, as his wife and enlisted the help of Bathsheba, Solomon viewed this as treachery and ordered Benaiah[1] to put Adonijah to death.

📖 (3:4; 1 Kings 1:5–13, 18, 24–25, 41–42, 50–53; 2:13–25, 28; 1 Chronicles 3:2)

Haggith
(late C11th BC)

Wife of David. Mother of Adonijah[1].

📖 (3:4; 1 Kings 1:5, 11; 2:13; 1 Chronicles 3:2)

Shephatiah[1]
(born early C10th BC)
Son of David and Abital.
📖 (3:4; 1 Chronicles 3:3)

Abital
(late C11th BC)
Wife of David. Mother of
Shephatiah[1].
📖 (3:4; 1 Chronicles 3:3)

Ithream
(born early C10th BC)
Son of David and Eglah.
📖 (3:5; 1 Chronicles 3:3)

Eglah
(late C11th BC)
Wife of David. Mother of Ithream.
📖 (3:5; 1 Chronicles 3:3)

Rizpah
(late C11th BC)
Daughter of Aiah[2]. Concubine
of Saul[1]. Mother of Armoni and
Mephibosheth[2]. Ish-Bosheth
challenged Abner[1] about his
relationship with Rizpah. Her two
sons were handed over by David
to the Gibeonites, who killed them
and displayed their bodies on a hill.
Rizpah laid out sackcloth and kept
watch over their bodies, ensuring
that birds and wild animals did not
touch them. Her actions provoked
David to recover the bones of Saul
and Jonathan[2] and Rizpah's sons,
along with the five sons of Merab
who had also been killed.
📖 (3:7; 21:8, 10–11)

Aiah[2]
(mid C11th BC)
Father of Rizpah.
📖 (3:7; 21:8, 10–11)

Baanah[1], Rekab[1] (Recab)
(died 1008 BC)
Sons of Rimmon[1]. They were the
two leaders of Ish-Bosheth's raiding
bands but they turned against the

house of Saul[1] once Abner[1] died.
They tried to impress David by
killing Ish-Bosheth and presenting
his head to David. David, however,
ordered their killing on account of
this treachery against Saul's son.
Their bodies, with hands and feet
removed, were hung by a pool in
Hebron where David was residing.
📖 (4:2, 5–12)

Rimmon
(mid C11th BC)
Father of Baanah[1] and Rekab[1].
From Beeroth and the tribe of
Benjamin.
📖 (4:2, 5, 9)

Mephibosheth[1]/Merib-Baal
(1015–mid C10th BC)
Father of Mika[1]. Son of
Jonathan[2]. Grandson of Saul[1].
He was five years old when Saul
and Jonathan died. When the news
of their deaths came, his nurse
picked him up to flee but he fell
and became lame. He lived in the
house of Makir[2] in Lo Debar until
David brought him to Jerusalem
to eat at his table as a son. David
showed him kindness because of
his love for Jonathan. David gave
him the land that belonged to Saul
and appointed Ziba and his sons
as Mephibosheth's servants, but
Ziba betrayed Mephibosheth by
suggesting to David that he was not
loyal to him, so Ziba acquired all
the belongings of the house of Saul.
However, Mephibosheth put David
right and showed his devotion to
David. David spared Mephibosheth
when the Gibeonites demanded that
descendants of Saul be handed over
to them.
📖 (4:4; 9:6–13; 16:1–4; 19:24–30; 21:7;
1 Chronicles 8:34; 9:40–41)

Hiram/Huram[2]
(reigned early–mid C10th BC)
King of Tyre who supplied materials
and personnel for the building of
David's palace in Jerusalem. Solomon

asked Hiram to supply cedar and skilled workmen to build a temple. Hiram praised the Lord in response and entered into a treaty with Solomon by which Hiram supplied all the materials Solomon needed and Solomon provided Hiram with wheat and olive oil. At the conclusion of his 20-year building programme, Solomon gave 20 towns in Galilee to Hiram but he was not pleased with them. However, Hiram's sailors later served in Solomon's merchant fleet, collecting gold, almug wood and precious stones from Ophir and elsewhere.

📖 (5:11; 1 Kings 5:1–12, 18; 9:11–14, 27; 10:11, 22; 1 Chronicles 14:1; 2 Chronicles 2:3, 11–16; 8:2, 18; 9:10, 21)

Shammua[2], Shobab[1], Nathan[1]
(born early C10th BC)

Sons of David and Bathsheba. Born during the 33 years when David reigned from Jerusalem. Nathan[1] is mentioned in Luke's genealogy of Jesus.

📖 (5:14; 1 Chronicles 3:5; 14:4; Zechariah 12:12; Luke 3:31)

Solomon
(c.990–930 BC; reigned 970–930 BC)

Son of David and Bathsheba. Married a daughter of Pharaoh (*see panel, p. 23*). Father of Rehoboam. Born when David reigned over all Israel from Jerusalem. Also given the name Jedidiah ('loved of the Lord'). David appointed Solomon as his successor and he ruled in Jerusalem for 40 years. He was anointed with oil by Zadok[1] at Gihon, with Nathan[2] and Benaiah[1] in attendance. Before David died, he charged Solomon to walk in obedience to the Lord. His throne was established firmly, especially when his brother Adonijah[1], who had earlier tried to take the throne himself, was put to death. The Lord appeared to Solomon in a dream at Gibeon, and Solomon, aware of

his youth, asked for wisdom. The Lord promised him wealth and honour as well. Solomon acted as a judge for the people, settling disputes (e.g., between two women, 1 Kings 3:16–28). He developed a bureaucracy to support the well-being of his people, appointing chief officials and district governors to distribute supplies. He made an alliance with Hiram and finished building the palace and then the temple in a 20-year building project. The temple's beauty and meticulous design bore evidence of Solomon's great wealth. The climax was when the ark was brought to the Most Holy Place and the glory of the Lord filled the temple. Solomon offered a prayer of dedication for the temple and prayed for God's blessing on the people. He built ships, and his fame spread and his riches multiplied. Even the Queen of Sheba visited him and was amazed. But Solomon's reign was blemished by some of the choices he made. He used forced labour for the temple building; he attracted adversaries; he built high places for pagan gods; he was led into sin by foreign women, many of whom were among his wives and concubines. He misjudged Jeroboam[1], one of his own officials, by promoting him before he rebelled against Solomon. He was buried in Jerusalem and his death instigated the start of the division of the kingdom. The book of Proverbs is associated with Solomon. His wise sayings were among those collected by Hezekiah[1]'s men. Similarly the Song of Songs is associated with him. He is mentioned in Matthew's genealogy of Jesus. Jesus uses Solomon as an example of splendour, wealth and wisdom.

📖 (5:14; 12:24; 1 Kings 1:10 – 11:43; 14:21; 2 Kings 21:7; 23:13; 24:13; 1 Chronicles 3:5; 14:4; 22:5–11; 23:1; 28:5–11, 20; 29:1, 19–28; 2 Chronicles 1:1 – 3:3; 4:11 – 5:6; 6:1 – 9:31; 10:2–6; 11:3, 17; 12:9; 13:6–7; 30:26; 33:7; 35:3–4; Psalms 72, 127 titles; Proverbs 1:1; 10:1; 25:1; Song of Songs

1:1, 5; 3:7, 9, 11; 8:11–12; Jeremiah 52:20; Matthew 1:6–7; 6:29; 12:42; Luke 11:31; 12:27; John 10:23; Acts 3:11; 5:12; 7:47)

Ibhar, Elishua, Nepheg[2], Japhia[2], Elishama[2], Eliada[1]/Beeliada, Eliphelet[1]
(born early C10th BC)

Sons of David. Born during the 33 years when David reigned over all Israel from Jerusalem.

📖 (5:15–16; 1 Chronicles 3:6–8; 14:5–7)

Uzzah[1]
(died c.1001 BC)

Son of Abinadab[1]. With his brother Ahio[1], he guided the cart which carried the ark of God when it was taken from Abinadab's house to Jerusalem. But at the threshing floor of Nakon the oxen stumbled and Uzzah reached out and touched the ark. The Lord struck him down for this irreverence and he died. David's mood turned from celebration to anger and fear. The procession to Jerusalem was aborted and the ark was taken to the house of Obed-Edom[1] instead.

📖 (6:3–8; 1 Chronicles 13:7)

Ahio[1]
(late C11th BC)

Son of Abinadab[1]. With his brother Uzzah[1], he guided the cart which carried the ark of God when it was taken from Abinadab's house to Jerusalem.

📖 (6:3, 6–7; 1 Chronicles 13:7)

Nakon (Nacon)
(late C11th BC)

Owner of the threshing floor where the oxen pulling the cart carrying the ark of God stumbled. The place was renamed Perez Uzzah (meaning 'outbreak against Uzzah') because Uzzah[1] died there.

📖 (6:6)

Obed-Edom[1]
(late C11th BC)

A Gittite. Owner of the house where David took the ark after the incident with Uzzah[1]. The ark stayed in his house for three months and Obed-Edom's household was blessed by God during that time.

📖 (6:10–12; 1 Chronicles 13:13–14; 15:25)

Nathan[2]
(early C10th BC)

Prophet of God who advised David and confirmed God's promise that David's throne would be established for ever. However, he told David that he would not be the one to build a temple for the Lord. By means of a parable he rebuked David for his adultery with Bathsheba and the murder of Uriah[1]. Upon David's confession, Nathan assured David that he would not die, because the Lord had removed his sin. However, Nathan announced that the son that had been born to Bathsheba would die. It was Nathan who gave Solomon the second name Jedidiah ('loved by the Lord') and who with Zadok[1] and Benaiah[1] was summoned by David to participate in Solomon's coronation ceremony at Gihon.

📖 (7:1–17; 12:1–15, 25; 1 Kings 1:8, 10–11, 22–24, 32, 34, 38, 44, 45; 1 Chronicles 17:1–15; 29:29; 2 Chronicles 9:29; 29:25; Psalm 51 title)

Hadadezer
(early C10th BC)

Son of Rehob[1]. King of Zobah. He suffered defeat at the hands of David, who struck down the Arameans who had come to help him and ransacked Hadadezer's towns, taking gold shields and bronze. Hadadezer had previously warred with Tou. When Hadadezer and the Arameans suffered a further defeat by David at Helam, other kings who were vassals of Hadadezer made peace with Israel.

📖 (8:3–5, 7–12; 10:16, 19; 1 Kings 11:23; 1 Chronicles 18:3–10; 19:19)

Rehob[1]
(late C11th BC)

Father of Hadadezer.

📖 (8:3, 12)

Tou
(early C10th BC)

Father of Joram[1]. King of Hamath, who had previously warred with Hadadezar, he sent Joram[1] to congratulate David on his victory over Hadadezer.

📖 (8:9–10; 1 Chronicles 18:9–10)

Joram[1]/Hadoram[2]
(early C10th BC)

Son of Tou. He was sent to David with gifts to congratulate him for defeating Hadadezer.

📖 (8:10; 1 Chronicles 18:10)

Jehoshaphat[1]
(early C10th BC)

Son of Alihud. He was an official of David's administration and acted as recorder (a role similar to a national historian). His role continued into the reign of Solomon.

📖 (8:16; 20:24; 1 Kings 4:3; 1 Chronicles 18:15)

Ahilud
(late C11th BC)

Father of Jehoshaphat[1] and Baana[1].

📖 (8:16; 20:24; 1 Kings 4:3, 12; 1 Chronicles 18:15)

Zadok[1]
(early C10th BC)

Son of Ahitub[2] (or grandson of Ahitub and son of Meraioth[2], see 1 Chronicles, p. 145). Father of Ahimaaz[2] and probably grandfather of Azariah[1]. A descendant of Aaron, he served as priest alongside Abiathar and Ahimelek[3] during David's reign. Before Absalom[1] arrived in Jerusalem Zadok and Abiathar took the ark of God back there on David's instructions and acted as spies for David, who had fled the city because of the growing strength of Absalom[1]'s followers. David sought their advice about his return. Zadok was loyal even when David reached old age and when Abiathar supported Adonijah[1]'s attempt to succeed David. Zadok was involved with the anointing of Solomon as king at Gihon. Solomon chose Zadok to serve him as priest.

📖 (8:17; 15:24–29, 35–36; 17:15; 18:19, 22, 27; 19:11; 20:25; 1 Kings 1:8, 26, 32–34, 38, 44–45; 2:35; 4:2, 4; 1 Chronicles 6:8, 53; 9:11; 15:11; 16:39; 18:16; 24:3, 31; 29:22; 2 Chronicles 31:10; Ezra 7:2; Ezekiel 40:46; 43:19; 44:15)

Ahitub[2]
(late C11th BC)

Son of Amariah[1]. Father of Zadok[1] the priest (or grandfather, see 1 Chronicles 9:11).

📖 (8:17; 1 Chronicles 6:7–8, 52; 9:11; 18:16, Ezra 7:2–3)

Seraiah[1]/Sheva[1]/Shavsha/ Shisha
(early C10th BC)

Among David's officials. Served as secretary.

📖 (8:17; 20:25; 1 Kings 4:3; 1 Chronicles 18:16)

Benaiah[1]
(early C10th BC)

Son of Jehoiada[1]. Father of Ammizabad. From Kabzeel. One of David's officials with authority over the Kerethites and Pelethites. He had 24,000 men in his army division, which was on duty for the third month. He later served Solomon. He was a 'valiant fighter' who performed 'great exploits'. He killed mighty men, including two Moabite warriors and an Egyptian as well as a lion. Although he was not among David's Three mighty warriors, nor among his Thirty mighty men, he was as famous as they were, and David esteemed him above his Thirty mighty men. He was in charge of David's bodyguard. He was loyal to David even when Adonijah[1] sought to succeed him. He witnessed the anointing of Solomon as David's successor. Benaiah offered a prayer of blessing on Solomon. Once Solomon's throne was established, Solomon ordered Benaiah to kill Adonijah for his treachery and Shimei[3] for his disobedience to the king's instructions.

📖 (8:18; 20:23; 23:20–23; 1 Kings 1:8, 10, 26, 32–38, 44; 2:34–35, 46; 4:4; 1 Chronicles 11:22–25; 18:17; 27:5–6, 34)

Jehoiada[1]
(late C11th BC)

Father of Benaiah[1] (although 1 Chronicles 27:34 suggests he was the son of Benaiah; probably due to the transposition of names).

📖 (8:18; 20:23; 23:20, 22; 1 Kings 1:8, 26, 32, 36, 38, 44; 2:25, 46; 4:4; 1 Chronicles 11:22, 24; 18:17; 27:5, 34)

Ziba
(late C11th BC)

Servant in the house of Saul[1]. David summoned him after Saul's death to enquire if Saul had any remaining relative to whom David could show kindness. Ziba told David that Jonathan[2]'s son Mephibosheth[1] was still alive. David appointed Ziba and his sons as Mephibosheth's servants. But Ziba turned against Mephibosheth and insinuated to David that he was not loyal to him. David discovered Ziba's deceit.

📖 (9:2–4, 9–12; 16:1–4; 19:17, 26, 29)

Makir[2]
(early C10th BC)

Son of Ammiel[2]. Owner of the house in Lo Debar where Mephibosheth[1] lived before David brought him to Jerusalem. He later supplied provisions for David and his men at Mahanaim.

📖 (9:4–5; 17:27)

Ammiel[2]
(late C11th BC)

Father of Makir[2].

📖 (9:4–5; 17:27)

Mika[1] (Mica)/Micah[2]
(early C10th BC)

Son of Mephibosheth[1]. Father of Pithon, Melek (Melech), Tarea and Ahaz[2].

📖 (9:12; 1 Chronicles 8:34–35; 9:40–41)

Hanun[1]
(early C10th BC)

Son of Nahash[1], whom he succeeded as king of the Ammonites. He brought disgrace on David's men who brought sympathy to him on his father's death, because he was ill-advised by his commanders. As a result, Joab[1] deployed some of his men under Abishai against them.

📖 (10:1–4; 1 Chronicles 19:2–6)

Shobak (Shobach)/Shophak (Shophach)
(early C10th BC)

Commander of Hadadezer's army when the Arameans were defeated by David at Helam.

📖 (10:16, 18; 1 Chronicles 19:16)

Bathsheba (Bathshua)
(born late C11th BC)

Daughter of Eliam[1]. Wife of Uriah[1] the Hittite and then David. Mother of Shammua[2], Shobab[1], Nathan[1] and Solomon. Described as a very beautiful woman, she aroused David's passions. David committed adultery with her and then murdered her husband Uriah in order to cover up his adultery. The incident resulted in the writing of one of the great penitential psalms. The first unnamed son of Bathsheba and David died as a result of the Lord's punishment upon David for his sin. When Adonijah[1] tried to set himself up as king in David's old age, Bathsheba alerted the king to Adonijah's intentions, which resulted in David arranging Solomon's coronation. At a later point Adonijah asked Bathsheba to help him secure Abishag as his wife by pleading with Solomon on his behalf. On this occasion Bathsheba's intervention alerted Solomon to Adonijah's evil intentions and he was put to death. Bathsheba is referred to as 'Uriah's wife' in Matthew's genealogy of Jesus.

(11:3, 26; 12:24; 1 Kings 1:11–21, 28–31; 2:13–22; 1 Chronicles 3:5 (NIV 2011 footnote has variant Bathshua); Psalm 51 title; Matthew 1:6)

Eliam[1]/Ammiel[3]
(mid C11th BC)

Father of Bathsheba.

(11:3; 1 Chronicles 3:5)

Uriah[1]
(born late C11th BC)

The Hittite; husband of Bathsheba. One of David's Thirty mighty men. When David slept with Bathsheba and she became pregnant, David arranged for Uriah to be sent home from battle, presumably so David's adulterous actions could be concealed. But Uriah was determined that he would not enter his house while the army was still engaged in battle. So David arranged for Joab[1] to place Uriah at the front of the battle line so he would be killed. His plan succeeded and Bathsheba mourned for her husband before she became David's wife. Nathan[2] rebuked David for his actions against Uriah.

(11:3–27; 12:9–10, 15; 23:39; 1 Kings 15:5; 1 Chronicles 11:41; Matthew 1:6)

Jerub-Besheth
(mid C12th BC)

See **Gideon** in Judges, p. 61.

(11:21)

Jedidiah
(c.990–930 BC; reigned 970–930 BC)

See **Solomon** in 2 Samuel, p. 81.

(12:25)

Tamar[2]
(early C10th BC)

Daughter of David and brother of Absalom[1]. Her half-brother Amnon[1] was captivated by her beauty and he tricked Tamar into entering his bedroom and then raped her. His love for Tamar then turned to anger and Tamar left weeping. When Absalom found out what had happened, he took Tamar into his house.

(13:1–33; 1 Chronicles 3:9)

Shimeah[1]
(late C11th BC)

See **Shammah[2]** in 1 Samuel, p. 73.

(13:3)

Jonadab[1]
(early C10th BC)

Son of Shimeah[1]. Advisor of Amnon[1]. He suggested a deceitful plan to enable Amnon to sleep with his sister Tamar[2]. This resulted in Tamar's rape and enmity between Amnon and his brother Absalom[1], which in turn led to Amnon's murder. It was Jonadab who explained to David that the report that all David's other sons had been killed by Absalom[1] was false and that only Amnon had died.

(13:3–5, 32–35)

Ammihud[4]
(late C11th BC)

Father of Talmia[2].

(13:37)

Tamar[3]
(mid C10th BC)

Daughter of Absalom[1]. Granddaughter of David. She is described as a 'beautiful woman'.

(14:27)

Ahithophel
(early C10th BC)

Father of Eliam[2]. From Giloh. A valued advisor to David who joined Absalom[1]'s conspiracy. When Absalom[1] returned to Jerusalem in David's absence, Ahithophel suggested that Absalom[1] should sleep with his father's concubines so that it was obvious to everyone that he was obnoxious in his father's eyes, thus increasing the resolve of his own men. He also advised Absalom[1] to attack David during the night, but Absalom[1] preferred to follow alternative advice offered by Hushai[1]. When Ahithophel discovered his advice had not been followed, he left Absalom[1], returned to his own home and hanged himself.

📖 (15:12, 31, 34; 16:15, 20–23; 17:1, 6–7, 14–15, 21–23; 23:34; 1 Chronicles 27:33–34)

Ittai
(early C10th BC)

A Gittite who was faithful to David and joined the march out from Jerusalem when Absalom[1]'s attack was expected. Later David put a third of his troops under Ittai's command.

📖 (15:19–22; 18:2, 5, 12)

Ahimaaz[2]
(early C10th BC)

Son of Zadok[1]. Father of Azariah[1]. Alongside Jonathan[3] he acted as an informant for David while David was on the run from Absalom[1]. They stayed in En Rogel, where messages from Jerusalem were conveyed to them, but Absalom[1] was informed so they left there and went to a house in Bahurim and hid in a well. Absalom[1]'s men unsuccessfully tried to find them and when it was safe to do so, they were able to warn David of the impending danger, so he crossed over the Jordan and waited for Absalom[1] there. When Absalom[1] died in battle, Ahimaaz asked Joab[1] if he could take the news to David. Joab instructed a Cushite to carry the news but Ahimaaz was allowed to follow him. Ahimaaz outran the Cushite and brought the good news of the victory for Joab's army. The Cushite arrived to convey the news of Absalom[1]'s death.

📖 (15:27, 36; 17:17, 20; 18:19–29; 1 Chronicles 6:8–9, 53)

Jonathan[3]
(early C10th BC)

Son of Abiathar. Alongside Ahimaaz[2] he acted as an informant for David while David was on the run from Absalom[1]. They stayed in En Rogel, where messages from Jerusalem were conveyed to them, but Absalom[1] was informed so they left there and went to a house in Bahurim and hid in a well. Absalom[1]'s men unsuccessfully tried to find them and when it was safe to do so, they were able to warn David of the impending danger, so he crossed over the Jordan and waited for Absalom[1] there. Later, Jonathan with his father Abiathar supported Adonijah's conspiracy against David and brought the news of Solomon's coronation to Adonijah.

📖 (15:27, 36; 17:17, 20; 1 Kings 1:42–43)

Hushai[1]
(early C10th BC)

From Archi, west of Bethel. He was David's confidant who met him at the summit of the Mount of Olives when David and the people arrived there mourning their departure from Jerusalem. David asked him to return to Jerusalem and pretend to be loyal to Absalom[1] in an attempt to gain information about his plans against David. Hushai succeeded in convincing Absalom[1] of his loyalty and even persuaded him to follow his advice against that of Ahithophel.

📖 (15:32, 37; 16:16–18; 17:5–8, 14–15; 1 Chronicles 27:33)

Shimei[3]
(early C10th BC)

Son of Gera[3]. A Benjamite, from Saul[1]'s family's clan. He cursed David and his men when they came to Bahurim and pelted them with stones. He accused David of being a murderer but David refused his men permission to kill him. When David returned to Jerusalem as king, Shimei begged mercy from David for his past actions and David reassured him he would not be put to death for his past misjudgment. However, David later charged Solomon to put Shimei to death. Solomon gave instructions to Shimei that he could stay in Jerusalem but not travel elsewhere. Shimei disobeyed these instructions by going to Gath to retrieve two runaway slaves. Solomon ordered Benaiah[1] to kill Shimei, and his death established Solomon's kingdom as secure.

📖 (16:5–13; 19:16–23; 1 Kings 2:8–9, 36–46)

Gera[3]
(late C11th BC)

Father of Shimei[3].

📖 (16:5; 19:16, 18; 1 Kings 2:8)

Amasa[1]
(died c.980 BC)

Son of Jether[2] and Abigail[2]. Joab[1]'s and David's cousin. He became the commander of Absalom[1]'s army. When Absalom[1] died, David welcomed him back as leader of his own army but he was killed by Joab's dagger at the great rock of Gibeon, leaving Joab once more in charge of the army. David instructed his son Solomon to avenge Amasa's blood.

📖 (17:25; 19:13; 20:4–13; 1 Kings 2:5, 32; 1 Chronicles 2:17)

Jether[2]/Ithra
(mid C11th BC)

Father of Amasa[1]. Husband of Abigail[2]. An Ishmaelite.

📖 (17:25; 1 Kings 2:5, 32; 1 Chronicles 2:17)

Abigail[2]
(mid C11th BC)

Daughter of Nahash[2]. Sister of Joab[1]'s mother Zeruiah. Wife of Jether[2]. Mother of Amasa[1]. (Although 1 Chronicles suggests she is the daughter of Jesse.)

📖 (17:25; 1 Chronicles 2:16–17)

Nahash[2]
(early C11th BC)

Father of Abigail[2]. Possibly the first husband of David's mother.

📖 (17:25)

Shobi
(early C10th BC)

Son of Nahash[1]. An Ammonite from Rabbah who lived in Mahanaim and offered practical support for David and his people when he was facing opposition from Absalom[1].

📖 (17:27–29)

Barzillai[1]
(c.1062–after 980 BC)

A Gileadite from Rogelim who offered practical support for David and his people when David was facing opposition from Absalom[1]. When he was 80 years old, David offered Barzillai the opportunity to go with him to Jerusalem to be cared for in the king's house but Barzillai preferred to return to his own home. David commissioned Solomon to continue to show kindness to Barzillai.

📖 (17:27; 19:31–39; 1 Kings 2:7)

Kimham
(early C10th BC)

Possibly a son of Barzillai[1]. He crossed the Jordan with David and went on to Gilgal, while Barzillai in his old age turned back home.

📖 (19:37–40)

Sheba[4]
(early C10th BC)

Son of Bikri from the hill country of Ephraim. A Benjamite called 'a troublemaker'. He persuaded the house of Israel to desert David. Once David returned to Jerusalem, he instructed Abishai to pursue Sheba, and he did this with the help of Joab[1], besieging Abel Beth Maakah. A wise woman advised David's men not to destroy the city for the sake of one man. So Sheba's head was thrown over the wall of the city and Joab and his men withdrew.

📖 (20:1–2, 6–7, 10, 13–22)

Bikri (Bicri)
(late C11th BC)

Father of Sheba[4].

📖 (20:1–2, 6–7, 10, 13, 21–22)

Adoniram
(died c.930 BC)

Son of Abda[1]. David's official in charge of forced labour. When the house of Israel rebelled against King Rehoboam, Adoniram was sent out to restore order but the Israelites stoned him to death.

📖 (20:24; 1 Kings 4:6; 5:14; 12:18; 2 Chronicles 10:18)

Sheva[1]
(early C10th BC)

See **Seraiah[1]** *in 2 Samuel, p. 83.*

📖 (20:25)

Ira[1]
(early C10th BC)

A Jairite. One of David's officials, he served as priest.

📖 (20:26; 1 Chronicles 11:40; 27:9)

Armoni, Mephibosheth[2]
(died c.978 BC)

Two sons of Saul[1] and his concubine Rizpah who were given by David to the Gibeonites so they could avenge Saul's household for the bloodshed for which he had been responsible. The Gibeonites killed and exposed the bodies of the seven relatives of Saul who were given to them, but David gathered up their bodies for burial.

📖 (21:8)

Barzillai[2]
(mid C11th BC)

Father of Adriel. A Meholathite.

📖 (21:8)

Ishbi-Benob
(died c.975 BC)

A Philistine warrior and a descendant of Rapha[1]. He had a huge spear and a sharp sword and vowed to kill David. He was struck down by Abishai. The incident brought about a new policy: David would not go out with his men in battle again.

📖 (21:16–17)

Rapha[1]
(unknown)

The ancestor of a series of named Philistine giants and warriors who warred against the Israelites in David's time.

📖 (21:16, 18, 20, 22; 1 Chronicles 20:6, 8)

Sibbekai (Sibbecai)
(early C10th BC)

A Hushathite who killed Saph, one of the descendants of Rapha[1]. Named among David's Thirty mighty men, he led the eighth army division of 24,000 men.

📖 (21:18; 23:27; 1 Chronicles 11:29; 20:4; 27:11)

Saph/Sippai
(died c.975 BC)

A Philistine warrior. Descendant of Rapha[1]. Killed by Sibbekai during David's wars against the Philistines.

📖 (21:18; 1 Chronicles 20:4)

Elhanan[1]
(early C10th BC)

Son of Jair[3] from Bethlehem who killed Lahmi, the brother of Goliath, in a battle against the Philistines at Gob.

📖 (21:19; 1 Chronicles 20:5)

Jair[3] (Jaare-Oregim, NIV 2011 footnote)
(late C11th BC)

Father of Elhanan[1].

📖 (21:19; 1 Chronicles 20:5)

Jonathan[4]
(early C10th BC)

Son of Shimeah[1]. Killed a giant from Gath with six fingers on each hand and six toes on each foot who had taunted the Israelites.

📖 (21:21; 1 Chronicles 20:7)

**Josheb-Basshebeth/
Jashobeam[1]**
(early C10th BC)

Chief of David's Three mighty warriors. A Tahkemonite (Hakmonite) who became famous because he killed 800 (or 300) men at one time by his spear.

📖 (23:8; 1 Chronicles 11:11)

Eleazar[3]
(early C10th BC)

Son of Dodai. Second of David's Three mighty warriors. Famous for his defeat of the Philistines at Pas Dammim when the Israelite troops retreated.

📖 (23:9–10; 1 Chronicles 11:12–14)

Dodai
(early C10th BC)

Father of Eleazar[3]. An Ahohite. In charge of the second division of David's army.

📖 (23:9; 1 Chronicles 11:12; 27:4)

Shammah[3]/Shagee
(early C10th BC)

Son of Agee. Father of Jonathan[5].

Third of David's Three mighty warriors. Famous for standing firm against the Philistines in a field even when the troops retreated. He won a great victory.

📖 (23:11–12, 32–33; 1 Chronicles 11:34)

Agee
(late C11th BC)

Father of Shammah[3]. A Hararite.

📖 (23:11)

Elhanan[2]
(early C10th BC)

Son of Dodo[2] from Bethlehem. Named among David's Thirty mighty men.

📖 (23:24; 1 Chronicles 11:26)

Dodo[2]
(late C11th BC)

Father of Elhanan[2]. From Bethlehem.

📖 (23:24; 1 Chronicles 11:26)

Shammah[4]/Shammoth, Elika
(early C10th BC)

Harodites named among David's Thirty mighty men.

📖 (23:25; 1 Chronicles 11:27)

Helez[1]
(early C10th BC)

A Paltite (Pelonite) and Ephraimite named among David's Thirty mighty men. He commanded the seventh division of David's army.

📖 (23:26; 1 Chronicles 11:27; 27:10)

Ira[2]
(early C10th BC)

Son of Ikkesh from Tekoa. Named among David's Thirty mighty men. He commanded the sixth division of David's army.

📖 (23:26; 1 Chronicles 11:28; 27:9)

Ikkesh
(late C11th BC)

Father of Ira[2]. From Tekoa.

📖 (23:26; 1 Chronicles 11:28; 27:9)

Abiezer[2]
(early C10th BC)

From Anathoth. Named among David's Thirty mighty men. He commanded the ninth division of David's army.

📖 (23:27; 1 Chronicles 11:28; 27:12)

Zalmon/Ilai
(early C10th BC)

An Ahohite. Named among David's Thirty mighty men.

📖 (23:28; 1 Chronicles 11:29)

Maharai
(early C10th BC)

A Netophathite and Zerahite. Named among David's Thirty mighty men. He commanded the tenth division of David's army.

📖 (23:28; 1 Chronicles 11:30; 27:13)

Heled
(early C10th BC)

Son of Baanah[2]. Named among David's Thirty mighty men.

📖 (23:29; 1 Chronicles 11:30)

Baanah[2]
(late C11th BC)

Father of Heled. A Netophathite.

📖 (23:29; 1 Chronicles 11:30)

Ithai
(early C10th BC)

Son of Ribai. Named among David's Thirty mighty men.

📖 (23:29; 1 Chronicles 11:31)

Ribai
(late C11th BC)

Father of Ithai. From Gibeah in Benjamite territory.

📖 (23:29; 1 Chronicles 11:31)

Benaiah[2]
(early C10th BC)

A Pirathonite and Ephraimite. Named among David's Thirty mighty men. Leader of the army division of 24,000 men that served in the eleventh month.

📖 (23:30; 1 Chronicles 11:31; 27:14)

Hiddai/Hurai
(early C10th BC)

From the ravines of Gaash. Named among David's Thirty mighty men.

📖 (23:30; 1 Chronicles 11:32)

Abi-Albon/Abiel[2]
(early C10th BC)

An Arbathite. Named among David's Thirty mighty men.

📖 (23:31; 1 Chronicles 11:32)

Azmaveth[1]
(early C10th BC)

A Barhumite. Named among David's Thirty mighty men.

📖 (23:31; 1 Chronicles 11:33)

Eliahba
(early C10th BC)

A Shaalbonite. Named among David's Thirty mighty men.

📖 (23:32; 1 Chronicles 11:33)

Jashen/Hashem
(late C11th BC)

The father of some of David's Thirty mighty men.

📖 (23:32; 1 Chronicles 11:34)

Jonathan[5]
(early C10th BC)

Son of Shammah[3]. Named among David's Thirty mighty men.

📖 (23:32–33; 1 Chronicles 11:34)

Ahiam
(early C10th BC)

Son of Sharar. Named among David's Thirty mighty men.

📖 (23:33; 1 Chronicles 11:35)

Sharar/Sakar[1] (Sacar)
(late C11th BC)

Father of Ahiam. A Hararite.

📖 (23:33; 1 Chronicles 11:35)

Eliphelet[2]
(early C10th BC)

Son of Ahasbai. Named among David's Thirty mighty men.

📖 (23:34)

Ahasbai
(late C11th BC)

Father of Eliphelet[2]. A Maakathite.

📖 (23:34)

Eliam[2]/Ahijah[6]
(early C10th BC)

Son of Ahithophel. One of David's Thirty mighty men.

📖 (23:34; 1 Chronicles 11:36)

Hezro
(early C10th BC)

From Carmel. Named among David's Thirty mighty men.

📖 (23:35; 1 Chronicles 11:37)

Paarai
(early C10th BC)

An Arbite. Named among David's Thirty mighty men.

📖 (23:35)

Igal[2]
(early C10th BC)

Son of Nathan[3]. Named among David's Thirty mighty men.

📖 (23:36)

Nathan[3]
(late C11th BC)

Father of Igal[2]. From Zobah.

📖 (23:36)

Hagri (Haggadi, NIV 2011 footnote)
(mid C11th BC)

Father of Nathan[3] and Mibhar.

📖 (23:36; 1 Chronicles 11:38)

Zelek
(early C10th BC)

An Ammonite. Named among David's Thirty mighty men.

📖 (23:37; 1 Chronicles 11:39)

Naharai
(early C10th BC)

A Beerothite and armour-bearer of Joab. Named among David's Thirty mighty men.

📖 (23:37; 1 Chronicles 11:39)

Ira[3]
(early C10th BC)

An Ithrite. Listed among David's Thirty mighty men.

📖 (23:38; 1 Chronicles 11:40)

Gareb
(early C10th BC)

An Ithrite. Named among David's Thirty mighty men.

📖 (23:38; 1 Chronicles 11:40)

Araunah
(early C10th BC)

A Jebusite who owned a threshing floor. The angel of the Lord that had brought a plague against Israel had reached here. Gad[2] advised David to build an altar to the Lord here. Araunah offered his threshing floor and oxen free of charge to David but David insisted on paying Araunah. David's offering was received and the plague was ended.

📖 (24:16, 18–25; 1 Chronicles 21:15–28; 2 Chronicles 3:1)

1 Kings

Abishag
(born c.985 BC)

A beautiful Shunammite girl who was David's nurse in his old age. Through Bathsheba, Adonijah[1] requested that Solomon allow Abishag to become his wife following David's death, but the request resulted in Solomon ordering that Adonijah be put to death.

📖 (1:3, 15; 2:13–25)

Shimei[4], Rei
(early C10th BC)
Two men who did not join
Adonijah[1]'s conspiracy but
supported Solomon's succession.

📖 (1:8)

Maakah[3]
(mid C11th BC)
See **Maok** *in 1 Samuel, p. 78.*

📖 (2:39)

Azariah[1]
(mid C10th BC)
Son (or grandson) of Zadok[1]. One
of Solomon's chief officials.

📖 (4:2; 1 Chronicles 6:8–9)

Elihoreph, Ahijah[2]
(mid C10th BC)
Sons of Shisha. They were among
Solomon's chief officials and served
as secretaries.

📖 (4:3)

Shisha
(early C10th BC)
See **Seraiah[1]** *in 2 Samuel, p. 83.*

📖 (4:3)

Azariah[2]
(mid C10th BC)
Son of Nathan[4]. One of Solomon's
chief officials who supervised the
district governors.

📖 (4:5)

Nathan[4]
(early C10th BC)
Father of Azariah[2] and Zabud.

📖 (4:5)

Zabud
(mid C10th BC)
Son of Nathan[4]. One of Solomon's
chief officials who served as a priest
and advisor.

📖 (4:5)

Ahishar
(mid C10th BC)
One of Solomon's chief officials who
served as palace administrator.

📖 (4:6)

Abda[1]
(late C11th BC)
Father of Adoniram.

📖 (4:6)

**Ben-Hur, Ben-Deker, Ben-Hesed,
Ben-Abinadab, Baana[1], Ben-
Geber, Ahinadab, Ahimaaz[3],
Baana[2], Jehoshaphat[2],
Shimei[5], Geber**
(mid C10th BC)
Solomon's 12 district governors
who were responsible for supplying
provisions to the king's household
on a monthly rota basis.

📖 (4:8–19)

Taphath
(mid C10th BC)
Daughter of Solomon and wife of
Ben-Abinadab.

📖 (4:11)

Iddo[1]
(early C10th BC)
Father of Ahinadab.

📖 (4:14)

Basemath[3]
(mid C10th BC)
Daughter of Solomon. Wife of
Ahimaaz[3].

📖 (4:15)

Hushai[2]
(early C10th BC)
Father of Baana[2].

📖 (4:16)

Paruah
(early C10th BC)
Father of Jehoshaphat[2].

📖 (4:17)

Ela
(early C10th BC)

Father of Shimei[5].

📖 (4:18)

Uri[2]
(early C10th BC)

Father of Geber.

📖 (4:19)

Ethan[1]
(early C10th BC)

A wise man who is compared to Solomon and whose wisdom is considered less than his. Known also as an 'Ezrahite', his name is connected to Psalm 89. Probably the same Ethan as the one listed with the sons of Zerah[3] in 1 Chronicles 2:6. *Possibly to be identified with* **Ethan[2]** *in 1 Chronicles, p. 121.*

📖 (4:31; Psalm 89 title)

Heman[1], Kalkol (Calcol), Darda
(early C10th BC)

Sons of Mahol. Wise men who are compared to Solomon and whose wisdom is considered less than his. They are probably the same people as those listed in 1 Chronicles 2:6 as the sons of Zerah[3]. It is likely that Heman was also known as an Ezrahite (see the title of Psalm 88).

📖 (4:31)

Mahol
(late C11th BC)

Father of Heman[1], Kalkol and Darda.

📖 (4:31)

Huram[3]/Huram-Abi
(mid C10th BC)

Craftsman sent from Tyre by King Hiram to work on the temple for King Solomon.

📖 (7:13–14, 40, 45; 2 Chronicles 2:13–14; 4:11–17)

Queen of Sheba
(mid C10th BC)

Visited Solomon in Jerusalem when she heard of his wisdom, wealth and relationship to the Lord. She brought symbols of her own wealth (including great quantities of spices) as gifts to Solomon but she was overwhelmed by his wealth and wisdom. She praised Solomon and rejoiced in the Lord's wisdom in raising up a king to maintain justice and righteousness. Solomon showered her with gifts from the royal stores before she returned home.

📖 (10:1, 4, 10, 13; 2 Chronicles 9:1, 3, 9, 12; Matthew 12:42; Luke 11:31)

Hadad[4]
(mid C10th BC)

An Edomite who had escaped from Edom as a boy when Joab[1]'s army had struck down all its male inhabitants. He had gone first to Paran and then down to Egypt, where he had found favour with the king of Egypt. Pharaoh gave the sister of Tahpenes (his own wife) in marriage to Hadad. Hadad returned to Edom and he became an adversary of Solomon.

📖 (11:14–25)

Queen Tahpenes
(mid C10th BC)

Wife of Pharaoh (*see panel, p. 23*). Her sister became Hadad[4]'s wife.

📖 (11:19–20)

Genubath
(late C10th BC)

Son of Hadad[4] and nephew of Tahpenes. He grew up with Pharaoh's own children in the royal palace.

📖 (11:20)

Rezon
(mid C10th BC)

Son of Eliada[2]. He had fled from Hadadezer, his master. When David had destroyed Hadadezer's army,

Rezon gathered his own band of fighters, who took control of Damascus and Aram. The Lord raised him up as an enemy of Solomon.

📖 (11:23)

Eliada[2]
(early C10th BC)

Father of Rezon.

📖 (11:23)

Kings of Israel and Judah

Dates are those of reigns; all dates are BC. Note that overlapping dates indicate periods of co-regency. In addition, as the royal year sometimes began in March/April and sometimes in September/October, it is not usually known whether an event occurred towards the end of one year or at the beginning of the next. For simplicity, the second of these two possibilities has been used in this table.

The united kingdom

1050–1010	Saul[1]
1010–970	David
970–930	Solomon
(930 The kingdom divides)	

Israel

930–909	Jeroboam I (Jeroboam[1])
909–908	Nadab[2]
908–885	Baasha
885–884	Elah[2]
884	Zimri[3]
884–880	Tibni
884–873	Omri[1]
873–853	Ahab[1]
853–852	Ahaziah[1]
852–841	Jehoram (Joram[2])
841–813	Jehu[2]
813–798	Jehoahaz[1]
798–781	Jehoash
792–753	Jeroboam II (Jeroboam[2])
753–752	Zechariah[1]
752	Shallum[1]
752–741	Menahem
741–739	Pekahiah
752–731	Pekah
731–722	Hoshea[2]
(722 Israel falls; people exiled)	

Judah

930–913	Rehoboam
913–910	Abijah[3]
910–869	Asa[1]
872–848	Jehoshaphat[3]
853–841	Jehoram[1]
841	Ahaziah[2]
841–835	Athaliah[1] (Queen)
835–796	Joash[3]
796–767	Amaziah[1]
791–739	Uzziah (Azariah[3]/Uzziah[1])
750–731	Jotham[2]
741–715	Ahaz[1]
728–686	Hezekiah[1]
696–642	Manasseh[2]
642–640	Amon[2]
640–609	Josiah[1]
609	Jehoahaz[2]
609–598	Jehoiakim
598–597	Jehoiachin
597–586	Zedekiah (Mattaniah[1]/Zedekiah[2])

See also Timeline of the Prophets, p. 203.

Jeroboam[1] (Jeroboam I)
(died 909 BC; reigned 930–909 BC)

Son of Nebat and Zeruah. Father of Nadab[2]. King of Israel. An Ephraimite from Zeredah. An official of Solomon, in charge of the labour force of the house of Joseph. Ahijah[3] told him that he would rule over the 10 tribes of Israel whereas only one tribe would be retained by Solomon and his descendants. When Solomon heard about this, he tried to kill Jeroboam, who fled to Egypt. He stayed there until Solomon died and was succeeded by his son Rehoboam. Rehoboam treated the Israelites harshly. Jeroboam settled in Shechem, in the hill country of Ephraim. He built up Peniel and set up golden calves in Bethel and Dan to deter the people from going to Jerusalem. Pagan worship developed among the Israelite tribes, leading to judgment from the Lord. Jeroboam did not heed the Lord's warnings. His own son died because of his pagan tendencies and wicked activities. He reigned over the Israelite tribes for 22 years and was succeeded by his son Nadab. During his reign he warred against Judah, which was led by Rehoboam, Abijah[3] and Asa[1]. Jeroboam's army was defeated by Abijah, and Jeroboam never really regained power before he died.

📖 (11:26–40; 12:2–15, 25–33; 13:1–10, 33–34; 14:1–20; 15:1, 6–7, 9, 25–30; 2 Kings 3:3; 9:9; 13:2; 2 Chronicles 9:29; 10:2–16; 11:4, 14; 12:15; 13:1–20)

Nebat
(early C10th BC)

Father of Jeroboam[1].

📖 (11:26; 12:2; 21:22; 22:52; 2 Kings 3:3;
14:24; 2 Chronicles 9:29; 10:2)

Zeruah
(early C10th BC)

Mother of Jeroboam[1].

📖 (11:26)

Ahijah[3]
(mid C10th BC)

A prophet based in Shiloh. He
ripped his cloak into 12 pieces,
representing the tribes of Israel, and
gave 10 pieces to Jeroboam[1] to
indicate that he would control the
10 tribes of Israel whereas Solomon's
descendants would rule only
Judah. When Rehoboam succeeded
Solomon, the kingdom divided
as Ahijah had foretold. When
Jeroboam's son Abijah[2] became ill,
Jeroboam sent his wife to enquire of
Ahijah what would happen. Despite
disguising herself, Abijah knew she
was Jeroboam's wife and told her
that her son would die because of the
evil ways of his father.

📖 (11:29–30; 12:15; 14:2–6, 18;
2 Chronicles 9:29; 10:15)

Shishak
(ruled Egypt c.945–924 BC)

King of Egypt during the conflict
between Jeroboam[1] and Rehoboam.
Following Ahijah[3]'s prophecy
Jeroboam stayed with Shishak
until Solomon's death. In the fifth
year of Rehoboam's reign, Shishak,
with supporting troops of Libyans,
Sukkites and Cushites, attacked
Jerusalem and took the treasures
of the royal palace and temple.
Shemaiah[1] explained that this had
happened because Rehoboam and
the leaders of Judah had abandoned
the Lord. Because Rehoboam
repented, Shishak did not totally
destroy Judah.

📖 (11:40; 14:25; 2 Chronicles 12:2–9)

Rehoboam
(971–913 BC; reigned 930–913 BC)

Son of Solomon and an Ammonite
woman called Naamah[2]. Husband
of Mahalath[2] and Maakah[4],
he had in total 18 wives and 60
concubines. He had 28 sons and 60
daughters. After Solomon's death
he went to Shechem to be anointed
king. There Jeroboam[1] asked him
to remove the heavy burdens that
Solomon had placed on the Israelites.
Rehoboam decided to place even
heavier expectations upon them.
This led to the division of the
kingdom, as only the tribes of Judah
and Benjamin remained loyal to
Rehoboam; the other tribes, under
Jeroboam, rebelled against him.
Rehoboam was 41 years old when
he became king and he ruled over
Judah from Jerusalem for 17 years.
During these years he showed some
signs of obedience to the Lord but he
was punished for leading Judah into
idolatry. In his fifth year, Jerusalem
was attacked by Egypt under Shishak.
When Rehoboam followed the ways
of Solomon he received support
from the priests and Levites, who
strengthened his rule and he showed
signs of his father's wisdom. He is
listed in Matthew's genealogy of
Jesus.

📖 (11:43; 12:1–27; 14:21–31;
1 Chronicles 3:10; 2 Chronicles 9:31;
10:1 – 12:16; Matthew 1:7)

Shemaiah[1]
(late C10th BC)

A prophet who told Rehoboam that
because Judah had abandoned the
Lord the people would be handed
over to Shishak. He kept genealogical
records.

📖 (12:22; 2 Chronicles 11:2; 12:5–8, 16)

Josiah[1]
(648–609 BC; reigned 640–609 BC)

Son of Amon[2] and Jedidah.
Father of Jehoahaz[2], Eliakim[2],
Zedekiah[2] and Shallum[3].
He became king after Amon's

assassination, at the age of eight years. He reigned over Judah for 31 years. His birth was predicted by a man of God who appeared to Jeroboam[1] at the site of idolatry in Bethel. He began to repair the temple and during this work the Book of the Law was found. The book was read to Josiah and he wept because his ancestors had not obeyed this Law book. A prophetess named Huldah told Josiah that his repentance meant that the disaster predicted for Judah would not happen in his lifetime. Josiah held a covenant renewal ceremony and instituted a programme of religious reform. He removed pagan influences from the temple, he desecrated sites where sacrifices were offered to the pagan gods Molek and Ashtoreth and he did away with idolatrous priests, mediums and spiritualists. In the eighteenth year of his reign he organized the celebration of the Passover. A similar celebration had not been seen since the days of Samuel. Tragically, Josiah was killed by Necho king of Egypt at Megiddo. He was succeeded by his son Jehoahaz. Jeremiah[6] composed laments for him. Zephaniah[4] prophesied during his reign. Josiah is mentioned in Matthew's genealogy of Jesus, appearing at the end of the list of pre-exilic kings.

(13:2; 2 Kings 21:24 – 23:30, 34; 1 Chronicles 3:14–15; 2 Chronicles 33:25 – 36:1; Jeremiah 1:1–3; 3:6; 22:11, 18; 25:1, 3; 26:1; 27:1; 35:1; 36:1–2, 9; 37:1; 45:1; 46:2; Zephaniah 1:1; Matthew 1:10–11)

Abijah[2]
(late C10th BC)

Son of Jeroboam[1]. Although he died because of the Lord's punishment on the sin of his father's house, Abijah is singled out as the only person in the family in whom the Lord 'found anything good'.

(14:1–17)

Nadab[2]
(died 908 BC; reigned 909–908 BC)

Son of Jeroboam[1]. He became king of Israel while Asa[1] was ruler of Judah. He led his people into sin. His reign was short because Baasha killed him and then succeeded him.

(14:20; 15:25–31)

Naamah[2]
(mid C10th BC)

Ammonite mother of Rehoboam.

(14:21, 31; 2 Chronicles 12:13)

Abijah[3]
(c.950–910 BC; reigned 913–910 BC)

Son of Rehoboam and Maakah[4]. Brother of Attai[3], Ziza[3] and Shelomith[5]. Father of Asa[1]. Became king of Judah in the eighteenth year of Jeroboam[1]'s reign and reigned for three years, throughout which he was at war with Jeroboam. He did not follow the Lord wholeheartedly but the Lord allowed Jerusalem to be secure during his reign. At Mount Zemaraim (in Ephraim) he addressed Jeroboam, reminding Israel that God was with David's descendants. Despite Jeroboam's superior military tactics, attacking the people of Judah from in front and behind, the Lord delivered the people of Judah, and Abijah took Bethel, Jeshanah and Ephron from Jeroboam. Jeroboam never recovered but Abijah's strength grew. He accumulated a total of 14 wives, 22 sons and 16 daughters. Abijah is mentioned in Matthew's genealogy of Jesus.

(14:31; 15:1–8; 1 Chronicles 3:10; 2 Chronicles 11:20–22; 12:16; 13:1 – 14:1; Matthew 1:7; Luke 1:5)

Asa[1]
(c.925–869 BC; reigned 910–869 BC)

Son of Abijah[3]. Father of Jehoshaphat[3]. He became king of Judah in the twelfth year of Jeroboam[1]'s reign. He ruled in Jerusalem for 41 years. Asa removed idols from Judah and was wholly committed to the Lord. He even removed his grandmother from her royal position because of her involvement with idolatry. Judah prospered and experienced periods of peace under Asa. He conducted successful military campaigns against the Cushites, recognizing his need of God's help. He warred with Baasha, who became king of Israel in Asa's third year of rule. He made an alliance with Ben-Hadad[1], the king of Aram, which symbolized his growing self-reliance and earned judgment from Hanani[1], which he responded to by imprisoning the prophet. He died in old age, probably as a result of disease that affected his feet and about which he did not ask God for help. He was honoured in his death by various funeral rites and was succeeded by his son Jehoshaphat[3]. Asa is mentioned in Matthew's genealogy of Jesus.

📖 (15:8–24, 28, 33; 16:8, 10, 15, 23, 29; 22:41, 43, 46; 1 Chronicles 3:10; 2 Chronicles 14:1–15; 15:2 – 16:14; 17:2; 20:32; 21:12; Jeremiah 41:9; Matthew 1:7–8)

Maakah[4] (Maacah)
(mid C10th BC)

Beloved wife of Rehoboam. Mother of Abijah[3], Attai[3], Ziza[3], and Shelomith[5]. Daughter of Abishalom or Uriel[3] of Gibeah. Grandmother of Asa[1]. Because she made an image for the worship of Asherah, Asa deposed her as queen mother.

📖 (15:2, 10, 13; 2 Chronicles 11:20–22; 13:2; 15:16)

Abishalom/Absalom[2]
(early C10th BC)

Father of Maakah[4]. Grandfather of Abijah[3] and great-grandfather of Asa[1].

📖 (15:2, 10)

Baasha
(died 885 BC; reigned 908–885 BC)

Son of Ahijah[4]. Father of Elah[2]. Baasha succeeded Nadab[2] as king of Israel by plotting his death in the third year of Asa[1]'s reign in Judah. He warred against Asa and lost towns and supplies to Asa following his alliance with Ben-Hadad[1] king of Aram. However, he killed all the remaining members of Jeroboam[1]'s family. He reigned for 24 years but became renowned for his evil ways, which matched those of Jeroboam. Jehu[1] received a prophecy about Baasha's demise on account of his sin and his family was wiped out by Zimri[3], one of his son's own officials who plotted against him.

📖 (15:16 – 16:13; 21:22; 2 Kings 9:9; 2 Chronicles 16:1–6; Jeremiah 41:9)

Ben-Hadad[1]
(early C9th BC)

Son of Tabrimmon. King of Aram during the reign of Asa[1]. Asa wanted to break Ben-Hadad's treaty with Baasha and sought his own alliance with him. Asa achieved this by sending him gifts of silver and gold. Ben-Hadad conquered a number of Israelite towns, taking Baasha's supplies and forcing him to withdraw to Tirzah.

📖 (15:18–21; 2 Chronicles 16:2–5)

Tabrimmon
(late C10th BC)

Father of Ben-Hadad[1]. Son of Hezion.

📖 (15:18)

Hezion
(mid C10th BC)

Father of Tabrimmon. Grandfather of Ben-Hadad[1].

📖 (15:18)

Jehoshaphat[3]
(c.907–848 BC; reigned 872–848 BC)

Son of Asa[1] and Azubah[1]. Father of Jehoram[1], Azariah[12], Jehiel[4], Zechariah[13], Azariahu, Michael[9] and Shephatiah[5]. He succeeded Asa[1] as king of Judah at the age of 35 and reigned for 25 years. His reign is described in mixed terms.

He made an alliance with Israel, whose regime under Ahab[1] was corrupt. Despite the warning of Micaiah[1], Jehoshaphat went into battle with Ahab to capture Ramoth Gilead from the king of Aram. The result was Ahab's death in battle. He also joined an alliance with Joram, king of Israel, and the king of Edom against Mesha[1]. This time Jehoshaphat consulted Elisha for advice. Although they were successful against Moab, they aroused extreme fury. On the other hand, Judah prospered during his reign because he did what was right in the Lord's eyes. He fortified cities in Judah, built up his army and accumulated wealth. Although he did not remove the sacrificial sites, he did rid the land of Asherah poles and male shrine prostitutes. He achieved peace and established a fleet of sailing boats, although they never set sail. His people held him in honour. He sent teachers and priests and Levites into the towns of Judah to teach the people about the Law of the Lord, which led to spiritual renewal. He secured a resounding victory over the Moabites and Ammonites, having encouraged the people of Judah to have faith in God for the victory. They prepared for the battle by singing praise to the Lord but never had to fight, because their invaders had fought among themselves; they only had to carry off the plunder. They praised God in the Valley of Berakah ('blessing') and other nations feared God on account of this event. Jehoshaphat led his people back to Jerusalem to continue the celebrations. Like his father he was buried in Jerusalem. He was succeeded by his son Jehoram. He is mentioned in Matthew's genealogy of Jesus.

📖 (15:24; 22:2–50; 2 Kings 1:17; 3:1–14; 8:16; 12:18; 1 Chronicles 3:10; 2 Chronicles 17:1 – 21:3, 12; 22:9; Joel 3:2, 12; Matthew 1:8)

Ahijah[4]
(mid C10th BC)
Father of Baasha.

📖 (15:27, 33; 21:22; 2 Kings 9:9)

Jehu[1]
(early–mid C9th BC)
Son of Hanani[1]. A prophet of the Lord. He brought words of judgment to Baasha because of his evil ways. He also challenged Jehoshaphat[3] about his alliance with Ahab[1], indicating that this had aroused God's anger, but at the same time he commended him for setting his heart on seeking God.

📖 (16:1–7, 12; 2 Chronicles 19:2–3; 20:34)

Hanani[1]
(late C10th BC)
Father of Jehu[1]. A prophet imprisoned by Asa[1] when he prophesied judgment on him.

📖 (16:1, 7; 2 Chronicles 16:7; 19:2; 20:34)

Elah[2]
(died 884 BC; reigned 885–884 BC)
Son of Baasha. He succeeded his father as king of Israel when Asa[1] was king of Judah. He reigned in Tirzah for two years before being killed by Zimri[3], who had plotted against him and took advantage of the opportunity to kill him when he was drunk. This fulfilled Jehu[1]'s prophecy against Baasha.

📖 (16:8–14)

Zimri[3]
(died 884 BC; reigned 884 BC)
An official of Elah[2] who looked after half of the chariots. He plotted against Elah and killed him. He proceeded to wipe out Baasha's family. He then succeeded Elah as king of Israel. He reigned in Tirzah for only seven days and killed himself when he set the palace on fire to avoid certain death at the hands of Omri[1], whom the people declared king when they heard that

Zimri had murdered Elah. He is remembered for his treachery against his master, which is why Jezebel taunted Jehu[2] by using his name.

(16:9–12, 15–20; 2 Kings 9:31)

Arza
(early C9th BC)

Elah[2]'s official in charge of the palace at Tirzah. Elah was drinking at Arza's house when Zimri[3] killed Elah and took the throne for himself.

(16:9)

Omri[1]
(died 873 BC; reigned 884–873 BC)

Father of Ahab[1]. The commander of the army of Israel that was encamped at Gibbethon when Zimri[3] took control of the palace at Tirzah. Enraged by Zimri's actions, the people pronounced Omri king of Israel. Omri led the army to Tirzah but Zimri had fled to the palace and set it ablaze and killed himself. Omri's reign began with the people divided, half supporting Tibni as king. But Omri had superior military strength and Tibni died, leaving Omri king of Israel. He reigned for 12 years but was evil, especially in respect to idol worship. He was buried in Samaria, which he had been responsible for building up as a fortified city. His granddaughter Athaliah[1] was the wife of Jehoram[1].

(16:16–30; 2 Kings 8:26; 2 Chronicles 22:2; Micah 6:16)

Tibni
(died 880 BC; reigned 884–880 BC)

Son of Ginath. He received some support to succeed Zimri[3] as king of Israel but Omri[1]'s supporters were stronger. Tibni died (presumably in conflict with Omri's followers).

(16:21–22)

Ginath
(mid C10th BC)

Father of Tibni.

(16:21)

Shemer[1]
(early C9th BC)

Owner of a hill which Omri[1] purchased from him for two talents of silver. Omri built the city of Samaria there.

(16:24)

Ahab[1]
(died 853 BC; reigned 873–853 BC)

Son of Omri[1]; husband of Jezebel; father of Ahaziah[1], Joram[2] and Joash[2] and at least one daughter called Athaliah[1]. King of Israel, he reigned in Samaria for 22 years. He outdid Jeroboam[1] in terms of his evil reputation by establishing an altar for the worship of Baal (a pagan god) in Samaria and setting up a pole to another pagan god, Asherah. He also set himself against the Lord's prophets, including Elijah[1]. God sent a drought in the land as judgment upon Ahab; the resulting famine was particularly fierce in Samaria. Despite Elijah's demonstration to Ahab on Mount Carmel that Baal was a worthless idol, Ahab refused to rely on God and planned more evil against Elijah through Jezebel. God enabled Ahab to defeat the army of Ben-Hadad[2] of Aram but he then chose to form an alliance with them instead of following the Lord's command to destroy them. Elijah also confronted Ahab about the injustice he meted out to Naboth, whose death he and Jezebel secured so they could obtain his vineyard. Elijah told Ahab he had aroused God's anger. This time Ahab responded with some level of repentance and the destruction of his house was delayed until after his death. He died at the hands of the king of Aram in Ramoth Gilead and was buried in Samaria. After his death, Jehu[2] fulfilled Elijah's prophecy against Ahab's house by wiping out every member of his family.

(16:28 – 17:1; 18:1–20; 18:41 – 19:1; 20:2–15, 33–34; 21:1–29; 22:20, 39– 53; 2 Kings 1:1; 3:1, 5; 8:16, 18, 25–29;

9:7–9, 25, 29; 10:1, 10–11, 17–18, 30;
21:3, 13; 2 Chronicles 18:1–34; 21:6,
13; 22:3–8; Micah 6:16)

Jezebel
(mid C9th BC)

Daughter of Ethbaal; wife of Ahab[1].
She took over in moments of Ahab's
weakness, suggesting that in many
ways he was a pawn in her hands.
A manipulative and powerful
woman, she was committed to
pagan idolatry; she killed many
prophets, was involved in witchcraft
and entertained the priests of the
pagan god Asherah at her table. She
was particularly malicious towards
Elijah[1], who fled for his life from
her. It was Jezebel who devised
the evil murder of Naboth for the
sake of acquiring his vineyard. Her
personal vanity is portrayed by her
attention to her appearance when
Jehu[2] came to Jezreel. This pride
was her downfall because Jehu had
come to destroy Ahab's household.
Jezebel was thrown down before Jehu
from a window. Horses trampled
her and dogs devoured her body as
Elijah had predicted. Her name is
used figuratively in Revelation to
represent the sin of idolatry.

📖 (16:31; 18:4, 13, 19; 19:1–2; 21:5–25;
2 Kings 9:7–10, 22, 30–37; Revelation
2:20)

Ethbaal
(early C9th BC)

Father of Jezebel. King of the
Sidonians.

📖 (16:31)

Hiel
(mid C9th BC)

Father of Abiram[2] and Segub[1].
From Bethel. He rebuilt Jericho
during the reign of Ahab.

📖 (16:34)

Abiram[2], Segub[1]
(mid C9th BC)

Sons of Hiel. Their involvement in

the rebuilding of Jericho cost them
their lives.

📖 (16:34; Joshua 6:26)

Elijah[1]
(mid C9th BC)

A prophet from Tishbe in Gilead.
He was active during the reign of
Ahab[1]. As directed by the Lord,
he himself drank at a brook and
was fed by ravens. He was able to
perform miracles through the power
of God, including the provision of
constant flour and oil during the
famine for the widow of Zarephath
and the restoration to life of a young
boy. He challenged the priests of
Baal (a pagan god) to present their
god for a contest against the God
of Israel on Mount Carmel and
demonstrated to them God's power.
He aroused the anger of Jezebel and
fled to a cave. He warned Ahab of
the coming drought and famine,
and these prophecies against Ahab
were fulfilled through Jehu[2] after
Ahab's death. He also told Ahaziah[2]
that he would die from his injuries.
Elijah did not experience physical
death but was taken up to heaven
in a whirlwind. Elisha was his
successor. By New Testament times
a forerunner of Jesus was expected
who was associated with Elijah. Jesus
explained that he himself was not
the expected Elijah figure but that
John the Baptist had performed this
prophetic role and prepared the way
for Jesus' own ministry. In James,
Elijah is used as an example of a man
who prayed with faith.

📖 (17:1 – 19:21; 21:17–29; 2 Kings
1:3–17; 2:1–15; 3:11; 9:36; 10:10, 17;
2 Chronicles 21:12; Malachi 4:5;
Matthew 11:14; 16:14; 17:3–12; 27:47,
49; Mark 6:15; 8:28; 9:4–13; 15:35–36;
Luke 1:17; 4:25–26; 9:8, 19, 33; John
1:21, 25; Romans 11:2; James 5:17–18)

Obadiah[1]
(mid C9th BC)

A believer in the Lord who was
in charge of Ahab[1]'s palace in

Samaria. He thwarted the evil plans of Jezebel to kill the Lord's prophets by hiding 100 prophets in two caves and supplying them with provisions. During the years of famine in Samaria, Ahab sent Obadiah to search the land for grass for the livestock. On his travels he met Elijah[1], who instructed him to tell Ahab of his whereabouts. Despite his fears for his personal safety, Obadiah was reassured by Elijah and did as he was instructed.

📖 (18:2–16)

Hazael
(ruled Syria c.843–798 BC)

An official of Ben-Hadad[2]. Along with Jehu[2] his role was to bring judgment on the house of Ahab[1]. The first step towards this was Hazael's role in the murder of his predecessor as king, Ben-Hadad[2]. Hazael executed God's punishment on Israel as Elisha predicted and took over their territory in Gilead. He also captured Gath but he did not attack Judah because Joash[3] sent him gifts to win his favour. On his death Hazael was succeeded by his son Ben-Hadad[3].

📖 (19:15–17; 2 Kings 8:8–15, 28–29; 9:14–15; 10:32; 12:17–18; 13:3, 22–25; 2 Chronicles 22:5–6; Amos 1:4)

Jehu[2]
(died 813 BC; reigned 841–813 BC)

Descendant of Nimshi. Son of Jehoshaphat[4]. Commander of the army of Joram[2]. Elijah was instructed to anoint him as king over Israel but this actually took place in Ramoth Gilead by one of Elisha's young prophetic companions. Following his anointing, the people declared him king. Jehu met the kings of Judah (Ahaziah[1]) and Israel (Joram[2]) in Jezreel. There he killed Joram with an arrow that pierced his heart. Ahaziah fled but Jehu's men wounded him and he died later in Megiddo. Jehu became king and reigned for 28 years. God appointed him to wipe out the family of Ahab[1] and he oversaw the deaths of Jezebel and Ahab's children (the 70 royal princes) in Samaria, and other relatives too. Next he brought together the worshippers of the pagan god Baal and killed them all. This secured the promise of God that Jehu's descendants would rule in Israel for four generations, but Jehu then began to turn his back on God. Hazael succeeded in taking territory from Israel, and Jehu's power diminished. He was buried in Samaria and succeeded by his son Jehoahaz[1].

📖 (19:16–17; 2 Kings 9:2 – 10:36; 12:1; 13:1; 14:8; 15:12; 2 Chronicles 22:7–9; 25:17; Hosea 1:4)

Nimshi
(late C10th BC)

Ancestor, probably grandfather, of Jehu[2].

📖 (19:16; 2 Kings 9:2, 14, 20; 2 Chronicles 22:7)

Elisha
(c.870–795 BC)

Son of Shaphat[2]. First Elijah[1]'s servant, then his successor. He witnessed Elijah being taken up into heaven and put on Elijah's cloak, symbolizing his role as Elijah's successor. As a prophet of the Lord, he had a powerful ministry which incorporated prophetic words, pictures and miraculous deeds. His miracles included the cleaning of a city's water supplies; supplying a widow with overflowing oil; restoring to life the son of a Shunammite woman; making a stew edible for his company of prophets in Gilgal; multiplying 20 bread rolls; and causing an iron axe to float. He pronounced a curse on young men who jeered at him, which resulted in them being mauled to death by bears. Ahab[1] and Jehoshaphat[3] sought advice from Elisha following their decision to fight the Moabites. He protected Israel from the raids of the king of Aram and also declared that food would be common in Samaria at a time when the siege imposed on the city by the Arameans had caused desperate famine. He also denounced the kings of Israel for their unbelief and pronounced judgment on them. He showed compassion to the poor and the hungry, demonstrating God's concern for people from all the nations, not least by healing Naaman[2], the Syrian army commander, of his leprosy by instructing him to dip in the Jordan seven times. Elisha ordered one of the prophets in his company to anoint Jehu[2] as king of Israel, thus enabling him to fulfil his role of wiping out the family of Ahab. On his deathbed he commissioned Jehoash king of Israel, who was weeping over him, to destroy the Arameans. Elisha was buried and even after his death his body restored life to an Israelite man (2 Kings 13:21).

📖 (19:16–21; 2 Kings 2:1–24; 3:11–20; 4:1–17, 29–43; 5:8 – 7:2; 8:1–14; 9:1–3; 13:14–21; Luke 4:27)

Shaphat[2]
(early C9th BC)

Father of Elisha. From Abel Meholah.

📖 (19:16, 19; 2 Kings 3:11; 6:31)

Ben-Hadad[2]
(ruled Syria c.860–843 BC)

King of Aram (Syria) who went with 32 kings and horses and chariots to besiege Samaria. He wanted Ahab[1] to hand over his treasure, his wives and children and to allow him to ransack the properties of the king and his officials. When Ahab would not meet his demands, he prepared to attack Samaria, but Ahab's armies inflicted losses on them even though Ben-Hadad escaped on horseback. The following spring Ben-Hadad attacked the Israelites again in Aphek. The Israelites inflicted further losses on them. Ben-Hadad escaped by hiding in an inner room in the city of Aphek. He begged Ahab to spare his life and promised to return

to Israel cities which his father had taken. On this basis they made a treaty of friendship which provoked a warning from the prophets. Although they originally worked together to defend themselves against the Assyrians, Ahab died at Syrian hands when he tried to repossess Ramoth Gilead. When Ben-Hadad became ill, he sent Hazael to Elisha to find out if he would recover. Elisha replied that he knew that Ben-Hadad would die. In fact Hazael murdered him by suffocation and succeeded him as king.

📖 (20:1–21, 26–34; 2 Kings 6:24; 8:7–9, 14–15)

Naboth
(mid C9th BC)

From Jezreel. An owner of a vineyard which Ahab[1] wanted to acquire. Ahab's wife Jezebel secured it for him by arranging for Naboth to be falsely accused of treachery against God and the king. Naboth was killed and the vineyard was taken over by Ahab. The prophet Elijah[1] condemned Ahab for this and warned that his family would be wiped out for their evil deeds. Joram's body was thrown into the field belonging to Naboth.

📖 (21:1–29; 2 Kings 9:21–26)

Micaiah[1]
(mid C9th BC)

Son of Imlah. A faithful prophet. He warned Ahab[1] and Jehoshaphat[3] not to try to take Ramoth Gilead from the king of Aram even though other prophets were assuring them they would be victorious. For his trouble, Micaiah was placed in prison and was given only bread and water to live on but his warning was vindicated because Ahab died during this conflict. This is possibly the same Micaiah who assumed a teaching role in Judah during Jehoshaphat's reign.

📖 (22:8–28; 2 Chronicles 17:7; 18:7–27)

Imlah
(early C9th BC)

Father of Micaiah[1].

📖 (22:8–9; 2 Chronicles 18:7–8)

Zedekiah[1]
(mid C9th BC)

Son of Kenaanah[1]. He prophesied before Ahab[1] and Jehoshaphat[3] and told them that they should go up against the king of Aram and take Ramoth Gilead because they would be victorious. He made two iron horns and said they would gore the Arameans. Micaiah[1] offered a contrasting prophecy, which led Zedekiah[1] to slap him in the face and insult him.

📖 (22:10–12, 24; 2 Chronicles 18:10, 23–24)

Kenaanah[1]
(early C9th BC)

Father of Zedekiah[1].

📖 (22:11, 24; 2 Chronicles 18:10, 23)

Amon[1]
(mid C9th BC)

Ruler of the city of Samaria. At Ahab's command he imprisoned Micaiah[1].

📖 (22:26–27; 2 Chronicles 18:25–26)

Joash[2]
(mid C9th BC)

Son of Ahab[1]. He received instructions from Ahab to secure Micaiah[1] in prison.

📖 (22:26–27; 2 Chronicles 18:25–26)

Ahaziah[1]
(c.875–852 BC; reigned 853–852 BC)

Son of Ahab[1]. Succeeded his father as king of Israel at the age of 22 and reigned for two years. He tried to persuade Jehoshaphat[3] to allow his men to sail with Jehoshaphat's trading ships but he was unsuccessful. He continued in the idolatrous ways of his parents and aroused God's anger. He fell through a window and injured himself. He asked his messengers to ask the pagan god of Ekron (Baal-Zebub) if he would recover. The messengers encountered Elijah[1], who condemned Ahaziah for not consulting the Lord God of Israel. He died as Elijah had predicted without a son.

📖 (22:40, 49–53; 2 Kings 1:2–18)

Azubah[1]
(early C9th BC)

Mother of Jehoshaphat[3]. Daughter of Shilhi.

📖 (22:42; 2 Chronicles 20:31)

Shilhi
(late C10th BC)

Father of Azubah[1] and grandfather of Jehoshaphat[3].

📖 (22:42; 2 Chronicles 20:31)

Jehoram[1]
(c.885–841 BC; reigned 853–841 BC)

Son of Jehoshaphat[3]. Father of Ahaziah[2] and a daughter called Jehosheba. He succeeded his father as king of Judah and reigned for eight years. He was an evil king who killed his brothers and officials in Judah. He was judged as unfit to lead Judah and his behaviour is compared to that of Ahab[1]. He married Ahab's daughter Athaliah[1], which brought dire spiritual and political consequences to Judah, not least because it led to his alliance with Joram[2], his brother-in-law, who became king of Israel. His reign was disturbed by revolts from the Edomites and the inhabitants of Libnah. Because of the Lord's promise to David, he did not wipe out Jehoram's family, despite his evil deeds. The prophet Elijah[1] denounced his sin and indicated that his judgment would come in the form of an incurable bowel disease. He died in pain and without honour or regret and was succeeded by his son Ahaziah[2].

📖 (22:50; 2 Kings 8:16–25, 29; 11:2; 12:18; 1 Chronicles 3:11; 2 Chronicles 21:1–20; 22:1, 6, 11; Matthew 1:8)

2 Kings

Joram[2]
(died 841 BC; reigned 852–841 BC)

Son of Ahab[1] and Jezebel. He succeeded Ahaziah[1] as king of Israel and reigned for 12 years. He removed some pagan worship of the god Baal but still did 'evil in the eyes of the Lord'. He mobilized his army and those of Judah and Edom when Mesha[1] rebelled against him. With this support victory was secured, though it evoked Moabite fury. He later joined with Ahaziah[2] against the Arameans at Ramoth. He was injured and returned to Jezreel to recover. Jehu[2] killed Joram with an arrow shot that pierced his heart. His death reflects the judgment already pronounced on Ahab's family.

📖 (1:17; 3:1, 4–27; 8:16, 25, 28–29; 9:14–17, 21–24, 29; 2 Chronicles 22:5–7)

Mesha[1]
(mid C9th BC)

King of Moab who led the Moabites in rebellion against Joram[2]. He was defeated by the coalition of Judah, Israel and Edom.

📖 (3:4–27)

Gehazi
(mid C9th BC)

Servant of Elisha. He alerted Elisha to the childless status of the Shunammite woman, who subsequently had a son. When the boy died, Elisha told Gehazi to take his staff and touch it upon the boy's face, but to no avail. Gehazi witnessed the miracle when Elisha revived the child. Seven years later he was instrumental in the restoration of the woman's land. After Naaman[2] was healed from his leprosy, Gehazi acquired gifts from Naaman. He lied to Elisha about what he had done and was himself afflicted with leprosy.

📖 (4:12–36; 5:20–27; 8:4–5)

Naaman[2]
(mid C9th BC)

Commander of the Syrian army. He was highly regarded but had leprosy. Through the intervention of his wife's servant girl, Naaman was sent from Aram to the king of Israel then on to Elisha to be healed. Elisha instructed Naaman to wash seven times in the Jordan River. The idea was repugnant to Naaman but he finally complied and was healed. He declared his faith in God and offered gifts to Elisha but they were refused. Naaman asked Elisha to pardon him for his involvement with the worship of Rimmon, a pagan god. Gehazi was cross about the leniency Elisha showed to Naaman. He pursued Naaman, who gave him gifts for the young prophets who Gehazi falsely claimed needed money and clothes. In Luke's Gospel Naaman is mentioned by Jesus as an example of someone outside Israel who accepted the ministry of God's servant and was healed.

📖 (5:1–23; Luke 4:27)

Ahaziah[2]
(c.863–841 BC; reigned 841 BC)

Son of Jehoram[1] and Athaliah[1]. Brother of Jehosheba. Father of Joash[3]. He succeeded his father as king of Judah when he was 22 years old. He reigned for one year. He joined with Joram[2] in war against Hazael at Ramoth, during which Joram was injured. When Ahaziah went to visit Joram in Jezreel, Jehu[2] killed both Joram and Ahaziah. Ahaziah died at Megiddo but was buried in Jerusalem.

📖 (8:25–29; 9:27–29; 13:1; 1 Chronicles 3:11)

Athaliah[1]
(died 835 BC; reigned 841–835 BC)

Daughter of Ahab[1]. Granddaughter of Omri[1]. Wife of Jehoram[1] and mother of Azariah[2]; by her marriage she brought the houses of Israel and Judah together. After Ahaziah[2]'s death, she put to death the rest of Judah's royal family, except Ahaziah's son Joash[3]. She ruled Judah for six years until she was put to death at the command of Jehoiada[2] following her outcry against Joash, who had been anointed king. The people rejoiced at her death. Her family was notorious: her sons had taken sacred items for use in Baal worship.

📖 (8:26; 11:1–3, 13–16, 20; 2 Chronicles 22:2, 10–12; 23:12–15, 21; 24:7)

Jehoshaphat[4]
(early C9th BC)

Son of Nimshi. Father of Jehu[2].

📖 (9:2, 14)

Bidkar
(mid C9th BC)

Jehu[2]'s chariot officer who picked up the body of Joram[2] and threw it onto Naboth's field.

📖 (9:25)

Jehonadab (also Jonadab[2], NIV 2011 footnote)
(mid C9th BC)

Son of Rekab[2]. Jehu[2] invited him to join him in his chariot to witness him destroy the rest of Ahab[1]'s family and the worshippers of Baal in Samaria.

📖 (10:15, 23; Jeremiah 35:6, 8, 10, 14, 16, 19)

Rekab[2] (Recab)
(early C9th BC)

Father of Jehonadab.

📖 (10:15; Jeremiah 35:6, 8, 14, 16, 19)

Jehoahaz[1]
(died 798 BC; reigned 813–798 BC)

Son of Jehu[2]. Father of Jehoash. He succeeded his father in the twenty-third year of Joash[3]'s rule and reigned over Israel for 17 years. He did not please the Lord and consequently Israel was subject to Hazael and his son Ben-Hadad[3]. The oppression was severe, leading Jehoahaz to seek the Lord's

help. Israel was delivered but was weakened by the loss of its army. Jehoahaz's turning to the Lord was only half-hearted and symbols of idol worship were not removed from Samaria.

📖 (10:35; 13:1–10, 22, 25; 14:1, 8, 17; 2 Chronicles 25:17, 25)

Jehosheba
(mid C9th BC)

Daughter of Jehoram[1]. Sister of Ahaziah[2]. Aunt of Joash[3]. Wife of Jehoida[2]. When Athaliah[1] set out to kill all the royal family of Judah, Jehosheba hid Joash and his nurse in a bedroom, so preserving the royal family line. She cared for him for six years in the temple courts.

📖 (11:2; 2 Chronicles 22:11)

Joash[3]
(842–796 BC; reigned 835–796 BC)

Son of Ahaziah[2] and Zibiah. Father of Amaziah[1]. When his grandmother Athaliah[1] tried to wipe out the royal family, Joash was hidden by Jehosheba. His uncle Jehoiada[2] arranged his coronation ceremony six years later. Joash became king at the age of seven years. He ruled Judah for 40 years and began the slow process of repairing the temple in Jerusalem. Joash reorganized the finances of the project and skilled workers were recruited. When Hazael decided to attack Jerusalem, Joash sent him the sacred temple treasures to persuade him to withdraw. After Jehoiada's death, Joash was led astray by his officials, who resumed their worship of idols. When Zechariah[14] warned him about his disobedience to God, Joash ordered Zechariah's death. The consequence of his treachery against Jehoiada's family was that he himself was assassinated at Beth Millo by his own officials. He was buried in Jerusalem but not in the tomb of the kings.

📖 (11:2–21; 12:1–21; 1 Chronicles 3:11; 2 Chronicles 22:10 – 24:27)

Jehoiada[2]
(mid C9th BC)

Husband of Jehosheba. Priest in Jerusalem. Father of Zechariah[14]. He organized the coronation of Joash[3] by bringing him out of hiding. Then he arranged Athaliah[1]'s death. Jehoiada led the king and the people in a covenant commitment of loyalty to the Lord, and the temple of Baal was destroyed. Jehoiada remained Joash's advisor and chose his two wives for him. He advised and supported Joash in the repair of the temple, and worship was renewed. He was 130 years old when he died. He was buried with the kings in Jerusalem in recognition of his service for God.

(11:4–20; 12:2, 7, 9; 2 Chronicles 22:11; 23:1–20; 24:2–25; Jeremiah 29:26)

Mattan[1]
(mid C9th BC)

The priest of the pagan god Baal who was killed in front of the altars when Jehoiada[2] destroyed Baal's temple.

(11:18; 2 Chronicles 23:17)

Zibiah
(mid C9th BC)

Mother of Joash[3]. She came from Beersheba.

(12:1; 2 Chronicles 24:1)

Jozabad[1]/Zabad[1], Jehozabad[1]
(late C9th BC)

Sons of Shomer[1]. They were Joash[3]'s officials but were responsible for his murder. Joash's son Amaziah[1] executed them for their treachery.

(12:21; 2 Chronicles 24:26; 25:3)

Shimeath
(mid C9th BC)

Mother of Jozabad[1]/Zabad[1]. An Ammonite.

(12:21; 2 Chronicles 24:26)

Shomer[1]/Shimrith
(mid C9th BC)

Mother of Jehozabad[1]. A Moabite.

(12:21; 2 Chronicles 24:26)

Amaziah[1]
(c.821–767 BC; reigned 796–767 BC)

Son of Joash[3] and Jehoaddan. Father of Azariah[3]. He was 25 years old when he succeeded Joash[3] as king of Judah. He reigned for 29 years, combining righteous actions with maintaining the high places of idol worship. He put to death the officials who had assassinated his father. He reorganized military service and conscripted men from Ephraim, until a man of God told him to send home the troops from Ephraim. He defeated 10,000 Edomites in the Valley of Salt but also brought back the gods of Seir. Another prophet warned Amaziah that his action would lead to God's punishment. He then incited war with Jehoash. Judah was defeated, its army fled; Amaziah was captured at Beth Shemesh; and the city wall of Jerusalem was penetrated. After Jehoash's death, Amaziah lived for 15 years but when men conspired against him in Jerusalem he fled to Lachish, where he was killed. His body was returned to Jerusalem by horse and he was buried with his ancestors.

(12:21; 14:1–22; 1 Chronicles 3:12; 2 Chronicles 24:27 – 26:2)

Ben-Hadad[3]
(ruled Syria c.796–770 BC)

Son of Hazael. He continued his father's evil ways and God used him to punish Israel. He was defeated eventually because of God's judgment on the nations that surrounded Israel.

(13:3; Jeremiah 49:27; Amos 1:4)

Jehoash
(died c.781 BC; reigned 798–781 BC)

Son of Jehoahaz[1]. Father of Jeroboam[2]. He succeeded his father as king of Israel and ruled for 16 years. He did evil in the Lord's sight. On his deathbed Elisha promised Jehoash that he would have three victories over Aram. These victories led to the recapture of the Israelite towns that Hazael had taken. Jehoash tried to avoid conflict with Amaziah[1], but Amaziah was determined to meet him in battle. Jehoash captured Amaziah, broke through the wall of Jerusalem and took treasures as well as hostages before returning to Samaria. He was buried in Samaria with the kings of Israel.

📖 (13:10 – 14:1, 8–17; 2 Chronicles 25:17–25; Hosea 1:1; Amos 1:1)

Jeroboam[2]
(died c.753 BC; reigned 792–753 BC)

Son of Jehoash. Father of Zechariah[1]. Succeeded his father as king of Israel and reigned for 41 years. He did evil in the Lord's sight. He did, however, restore the boundaries of Israel from Lebo Hamath to the Dead Sea and recovered both Damascus and Hamath. The Lord brought deliverance for Israel through Jeroboam; his military successes restored territory and prosperity. Amos[1] and Hosea considered that this prosperity brought inequality between the rich and the poor as well as religious complacency.

📖 (13:13; 14:23 – 15:1, 8; Hosea 1:1; Amos 1:1; 7:9–11)

Jehoaddan (Jehoaddin)
(late C9th BC)

Wife of King Joash[3]. Mother of Amaziah[1]. She came from Jerusalem.

📖 (14:2; 2 Chronicles 25:1)

Azariah[3]/Uzziah[1]
(c.807–739 BC; reigned 791–739 BC)

Son of Amaziah[1] and Jekoliah. Father of Jotham[2]. He succeeded his father as king of Judah when he was 16 years old. He reigned for 52 years and rebuilt Elath, restoring it to Judah. He combined righteous actions with maintaining the high places of idol worship. He was successful in military campaigns against the Philistines, Arabs and Meunites. He was honoured by the Ammonites and his reputation reached Egypt. He fortified Jerusalem, dug cisterns and cultivated the land. He provided his army with good-quality armour and weapons. He became proud, however, and started to usurp roles in the temple reserved for priests. Azariah[15] challenged him but his angry response meant he was afflicted with leprosy, so he lived in a separate house while his son Jotham[2] took charge of the palace. He was buried in Jerusalem. The prophets Isaiah, Hosea and Amos[1] prophesied during his reign. Uzziah is mentioned in Matthew's genealogy of Jesus.

📖 (14:21–22; 15:1–8, 13, 17, 23, 27, 30–34; 1 Chronicles 3:12; 2 Chronicles 26:1–23; 27:2; Isaiah 1:1; 6:1; 7:1; Hosea 1:1; Amos 1:1; Zechariah 14:5; Matthew 1:8–9)

Jonah[1]
(mid C8th BC)

See **Jonah[1]** in *Jonah, p. 214.*

📖 (14:25)

Amittai
(early C8th BC)

Father of Jonah[1].

📖 (14:25; Jonah 1:1)

Zechariah[1]
(died 752 BC; reigned 753–752 BC)

Son of Jeroboam[2]. He ruled Israel for six months. He did evil in the Lord's sight. He was publicly assassinated by Shallum[1].

📖 (14:29; 15:8–12)

Jekoliah (Jecoliah)
(early C8th BC)

Wife of King Amaziah[1]. Mother of Azariah[3]. She came from Jerusalem.

📖 (15:2; 2 Chronicles 26:3)

Jotham[2]
(c.775–731 BC; reigned 750–731 BC)

Son of Azariah[3] and Jerusha. Father of Ahaz[1]. He looked after the palace affairs in his youth while his father lived in a separate house because of his leprosy. He became king of Judah at 25 years old. He reigned for 16 years and then lived on for another 4 years after being deposed in a major power struggle. The pro-Assyrian Ahaz, who was nominally co-regent from 741 BC, seems to have taken control in 735 (Jotham's 16th year), from which Ahaz's sole reign is dated. He 'did what was right in the eyes of the LORD', though he did not remove the pagan high places of worship. He carried out extensive work on the wall of Jerusalem; he rebuilt the Upper Gate of the temple and built new towns and forts. He conquered the Ammonites, who brought him tribute for three years. Isaiah, Hosea and Micah[5] prophesied during his reign. He is mentioned in Matthew's genealogy of Jesus.

📖 (15:5, 7, 30, 32–38; 16:1; 1 Chronicles 3:12; 5:17; 2 Chronicles 26:21 – 27:9; Isaiah 1:1; 7:1; Hosea 1:1; Micah 1:1; Matthew 1:9)

Shallum[1]
(died 752 BC; reigned 752 BC)

Son of Jabesh. He assassinated Zechariah[1] and succeeded him as king of Israel. He ruled in Samaria for one month before Menahem assassinated him.

📖 (15:10–15)

Jabesh
(early C8th BC)

Father of Shallum[1].

📖 (15:10–14)

Uzziah[1]
(c.807–739 BC; reigned 791–739 BC)

See **Azariah[3]** in 2 Kings, p. 108.

📖 (15:13)

Menahem
(died c.741 BC; reigned 752–741 BC)

Son of Gadi. Father of Pekahiah. He assassinated Shallum[1] in Samaria and succeeded him as king of Israel. He ruled for 10 years and 'did evil in the eyes of the LORD'. He attacked Tiphsah and 'ripped open' all the pregnant women there. Taking money from wealthy Israelites, he paid tribute to Pul the king of Assyria to secure his withdrawal.

📖 (15:14–23)

Gadi
(early C8th BC)

Father of Menahem.

📖 (15:14, 17)

Pul/Tiglath-Pileser
(ruled Assyria 745–727 BC)

King of Assyria who invaded Israel during the reign of Menahem. He withdrew on payment of tribute money. During Pekah's reign he took over Israel's towns and villages, including Gilead, Galilee and Naphtali, deporting the Reubenites, the Gadites and the half-tribe of Manasseh[1] to exile in Assyria. Ahaz[1] asked Tiglath-Pileser for help when the king of Israel joined with the king of Syria but this brought him even more trouble.

📖 (15:19–20, 29; 16:7–10; 1 Chronicles 5:6, 26; 2 Chronicles 28:16–21)

Pekahiah
(died 739 BC; reigned 741–739 BC)

Son of Menahem. He succeeded his father and ruled Israel for two years. He followed the sinful ways of Jeroboam[1] and was assassinated by Pekah in the citadel of the royal palace in Samaria.

📖 (15:22–26)

Pekah
(died 731 BC; reigned 752–731 BC)

Son of Remaliah. He was one of Pekahiah's officials but he assassinated him and then succeeded him as king of Israel. He ruled for a total of 20 years. He followed the sinful ways of Jeroboam[1]. During his reign Israel suffered loss of territory and people as Pul advanced. He joined with Rezin[1] to attack Ahaz[1] but they did not overpower him. However, on another occasion he inflicted heavy casualties on Judah. He was assassinated by Hoshea[2].

📖 (15:25, 27–32, 37; 16:1, 5; 2 Chronicles 28:6; Isaiah 7:1)

Remaliah
(early C8th BC)

Father of Pekah.

📖 (15:25, 27, 30, 32, 37; 2 Chronicles 28:6; Isaiah 7:1, 4–9; 8:6)

Argob, Arieh
(mid C8th BC)

These men were assassinated with Pekahiah by Pekah.

📖 (15:25)

Tiglath-Pileser
(ruled Assyria 745–727 BC)

See **Pul** *in 2 Kings, p. 109.*

📖 (15:29)

Hoshea[2]
(reigned 731–722 BC)

Son of Elah[3]. He assassinated Pekah and succeeded him as king of Israel. He reigned for nine years, during which he paid tribute to Shalmaneser. However, Shalmaneser discovered he was a traitor and imprisoned him. Shalmaneser captured Samaria and deported the Israelites to Assyria. Hoshea was Israel's last king.

📖 (15:30; 17:1–6; 18:1, 9–10)

Elah[3]
(early C8th BC)

Father of Hoshea[2].

📖 (15:30; 17:1; 18:1)

Jerusha
(early C8th BC)

Mother of Jotham[2]. Daughter of Zadok[2].

📖 (15:33; 2 Chronicles 27:1)

Zadok[2]
(late C9th BC)

Father of Jerusha.

📖 (15:33; 2 Chronicles 27:1)

Rezin[1]
(ruled Aram c.740–732 BC)

King of Aram who joined with Pekah in attacking Judah. He took back Elath for the Edomites by driving out Judah. Ahaz[1] persuaded the king of Assyria to help him resist Rezin and in a show of strength he attacked Damascus and put Rezin to death.

📖 (15:37; 16:5–6; Isaiah 7:1, 4, 8; 8:6)

Ahaz[1]
(c.755–715 BC; reigned 741–715 BC)

Son of Jotham[2]. Father of Hezekiah[1] and other children, including Maaseiah[4]. He succeeded his father at 20 years old. After the death of his father in

731 BC he ruled Judah for 16 years but 'did not do what was right in the eyes of the LORD his God'. He sacrificed his own children in fire and engaged in pagan worship. When Rezin[1] and Pekah formed an alliance against him he was defeated. Ahaz paid Pul tribute money to engage his help. He asked Uriah[2] to make an altar in Jerusalem to impress Pul but Pul only brought him trouble. As things deteriorated for Ahaz, he became more unfaithful to God. He shut the doors to the temple and set up altars to other gods on street corners in Jerusalem and in every town in Judah. He was buried in Jerusalem but not in the tombs of the kings. Isaiah, Hosea and Micah[5] prophesied during his reign. He is mentioned in Matthew's genealogy of Jesus.

📖 (15:38 – 17:1; 18:1; 20:11; 23:12; 1 Chronicles 3:13; 2 Chronicles 27:9 – 28:27; 29:19; Isaiah 1:1; 7:1–12; 14:28; 38:8; Hosea 1:1; Micah 1:1; Matthew 1:9)

Uriah[2]
(late C8th BC)

Priest in the time of Ahaz[1] who was willing to follow Ahaz's instructions for temple worship and new altars. His actions were indicative of the fear in Judah at its vulnerability and the demise of the faith.

📖 (16:10–16)

Hezekiah[1]
(c.740–686 BC; reigned 728–686 BC)

Son of Ahaz[1] and Abijah[4]. Father of Manasseh[3]. Although co-regent from the age of 12, in 715 BC he succeeded his father to become sole king of Judah when he was 25 years old. He reigned for 29 years and followed the ways of David. He made mistakes but he was wholeheartedly committed to the Lord. His campaign for religious reform included removing every symbol of pagan worship; reconsecrating the priests and the temple; and using musical instruments and the songs of praise written by David and Asaph[2]. He assembled people from all over Judah to celebrate the Passover in Jerusalem. Hezekiah prayed for the people and reinstituted gifts for the priests and the Levites, and the people responded generously. Politically he defeated the Philistines and was not intimidated by the king of Assyria. When Sennacherib taunted the inhabitants of Jerusalem, asking them to trust him rather than Hezekiah and his God, Hezekiah wept and prayed in the temple and sought advice from Isaiah. Isaiah reassured Hezekiah that Jerusalem would not be defeated by the Assyrians. Some time later Hezekiah was ill and about to die but again he prayed to the Lord and 15 years were added to his life. He became wealthy and cared for his people. He increased the city's defences and constructed a water channel from the Gihon spring to the Pool of Siloam. His people honoured him in his death, and he was buried in the tombs of David's descendants. Some of the Proverbs of Solomon were collected during his reign. Isaiah, Hosea and Micah[5] prophesied during his reign. Jeremiah[6] commends Hezekiah for his fear of the Lord. Hezekiah is mentioned in Matthew's genealogy of Jesus.

📖 (16:20; 18:1 – 20:21; 21:3; 1 Chronicles 3:13; 4:41; 2 Chronicles 28:27 – 32:33; 33:3; Proverbs 25:1; Isaiah 1:1; 36:1 – 39:8; Jeremiah 15:4; 26:18–19; Hosea 1:1; Micah 1:1; Matthew 1:9–10)

Pagan gods

The Bible teaches that there is only one true God who is the maker of heaven and earth and eternal in his being. However, the Bible acknowledges that people have worshipped other gods. Some of these took the form of idols or images; others were purely mythical.

Old Testament			
Adrammelek and Anammelek	gods of Sepharvaim		2 Kings 17:31
Amon	chief god of Egypt		Jeremiah 46:25
Apis	bull-god of Egypt		Jeremiah 46:15 (some versions)
Asherah	Canaanite goddess	associated with wooden poles	Exodus 34:13–14
Ashima	Syrian god		2 Kings 17:30
Ashtoreth	Canaanite goddess of war and fertility	also called *Ishtar, Astarte, Venus, Queen of heaven* Jeremiah 7:18; 44:17–19, 25	Judges 2:12–13
Baal	Canaanite and Phoenician god of rain and fertility	means 'lord'	Judges 2:10–13
Baal-Berith	Caananite god	'lord of the covenant'; also called *El Berith* Judges 9:46	Judges 8:33; 9:4
Baal-Zebub	god of the Philistines	*Beelzebub* is the Greek form of the name *Baal-Zebub*, meaning 'lord of the flies'	2 Kings 1:2–17; Matthew 12:24
Bel	chief god of Babylon; the sun god	also called *Marduk*	Isaiah 46:1
Chemosh	chief god of Moab	also called *Milkom* in Hebrew	1 Kings 11:7
Dagon	Philistine god		Judges 16:23
Molek	chief god of Ammon	also called *Milkom*	1 Kings 11:4–5
Nebo		also called *Nabu*	Isaiah 46:1

Nergal	god of war, death and plague		2 Kings 19:37
Nibhaz	Elamite god		2 Kings 17:31
Nisrok	pagan god worshipped by Sennacherib	(Nisroch)	2 Kings 19:37; Isaiah 37:38
Rimmon	Aramean god of storm	also called *Hadad*	2 Kings 5:18; Zechariah 12:11
Sukkoth Benoth			2 Kings 17:30
Tammuz	Babylonian fertility god		Ezekiel 8:14
Tartak			2 Kings 17:31

New Testament			
Artemis	Greek name for Roman goddess Diana		Acts 19:24–35
Castor and Pollux	Twin gods, sons of Zeus and guardians of sailors		Acts 28:11
Rephan			Acts 7:43
Zeus and Hermes	Greek gods	Zeus: patron god of Lystra; Hermes: Roman god Mercury	Acts 14:12–13

Shalmaneser
(ruled Assyria 727–722 BC)

King of Assyria who was angry because Hoshea[2] had turned to Egypt for help. He imprisoned Hoshea, and, in Hezekiah[1]'s reign, he laid siege against Samaria and three years later took the people into exile.

📖 (17:3–6, 24–41; 18:9–12)

So
(ruled Egypt c.730–716 BC)

King of Egypt. Hoshea[2] sought his help against the Assyrians.
Possibly to be identified with Shabaka or Osorkon IV (see panel, p. 23).

📖 (17:4)

Abijah[4]
(mid C8th BC)

Mother of Hezekiah[1]. Wife of Ahaz[1]. Daughter of Zechariah[2].

📖 (18:2; 2 Chronicles 29:1)

Zechariah[2]
(early C8th BC)

Father of Abijah[4]. Grandfather of Hezekiah[1].

📖 (18:2; 2 Chronicles 29:1)

Assyrian rulers

Tiglath-Pileser I	1115–1077 BC
Tukulti-Ninurta I	890–884 BC
Ashurnasirpal II	883–859 BC
Shalmaneser III	859–824 BC
Samsi-Adad V	823–811 BC
Adad-Nirari III	810–783 BC
Shalmaneser IV	782–773 BC
Ashurdan III	772–755 BC
Ashurnirari V	754–745 BC
Tiglath-Pileser III	745–727 BC
Shalmaneser V	727–722 BC
Sargon II	722–705 BC
Sennacherib	705–681 BC
Esarhaddon	681–669 BC
Ashurbanipal	669–c.627 BC

(Adapted from John Drane, *Introducing the Old Testament*, Lion Publishing, 2000)

Sennacherib
(ruled Assyria 705–681 BC)

King of Assyria during Hezekiah[1]'s reign. He captured the fortified cities of Judah but Hezekiah paid him off with tribute money. He sent three of his chief officials to Jerusalem to taunt the inhabitants of Jerusalem. But the field commander was sidetracked by fighting in Libnah, and Sennacherib sent another message to Hezekiah to taunt him further. Isaiah reassured Hezekiah that he had nothing to fear. That night an angel of the Lord put to death 185,000 in the Assyrian camp and Sennacherib withdrew to Nineveh. Sennacherib was murdered by his two sons while he worshipped his pagan god Nisrok.

📖 (18:13 – 19:37; 2 Chronicles 32:1–2, 9–22; Isaiah 36:1 – 37:38)

Eliakim[1], Shebna, Joah[1]
(late C8th BC)

Palace administrator, secretary and recorder during Hezekiah[1]'s reign. They went out to the aqueduct of the Upper Pool, on the road to the Washerman's Field, to meet the three officials of Sennacherib. The threatening words of Sennacherib's officials disturbed them and they reported to Hezekiah. Hezekiah sent them to Isaiah, who gave them a reassuring message.

📖 (18:18, 26, 37; 19:2–7; Isaiah 22:15, 20–24; 36:3, 11, 22; 37:2)

Hilkiah[1]
(mid C8th BC)

Father of Eliakim[1].

📖 (18:18, 26, 37; Isaiah 22:20; 36:3, 22)

Asaph[1]
(mid C8th BC)

Father of Joah[1].

(18:18, 37; Isaiah 36:3, 22)

Isaiah
(prophesied c.739–700 BC)

Son of Amoz. Father of Shear-Jashub and Maher-Shalal-Hash-Baz. Prophet in Jerusalem during the reigns of Azariah[3]/Uzziah[1], Jotham[2], Ahaz[1] and Hezekiah[1]. He urged Ahaz to have faith in God when faced by the coalition of Rezin[1] and Pekah. When Hezekiah consulted him about the threat from Sennacherib, Isaiah reassured him. Later Hezekiah consulted him about what he feared was a terminal illness and Isaiah told him that 15 years would be added to his life. He warned Hezekiah that one day the Babylonians would force his descendants into exile. The book of Isaiah records Isaiah's vision of the Lord and his call in the year of Uzziah's death (chapter 6). His prophecies anticipate a new ruler from the line of David who will reassemble the scattered people of Judah (chapter 11). Chapter 40 onwards considers the situation of God's people following the exile to Babylon. The prophecies anticipate the coming of a servant of the Lord to rescue his people. The last prophecies anticipate the return of God's people from exile and celebrate their role as light to the nations. The prophecies of Isaiah are frequently quoted in the New Testament, especially with the purpose of validating the ministry of John the Baptist and Jesus.

(19:2–7, 20–34; 20:1–11, 14–19; 2 Chronicles 26:22; 32:20, 32; Isaiah 1:1; 2:1; 7:3, 13; 13:1; 20:2–3; 37:2–6, 21; 38:1–4, 21; 39:3–5; Matthew 3:3; 4:14; 8:17; 12:17; 13:14–15; 15:7–9; John 1:23; 12:38–41; Acts 8:28–33; 28:25–27; Romans 9:27–29; 10:16, 20–21; 11:8; 15:12)

Amoz
(mid C8th BC)

Father of Isaiah.

(19:2, 20; 2 Chronicles 26:22; Isaiah 1:1; 2:1; 38:1)

Tirhakah
(ruled Cush c.690–664 BC)

King of Cush who marched out against Sennacherib during Hezekiah's reign.

(19:9; Isaiah 37:9)

Adrammelek, Sharezer[1]
(early C7th BC)

Sons of Sennacherib who murdered their father in the temple of the pagan god Nisrok. They escaped to Ararat.

(19:37; Isaiah 37:38)

Esarhaddon
(ruled Assyria c.681–669 BC)

Son of Sennacherib. He succeeded his father as king after his two brothers had murdered him. In Ezra[1]'s day some of the people whom Esarhaddon had taken to Jerusalem were residing among the returned Israelite exiles.

(19:37; Ezra 4:2; Isaiah 37:38)

Marduk-Baladan (Merodach-Baladan)
(ruled Babylon c.720–709, 703 BC)

Son of Baladan. King of Babylon during Hezekiah[1]'s reign. He sent letters and a gift to Hezekiah during his illness. Isaiah warned Hezekiah at this time that the Babylonians would come again to take everything belonging to Hezekiah's kingdom, including his descendants into exile.

(20:12–18; Isaiah 39:1)

Baladan
(mid C8th BC)

Father of Marduk-Baladan.

(20:12; Isaiah 39:1)

Manasseh[2]
(c.708–642 BC; reigned 696–642 BC)

Son of Hezekiah[1] and Hephzibah. Father of Amon[2]. At 12 years old he succeeded his father as king of Judah and reigned for 55 years. He rebuilt the places of idol worship that Hezekiah had destroyed. In the temple courts he erected altars to the stars and an Asherah pole. He practised divination and consulted mediums and sacrificed his own son in fire. Through faithful prophets the Lord spoke words of judgment on Manasseh and Jerusalem. The Assyrian army commanders took Manasseh prisoner to Babylon. In his distress he humbled himself before God and received mercy from the Lord and he returned to Jerusalem. He strengthened the city's defences and removed the pagan altars he had erected. He then led the people in worship and obedience to God. He was buried in the palace garden of Uzza[1]. Manasseh is mentioned in Matthew's genealogy of Jesus.

📖 (20:21 – 21:18; 23:12, 26; 24:3;
    1 Chronicles 3:13; 2 Chronicles 32:33 –
    33:23; Jeremiah 15:4; Matthew 1:10)

Hephzibah
(late C8th BC)

Mother of Manasseh[2]. Wife of Hezekiah[1].

📖 (21:1)

Uzza[1]
(unknown)

The palace garden where Manasseh[2] was buried was named after this man.

📖 (21:18, 26)

Amon[2]
(c.664–640 BC; reigned 642–640 BC)

Son of Manasseh[2] and Meshullemeth. Father of Josiah[1]. At 22 years old he succeeded his father and ruled Judah for two years. He 'did evil in the eyes of the LORD' and did not repent like Manasseh. He was assassinated as a result of a conspiracy among his officials in his palace. He was buried in the palace garden of Uzza[1]. He is mentioned in Matthew's genealogy of Jesus.

📖 (21:18–26; 1 Chronicles 3:14;
    2 Chronicles 33:20–25; Jeremiah 1:2;
    25:3; Zephaniah 1:1; Matthew 1:10)

Meshullemeth
(early C7th BC)

Mother of Amon[2]. Daughter of Haruz.

📖 (21:19)

Haruz
(late C8th BC)

Father of Meshullemeth. Grandfather of Amon[2].

📖 (21:19)

Josiah[1]
(648–609 BC; reigned 640–609 BC)

*See **Josiah[1]** in 1 Kings, p. 96.*

📖 (21:26)

Jedidah
(mid C7th BC)

Mother of Josiah[1]. Wife of Amon[2]. Daughter of Adaiah[1]. From Bozkath.

📖 (22:1)

Adaiah[1]
(early C7th BC)

Father of Jedidah. Grandfather of Josiah[1].

📖 (22:1)

Shaphan[1]
(mid C7th BC)

Son of Azaliah. Secretary of Josiah[1]. Father of Ahikam and Elasah[2]. When the Book of the Law was recovered, he read it to Josiah and went with Hilkiah[2], Ahikam, Akbor[2] and Asaiah to enquire more about it from Huldah.

📖 (22:3–14; 25:22; 2 Chronicles 34:8,
    15–22; Jeremiah 26:24; 29:3; 36:10–12;
    39:14; 40:5–11; 41:2; 43:6)

Azaliah
(mid C7th BC)

Father of Shaphan[1]. Son of Meshullam[1].

(22:3; 2 Chronicles 34:8)

Meshullam[1]
(early C7th BC)

Father of Azaliah. Grandfather of Shaphan[1].

(22:3; 2 Chronicles 34:12–13)

Hilkiah[2]
(late C7th BC)

Son of Shallum[6]. Father of Azariah[8]. High priest in Jerusalem during Josiah[1]'s reign. Hilkiah paid the wages of the workmen repairing the temple. He found the Book of the Law during the rebuilding work. Josiah asked Hilkiah[2] to go with Shaphan[1] and others to find out more about it from Huldah.

(22:4–14; 1 Chronicles 6:13; 2 Chronicles 34:9–22; 35:8)

Ahikam
(late C7th BC)

Son of Shaphan[1]. Father of Gedaliah[2]. He accompanied his father and others when Josiah[1] sent them to Huldah to enquire about the Book of the Law. He supported Jeremiah[6] when he was under threat of death.

(22:12; 25:22; Jeremiah 26:24; 39:14; 40:5–11; 41:1–18; 43:6)

Akbor[2] (Acbor)/Abdon[4]
(late C7th BC)

Son of Micaiah[2]. Father of Elnathan[5]. He went with Shaphan[1] and others when Josiah[1] sent them to Huldah to enquire about the Book of the Law. *Called 'Adbon son of Micah', see* **Abdon[4]** *in 2 Chronicles, p. 166.*

(22:12; Jeremiah 26:22; 36:12)

Micaiah[2]/Micah[6]
(mid C7th BC)

Father of Akbor[2].

(22:12; 2 Chronicles 34:20)

Asaiah[1]
(late C7th BC)

He went with Shaphan[1] and others when Josiah[1] sent them to Huldah to enquire about the Book of the Law.

(22:12)

Huldah
(late C7th BC)

Wife of Shallum[2]. The prophetess who lived in the New Quarter in Jerusalem, whom Josiah[1]'s officials consulted about the Book of the Law. She confirmed the Lord's displeasure that the people of Judah had neglected the covenant. She assured Josiah that the coming destruction would not occur in his lifetime.

(22:14; 2 Chronicles 34:22)

Shallum[2]
(late C7th BC)

Son of Tikvah[1]. Grandson of Harhas. Husband of Huldah. He looked after the royal wardrobe.

(22:14; 2 Chronicles 34:22; Jeremiah 32:7)

Tikvah[1]/Tokhath
(mid C7th BC)

Father of Shallum[2]. Son of Harhas.

(22:14; 2 Chronicles 34:22)

Harhas/Hasrah
(early C7th BC)

Father of Tikvah[1]. Grandfather of Shallum[2].

(22:14; 2 Chronicles 34:22)

Nathan-Melek (Nathan-Melech)
(late C7th BC)

An official during Josiah[1]'s reign who had a room near the court of the temple.

(23:11)

Necho (Neco)
(ruled Egypt c.610–595 BC)

An Egyptian Pharaoh (*see panel, p. 23*) during Josiah's reign. At Megiddo he killed Josiah[1], who had gone out to meet him in battle. Necho wanted to avoid conflict with Josiah but Josiah would not be persuaded to back down. Necho was on his way to help the king of Assyria at that time and it is possible that Josiah feared this coalition. Necho put Josiah's son Jehoahaz[2] in chains so he could not reign and he imposed heavy taxes on Judah. Necho's authority is evident because he placed Eliakim[2], Jehoahaz's brother, on the throne. He changed Eliakim's name to Jehoiakim and took Jehoahaz to Egypt to die. Jehoiakim had to meet Necho's demands for silver and gold but Necho himself was defeated at Carchemish on the River Euphrates by Nebuchadnezzar.

📖 (23:29, 33–35; 2 Chronicles 35:20–22; 36:4; Jeremiah 46:2)

Jehoahaz[2]/Shallum[3]
(born c.632 BC; reigned 609 BC)

Son of Josiah[1] and Hamutal. Grandson of Amon[2] and Jeremiah[1]. Jehoahaz succeeded his father at the age of 23 but he ruled Judah for only three months because Necho chained him and took him to Egypt and appointed his brother Eliakim[2] as king in his place. Jehoahaz died in Egypt as Jeremiah[6] prophesied because he had turned away from the righteous and just ways of his father.

📖 (23:30–34; 1 Chronicles 3:15; 2 Chronicles 36:1–4; Jeremiah 22:11–17)

Hamutal
(late C7th BC)

Wife of Josiah[1]. Mother of Jehoahaz[2] and Zedekiah[2]. Daughter of Jeremiah[1]. From Libnah.

📖 (23:31; 24:18)

Jeremiah[1]
(mid C7th BC)

Father of Hamutal.

📖 (23:31; 24:18)

Eliakim[2]/Jehoiakim
(c.634–598 BC; reigned 609–598 BC)

Son of Josiah[1] and Zebidah. Father of Jehoiachin. Made king of Judah by Pharaoh Necho at the age of 25, he reigned for 11 years. Necho changed his name from Eliakim to Jehoakim and demanded tribute money from him. He 'did evil in the eyes of the LORD' and became Nebuchadnezzar's vassal for three years. Things only got worse for him because the Babylonians were joined by Arameans, Moabites and Ammonites who set out to destroy Judah. Jeremiah[6] prophesied about his shameful death on account of his pride before the Lord. He was taken away from Jerusalem to Babylon in shackles by Nebuchadnezzar.

📖 (23:34 – 24:6, 19; 1 Chronicles 3:15–16; 2 Chronicles 36:4–8; Jeremiah 1:3; 22:18–23; 24:1; 25:1; 26:1, 21–23; 27:20; 28:4; 35:1; 36:1, 9, 28–32; 37:1; 45:1; 46:2; 52:2; Daniel 1:1–2)

Zebidah
(late C7th BC)

Wife of Josiah[1]. Mother of Eliakim[2]. Daughter of Pedaiah[1].

📖 (23:36)

Pedaiah[1]
(mid C7th BC)

Father of Zebidah. Grandfather of Eliakim[2].

📖 (23:36)

Jehoiachin/Jeconiah
(born c.616 BC, died after 560 BC; reigned 598–597 BC)

Son of Eliakim[2] and Nehushta. Father of Shealtiel. Succeeded his father as king of Judah at 18 years old but only reigned for three months. He surrendered to Nebuchadnezzar when he advanced on Jerusalem and was taken captive to Babylon with Mordecai[2]. Nebuchadnezzar made Zedekiah[2] king in his place. After 37 years of exile he was released from prison and treated with honour by Awel-Marduk, king of Babylon. From then on he ate at the king's table and was given an allowance. Jeremiah[6] prophesied that Jehoiachin and his mother would die in exile. Ezekiel's visions were received during Jehoiachin's fifth year in exile. He is called Jeconiah in Matthew's genealogy of Jesus.

📖 (24:6–16; 25:27–30; 1 Chronicles 3:16–17; 2 Chronicles 36:8–10; Esther 2:6; Jeremiah 22:24–30; 24:1; 27:20; 28:4; 29:2; 37:1; 52:31–34; Ezekiel 1:2; Matthew 1:11–12)

Nehushta
(late C7th BC)

Mother of Jehoiachin. Daughter of Elnathan[1]. She was among those who surrendered to Nebuchadnezzar and was taken off into exile in Babylon.

📖 (24:8–12; Jeremiah 22:26; 29:2)

Elnathan[1]
(mid C7th BC)

Father of Nehushta. Grandfather of Jehoiachin.

📖 (24:8)

Nebuchadnezzar
(ruled Babylon 605–562 BC)

King of Babylon who defeated Necho. Eliakim[2]/Jehoiakim was Nebuchadnezzar's vassal for three years but when he rebelled, Nebuchadnezzar captured Jerusalem and took Jehoiakim, along with people and treasures, into Babylonian exile. He made Mattaniah[1] king in Jehoiakim's place, changing his name to Zedekiah[2]. When Zedekiah rebelled against him, Nebuchadnezzar besieged Jerusalem for two years, which led to a severe lack of food. Zedekiah tried to break out of the city, but Nebuchadnezzar's army overtook him on the plains of Jericho. They

killed his sons, gouged out his eyes and put him in shackles in Babylon. Nebuzaradan then took all but the very poorest people of Judah into exile. Nebuchadnezzar appointed Gedaliah[1] over the people left in Judah. Included among those he took into exile were Jozadak and Mordecai[2]. He won victories over the people of Tyre and Egypt. The story of Daniel[5] is set in the court of Nebuchadnezzar in Babylon. He was a powerful king whose splendour was coupled with pride and a fiery temper. His responses sometimes suggest that he understood something of the greatness of the God of the Jews.

📖 (24:1–17; 25:1–26; 1 Chronicles 6:15; 2 Chronicles 36:6–21; Ezra 1:7; 2:1; 5:12–14; 6:5; Nehemiah 7:6; Esther 2:6; Jeremiah 21:2, 7; 22:25; 24:1; 25:1, 9–11; 27:6–8, 20; 28:3, 11, 14; 29:1–3, 21; 32:1, 28; 34:1; 35:11; 37:1; 39:1–11; 43:10; 44:30; 46:2, 13, 26; 49:28–30; 50:17; 51:34; 52:4, 12, 28–29; Ezekiel 26:7; 29:18–19; 30:10; Daniel 1:1, 18; 2:1, 28, 46; 3:1–28; 4:1–18, 28–37; 5:2,11, 18)

Mattaniah[1]/Zedekiah[2]
(born c.618 BC; reigned 597–586 BC)

Son of Josiah[1] and Hamutal. Uncle of Jehoiachin. Last king of Judah. Nebuchadnezzar appointed him as king in place of Jehoiachin when he was 21 years old and then changed his name from Mattaniah to Zedekiah. He reigned in Jerusalem for 11 years but 'did evil in the eyes of the LORD'. Jeremiah[6] warned him to accept that the Babylonians would capture Jerusalem. Zedekiah provided Jeremiah with some provisions in the courtyard of the guard. Jerusalem fell to Nebuchadnezzar during his reign, and Zedekiah was shackled, his eyes were gouged out and he was taken prisoner to Babylon, where he died.

📖 (24:17–20; 25:2,7; 1 Chronicles 3:16; 2 Chronicles 36:10–14; Jeremiah 1:3; 21:1–7; 24:8; 27:1, 3, 12; 28:1; 32:1–5; 34:1–8, 21–22; 37:1–3, 17–21; 38:14–24; 39:1–7; 44:30; 49:34; 51:59; 52:1–11)

Nebuzaradan
(early C6th BC)

Commander of Nebuchadnezzar's imperial guard. He was responsible for the ransacking of Jerusalem and the physical removal of people from Judah into exile. He also took Seraiah[2], Zephaniah[1] and three doorkeepers from the temple, along with other royal advisors, to Nebuchadnezzar at Riblah, Babylon, where they were executed. He had Jeremiah[6] released from chains when he was en route to Babylon and supplied him with provisions before allowing him to return to Gedaliah[1]'s care at Mizpah. He returned to Jerusalem at a later date to remove more people to Babylon.

(25:8–21; Jeremiah 39:9–13; 40:1–5; 41:10; 43:6; 52:12–30)

Seraiah[2]
(died 586 BC)

Son of Azariah[8]. Father of Jehozadak. Chief priest when Nebuzaradan ransacked Jerusalem. He was taken prisoner and presented to Nebuchadnezzar at Riblah, where he was executed.

(25:18; 1 Chronicles 6:14; Jeremiah 52:24–27)

Zephaniah[1]
(died 586 BC)

Priest second to Seraiah[2] when Nebuzaradan ransacked Jerusalem. He was taken prisoner and presented to Nebuchadnezzar at Riblah, where he was executed.

(25:18; Jeremiah 52:24–27)

Gedaliah[1]
(early C6th BC)

Son of Ahikam. Appointed by Nebuchadnezzar as governor over those who remained in Judah after the exile. When Jeremiah[6] was allowed to return to Jerusalem he was sent to Gedaliah. Gedaliah tried to encourage the people to settle down and not be fearful. But Ishmael[2] came with 10 men to Mizpah and assassinated Gedaliah and his supporters. The rest of the people fled to Egypt, fearful of Babylonian revenge.

(25:22–26; Jeremiah 39:14; 40:5 – 41:10, 16–18; 43:6)

Ishmael[2]
(early C6th BC)

Son of Nethaniah[1]. An army official who went to Gedaliah[1] at Mizpah to seek reassurance. He returned later with 10 men and killed Gedaliah and his supporters.

(25:23–26; Jeremiah 40:8; 40:13 – 41:18)

Nethaniah[1]
(late C7th BC)

Father of Ishmael[2].

(25:23; Jeremiah 40:14–15; 41:1–2, 6, 10, 12, 15, 16, 18)

Johanan[1]
(early C6th BC)

Son of Kareah. An army official who went to Gedaliah[1] at Mizpah to seek reassurance. He tried to warn Gedaliah that Ishmael[2] was planning to assassinate him but Gedaliah did not believe him. After Gedaliah's death many people turned to Johanan. Contrary to Jeremiah[6]'s advice, he took the people (and Jeremiah and Baruch) to Egypt because they were fearful of Babylonian retaliation for Gedaliah's death.

(25:23; Jeremiah 40:8, 13–16; 41:1 – 43:7)

Kareah
(late C7th BC)

Father of Johanan[1] and Jonathan[15].

(25:23; Jeremiah 40:8, 13–16; 41:11– 16; 42:1, 8; 43:4)

Seraiah[3]
(early C6th BC)

Son of Tanhumeth. An army official who went to Gedaliah[1] at Mizpah to seek reassurance.

📖 (25:23; Jeremiah 40:8)

Tanhumeth
(late C7th BC)

Father of Seraiah[3]. A Netophathite.

📖 (25:23; Jeremiah 40:8)

Jaazaniah[1]
(early C6th BC)

Son of a Maakathite. An army official who went to Gedaliah[1] at Mizpah to seek reassurance.

📖 (25:23; Jeremiah 40:8)

Elishama[3]
(mid C7th BC)

Father of Nethaniah[1]. Grandfather of Ishmael[2].

📖 (25:25)

Awel-Marduk (Evil-Merodach)
(ruled Babylon 562–560 BC)

King of Babylon who released Jehoiachin from prison and gave him a seat of honour at his table as well as an allowance for the rest of his life.

📖 (25:27; Jeremiah 52:31)

1 Chronicles

Many of the dates in the genealogies in 1 Chronicles 1–9 are highly speculative. In addition to the assumptions referred to in the note preceding the entry on Abraham (see p. 20) (that the descent into Egypt occurred in 1662 BC and the exodus in 1447 BC), it is often unclear whether 'son' and 'father' refers to one generation or to more than one (hence 'descendant' or 'ancestor'), or to a political rather than a biological link. Generations in linear genealogies are often missed out (but there is usually no way of knowing where the gap is), and some whole genealogies are unconnected with any others or with any historical event that we can date. Some names may refer to places or clans rather than individuals. If the same name recurs, it is often hard to know whether the same individual is being referred to or someone else of the same name. Frequently the Hebrew is ambiguous as to which antecedent name is being referred back to when a relationship is being described. Where there are no other constraints, this book assumes an average of three generations per century, although in practice this will often be an underestimate. In consultation with the commentaries, the fragmentary evidence is dealt with as carefully as possible, but all these dates must be treated with extreme caution.

Ethan[1]
(early C10th BC)

See **Ethan[1]** in 1 Kings, p. 93.

📖 (2:6)

Heman[1], Kalkol (Calcol), Darda
(early C10th BC)

See **1 Kings**, p. 93.

📖 (2:6)

Ethan[2]
(early C10th BC)

Father of Azariah[4]. Possibly the same person as Ethan[1].

📖 (2:8)

Achar
(late C15th BC)
See **Achan** *in Joshua, p. 58.*
(2:7)

Azariah[4]
(mid C10th BC)
Son of Ethan[2]. Descendant of Zerah[3].
(2:8)

Jerahmeel[1]
(early C16th BC)
Son of Hezron[2]. Grandson of Perez. Brother of Ram[1] and Caleb[2].
(2:9, 25, 42)

Caleb[2]
(early C16th BC)
Son of Hezron[2]. Grandson of Perez. Brother of Jerahmeel[1] and Ram[1]. Married Azubah[2] and Ephrath.
(2:9, 42, 46–50)

Nethanel[2], Raddai, Ozem[1]
(mid C11th BC)
Sons of Jesse. Grandsons of Obed[1]. Brothers of David.
(2:14–15)

Azubah[2]
(early C16th BC)
First wife of Caleb[2]. Mother of Jesher, Shobab[2] and Ardon.
(2:18)

Jerioth
(early C16th BC)
Either a concubine or wife of Caleb[2], through whom he had children.
(2:18)

Jesher, Shobab[2], Ardon
(mid C16th BC)
Sons of Azubah[2] and Caleb[2].
(2:18)

Ephrath
(early C16th BC)
Became wife of Caleb[2] following Azubah[2]'s death. Mother of Hur[1].
(2:19)

Segub[2]
(early C16th BC)
Son of Hezron[2]. His mother was the daughter of Makir[1]. Father of [1].
(2:21–22)

Abijah[5]
(late C17th BC)
Wife of Hezron[2]. Mother of Ashhur.
(2:24)

Ashhur
(early C16th BC)
Son of Hezron[2] and Abijah[5]. Father of Tekoa.
(2:24; 4:5)

Tekoa
(mid C16th BC)
Son of Ashhur. Alternatively, the place where Ashhur was governor.
(2:24; 4:5)

Ram[2], Bunah, Oren, Ozem[2], Ahijah[5]
(mid C16th BC)
Sons of Jerahmeel[1]. Grandsons of Hezron[2].
(2:25, 27)

Atarah
(early C16th BC)
Wife of Jerahmeel[1]. Mother of Onam[2].
(2:26)

Onam[2]
(mid C16th BC)
Son of Jerahmeel[1] and Atarah. Father of Shammai[1] and Jada.
(2:26)

Maaz, Jamin[2], Eker
(late C16th BC)
Sons of Ram[2]. Grandsons of Jerahmeel[1].
📖 (2:27)

Shammai[1], Jada
(late C16th BC)
Sons of Onam[2]. Grandsons of Jerahmeel[1].
📖 (2:28, 32)

Nadab[3], Abishur
(mid C16th BC)
Sons of Shammai[1]. Grandsons of Onam[2].
📖 (2:28–29)

Abihail[2]
(mid C16th BC)
Wife of Abishur. Mother of Ahban and Molid.
📖 (2:29)

Ahban, Molid
(mid C15th BC)
Sons of Abishur and Abihail[2].
📖 (2:29)

Seled, Appaim
(mid C15th BC)
Sons of Nadab[3]. Grandsons of Shammai[1].
📖 (2:30)

Ishi[1]
(late C15th BC)
Son of Appaim. Grandson of Nadab[3]. Father of Sheshan.
📖 (2:31)

Sheshan
(early C14th BC)
Son of Ishi[1]. Grandson of Appaim. Father of Ahlai[1] and (an)other unnamed daughter(s). His family name was preserved by his servant Jarha.
📖 (2:31, 34–35)

Ahlai[1]
(mid C14th BC)
Daughter of Sheshan.
📖 (2:31, 35)

Jether[3]
(early C15th BC)
Son of Jada. Grandson of Onam[2].
📖 (2:32)

Jonathan[6]
(early C15th BC)
Son of Jada. Grandson of Onam[2]. Father of Peleth[2] and Zaza.
📖 (2:32–33)

Peleth[2], Zaza
(mid C15th BC)
Sons of Jonathan[6]. Grandsons of Jada.
📖 (2:33)

Jarha
(mid C14th BC)
Father of Attai[1]. Egyptian servant of Sheshan who married Sheshan's daughter so her father's family name could be preserved.
📖 (2:34–35)

Attai[1]
(late C14th BC)
Son of Jarha and Sheshan's daughter. Father of Nathan[5].
📖 (2:35–36)

Nathan[5]
(early C13th BC)
Son of Attai[1]. Grandson of Jarha. Father of Zabad[2].
📖 (2:36)

Zabad[2]
(mid C13th BC)
Son of Nathan[5]. Grandson of Attai[1]. Father of Ephlal.
📖 (2:36–37)

Ephlal
(late C13th BC)

Son of Zabad[2]. Grandson of Nathan[5]. Father of Obed[2].

📖 (2:37)

Obed[2]
(early C12th BC)

Son of Ephlal. Grandson of Zabad[2]. Father of Jehu[3].

📖 (2:37–38)

Jehu[3]
(mid C12th BC)

Son of Obed[2]. Grandson of Ephlal. Father of Azariah[5].

📖 (2:38)

Azariah[5]
(late C12th BC)

Son of Jehu[3]. Grandson of Obed[2]. Father of Helez[2].

📖 (2:38–39)

Helez[2]
(early C11th BC)

Son of Azariah[5]. Grandson of Jehu[3]. Father of Eleasah[1].

📖 (2:39)

Eleasah[1]
(mid C11th BC)

Son of Helez[2]. Grandson of Azariah[5]. Father of Sismai.

📖 (2:39–40)

Sismai
(late C11th BC)

Son of Eleasah[1]. Grandson of Helez[2]. Father of Shallum[4].

📖 (2:40)

Shallum[4]
(early C10th BC)

Son of Sismai. Grandson of Eleasah[1]. Father of Jekamiah[1].

📖 (2:40–41)

Jekamiah[1]
(mid C10th BC)

Son of Shallum[4]. Grandson of Sismai. Father of Elishama[4].

📖 (2:41)

Elishama[4]
(late C10th BC)

Son of Jekamiah[1]. Grandson of Shallum[4].

📖 (2:41)

Mesha[2]
(mid C16th BC)

Firstborn son of Caleb[2]. Father of Ziph[1].

📖 (2:42)

Ziph[1]
(late C16th BC)

Son of Mesha[2]. Grandson of Caleb[2].

📖 (2:42)

Mareshah[1]
(mid C16th BC)

Son of Caleb[2]. Father of Hebron[2].

📖 (2:42)

Hebron[2]
(late C16th BC)

Son of Mareshah[1]. Grandson of Caleb[2]. Father of Korah[4], Tappuah, Rekem[2] and Shema[1].

📖 (2:42–43)

Korah[4], Tappuah
(early C15th BC)

Sons of Hebron[2].

📖 (2:43)

Rekem[2]
(early C15th BC)

Son of Hebron[2]. Father of Shammai[2].

📖 (2:43–44)

Shema[1]
(early C15th BC)
Son of Hebron[2]. Father of Raham.
📖 (2:43–44)

Raham
(mid C15th BC)
Son of Shema[1]. Father of Jorkeam.
📖 (2:44)

Jorkeam
(late C15th BC)
Son of Raham.
📖 (2:44)

Shammai[2]
(mid C15th BC)
Son of Rekem[2].
📖 (2:44–45)

Maon
(late C15th BC)
Son of Shammai[2]. Father/founder of Beth Zur.
📖 (2:45)

Ephah[2]
(early C16th BC)
Concubine of Caleb[2]. Mother of Haran[2], Moza[1] and Gazez[1].
📖 (2:46)

Haran[2], Moza[1], Gazez[1]
(mid C16th BC)
Sons of Caleb[2] and Ephah[2].
📖 (2:46)

Gazez[2]
(late C16th BC)
Son of Haran[2]. Grandson of Caleb[2].
📖 (2:46)

Jahdai
(mid C16th BC)
A descendant of Caleb[2].
📖 (2:47)

Regem, Jotham[3], Geshan, Pelet[1], Ephah[3], Shaaph[1]
(late C16th BC)
Sons of Jahdai.
📖 (2:47)

Maakah[5] (Maacah)
(early C16th BC)
Concubine of Caleb[2]. Mother of Sheber, Tirhanah, Shaaph[2], Sheva[2] and possibly also Aksah[2].
📖 (2:48–49)

Sheber, Tirhanah, Shaaph[2]
(mid C16th BC)
Sons of Caleb[2] and Maakah[5].
📖 (2:49)

Madmannah
(late C16th BC)
Son of Shaaph[2]. Grandson of Caleb[2] and Maakah[5].
📖 (2:49)

Sheva[2]
(mid C16th BC)
Son of Caleb[2] and Maakah[5].
📖 (2:49)

Makbenah, Gibea
(late C16th BC)
Sons of Sheva[2]. Grandsons of Caleb[2] and Maakah[5].
📖 (2:49)

Aksah[2] (Acsah)
(mid C16th BC)
Daughter of Caleb[2] and possibly Maakah[5].
📖 (2:49)

Hur[3]
(mid C16th BC)
Father of Shobal[2], Salma, Hareph and Reaiah[1].
📖 (2:50; 4:1)

Shobal[2]
(late C16th BC)
Son of Hur[3]. Governor of Kiriath Jearim. Grandfather of Jahath.
📖 (2:50; 4:1–2)

Salma
(late C16th BC)
Son of Hur[3]. Governor of Bethlehem.
📖 (2:51)

Hareph
(late C16th BC)
Son of Hur[3]. Governor of Beth Gader.
📖 (2:51)

Haroeh
(early C15th BC)
Descendant of Shobal[2].
📖 (2:52)

Hammath
(unknown)
Ancestor of the Kenites. Governor of Beth Rekab.
📖 (2:55)

Daniel[1]
(born late C11th BC)
See **Kileab** *in 2 Samuel, p. 79.*
📖 (3:1)

Eliphelet[3]/Elpelet
(born early C10th BC)
Son of David. Born in Jerusalem.
📖 (3:6; 14:5)

Nogah
(born early C10th BC)
Son of David. Born in Jerusalem.
📖 (3:7; 14:6)

Johanan[2]
(late C7th BC)
Firstborn son of Josiah[1].
📖 (3:15)

Shallum[3]/Jehoahaz[2]
See **Jehoahaz[2]/Shallum[3]**, *p. 118.*
📖 (3:15)

Zedekiah[3]
(born late C7th BC)
Son of Jehoiakim.
📖 (3:16)

Shealtiel
(born c.600 BC)
Son of Jehoiachin.
📖 (3:17; Ezra 3:2, 8; 5:2; Haggai 1:1)

Malkiram, Pedaiah[2], Shenazzar, Jekamiah[2], Hoshama, Nedabiah
(early C6th BC)
Descendants of Jehoiachin.
📖 (3:18)

Zerubbabel
(early C6th BC)
Son of Pedaiah[2] and frequently referred to as the son of Shealtiel. Governor of post-exilic Judah, he had returned with Joshua[3] and the people from Babylonian exile. He was responsible for the rebuilding of the altar and the re-establishment of worship there. He is mentioned in Matthew's and Luke's genealogies of Jesus.
📖 (3:19; Ezra 2:2; 3:2, 8; 5:2; Nehemiah 12:1; Haggai 1:1; 2:23; Matthew 1:12–13; Luke 3:27)

Shimei[6]
(early C6th BC)
Son of Pedaiah[2].
📖 (3:19)

Meshullam[2], Hananiah[1]
(mid C6th BC)
Sons of Zerubbabel. Grandsons of Pedaiah[2].
📖 (3:19)

Shelomith[2]
(mid C6th BC)
Daughter of Zerubbabel. Granddaughter of Pedaiah[2].
📖 (3:19)

Hashubah, Ohel, Berekiah[1], Hasadiah, Jushab-Hesed
(late C6th BC)
Descendants of Zerubbabel.
📖 (3:20)

Pelatiah[1], Jeshaiah[1], Rephaiah[1], Arnan, Obadiah[2], Shekaniah[1] (Shecaniah)
(late C6th BC)
Descendants of Hananiah[1].
📖 (3:21–22)

Shemaiah[2]
(early C5th BC)
Descendant of Shekaniah[1].
📖 (3:22)

Hattush[1]
(mid C5th BC)
Son of Shemaiah[2]. This is probably the same Hattush as the one who sealed the covenant of recommitment with Nehemiah[2] (Nehemiah 10:4).
📖 (3:22; Ezra 8:2)

Igal[3], Bariah, Neariah[1], Shaphat[3]
(mid C5th BC)
Sons of Shemaiah[2].
📖 (3:22–23)

Elioenai[1], Hizkiah, Azrikam[1]
(late C5th BC)
Sons of Neariah[1].
📖 (3:23–24)

Hodaviah[1], Eliashib[1], Pelaiah[1], Akkub[1], Johanan[3], Delaiah[1], Anani
(late C5th BC)
Sons of Elioenai[1].
📖 (3:24)

From the tribe of Judah[1]

Reaiah[1]
(early C15th BC)
Son of Shobal[2]. Descendant of Hur[3]. Father of Jahath[1].
📖 (4:2)

Jahath[1]
(mid C15th BC)
Son of Reaiah[1]. Father of Ahumai and Lahad.
📖 (4:2)

Ahumai, Lahad
(late C15th BC)
Sons of Jahath[1].
📖 (4:2)

Etam
(late C16th BC)
Descendant of Hur[3]. Father of Jezreel[1], Ishma, Idbash and Hazzelelponi.
📖 (4:3)

Jezreel[1], Ishma, Idbash
(early C15th BC)
Sons of Etam.
📖 (4:3)

Hazzelelponi
(early C15th BC)
Daughter of Etam.
📖 (4:3)

Penuel[1]
(late C16th BC)
Descendant of Hur[3]. Father of Gedor[1].
📖 (4:4)

Gedor[1]
(early C15th BC)
Son of Penuel[1].
📖 (4:4)

Ezer[2]
(late C16th BC)
Descendant of Hur[3]. Father of Hushah.
📖 (4:4)

Hushah
(early C15th BC)
Son of Ezer[2].
📖 (4:4)

Helah
(early C16th BC)
Wife of Ashhur. Mother of Zereth, Zohar[3], Ethnan and Koz.
📖 (4:5, 7)

Naarah
(early C16th BC)
Wife of Ashhur. Mother of Ahuzzam, Hepher[2], Temeni and Haahashtari.
📖 (4:5–6)

Ahuzzam, Hepher[2], Temeni, Haahashtari
(mid C16th BC)
Sons of Ashhur and Naarah.
📖 (4:6–7)

Zereth, Zohar[3], Ethnan, Koz
(mid C16th BC)
Sons of Ashhur and Helah.
📖 (4:8)

Anub, Hazzobebah
(late C16th BC)
Sons of Koz.
📖 (4:8)

Aharhel
(late C16th BC)
Son of Harum. Leader of a clan of Judah[1] related to Koz.
📖 (4:8)

Harum
(mid C16th BC)
Father of Aharhel.
📖 (4:8)

Jabez
(unknown)
A descendant of Judah[1] whose parents are unknown. He is remembered for his prayer that the Lord would bless him. God granted his request.
📖 (4:9–10)

Kelub[1]
(unknown)
Father of Mehir. Brother of Shuhah. Descendant of Judah.
📖 (4:11)

Shuhah
(unknown)
Brother of Kelub[1].
📖 (4:11)

Mehir
(unknown)
Son of Kelub[1]. Father of Eshton.
📖 (4:11)

Eshton
(unknown)
Son of Mehir. Father of Beth Rapha, Paseah[1] and Tehinnah.
📖 (4:11–12)

Beth Rapha, Paseah[1]
(unknown)
Sons of Eshton.
📖 (4:12)

Tehinnah
(unknown)
Son of Eshton. Founder of Ir Nahash. Lived in Rekah (Recah).
📖 (4:12)

Seraiah[4]
(mid C14th BC)
Son of Kenaz[3]. Father of Joab[2].
📖 (4:13–14)

Hathath, Meonothai
(late C14th BC)
Sons of Othniel.
📖 (4:13–14)

Ophrah
(early C13th BC)
Son of Meonothai.
📖 (4:14)

Joab[2]
(late C14th BC)
Son of Seraiah[4]. Governor of the
Valley of Harashim.
📖 (4:14)

Iru, Elah[4], Naam
(late C15th BC)
Sons of Caleb[1].
📖 (4:15)

Kenaz[4]
(early C14th BC)
Son of Elah[4].
📖 (4:15)

Jehallelel[1]
(? C15th BC)
Father of Ziph[2], Ziphah, Tiria and
Asarel.
📖 (4:16)

Ziph[2], Ziphah, Tiria, Asarel
(? C15th BC)
Sons of Jehallelel[1].
📖 (4:16)

Ezrah
(? C15th BC)
Father of Jether[4], Mered, Epher[2]
and Jalon.
📖 (4:17)

Jether[4], Epher[2], Jalon
(? C15th BC)
Sons of Ezrah.
📖 (4:17)

Mered
(? C15th BC)
Son of Ezrah. Father of Miriam[2],
Shammai[3], Ishbah, Jered, Heber[3]
and Jekuthiel.
📖 (4:17)

Miriam[2]
(? C14th BC)
Daughter of Mered.
📖 (4:17)

Shammai[3], Ishbah
(? C14th BC)
Sons of Mered.
📖 (4:17)

Eshtemoa[1]
(? C14th BC)
Son of Ishbah.
📖 (4:17)

Jered, Heber[3], Jekuthiel
(? C14th BC)
Sons of Mered and his wife from the
tribe of Judah[1].
📖 (4:18)

Gedor[2]
(? C14th BC)
Son of Jered.
📖 (4:18)

Soko (Soco)
(? C14th BC)
Son of Heber[3] or possibly a town
Heber founded.
📖 (4:18)

Zanoah
(? C14th BC)
Son of Jekuthiel.
📖 (4:18)

Bithiah
(? C15th BC)
Daughter of Pharaoh. Wife of Mered.
📖 (4:18)

Hodiah[1]
(? C15th BC)
Husband of the sister of Naham. Mentioned among the clan names of Judah.
📖 (4:19)

Naham
(? C15th BC)
Sister of Hodiah[1]'s wife.
📖 (4:19)

Keilah
(? C14th BC)
Grandson of Hodiah[1]. A Garmite mentioned among the clan names of Judah[1].
📖 (4:19)

Eshtemoa[2]
(? C14th BC)
Son or grandson of Hodiah[1]. A Maakathite mentioned among the clan names of the tribes of Judah[1].
📖 (4:19)

Shimon
(? C15th BC)
Mentioned among the clan names of Judah[1].
📖 (4:20)

Amnon[2], Rinnah, Ben-Hanan, Tilon
(? C15th BC)
Sons of Shimon.
📖 (4:20)

Ishi[2]
(? C15th BC)
Mentioned among the clan names of Judah[1].
📖 (4:20)

Zoheth, Ben-Zoheth
(? C15th BC)
Descendants of Ishi[2].
📖 (4:20)

Er[2]
(late C17th BC)
Son of Shelah[2]. Father of Lekah, Laadah and Jokim.
📖 (4:21)

Lekah (Lecah)
(early C16th BC)
Son of Er[2].
📖 (4:21)

Laadah
(early C16th BC)
Son of Er[2]. Father of Mareshah[2].
📖 (4:21)

Mareshah[2]
(mid C16th BC)
Son of Laadah.
📖 (4:21)

Jokim, Joash[4], Saraph
(? C16th BC)
Mentioned among the clan names of Judah[1], among the relatives of Shelah[2].
📖 (4:22)

From the tribe of Simeon[1]

Jarib[1]
(early C17th BC)
Descendant of Simeon[1].
See **Jakin[1]** in Genesis, p. 39.
📖 (4:24)

Shallum[5]
(mid C17th BC)
Son of Shaul[2]. Father of Mibsam[2].
📖 (4:25)

Mibsam[2]
(late C17th BC)
Son of Shallum[5]. Father of Mishma[2].
📖 (4:25)

Mishma[2]
(early C16th BC)
Son of Mibsam[2]. Father of Hammuel.
📖 (4:25–26)

Hammuel
(mid C16th BC)
Son of Mishma[2]. Father of Zakkur[2].
📖 (4:26)

Zakkur[2] (Zaccur)
(late C16th BC)
Son of Hammuel.
📖 (4:26)

Shimei[7]
(early C15th BC)
Son of Zakkur[2]. Father of 16 sons and 6 daughters but because his brothers had few children the clan remained small.
📖 (4:26–27)

Meshobab, Jamlech, Joshah, Joel[2], Jehu[4], Elioenai[2], Jaakobah, Jeshohaiah, Asaiah[2], Adiel[1], Jesimiel, Benaiah[3], Ziza[1]
(late C8th BC)
Descendants of Simeon[1] and clan leaders whose families increased and occupied spacious and peaceful territory.
📖 (4:34)

Amaziah[2]
(mid C8th BC)
Father of Joshah.
📖 (4:34)

Joshibiah
(mid C8th BC)
Father of Jehu[4].
📖 (4:35)

Seraiah[5]
(early C8th BC)
Father of Joshibiah.
📖 (4:35)

Asiel
(late C9th BC)
Father of Seraiah[5].
📖 (4:35)

Shiphi
(mid C8th BC)
Father of Ziza[1]. Son of Allon.
📖 (4:37)

Allon
(early C8th BC)
Father of Shiphi. Son of Jedaiah[1].
📖 (4:37)

Jedaiah[1]
(late C9th BC)
Father of Allon. Son of Shimri[1].
📖 (4:37)

Shimri[1]
(mid C9th BC)
Father of Jedaiah[1]. Son of Shemaiah[3].
📖 (4:37)

Shemaiah[3]
(early C9th BC)
Father of Shimri[1].
📖 (4:37)

Pelatiah[2], Neariah[2], Rephaiah[2], Uzziel[2]
(late C8th BC)
Sons of Ishi[3]. The brothers led 500 Simeonites to invade the hill country of Seir. They killed the Amalekites who escaped, and settled there.
📖 (4:42–43)

Ishi[3]
(mid C8th BC)
Father of Pelatiah[2], Neariah[2], Rephaiah[2] and Uzziel[2].
📖 (4:42)

From the tribe of Reuben

Joel[3]
(mid C10th BC)
Father of Shemaiah[4] and Shema[2]. His descendants defeated the Hagrites during Saul[1]'s reign.
📖 (5:4, 8)

Shemaiah[4]
(late C10th BC)
Son of Joel[3].
📖 (5:4)

Gog[1]
(early C9th BC)
Son of Shemaiah[4]. Father of Shimei[8].
📖 (5:4)

Shimei[8]
(mid C9th BC)
Son of Gog[1]. Father of Micah[3].
📖 (5:4)

Micah[3]
(late C9th BC)
Son of Shimei[8]. Father of Reaiah[2].
📖 (5:5)

Reaiah[2]
(early C8th BC)
Son of Micah[3]. Father of Baal[1].
📖 (5:5)

Baal[1]
(mid C8th BC)
Son of Reaiah[2]. Father of Beerah.
📖 (5:5)

Beerah
(late C8th BC)
Son of Baal[1]. A leader of the Reubenites taken into exile by Tiglath-Pileser.
📖 (5:6)

Jeiel[1]
(mid C9th BC)
A Reubenite chief.
📖 (5:7)

Zechariah[3], Bela[3]
(mid C9th BC)
Reubenite clan leaders.
📖 (5:7–8)

Azaz
(early C9th BC)
Father of Bela[3]. Son of Shema[2].
📖 (5:8)

Shema[2]
(late C10th BC)
Father of Azaz. Son of Joel[3].
📖 (5:8)

From the tribe of Gad[1]

Joel[4]
(mid C8th BC)
Gadite chief in Bashan.
📖 (5:12)

Shapham
(mid C8th BC)
Second over the Gadites in Bashan.
📖 (5:12)

Janai, Shaphat[4]
(mid C8th BC)
Led the Gadites in Bashan, but under Joel[4] and Shapham.
📖 (5:12)

Michael[2], Meshullam[3], Sheba[5], Jorai, Jakan (Jacan), Zia, Eber[2]
(mid C8th BC)
Sons of Abihail[3]. Family leaders among the Gadites in Bashan.
📖 (5:13)

Abihail[3]
(early C8th BC)
Son of Huri. Father of Michael[2],
Meshullam[3], Sheba[5], Jorai, Jakan,
Zia and Eber[2].
📖 (5:14)

Huri
(late C9th BC)
Father of Abihail[3]. Son of Jaroah.
📖 (5:14)

Jaroah
(mid C9th BC)
Father of Huri. Son of Gilead[3].
📖 (5:14)

Gilead[3]
(early C9th BC)
Father of Jaroah. Son of Michael[3].
📖 (5:14)

Michael[3]
(late C10th BC)
Father of Gilead[3]. Son of Jeshishai.
📖 (5:14)

Jeshishai
(mid C10th BC)
Father of Michael[3]. Son of Jahdo.
📖 (5:14)

Jahdo
(early C10th BC)
Father of Jeshishai. Son of Buz[2].
📖 (5:14)

Buz[2]
(late C11th BC)
Father of Jahdo.
📖 (5:14)

Ahi[1]
(mid C8th BC)
Son of Abdiel. Head of a Gadite
family.
📖 (5:15)

Abdiel
(early C8th BC)
Father of Ahi[1]. Son of Guni[2].
📖 (5:15)

Guni[2]
(late C9th BC)
Father of Abdiel.
📖 (5:15)

Nodab
(mid C8th BC)
Among the Hagrite leaders who were
defeated by the Reubenites, Gadites
and half-tribe of Manasseh[1].
📖 (5:19)

From the half-tribe of Manasseh[1]

**Epher[3], Ishi[4], Eliel[1],
Azriel[1], Jeremiah[2],
Hodaviah[2], Jahdiel**
(mid C8th BC)
Well-known heads of families and
brave warriors. They were unfaithful
to God.
📖 (5:24)

From the tribe of Levi[1]

Abishua[1]
(early C14th BC)
Son of Phinehas[1]. Father of Bukki[2].
📖 (6:4–5)

Bukki[2]
(late C14th BC)
Son of Abishua[1]. Father of Uzzi[1].
📖 (6:5)

Uzzi[1]
(early C13th BC)
Son of Bukki[2]. Father of
Zerahiah[1].
📖 (6:5–6)

Zerahiah[1]
(late C13th BC)
Son of Uzzi[1]. Father of Meraioth[1].
📖 (6:6)

Meraioth[1]
(early C12th BC)
Son of Zerahiah[1]. Father of Amariah[1].
📖 (6:6–7)

Amariah[1]
(late C12th BC)
Son of Meraioth[1]. Father of Ahitub[2].
📖 (6:7)

Azariah[6]
(mid C10th BC)
Son of Ahimaaz[2]. Father of Johanan[4].
📖 (6:9)

Johanan[4]
(late C10th BC)
Son of Azariah[6]. Father of Azariah[7]. Priest in Solomon's temple.
📖 (6:9–10)

Azariah[7]
(early C9th BC)
Son of Johanan[4]. Father of Amariah[2].
📖 (6:10–11)

Amariah[2]
(mid C9th BC)
Son of Azariah[7]. Father of Ahitub[3].
📖 (6:11)

Ahitub[3]
(late C9th BC)
Son of Amariah[2]. Father of Zadok[3].
📖 (6:11–12)

Zadok[3]
(early C8th BC)
Son of Ahitub[3]. Father of Shallum[6].
📖 (6:12)

Shallum[6]
(late C8th–early C7th BC)
Son of Zadok[3]. Father of Hilkiah[2].
📖 (6:12–13)

Azariah[8]
(late C7th BC)
Son of Hilkiah[2]. Father of Seraiah[2].
📖 (6:13–14)

Jozadak/Jehozadak
(early C6th BC)
Son of Seraiah[2]. Deported into exile by Nebuchadnezzar.
📖 (6:14–15)

Jahath[2]
(?late C17th BC)
Son of Libni[1]. Grandson of Gershon. Father of Zimmah[1].
📖 (6:20)

Zimmah[1]
(?late C16th BC)
Son of Jahath[2]. Father of Joah[2]. (The reference in 2 Chronicles 29 may possibly be to a further Zimmah.)
📖 (6:20; 2 Chronicles 29:12)

Joah[2]
(early C15th BC)
Son of Zimmah[1]. Father of Iddo[2] and Eden. He was involved in the purification of the temple in Hezekiah[1]'s reign. (The reference in 2 Chronicles 29 may possibly be to a further Joah.)
📖 (6:21; 2 Chronicles 29:12)

Iddo[2]
(late C15th BC)
Son of Joah[2]. Father of Zerah[4].
📖 (6:21)

Zerah[4]
(early C14th BC)
Son of Iddo[2]. Father of Jeatherai.
📖 (6:21)

Jeatherai
(late C14th BC)
Son of Zerah[4].
📖 (6:21)

Amminadab[2]
(mid C17th BC)
Son of Kohath. Grandson of Levi[1]. Father of Korah[5]. Possibly the same person who is called Izhar in 1 Chronicles 6:2, 18 and Exodus 6:18, 29.
📖 (6:22)

Korah[5]
(late C17th BC)
Son of Amminadab[2]. Father of Assir[2]. Possibly the same person as Korah[3].
📖 (6:22)

Assir[2]
(early C16th BC)
Son of Korah[5]. Father of Elkanah[3].
📖 (6:22)

Elkanah[3]
(early C16th BC)
Son of Assir[2]. Father of Ebiasaph.
📖 (6:23)

Ebiasaph
(early C16th BC)
Son of Elkanah[3]. Father of Assir[3]. Probably but not definitely the same person as Abiasaph.
See **Abiasaph** *in Exodus, p. 45.*
📖 (6:23, 37; 9:19)

Assir[3]
(mid C16th BC)
Son of Ebiasaph. Father of Tahath[1].
📖 (6:23)

Tahath[1]
(late C16th BC)
Son of Assir[3]. Father of Uriel[1].
📖 (6:24)

Uriel[1]
(early C15th BC)
Son of Tahath[1]. Father of Uzziah[2].
📖 (6:24)

Uzziah[2]
(mid C15th BC)
Son of Uriel[1]. Father of Shaul[3].
📖 (6:24)

Shaul[3]
(late C15th BC)
Son of Uzziah[2].
📖 (6:24)

Elkanah[4]
(early C14th BC)
Descendant of Kohath. An ancestor of Samuel.
📖 (6:25)

Amasai[1]
(mid C14th BC)
Descendant of Elkanah[4]. Possibly to be identified with Amasai[2].
📖 (6:25, 35)

Ahimoth
(late C14th BC)
Descendant of Elkanah[4].
📖 (6:25)

Elkanah[5]
(early C13th BC)
Descendant of Elkanah[4].
📖 (6:26)

Zophai
(mid C13th BC)
Son of Elkanah[5]. Father of Nahath[2].
📖 (6:26)

Nahath[2]
(late C13th BC)
Son of Zophai. Father of Eliab[4].
📖 (6:26)

Eliab[4]
(early C12th BC)
Son of Nahath[2]. Father of Jeroham[1]. Possibly called Elihu[1] in 1 Samuel 1:1.
📖 (6:27)

Libni[2]
(late C17th BC)
Son of Mahli[1]. Grandson of Merari. Father of Shimei[9].
📖 (6:29)

Shimei[9]
(early C16th BC)
Son of Libni[2]. Father of Uzzah[2].
📖 (6:29)

Uzzah[2]
(mid C16th BC)
Son of Shimei[9]. Father of Shimea[2].
📖 (6:29)

Shimea[2]
(late C16th BC)
Son of Uzzah[2]. Father of Haggiah.
📖 (6:30)

Haggiah
(early C15th BC)
Son of Shimea[2]. Father of Asaiah[3].
📖 (6:30)

Asaiah[3]
(mid C15th BC)
Son of Haggiah.
📖 (6:30)

Heman[2]
(early C10th BC)
Temple musician appointed by David. A descendant of Kohath. Son of Joel[1]. Grandson of Samuel. The king's seer whom God honoured by giving him 14 sons and 3 daughters.
📖 (6:33; 25:1, 4–6)

Eliel[2]
(early C12th BC)
Ancestor of Heman[2].
See **Elihu[1]** *in 1 Samuel, p. 67.*
📖 (6:34)

Toah
(late C13th BC)
See **Tohu** *in 1 Samuel, p. 67.*
📖 (6:34)

Elkanah[6]
(early C13th BC)
Father of Zuph. Son of Mahath[1].
📖 (6:35)

Mahath[1]
(late C14th BC)
Father of Elkanah[6]. Son of Amasai[2].
📖 (6:35)

Amasai[2]
(mid C14th BC)
Father of Mahath[1]. Son of Elkanah[7]. Possibly to be identified with Amasai[1].
📖 (6:35)

Elkanah[7]
(early C14th BC)
Father of Amasai[2]. Son of Joel[5].
📖 (6:36)

Joel[5]
(late C15th BC)
Father of Elkanah[7]. Son of Azariah[9].
📖 (6:36)

Azariah[9]
(mid C15th BC)
Father of Joel[5]. Son of Zephaniah[2].
📖 (6:36)

Zephaniah[2]
(early C15th BC)
Father of Azariah[9]. Son of Tahath[1].
📖 (6:36)

Asaph[2]
(early C10th BC)
Temple musician appointed by David. Son of Berekiah[2]. Grandson of Shimea[3].
📖 (6:39; 16:7, 37; 25:1–2, 6, 9; 2 Chronicles 5:12; 20:14; 29:13, 30; 35:15; Ezra 2:41; 3:10; Nehemiah 7:44; 11:17; 12:35, 46; Psalms 50; 73–83 titles)

Berekiah[2]
(? C11th BC)
Father of Asaph[2]. Son of Shimea[3]. *Possibly the same person as Berekiah[4] in 1 Chronicles, p. 152.*
📖 (6:39)

Shimea[3]
(? late C12th BC)
Father of Berekiah[2]. Son of Michael[4].
📖 (6:39)

Michael[4]
(? early C12th BC)
Father of Shimea[3]. Son of Baaseiah.
📖 (6:40)

Baaseiah
(? late C13th BC)
Father of Michael[4]. Son of Malkijah[1].
📖 (6:40)

Malkijah[1]
(? early C13th BC)
Father of Baaseiah. Son of Ethni.
📖 (6:40)

Ethni
(? late C14th BC)
Father of Malkijah[1]. Son of Zerah[5].
📖 (6:41)

Zerah[5]
(? early C14th BC)
Father of Ethni. Son of Adaiah[2].
📖 (6:41)

Adaiah[2]
(? late C15th BC)
Father of Zerah[5]. Son of Ethan[3].
📖 (6:41)

Ethan[3]
(? early C15th BC)
Father of Adaiah[2]. Son of Zimmah[2].
📖 (6:42)

Zimmah[2]
(? late C16th BC)
Father of Ethan[3]. Son of Shimei[10].
📖 (6:42)

Shimei[10]
(? early C16th BC)
Father of Zimmah[2]. Son of Jahath[3].
📖 (6:42)

Jahath[3]
(? late C17th BC)
Father of Shimei[10]. Son of Gershon.
📖 (6:43)

Ethan[4]
(early C10th BC)
A Merarite appointed by David to serve with Heman[2] and Asaph[2] as temple musicians. Son of Kishi.
📖 (6:44)

Kishi
(? late C11th BC)
Father of Ethan[4]. Son of Abdi[1].
📖 (6:44)

Abdi[1]
(? early C11th BC)
Father of Kishi. Son of Malluk[1].
📖 (6:44)

Malluk[1] (Malluch)
(? late C12th BC)
Father of Abdi[1]. Son of
Hashabiah[1].
📖 (6:44)

Hashabiah[1]
(? early C12th BC)
Father of Malluk[1]. Son of
Amaziah[3].
📖 (6:45)

Amaziah[3]
(? late C13th BC)
Father of Hashabiah[1]. Son of
Hilkiah[3].
📖 (6:45)

Hilkiah[3]
(? early C13th BC)
Father of Amaziah[3]. Son of
Amzi[1].
📖 (6:45)

Amzi[1]
(? C14th BC)
Father of Hilkiah[3]. Son of Bani[1].
📖 (6:46)

Bani[1]
(? C15th BC)
Father of Amzi[1]. Son of Shemer[2].
📖 (6:46)

Shemer[2]
(? C16th BC)
Father of Bani[1]. Son of Mahli[2].
📖 (6:46)

Mahli[2]
(? C17th BC)
Father of Shemer[2]. Son of Mushi.
📖 (6:47)

From the tribe of Issachar[1]

Uzzi[2], Rephaiah[3], Jeriel, Jahmai, Ibsam
(mid C17th BC)
Sons of Tola[1]. Grandsons of
Issachar[1].
📖 (7:2)

Izrahiah
(late C17th BC)
Son of Uzzi[2]. Grandson of Tola[1].
📖 (7:3)

Michael[5], Obadiah[3], Joel[6], Ishiah[1] (Isshiah)
(early C16th BC)
Sons of Izrahiah. Grandsons of
Uzzi[2].
📖 (7:3)

From the tribe of Benjamin[1]

Jediael[1]
(early C17th BC)
Son of Benjamin[1]. Father of
Bilhan[2].
📖 (7:6, 10–11)

Ezbon[2], Uzzi[3], Uzziel[3], Jerimoth[1], Iri
(mid C17th BC)
Sons of Bela[2]. Grandsons of
Benjamin[1].
📖 (7:7)

Zemirah, Joash[5], Eliezer[3], Elioenai[3], Omri[2], Jeremoth[1], Abijah[6], Anathoth[1], Alemeth[1]
(mid C17th BC)
Sons of Beker[1]. Grandsons of
Benjamin[1].
📖 (7:8)

Bilhan[2]
(mid C17th BC)
Son of Jediael[1]. Grandson of Benjamin[1]. Father of seven sons who were heads of families.
📖 (7:10–11)

Jeush[2], Benjamin[2], Ehud[2], Kenaanah[2], Zethan, Tarshish[2], Ahishahar
(late C17th BC)
Sons of Bilhan[2]. Grandsons of Jediael[1].
📖 (7:10–11)

Ir
(mid C17th BC)
Ancestor of the Shuppites and Huppites.
📖 (7:12)

Aher
(early C17th BC)
See **Ehi/Ahiram/Aher/Aharah** *in Genesis, p. 40.*
📖 (7:12)

From the tribe of Naphtali

All the names mentioned in this section already have an entry listed under an earlier book.

From the tribe of Manasseh[1]

Maakah[6] (Maacah)
(mid C17th BC)
Wife of Makir[1] the Gileadite. Mother of Peresh. (Also called Makir's sister.)
📖 (7:15–16)

Peresh
(late C17th BC)
Son of Makir[1] and Maakah[6].
📖 (7:16)

Sheresh
(late C17th BC)
Son of Makir[1]. Father of Ulam[1] and Rakem.
📖 (7:16)

Ulam[1], Rakem
(early C16th BC)
Sons of Sheresh.
📖 (7:16)

Bedan
(mid C16th BC)
Son of Ulam[1]. Grandson of Sheresh.
📖 (7:17)

Hammoleketh
(late C17th BC)
Sister of Gilead[1]. Mother of Ishhod, Abiezer[1] and Mahlah[2].
📖 (7:18)

Ishhod, Mahlah[2]
(early C16th BC)
Sons of Hammoleketh.
📖 (7:18)

Ahian, Shechem[3], Likhi, Aniam
(mid C16th BC)
Sons of Shemida.
📖 (7:19)

From the tribe of Ephraim

Bered
(late C17th BC)
Son of Shuthelah[1]. Father of Tahath[2].
📖 (7:20)

Tahath[2]
(early C16th BC)
Son of Bered. Father of Eleadah.
📖 (7:20)

Eleadah
(mid C16th BC)
Son of Tahath[2]. Father of Tahath[3].
📖 (7:20)

Tahath[3]
(late C16th BC)
Son of Eleadah. Father of Zabad[3].
📖 (7:20)

Zabad[3]
(early C15th BC)
Son of Tahath[3]. Father of
Shuthelah[2].
📖 (7:21)

Shuthelah[2]
(mid C15th BC)
Son of Zabad[3].
📖 (7:21)

Ezer[3], Elead
(mid C17th BC)
Sons of Ephraim who were killed by
the men of Gath.
📖 (7:21–22)

Beriah[2]
(mid C17th BC)
Son of Ephraim, born after the
deaths of Ezer[3] and Elead. Father of
Sheerah and Rephah.
📖 (7:23)

Sheerah
(late C17th BC)
Daughter of Beriah[2]. She built
Lower and Upper Beth Horon and
Uzzen Sheerah.
📖 (7:24)

Rephah
(mid C17th BC)
Son of Beriah[2]. Father of Resheph.
📖 (7:25)

Resheph
(late C17th BC)
Son of Rephah. Father of Telah.
📖 (7:25)

Telah
(late C17th BC)
Son of Resheph. Father of Tahan[2].
📖 (7:25)

Tahan[2]
(early C16th BC)
Son of Telah. Father of Ladan[1].
📖 (7:25)

Ladan[1]
(mid C16th BC)
Son of Tahan[2]. Father of
Ammihud[1]. Grandfather of
Elishama[1].
📖 (7:26)

From the tribe of Asher

Birzaith
(late C17th BC)
Son of Malkiel. Grandson of
Beriah[1].
📖 (7:31)

Japhlet, Shomer[2], Hotham[1]
(late C17th BC)
Sons of Heber[1].
📖 (7:32–34)

Shua[2]
(late C17th BC)
Daughter of Heber[1].
📖 (7:32)

**Pasak (Pasach), Bimhal,
Ashvath**
(early C16th BC)
Sons of Japhlet.
📖 (7:33)

Ahi[2], Rohgah, Hubbah, Aram[3]
(early C16th BC)
Sons of Shomer[2].
📖 (7:34)

Helem[1]
(late C17th BC)
Brother of Shomer[2]. Probably the same person as Hotham[1].
📖 (7:35)

Zophah, Imna, Shelesh, Amal
(early C16th BC)
Sons of Helem[1]. Amal is possibly the same person as Ulla, 1 Chronicles 7:39.
📖 (7:35)

Suah, Harnepher, Shual, Beri, Imrah, Bezer[2], Hod, Shamma, Shilshah, Ithran[2], Beera
(mid C16th BC)
Sons of Zophah.
📖 (7:36–37)

Jether[5]
(mid C16th BC)
Descendant of the tribe of Asher. Possibly the same person as Ithran[2].
📖 (7:38)

Jephunneh[2], Pispah, Ara
(late C16th BC)
Sons of Jether[5].
📖 (7:38)

Ulla
(early C16th BC)
Descendant of the tribe of Asher. Possibly the same person as Amal, 1 Chronicles 7:35.
📖 (7:39)

Arah[1], Hanniel[2], Rizia
(mid C16th BC)
Sons of Ulla.
📖 (7:39)

From the tribe of Benjamin[1] – the genealogy of King Saul[1]

Aharah
(early C17th BC)
See **Ehi/Ahiram/Aher/Aharah** *in Genesis, p. 40.*
📖 (8:1)

Nohah
(early C17th BC)
Fourth son of Benjamin[1].
📖 (8:2)

Rapha[2]
(early C17th BC)
Fifth son of Benjamin[1].
📖 (8:2)

Addar, Gera[4], Abihud, Abishua[2], Ahoah, Shephuphan[2]
(mid C17th BC)
Sons of Bela[2]. Grandsons of Benjamin[1].
📖 (8:3–5)

Gera[5]
(early C13th BC)
Descendant of Ehud[1]. Father of Uzza[2] and Ahihud[2]. One of the Benjamite family leaders in Geba who organized the deportation to Manahath. Possibly to be identified with Gera[4].
📖 (8:5, 7)

Naaman[3], Ahijah[6]
(early C13th BC)
Descendants of Ehud[1]. They were the Benjamite family leaders in Geba who were deported to Manahath.
📖 (8:7)

Uzza[2], Ahihud[2]
(mid C13th BC)
Sons of Gera[5].
📖 (8:7)

Shaharaim
(early C10th BC)

He lived in Moab. He divorced his first wife Hushim[2] and his second wife Baara, before his third wife Hodesh bore him seven more sons.

📖 (8:8)

Hushim[2]
(early C10th BC)

First wife of Shaharaim. Mother of Abitub and Elpaal.

📖 (8:8, 11)

Baara
(early C10th BC)

Second wife of Shaharaim.

📖 (8:8)

Hodesh
(early C10th BC)

Third wife of Shaharaim. Mother of seven sons.

📖 (8:9)

Jobab[4], Zibia, Mesha[3], Malkam (Malcam), Jeuz, Sakia, Mirmah
(mid C10th BC)

Sons of Shaharaim and Hodesh. They became family leaders.

📖 (8:9–10)

Abitub, Elpaal
(mid C10th BC)

Sons of Shaharaim and Hushim[2]. Elpaal had 12 sons.

📖 (8:11–12, 17)

Eber[3], Misham, Shemed
(late C10th BC)

Sons of Elpaal. Shemed was responsible for building Ono and Lod.

📖 (8:12)

Beriah[3], Shema[3]/Shimei[11]
(mid C10th BC)

Sons of Elpaal. Each had nine sons.

They became heads of families in Aijalon and drove out the citizens of Gath.

📖 (8:13–16, 19–21)

Ahio[2], Shashak, Jeremoth[2], Zebadiah[1], Arad, Eder[1], Michael[6], Ishpah, Joha[1]
(late C10th BC)

Sons of Beriah[3].

📖 (8:14–16)

Zebadiah[2], Meshullam[4], Hizki, Heber[4], Ishmerai, Izliah, Jobab[5]
(late C10th BC)

Sons of Elpaal.

📖 (8:17–18)

Jakim[1], Zikri[2], Zabdi[1], Elienai, Zillethai[1], Eliel[3], Adaiah[3], Beraiah, Shimrath
(late C10th BC)

Sons of Shimei[11].

📖 (8:19–21)

Shimei[11]
(mid C10th BC)

See **Shema[3]** in 1 Chronicles, p. 142 (left).

📖 (8:21)

Ishpan, Eber[4], Eliel[4], Abdon[2], Zikri[3], Hanan[1], Hananiah[2], Elam[2], Anthothijah, Iphdeiah, Penuel[2]
(late C10th BC)

Sons of Shashak.

📖 (8:22–25)

Shamsherai, Shehariah, Athaliah[2], Jaareshiah, Elijah[2], Zikri[4]
(late C10th BC)

Sons of Jeroham[2].

📖 (8:26–27)

Jeroham[2]
(mid C10th BC)
Family chief who lived in Jerusalem. Father of six sons.

📖 (8:26–27)

Jeiel[2]
(mid C12th BC)
Father or leader of Gibeon. Husband of Maakah[7] (Maacah). Father of 10 sons.

📖 (8:29; 9:35)

Maakah[7] (Maacah)
(mid C12th BC)
Wife of Jeiel[2] and mother of Ner, Saul[1]'s grandfather.

📖 (8:29; 9:35)

Abdon[3], Zur[2], Kish[2], Baal[2], Nadab[4], Gedor[3], Ahio[3], Zeker/Zechariah[4], Mikloth[1]
(late C12th BC)
Sons of Jeiel[2] and Maakah[7].

📖 (8:30–32; 9:36–38)

Ner[2]
(mid C12th BC)
Son of Jeiel[2] and Maakah[7]. *See* **Kish[1]** *in 1 Samuel, p. 69.*

📖 (8:30, 33)

Shimeah[2]/Shimeam
(early C11th BC)
Son of Mikloth[1].

📖 (8:32; 9:38)

Esh-Baal
(1050–1003 BC)
See **Ish-Bosheth** *in 2 Samuel, p. 78.*

📖 (8:33; 9:39)

Pithon, Melek (Melech), Tarea (Tahrea), Ahaz[2]
(mid C10th BC)
Sons of Micah[2].

📖 (8:35–36; 9:41–42)

Jehoaddah/Jadah
(late C10th BC)
Son of Ahaz[2]. Father of Alemeth[2], Azmaveth[2] and Zimri[4].

📖 (8:36; 9:42)

Alemeth[2], Azmaveth[2], Zimri[4]
(early C9th BC)
Sons of Jehoaddah.

📖 (8:36; 9:42)

Moza[2]
(mid C9th BC)
Son of Zimri[4]. Father of Binea.

📖 (8:36–37; 9:43)

Binea
(late C9th BC)
Son of Moza[2]. Father of Raphah.

📖 (8:37; 9:43)

Raphah/Rephaiah[4]
(early C8th BC)
Son of Binea. Father of Eleasah[2].

📖 (8:37; 9:43)

Eleasah[2]
(mid C8th BC)
Son of Raphah. Father of Azel.

📖 (8:37; 9:43)

Azel
(late C8th BC)
Son of Eleasah[2]. Father of six sons. Brother of Eshek.

📖 (8:37–38; 9:43–44)

Azrikam[2], Bokeru, Ishmael[3], Sheariah, Obadiah[4], Hanan[2]
(early C7th BC)
Sons of Azel.

📖 (8:38; 9:44)

Eshek
(late C8th BC)
Brother of Azel. Father of Ulam[2], Jeush[3] and Eliphelet[4].

📖 (8:39)

Ulam[2], Jeush[3], Eliphelet[4]
(early C7th BC)

Sons of Eshek. They were brave warriors and skilled with the bow. Between them they had 150 sons and grandsons.

📖 (8:39)

Returnees to Jerusalem from different tribes

Uthai[1]
(mid C6th BC)

Son of Ammihud[5]. Descendant of Perez son of Judah[1]. He resettled in Jerusalem after the exile to Babylon.

📖 (9:4)

Ammihud[5]
(early C6th BC)

Father of Uthai[1]. Son of Omri[3]. Descendant of Perez son of Judah[1]. He resettled in Jerusalem after the exile to Babylon.

📖 (9:4)

Omri[3]
(late C7th BC)

Father of Ammihud[5]. Son of Imri[1]. Descendant of Perez son of Judah[1]. He resettled in Jerusalem after the exile to Babylon.

📖 (9:4)

Imri[1]
(mid C7th BC)

Father of Omri[3]. Son of Bani[2]. Descendant of Perez son of Judah[1]. He resettled in Jerusalem after the exile to Babylon.

📖 (9:4)

Bani[2]
(early C7th BC)

Father of Imri[1]. Descendant of Perez son of Judah[1]. He resettled in Jerusalem after the exile to Babylon.

📖 (9:4)

Asaiah[4]
(mid C6th BC)

Firstborn of the Shilonites who, with his sons, was among the first group to resettle in Jerusalem after the exile in Babylon.

📖 (9:5)

Jeuel[1]
(mid C6th BC)

From the Zerahites. Among the first group to resettle in Jerusalem after the exile in Babylon.

📖 (9:6)

Sallu[1]
(mid C6th BC)

Son of Meshullam[5]. Among the first Benjamites to resettle in Jerusalem after the exile in Babylon.

📖 (9:7)

Meshullam[5]
(early C6th BC)

Father of Sallu[1]. Son of Hodaviah[3].

📖 (9:7)

Hodaviah[3]
(late C7th BC)

Father of Meshullam[5]. Son of Hassenuah[1].

📖 (9:7)

Hassenuah[1]
(mid C7th BC)

Father of Hodaviah[3].

📖 (9:7)

Ibneiah
(mid C6th BC)

Son of Jeroham[3]. Among the first Benjamites to resettle in Jerusalem after the exile in Babylon.

📖 (9:8)

Jeroham[3]
(early C6th BC)

Father of Ibneiah.

📖 (9:8)

Elah[5]
(mid C6th BC)
Son of Uzzi[4]. Among the first Benjamites to resettle in Jerusalem after the exile in Babylon.
📖 (9:8)

Uzzi[4]
(early C6th BC)
Father of Elah[5]. Son of Mikri.
📖 (9:8)

Mikri (Micri)
(late C7th BC)
Father of Uzzi[4].
📖 (9:8)

Meshullam[6]
(mid C6th BC)
Son of Shephatiah[2]. Among the first Benjamites to resettle in Jerusalem after the exile in Babylon.
📖 (9:8)

Shephatiah[2]
(early C6th BC)
Father of Meshullam[6]. Son of Reuel[3].
📖 (9:8)

Reuel[3]
(late C7th BC)
Father of Shephatiah[2]. Son of Ibnijah.
📖 (9:8)

Ibnijah
(mid C7th BC)
Father of Reuel[3].
📖 (9:8)

Jedaiah[2], Jehoiarib[1], Jakin[2], Azariah[10]
(mid C6th BC)
Priests who were among the first group to resettle in Jerusalem after the exile in Babylon.
📖 (9:10–11)

Hilkiah[4]
(early C6th BC)
Father of Azariah[10]. Son of Meshullam[7].
📖 (9:11)

Meshullam[7]
(late C7th BC)
Father of Hilkiah[4]. Son of Zadok[4].
📖 (9:11)

Zadok[4]
(mid C7th BC)
Father of Meshullam[7]. Son of Meraioth[2].
📖 (9:11)

Meraioth[2]
(early C7th BC)
Father of Zadok[4]. Son of Ahitub[2].
📖 (9:11)

Adaiah[4]
(mid C6th BC)
Son of Jeroham[4]. A priest who was among the first group to resettle in Jerusalem after the exile in Babylon.
📖 (9:12)

Jeroham[4]
(early C6th BC)
Father of Adaiah[4]. Son of Pashhur[1].
📖 (9:12)

Pashhur[1]
(late C7th BC)
Father of Jeroham[4]. Son of Malkijah[2].
See **Zephaniah[3]** *in Jeremiah, p. 204.*
📖 (9:12).

Malkijah[2]
(mid C7th BC)
Father of Pashhur[1].
📖 (9:12)

Maasai
(mid C6th BC)
Son of Adiel[2]. A priest who was among the first group to resettle in Jerusalem after the exile in Babylon.
📖 (9:12)

Adiel[2]
(early C6th BC)
Father of Maasai. Son of Jahzerah.
📖 (9:12)

Jahzerah
(late C7th BC)
Father of Adiel[2]. Son of Meshullam[8].
📖 (9:12)

Meshullam[8]
(mid C7th BC)
Father of Jahzerah. Son of Meshillemith.
📖 (9:12)

Meshillemith
(early C7th BC)
Father of Meshullam[8]. Son of Immer[1].
📖 (9:12)

Immer[1]
(late C8th BC)
Father of Meshillemith.
📖 (9:12)

Shemaiah[5]
(mid C6th BC)
Son of Hasshub[1]. A Levite who was among the first group to resettle in Jerusalem after the exile in Babylon.
📖 (9:14)

Hasshub[1]
(early C6th BC)
Father of Shemaiah[5]. Son of Azrikam[3].
📖 (9:14)

Azrikam[3]
(late C7th BC)
Father of Hasshub[1]. Son of Hashabiah[2].
📖 (9:14)

Hashabiah[2]
(mid C7th BC)
Father of Azrikam[3]. A Merarite.
📖 (9:14)

Bakbakkar, Heresh, Galal[1], Mattaniah[2]
(mid C6th BC)
Levites who were among the first group to resettle in Jerusalem after the exile in Babylon.
📖 (9:15)

Mika[2] (Mica)
(early C6th BC)
Father of Mattaniah[2]. Son of Zikri[5].
📖 (9:15)

Zikri[5] (Zicri)
(late C7th BC)
Father of Mika[2]. Son of Asaph[3].
📖 (9:15)

Asaph[3]
(mid C7th BC)
Father of Zikri[5].
📖 (9:15)

Obadiah[5]
(mid C6th BC)
Descendant of Shemaiah[6]. A Levite who was among the first group to resettle in Jerusalem after the exile in Babylon.
📖 (9:16)

Shemaiah[6]
(late C8th BC)
Ancestor of Obadiah[5]. Son of Galal[2].
📖 (9:16; 2 Chronicles 29:14–36)

Galal[2]
(? C9th BC)
Father of Shemaiah[6]. Son of
Jeduthun.
📖 (9:16)

Jeduthun
(early C10th BC)
Father of Galal[2]. He was a priest
who was appointed to give thanks
and to play instruments for sacred
songs. His sons served at the temple
gates.
📖 (9:16; 16:41; 2 Chronicles 29:14–36)

Berekiah[3]
(mid C6th BC)
Son of Asa[2]. A Levite who was
among the first group to resettle in
Jerusalem after the exile in Babylon.
📖 (9:16)

Asa[2]
(early C6th BC)
Son of Elkanah[8]. Father of
Berekiah[3].
📖 (9:16)

Elkanah[8]
(late C7th BC)
Father of Asa[2].
📖 (9:16)

**Shallum[7], Akkub[2], Talmon,
Ahiman[2], Shallum[8]**
(mid C6th BC)
Gatekeepers who were among the
first group to resettle in Jerusalem
after the exile in Babylon.
📖 (9:17–19)

Kore[1]
(early C6th BC)
Father of Shallum[8]. Descendant of
Ebiasaph and Korah[3].
📖 (9:19)

Zechariah[5]
(mid C6th BC)
Firstborn son of Meshelemiah[1].

A gatekeeper at the tent of meeting
who was among the first group to
resettle in Jerusalem after the exile in
Babylon. He was given responsibility
for the North Gate. He was known as
a wise counsellor.
📖 (9:21; 26:2, 14)

Meshelemiah[1]
(early C6th BC)
Father of Zechariah[5] and six other
sons. Son of Kore[1]. He or his
descendants were the gatekeepers
at the entrance of the tent after the
exile.
📖 (9:21; 26:1–2, 9)

Mattithiah[1]
(mid C6th BC)
A Levite and firstborn son
of Shallum[9] who assumed
responsibility for baking offering
bread in the temple when the first
group of exiles returned to Jerusalem
from Babylon.
📖 (9:31)

Shallum[9]
(early C6th BC)
Father of Mattithiah[1]. A Korahite.
📖 (9:31)

Zechariah[4]
(late C12th BC)
See **Zeker/Zechariah[4]** in
1 Chronicles, p. 143.
📖 (9:37)

Shimeam
(early C11th BC)
See **Shimeah[2]/Shimeam** in
1 Chronicles, p. 143.
📖 (9:38)

Tahrea
(mid C10th BC)
See **Tarea** in *1 Chronicles, p. 143.*
📖 (9:41)

Jadah
(late C10th BC)

See **Jehoaddah/Jadah** *in
1 Chronicles, p. 143.*

📖 (9:42)

Rephaiah[4]
(early C8th BC)

See **Raphah/Rephaiah[4]** *in
1 Chronicles, p. 143.*

📖 (9:43)

Jashobeam[2]
(early C10th BC)

Also called **Josheb-Basshebeth**,
see 2 Samuel, p.89.

📖 (11:11)

Shammoth
(early C10th BC)

Also called **Shammah[4]**,
see 2 Samuel, p. 89.

📖 (11:27)

Ilai
(early C10th BC)

Also called **Zalmon**, *see 2 Samuel,
p. 90.*

📖 (11:29)

Hurai
(early C10th BC)

Also called **Hiddai**, *see 2 Samuel,
p. 90.*

📖 (11:32)

Abiel[2]
(early C10th BC)

Also called **Abi-Albon**, *see 2 Samuel,
p. 90.*

📖 (11:32)

Hashem
(late C11th BC)

Also called **Jashen**, *see 2 Samuel,
p. 90.*

📖 (11:34)

Sakar[1] (Sacar)
(late C11th BC)

Also called **Sharar**, *see 2 Samuel,
p. 90.*

📖 (11:35)

Eliphal
(early C10th BC)

Son of Ur. One of David's mighty
warriors.

📖 (11:35)

Ur
(late C11th BC)

Father of Eliphal.

📖 (11:35)

Hepher[3]
(early C10th BC)

A Mekerathite. One of David's
mighty warriors.

📖 (11:36)

Ahijah[7]
(early C10th BC)

A Pelonite.

See **Eliam[2]** *in 1 Samuel, p. 91.*

📖 (11:36)

Naarai
(early C10th BC)

Son of Ezbai. One of David's mighty
warriors.

📖 (11:37)

Ezbai
(late C11th BC)

Father of Naarai.

📖 (11:37)

Joel[7]
(early C10th BC)

Brother of Nathan[6]. One of David's
mighty warriors.

📖 (11:38)

Nathan[6]
(early C10th BC)
Brother of Joel[7].
📖 (11:38)

Mibhar
(early C10th BC)
Son of Hagri. One of David's mighty warriors.
📖 (11:38)

Zabad[4]
(early C10th BC)
Son of Ahlai[2]. One of David's mighty warriors.
📖 (11:41)

Ahlai[2]
(late C11th BC)
Father of Zabad[4].
📖 (11:41)

Adina
(early C10th BC)
Son of Shiza. One of David's mighty warriors who was the chief of the Reubenites.
📖 (11:42)

Shiza
(late C11th BC)
Father of Adina.
📖 (11:42)

Hanan[3]
(early C10th BC)
Son of Maakah[8]. One of David's mighty warriors.
📖 (11:43)

Maakah[8] (Maacah)
(late C11th BC)
Father of Hanan[3].
📖 (11:43)

Joshaphat[1]
(early C10th BC)
A Mithnite. One of David's

mighty warriors.
📖 (11:43)

Uzzia
(early C10th BC)
An Ashterathite. One of David's mighty warriors.
📖 (11:44)

Shama
(early C10th BC)
Son of Hotham[2]. Brother of Jeiel[3]. One of David's mighty warriors.
📖 (11:44)

Jeiel[3]
(early C10th BC)
Son of Hotham[2]. Brother of Shama. One of David's mighty warriors.
📖 (11:44)

Hotham[2]
(late C11th BC)
Father of Shama and Jeiel[3]. An Aroerite.
📖 (11:44)

Jediael[2]
(early C10th BC)
Son of Shimri[2]. One of David's mighty warriors.
📖 (11:45)

Shimri[2]
(late C11th BC)
Father of Jediael[2].
📖 (11:45)

Joha[2]
(early C10th BC)
A Tizite. Brother of Jediael[2].
📖 (11:45)

Eliel[5]
(early C10th BC)
A Mahavite. One of David's mighty warriors.
📖 (11:46)

Jeribai
(early C10th BC)

Son of Elnaam. Brother of Joshaviah. One of David's mighty warriors.

📖 (11:46)

Joshaviah
(early C10th BC)

Son of Elnaam. Brother of Jeribai. One of David's mighty warriors.

📖 (11:46)

Elnaam
(late C11th BC)

Father of Jeribai and Joshaviah.

📖 (11:46)

Ithmah
(early C10th BC)

A Moabite. One of David's mighty warriors.

📖 (11:46)

Eliel[6], Obed[3]
(early C10th BC)

Among David's mighty warriors.

📖 (11:47)

Jaasiel[1]
(early C10th BC)

A Mezobaite. One of David's mighty warriors.

📖 (11:47)

Ahiezer[2]
(late C11th BC)

Son of Shemaah. The chief of Saul[1]'s relatives, who was skilled with the bow and sling. He came to David at Ziglag.

📖 (12:3)

Joash[6]
(late C11th BC)

Son of Shemaah. One of Saul[1]'s relatives, who was skilled with the bow and sling. He came to David at Ziglag.

📖 (12:3)

Shemaah
(mid C11th BC)

Father of Ahiezer[2] and Joash[6]. A Gibeathite.

📖 (12:3)

Jeziel, Pelet[2]
(late C11th BC)

Sons of Azmaveth[3]. Among Saul[1]'s relatives who were skilled with the bow and sling. They came to David at Ziglag.

📖 (12:3)

Azmaveth[3]
(mid C11th BC)

Father of Jezliel and Pelet[2].

📖 (12:3)

Berakah (Beracah)
(late C11th BC)

One of Saul[1]'s relatives, who was skilled with the bow and sling. He came to David at Ziglag.

📖 (12:3)

Jehu[5]
(late C11th BC)

An Anathothite. One of Saul[1]'s relatives, who was skilled with the bow and sling. He came to David at Ziglag.

📖 (12:3)

Ishmaiah[1]
(late C11th BC)

A Gibeonite and the leader of David's Thirty mighty men. One of Saul[1]'s relatives who was skilled with the bow and sling. He came to David at Ziglag.

📖 (12:4)

Jeremiah[3], Jahaziel[1], Johanan[5], Jozabad[2], Eluzai, Jerimoth[2], Bealiah, Shemariah[1], Shephatiah[3]
(late C11th BC)

Among Saul[1]'s relatives who were skilled with the bow and sling. They came to David at Ziglag.

📖 (12:4–5)

Elkanah[9], Ishiah[2] (Isshiah), Azarel[1], Joezer, Jashobeam[3]
(late C11th BC)

Korahites among Saul[1]'s relatives. They were skilled with the bow and sling. They came to David at Ziglag.

📖 (12:6)

Joelah, Zebadiah[3]
(late C11th BC)

Sons of Jeroham[5]. Among Saul[1]'s relatives who were skilled with the bow and sling. They came to David at Ziglag.

📖 (12:7)

Jeroham[5]
(mid C11th BC)

Father of Joelah and Zebadiah[3]. From Gedor.

📖 (12:7)

Ezer[4]
(late C11th BC)

Chief of the Gadite warriors. Skilled in spear and shield, he defected to David.

📖 (12:9)

Obadiah[6], Eliab[5], Mishmannah, Jeremiah[4], Attai[2], Eliel[7], Johanan[6], Elzabad[1], Jeremiah[5], Makbannai (Macbannai)
(late C11th BC)

Leaders of the Gadite warriors. Skilled in spear and shield, fierce and fast warriors, they defected to David.

📖 (12:9–13)

Adnah[1], Jozabad[3], Jediael[3], Michael[7], Jozabad[4], Elihu[2], Zillethai[2]
(late C11th BC)

Leaders of army units in Manasseh[1]. They were brave warriors who defected to David at Ziklag.

📖 (12:19–22)

Elpelet
(born early C10th BC)

See **Eliphelet[3]/Elpelet** in *1 Chronicles, p. 126.*

📖 (14:5)

Beeliada
(early C10th BC)

See **Eliada[1]/Beeliada** in *2 Samuel, p. 82.*

📖 (14:7)

Uriel[2]
(late C11th BC)

Leader of the Levitical family of Kohath. He brought the ark back to Jerusalem under the instructions of King David.

📖 (15:5, 11)

Joel[8]
(late C11th BC)

Leader of the Levitical family of Gershon. He brought the ark back to Jerusalem under the instructions of King David.

📖 (15:7, 11)

Shemaiah[7]
(late C11th BC)

Leader of the Levitical family of Elizaphan[2]. He brought the ark back to Jerusalem under the instructions of King David.

📖 (15:8, 11)

Eliel[8]
(late C11th BC)

Leader of the Levitical family of Hebron[1]. He brought the ark back to Jerusalem under the instructions of King David.

📖 (15:9, 11)

Amminadab[3]
(late C11th BC)

Leader of the Levitical family of Uzziel[1]. He brought the ark back to Jerusalem under the instructions of King David.

📖 (15:10–11)

Ethan[5]
(late C11th BC)

Son of Kushaiah. Appointed from the Levites as a musician to accompany the return of the ark to Jerusalem.

📖 (15:17, 19)

Kushaiah
(mid C11th BC)

Father of Ethan[5].

📖 (15:17)

Zechariah[6], Jaaziel (Aziel, NIV 2011 footnote v.20), Shemiramoth[1], Jehiel[1], Unni[1], Eliab[6], Benaiah[4], Maaseiah[1], Mattithiah[2], Eliphelehu, Mikneiah, Obed-Edom[2], Jeiel[4]
(late C11th BC)

Gatekeepers appointed from the Levites as musicians to accompany the return of the ark to Jerusalem.

📖 (15:18, 20–21; 16:5)

Azaziah[1]
(late C11th BC)

Appointed from the Levites to play the harp to accompany the return of the ark to Jerusalem.

📖 (15:21)

Kenaniah[1]
(late C11th BC)

Head Levite. He was responsible for the choirs and the singing that accompanied the ark on its return to Jerusalem.

📖 (15:22, 27)

Berekiah[4]
(late C11th BC)

Appointed to serve as a doorkeeper for the ark when it was returned to Jerusalem.
Possibly the same person as
Berekiah[2] *in 1 Chronicles, p. 137.*

📖 (15:23)

Elkanah[10]
(late C11th BC)

Appointed to serve as a doorkeeper for the ark when it was returned to Jerusalem.

📖 (15:23)

Shebaniah[1], Joshaphat[2], Nethanel[3], Amasai[3], Zechariah[7], Benaiah[5], Eliezer[4]
(late C11th BC)

Priests who blew the trumpets before the ark when it was returned to Jerusalem.

📖 (15:24; 16:5)

Obed-Edom[3], Jehiah
(late C11th BC)

Appointed to serve as doorkeepers for the ark when it was returned to Jerusalem.

📖 (15:24)

Jahaziel[2]
(late C11th BC)

A priest who blew trumpets before the ark when it was returned to Jerusalem.

📖 (16:6)

Hosah[1]
(late C11th BC)

A gatekeeper of the ark when it was returned to Jerusalem.

📖 (16:38)

Heman[3]
(early C10th BC)

Priest appointed to give thanks and to play instruments for sacred songs.

📖 (16:41)

Ahimelek[3] (Ahimelech)
(early C10th BC)

Son of Abiathar. A priest during David's reign.

📖 (18:16)

Shophak (Shophach)
(early C10th BC)

See **Shobak (Shobach)** *in 2 Samuel, p. 84.*

📖 (19:16)

Lahmi
(early C10th BC)

The brother of Goliath the Gittite.

📖 (20:5)

Shimea[1]
(late C11th BC)

See **Shimeah[1]** *in 1 Samuel, p. 73.*

📖 (20:7)

Ladan[2]
(late C11th BC)

Father of Jehiel[2], Zetham and Joel[9]. A Gershonite Levite whom David appointed for temple service at the end of his reign. His descendants were put in charge of the temple treasuries.

📖 (23:7–8; 26:21–22)

Shimei[12]
(late C11th BC)

Father of Shelomoth[1], Haziel and Haran[3]. A Gershonite Levite whom David appointed for temple service at the end of his reign.

📖 (23:7, 9–10)

Jehiel[2]/Jehieli, Zetham, Joel[9]
(early C10th BC)

Sons of Ladan[2]. Gershonite Levites whom David appointed for temple service at the end of his reign. They looked after the temple treasuries.

📖 (23:8; 26:22; 29:8)

Shelomoth[1], Haziel, Haran[3]
(early C10th BC)

Sons of Shimei[12]. Gershonite Levites and family heads whom David appointed for temple service at the end of his reign.

📖 (23:9)

Jahath[4], Ziza[2], Jeush[4], Beriah[4]
(early C10th BC)

Sons of Shimei[12]. Gershonite Levites whom David appointed for temple service at the end of his reign.

📖 (23:10–11)

Shubael[1]
(mid C15th BC)

First son of Gershom[1]. Grandson of Moses. Father of Jehdeiah[1]. He was appointed in charge of the temple treasuries.

📖 (23:16; 24:20; 26:24)

Rehabiah
(mid C15th BC)

Only son of Eliezer[1]. Grandson of Moses. Father of Ishiah[4] (Isshiah), and numerous other sons. Ancestor of Jeshaiah[3].

📖 (23:17; 24:21; 26:25)

Shelomith[3]
(late C16th BC)

First son of Izhar. Grandson of Kohath.

📖 (23:18)

Jeriah
(late C16th BC)

First son of Hebron[1]. Grandson of Kohath. David appointed the Hebronites with Jeriah at their head to oversee the worship and royal service of the Reubenites, Gadites and the half-tribe of Manasseh[1].

📖 (23:19; 24:23; 26:31–32)

Amariah[3], Jahaziel[3], Jekameam
(late C16th BC)

Sons of Hebron[1]. Grandsons of Kohath.

📖 (23:19; 24:23)

Micah[4]
(late C16th BC)

Firstborn son of Uzziel[1]. Grandson of Kohath. Father of Shamir.

📖 (23:20; 24:24)

Ishiah[3] (Isshiah)
(late C16th BC)

Second son of Uzziel[1]. Grandson of Kohath. Father of Zechariah[8].

📖 (23:20; 24:25)

Eleazar[4], Kish[3]
(late C16th BC)

Sons of Mahli[1]. Grandsons of Merari.

📖 (23:21–22)

Eder[2], Jerimoth[3]
(late C16th BC)

Sons of Mushi.

📖 (23:23)

Shemaiah[8]
(early C10th BC)

Son of Nethanel[4]. A Levite scribe at the end of David's reign. He recorded the names and divisions of priests to serve in the temple.

📖 (24:6)

Nethanel[4]
(late C11th BC)

Father of Shemaiah[8].

📖 (24:6)

Jehoiarib[2]
(early C10th BC)

One of the 24 heads of families from Eleazar[1] and Ithamar's descendants who were appointed by David to serve as priests in the temple. Possibly the same person as Jehiarib[1].

📖 (24:7)

Jedaiah[3]
(early C10th BC)

One of the 24 heads of families from Eleazar[1] and Ithamar's descendants who were appointed by David to serve as priests in the temple. Possibly the same person as Jedaiah[2].

📖 (24:7)

Harim[1], Seorim, Malkijah[3], Mijamin[1], Hakkoz[1], Abijah[7], Jeshua[1], Shekaniah[2], Eliashib[2], Jakim[2], Huppah, Jeshebeab, Bilgah[1], Immer[2], Hezir[1], Happizzez, Pethahiah[1], Jehezkel, Jakin[3], Gamul, Delaiah[2], Maaziah[1]
(early C10th BC)

Along with Jehoiarib[2] and Jedaiah[3], these men made up the 24 heads of families from Eleazar[1] and Ithamar's descendants who were appointed by David to serve as priests in the temple.

📖 (24:8–18)

Jehdeiah[1]
(early C10th BC)

Descendant of Shubael[1].

📖 (24:20)

Shelomoth[2]
(late C11th BC)

An Izharite. Father of Jahath[5].

📖 (24:22)

Jahath[5]
(early C10th BC)

An Izharite. Son of Shelomoth[2].

📖 (24:22)

Shamir
(early C10th BC)

Descendant of Micah[4].

📖 (24:24)

Ishiah[4] (Isshiah)
(late C15th BC)
Son of Rehabiah.
📖 (24:21)

Zechariah[8]
(early C10th BC)
Descendant of Ishiah[4].
📖 (24:25)

Jaaziah
(late C11th BC)
A Merarite. Father of Beno, Shoham,
Zakkur[3] and Ibri.
📖 (24:26–27)

Beno, Shoham, Zakkur[3], Ibri
(early C10th BC)
Merarites. Sons of Jaaziah.
📖 (24:27)

Jerahmeel[2]
(early C10th BC)
A Levite. Descendant of Kish[3].
📖 (24:29)

Zakkur[4], Joseph[3], Nethaniah[2], Asarelah
(early C10th BC)
Sons of Asaph[2]. In David's reign
they served under their father's
supervision. Their ministry included
prophesying accompanied by music.
📖 (25:2)

Gedaliah[2], Zeri/Izri, Jeshaiah[2], Shimei[13], Hashabiah[3]
(early C10th BC)
Sons of Jeduthun. In David's reign
they served under their father's
supervision. Their ministry included
prophesying and praising the Lord
using a harp.
📖 (25:3)

Mattithiah[3]
(early C10th BC)
Son of Jeduthun. In David's reign he
served under his father's supervision.

His ministry included prophesying
and praising the Lord using a harp.
He is possibly the same person as
Mattithiah[2].
📖 (25:3)

Bukkiah, Mattaniah[3]
(early C10th BC)
Sons of Heman[3]. In David's reign
they served under their father's
supervision. Their ministry included
prophesying accompanied by musical
instruments.
📖 (25:4)

Uzziel[4]/Azarel[2]
(early C10th BC)
Son of Heman[3]. In David's reign
he was appointed to the service of
prophesying accompanied by musical
instruments.
📖 (25:4, 18)

Shubael[2], Jerimoth[4], Hananiah[3], Hanani[2], Eliathah, Giddalti, Romamti-Ezer, Joshbekashah, Mallothi, Hothir, Mahazioth
(early C10th BC)
Sons of Heman[3]. In David's reign
they served under their father's
supervision. Their ministry included
prophesying accompanied by musical
instruments.
📖 (25:4)

Izri
(early C10th BC)
See **Zeri/Izri** in 1 Chronicles, p. 155 (left).
📖 (25:11)

Jesarelah
(early C10th BC)
See **Asarelah** in 1 Chronicles, p. 155 (left).
📖 (25:14)

Azarel[2]
(early C10th BC)
See **Uzziel[4]/Azarel[2]** in
1 Chronicles, p. 155 (left).
📖 (25:18)

Jediael[4], Zebadiah[4], Jathniel, Elam[3], Jehohanan[1], Eliehoenai[1]
(early C10th BC)

Sons of Meshelemiah. They formed a division of the Korahite temple gatekeepers. They were responsible for the East Gate.

📖 (26:2–3, 14)

Obed-Edom[4]
(late C11th BC)

A family head of Korahite temple gatekeepers. He had 8 sons and 62 descendants, who were strong and capable. He was given responsibility for the South Gate. God blessed him.

📖 (26:4, 6–8, 15)

Shemaiah[9]
(early C10th BC)

Firstborn son of Obed-Edom[4]. One of the Korahite temple gatekeepers. With his brothers he looked after the storehouse. He had four strong and capable sons also involved in this work.

📖 (26:4, 6–8, 15)

Jehozabad[2], Joah[3], Sakar[2] (Sacar), Nethanel[5], Ammiel[4], Issachar[2], Peullethai
(early C10th BC)

Sons of Obed-Edom[4]. One of the divisions of Korahite temple gatekeepers. They looked after the storehouse.

📖 (26:4, 15)

Othni, Rephael, Obed[4], Elzabad[2]
(early C10th BC)

Sons of Shemaiah[9]. Grandsons of Obed-Edom[4]. They were capable and strong leaders in their family.

📖 (26:7–8)

Elihu[3], Semakiah
(early C10th BC)

Relatives of Shemaiah[9]. Able men.

📖 (26:7–8)

Hosah[2]
(late C11th BC)

A Merarite temple gatekeeper given charge of the West Gate and the Shalleketh Gate with Shuppim. He had 13 relatives who shared this work. Possibly the same person as Hosah[1].

📖 (26:10, 16)

Shimri[3]
(early C10th BC)

Son of Hosah[2] who was appointed as first among his brothers even though he was not the firstborn. A temple gatekeeper.

📖 (26:10)

Hilkiah[5], Tabaliah, Zechariah[9]
(early C10th BC)

Sons of Hosah[2]. Together they formed a division of the temple gatekeepers.

📖 (26:11)

Shelemiah[1]/Meshelemiah[2]
(early C10th BC)

Keeper at the East Gate in David's time.
Possibly to be identified with **Meshelemiah[1]** *in 1 Chronicles, p. 147.*

📖 (26:14)

Shuppim
(early C10th BC)

A temple gatekeeper. With Hosah[2], he was given responsibility for the West Gate and the Shalleketh Gate.

📖 (26:16)

Jehieli
(early C10th BC)

See **Jehiel[2]/Jehieli** *in 1 Chronicles, p. 153.*

📖 (26:21–22)

Jeshaiah[3]
(early C11th BC)
Descendant of Rehabiah. Father of Joram[3].
(26:25)

Joram[3]
(mid C11th BC)
Son of Jeshaiah[3]. Father of Zikri[6].
(26:25)

Zikri[6] (Zicri)
(late C11th BC)
Son of Joram[3]. Father of Shelomith[4].
(26:25)

Shelomith[4]
(early C10th BC)
Son of Zikri[6]. In charge of all the treasures dedicated to the temple.
(26:25–28)

Kenaniah[2]
(early C10th BC)
An Izharite whose family served as officials and judges. Possibly the same person as Kenaniah[1].
(26:29)

Hashabiah[4]
(early C10th BC)
A Hebronite family head. He was responsible for 1,700 relatives in the work for the Lord and the king west of the Jordan.
(26:30)

Zabdiel[1]
(late C11th BC)
Father of Jashobeam[2].
(27:2)

Mikloth[2]
(early C10th BC)
Leader of the army division of 24,000 men that served in the second month.
(27:4)

Ammizabad
(early C10th BC)
Son of Benaiah[1]. Leader of the army division of 24,000 men that served in the third month.
(27:6)

Zebadiah[5]
(early C10th BC)
Son of Asahel[1]. He succeeded his father as leader of the army division of 24,000 men that served in the fourth month.
(27:7)

Shamhuth
(early C10th BC)
An Izrahite. Leader of the army division of 24,000 men that served in the fifth month.
(27:8)

Heldai[1]
(early C10th BC)
A Netophathite from the family of Othniel. Leader of the army division of 24,000 men that served in the twelfth month.
(27:15)

Eliezer[5]
(early C10th BC)
Son of Zikri[7]. Served as leader over the tribe of Reuben during David's reign.
(27:16)

Zikri[7] (Zicri)
(late C11th BC)
Father of Eliezer[5].
(27:16)

Shephatiah[4]
(early C10th BC)
Son of Maakah[9]. Served as leader over the tribe of Simeon[1] during David's reign.
(27:16)

Maakah[9] (Maacah)
(late C11th BC)
Father of Shephatiah[4].
📖 (27:16)

Hashabiah[5]
(early C10th BC)
Son of Kemuel[3]. Served as leader over the tribe of Levi[1] during David's reign.
📖 (27:17)

Kemuel[3]
(late C11th BC)
Father of Hashabiah[5].
📖 (27:17)

Zadok[5]
(early C10th BC)
Served as leader over the tribe of Aaron during David's reign. Possibly the same person as an earlier Zadok.
📖 (27:17)

Elihu[4]
(early C10th BC)
Brother of David. Served as leader over the tribe of Judah[1] during David's reign.
📖 (27:18)

Omri[4]
(early C10th BC)
Son of Michael[8]. Served as leader over the tribe of Issachar[1] during David's reign.
📖 (27:18)

Michael[8]
(late C11th BC)
Father of Omri[4].
📖 (27:18)

Ishmaiah[2]
(early C10th BC)
Son of Obadiah[7]. Served as leader over the tribe of Zebulun[1] during David's reign.
📖 (27:19)

Obadiah[7]
(late C11th BC)
Father of Ishmaiah[2].
📖 (27:19)

Jerimoth[5]
(early C10th BC)
Son of Azriel[2]. Served as leader over the tribe of Naphtali during David's reign.
📖 (27:19)

Azriel[2]
(late C11th BC)
Father of Jerimoth[5].
📖 (27:19)

Hoshea[3]
(early C10th BC)
Son of Azaziah[2]. Served as leader over the tribe of Ephraim during David's reign.
📖 (27:20)

Azaziah[2]
(late C11th BC)
Father of Hoshea[3].
📖 (27:20)

Joel[10]
(early C10th BC)
Son of Pedaiah[3]. Served as leader over the tribe of Manasseh[1] during David's reign.
📖 (27:20)

Pedaiah[3]
(late C11th BC)
Father of Joel[10].
📖 (27:20)

Iddo[3]
(early C10th BC)
Son of Zechariah[10]. Served as leader over the half-tribe of Manasseh[1] in Gilead during David's reign.
📖 (27:21)

Zechariah[10]
(late C11th BC)
Father of Iddo[3].
📖 (27:21)

Jaasiel[2]
(early C10th BC)
Son of Abner[2]. Served as leader over the tribe of Benjamin[1] during David's reign.
📖 (27:21)

Abner[2]
(late C11th BC)
Father of Jaasiel[2]. Possibly to be identified with Abner[1].
📖 (27:21)

Azarel[3]
(early C10th BC)
Son of Jeroham[6]. Served as leader over the tribe of Dan during David's reign.
📖 (27:22)

Jeroham[6]
(late C11th BC)
Father of Azarel[3].
📖 (27:22)

Azmaveth[4]
(early C10th BC)
Son of Adiel[3]. An official in David's reign with charge over the royal storehouses.
📖 (27:25)

Adiel[3]
(late C11th BC)
Father of Azmaveth[4].
📖 (27:25)

Jonathan[7]
(early C10th BC)
Son of Uzziah[3]. An official in David's reign with charge over the royal storehouses in towns, villages and watchtowers.
📖 (27:25)

Uzziah[3]
(late C11th BC)
Father of Jonathan[7].
📖 (27:25)

Ezri
(early C10th BC)
Son of Kelub[2]. An official in David's reign with charge over the land farmers.
📖 (27:26)

Kelub[2]
(late C11th BC)
Father of Ezri.
📖 (27:26)

Shimei[14]
(early C10th BC)
A Ramathite official in David's reign in charge of the vineyards.
📖 (27:27)

Zabdi[2]
(late C11th BC)
A Shiphmite official in David's reign in charge of wine-making.
📖 (27:27)

Baal-Hanan[2]
(early C10th BC)
A Gederite official in David's reign in charge of the olive and sycamore-fig trees.
📖 (27:28)

Joash[7]
(early C10th BC)
An official in David's reign in charge of olive oil supplies.
📖 (27:28)

Shitrai
(early C10th BC)
A Sharonite official in David's reign in charge of the herds of Sharon.
📖 (27:29)

Shaphat[5]
(early C10th BC)

Son of Adlai. An official in David's reign in charge of the valley herds.

📖 (27:29)

Adlai
(late C11th BC)

Father of Shaphat[5].

📖 (27:29)

Obil
(early C10th BC)

An Ishmaelite official in David's reign in charge of the camels.

📖 (27:30)

Jehdeiah[2]
(early C10th BC)

A Meronothite official in David's reign in charge of the donkeys.

📖 (27:30)

Jaziz
(early C10th BC)

A Hagrite official in David's reign in charge of the flocks.

📖 (27:31)

Jonathan[8]
(late C11th BC)

David's uncle who was a scribe known for his wisdom and counselling skills.

📖 (27:32)

Jehiel[3]
(early C10th BC)

Son of Hakmoni. An official in David's reign who looked after the king's sons.

📖 (27:32)

Hakmoni (Hacmoni)
(late C11th BC)

Father of Jehiel[3].

📖 (27:32)

Jehoiada[3]
(early C10th BC)

Son of Benaiah[1]. Succeeded Ahithophel as counsellor to King David.
Possibly the same person as
Jehoiada[1] *in 2 Samuel, p. 84.*

📖 (27:34)

2 Chronicles

Iddo[4]
(late C10th BC)

A prophet and keeper of genealogical records during the reigns of Solomon, Jeroboam and Rehoboam.

📖 (9:29; 12:15)

Mahalath[2]
(mid C10th BC)

Daughter of Jerimoth[6] and Abihail[4]. Granddaughter of King David. Wife of Rehoboam. Mother of Jeush[5], Shemariah[2] and Zaham.

📖 (11:18)

Jerimoth[6]
(early C10th BC)

Son of David. Father of Mahalath[2]. Husband of Abihail[4].

📖 (11:18)

Abihail[4]
(early C10th BC)

Wife of Jerimoth[6]. Daughter of Eliab[3]. Granddaughter of Jesse.

📖 (11:18)

Jeush[5], Shemariah[2], Zaham
(late C10th BC)

Sons of Rehoboam and Mahalath[2].

📖 (11:19)

Attai[3], Ziza[3], Shelomith[5]
(late C10th BC)

Sons of Rehoboam and Maakah[4].

📖 (11:20)

Absalom[2]
(early C10th BC)

See **Abishalom** in 1 Kings, p. 98.

📖 (11:20)

Uriel[3]
(early C10th BC)

An ancestor (possibly grandfather) of Maakah[4]. From Gibeah.

📖 (13:2)

Zerah[6]
(early C9th BC)

A Cushite. He led the Cushites against Judah during Asa[1]'s reign but suffered a heavy defeat.

📖 (14:9–15)

Azariah[11]
(early C9th BC)

Son of Oded[1]. A prophet who delivered God's word to Asa[1]. Asa heeded his words and the result for Judah was spiritual renewal, rejoicing and rest from their enemies.

📖 (15:1–9)

Oded[1]
(late C10th BC)

Father of Azariah[11].

📖 (15:1, 8)

Hanani[3]
(early C9th BC)

A prophet during the last years of Asa[1]'s reign. He was imprisoned because Asa objected to his message that God would punish Judah for their lack of trust in God which had led to reliance on the king of Aram.

📖 (16:7–10)

Ben-Hail, Obadiah[8], Zechariah[11], Nethanel[6], Micaiah[3]
(mid C9th BC)

Jehoshaphat[3]'s officials who went out into the towns of Judah to teach them from the Book of the Law.

The result was peace and prosperity in Judah.

📖 (17:7–9)

Shemaiah[10], Nethaniah[3], Zebadiah[6], Asahel[2], Shemiramoth[2], Jehonathan[1], Adonijah[2], Tobijah[1], Tob-Adonijah
(mid C9th BC)

Levites whom Jehoshaphat[3] sent out with his officials to teach from the Book of the Law, leading to peace and prosperity in Judah.

📖 (17:8–9)

Elishama[5], Jehoram[2]
(mid C9th BC)

Priests whom Jehoshaphat[3] sent out, along with his officials, to teach from the Book of the Law, leading to peace and prosperity in Judah.

📖 (17:8–9)

Adnah[2], Jehohanan[2]
(mid C9th BC)

Commanders among the experienced fighting men whom Jehoshaphat[3] stationed in Jerusalem.

📖 (17:14–15)

Amasiah
(mid C9th BC)

Son of Zikri[8]. A commander among the experienced fighting men whom Jehoshaphat[3] stationed in Jerusalem.

📖 (17:16)

Zikri[8] (Zicri)
(early C9th BC)

Father of Amasiah.

📖 (17:16)

Eliada[3]
(mid C9th BC)

A commander and valiant soldier among the experienced fighting men whom Jehoshaphat[3] stationed in Jerusalem.

📖 (17:17)

Jehozabad[3]
(mid C9th BC)

A commander among the experienced fighting men whom Jehoshaphat[3] stationed in Jerusalem.

📖 (17:18)

Amariah[4]
(mid C9th BC)

A chief priest during the reign of Jehoshaphat[3].

📖 (19:11)

Zebadiah[7]
(mid C9th BC)

Son of Ishmael[4]. Leader of the tribe of Judah. Jehoshaphat[3] appointed him to deal with matters relating to the king on behalf of the people. This, among other appointments, was intended to secure the people's return to the Lord.

📖 (19:11)

Ishmael[4]
(early C9th BC)

Father of Zebadiah[7].

📖 (19:11)

Jahaziel[4]
(mid C9th BC)

Son of Zechariah[12] and Levite descendant of Asaph[2]. When the Spirit of the Lord came on him, he stood before all the assembly at the temple and encouraged Jehoshaphat[3] not to be afraid of the army from Edom who were invading Judah. The Ammonites, Moabites and Seirites ended up destroying each other and the people of Judah blessed the Lord.

📖 (20:14–26)

Zechariah[12]
(early C9th BC)

Son of Benaiah[6]. Father of Jahaziel[4] and Levite descendant of Asaph[2].

📖 (20:14)

Benaiah[6]
(late C10th BC)

Son of Jeiel[5]. Father of Zechariah[12] and Levite descendant of Asaph[2].

📖 (20:14)

Jeiel[5]
(mid C10th BC)

Son of Mattaniah[4]. Father of Benaiah[6] and Levite descendant of Asaph[2].

📖 (20:14)

Mattaniah[4]
(early C10th BC)

Father of Jeiel[5] and Levite descendant of Asaph[2].

📖 (20:14)

Eliezer[6]
(mid C9th BC)

Son of Dodavahu. He prophesied against Jehoshaphat[3] when he made an alliance with Ahaziah[2].

📖 (20:37)

Dodavahu
(early C9th BC)

Father of Eliezer[6].

📖 (20:37)

Azariah[12], Jehiel[4], Zechariah[13], Azariahu, Michael[9], Shephatiah[5]
(mid C9th BC)

Sons of Jehoshaphat[3].

📖 (21:2)

Azariah[13]
(mid C9th BC)

Son of Jeroham[7]. A commander of an army unit of 100 who joined with Jehoiada[2] the priest as he secured Joash[3]'s coronation. The army units were in charge of security. They were also responsible for putting Athaliah[1] to death.

📖 (23:1, 9, 14, 20)

Jeroham[7]
(early C9th BC)
Father of Azariah[13].
📖 (23:1)

Ishmael[5]
(mid C9th BC)
Son of Jehohanan[3]. A commander of an army unit of 100 who joined with Jehoiada[2] the priest as he secured Joash[3]'s coronation. The army units were in charge of security. They were also responsible for putting Athaliah[1] to death.
📖 (23:1, 9, 14, 20)

Jehohanan[3]
(early C9th BC)
Father of Ishmael[5].
📖 (23:1)

Azariah[14], Maaseiah[2], Elishaphat
(mid C9th BC)
Commanders of army units of 100 men. They joined with Jehoiada[2] the priest as he secured Joash[3]'s coronation. The army units were in charge of security. They were also responsible for putting Athaliah[1] to death.
📖 (23:1, 9, 14, 20)

Obed[5]
(early C9th BC)
Father of Azariah[14].
📖 (23:1)

Adaiah[5]
(early C9th BC)
Father of Maaseiah[2].
📖 (23:1)

Zikri[9] (Zicri)
(early C9th BC)
Father of Elishaphat.
📖 (23:1)

Zechariah[14]
(late C9th BC)
Son of Jehoiada[2]. He was stoned to death in the courtyard of the temple on the command of Joash[3] because he prophesied that due to Joash's disobedience to the Lord, the Lord would abandon him and he would not prosper.
📖 (24:20–22)

Zabad[1]
(late C9th BC)
See **Jozabad[1]** *in 2 Kings, p. 107.*
📖 (24:26)

Shimrith
(mid C9th BC)
See **Shomer[1]** *in 2 Kings, p. 107.*
📖 (24:26)

Obed-Edom[5]
(early C8th BC)
His work involved caring for the gold and silver and other articles found in the temple of God in Jerusalem.
📖 (25:24)

Uzziah[1]
(c.807–739 BC; reigned 791–739 BC)
See **Azariah[3]** *in 2 Kings, p. 108.*
📖 (26:1)

Jeiel[6]
(early C8th BC)
Secretary to Uzziah[1].
📖 (26:11)

Maaseiah[3]
(early C8th BC)
One of Uzziah[1]'s officials. He looked after the army and was under the authority of Hananiah[4].
📖 (26:11)

Hananiah[4]
(early C8th BC)
A royal official during the reign of Uzziah[1].
📖 (26:11)

Zikri[10] (Zicri)
(mid C8th BC)

An Ephraimite warrior. During Ahaz[1]'s reign he killed Maaseiah[4], Azrikam[4] and Elkanah[11].

📖 (28:7)

Maaseiah[4]
(mid C8th BC)

Son of Ahaz[1]. He was killed by Zikri[10].

📖 (28:7)

Azrikam[4]
(mid C8th BC)

Officer in charge of the palace during Ahaz[1]'s reign. He was killed by Zikri[10].

📖 (28:7)

Elkanah[11]
(mid C8th BC)

Second in command to Ahaz[1]. He was killed by Zikri[10].

📖 (28:7)

Oded[2]
(mid C8th BC)

A prophet during the reigns of Ahaz[1] and Pekah. When the army of Israel under Pekah returned to Samaria having inflicted heavy losses on Ahaz and Judah, Oded confronted the army. He told them to release those they had taken prisoner and warned them that God's anger rested upon them.

📖 (28:9–11)

Azariah[15], Berekiah[5], Jehizkiah, Amasa[2]
(mid C8th BC)

These men were among the leaders who confronted the men of Israel who tried to take prisoners of war from Judah to Ephraim.

📖 (28:12)

Jehohanan[4]
(early C8th BC)

Father of Azariah[15].

📖 (28:12)

Meshillemoth[1]
(early C8th BC)

Father of Berekiah[5].

📖 (28:12)

Shallum[10]
(early C8th BC)

Father of Jehizkiah.

📖 (28:12)

Hadlai
(early C8th BC)

Father of Amasa[2].

📖 (28:12)

Kish[4]
(late C8th BC)

Son of Abdi[2]. A Merarite Levite. He purified the temple according to Hezekiah[1]'s instructions and the command of the Lord.

📖 (29:12, 15–36)

Abdi[2]
(mid C8th BC)

Father of Kish[4]. A Merarite.

📖 (29:12)

Azariah[16]
(late C8th BC)

Son of Jehallelel[2]. A Merarite Levite. He purified the temple according to Hezekiah[1]'s instructions and the command of the Lord.

📖 (29:12, 15–36)

Jehallelel[2]
(mid C8th BC)

Father of Azariah[16]. A Merarite.

📖 (29:12)

Zimmah[3]
(mid C8th BC)
Father of Joah[2].
📖 (29:12)

Eden
(late C8th BC)
Son of Joah[2]. A Gershonite Levite. He purified the temple according to Hezekiah[1]'s instructions and the command of the Lord. He assisted Kore[2] in the distribution of gifts to priests in the towns.
📖 (29:12, 15–36; 31:15)

Shimri[4], Jeiel[7]
(late C8th BC)
Levite descendants of Elizaphan[1]. They purified the temple according to Hezekiah[1]'s instructions and the command of the Lord.
📖 (29:13, 15–36)

Zechariah[15]
(late C8th BC)
A Levite descendant of Asaph[2]. He purified the temple according to Hezekiah[1]'s instructions and the command of the Lord.
📖 (29:13, 15–36)

Jehiel[5]
(late C8th BC)
A Levite descendant of Heman[3]. He purified the temple according to Hezekiah[1]'s instructions and the command of the Lord. He was appointed by Hezekiah and Azariah[17] to assist Konaniah[1] and Shimei[15] in looking after gifts brought to the temple storerooms.
📖 (29:13, 15–36; 31:13)

Shimei[15]
(late C8th BC)
A descendant of Heman[3]. He purified the temple according to Hezekiah[1]'s instructions and the command of the Lord.
📖 (29:13, 15–36)

Uzziel[5]
(late C8th BC)
A descendant of Jeduthun. He purified the temple according to Hezekiah[1]'s instructions and the command of the Lord.
📖 (29:15–36)

Azariah[17]
(late C8th BC)
From Zadok[1]'s family. Chief priest during the reign of Hezekiah[1]. Hezekiah consulted him about the offerings the people brought and together they appointed those who supervised the storerooms.
📖 (31:9–13)

Konaniah[1] (Conaniah)
(late C8th BC)
A Levite appointed by Hezekiah[1] and Azariah[17] to supervise the temple storerooms where tithes and gifts were brought following the spiritual revival under Hezekiah.
📖 (31:11–12)

Shimei[16]
(late C8th BC)
Brother of Konaniah[1]. He was appointed by Hezekiah[1] and Azariah[17] as second in rank to Konaniah in the role of temple storerooms supervisor.
📖 (31:11–12)

Azaziah[3], Nahath[3], Asahel[3], Jerimoth[7], Jozabad[5], Eliel[9], Ismakiah, Mahath[2], Benaiah[7]
(late C8th BC)
The assistants of Konaniah[1] and Shimei[16] who were appointed by Hezekiah[1] and Azariah[17] to look after gifts brought to the temple storerooms.
📖 (31:13)

Kore[2]
(late C8th BC)

Son of Imnah[2]. During the revival under Hezekiah[1] he looked after freewill offerings and their distribution, as well as consecrated gifts.

📖 (31:14)

Imnah[2]
(mid C8th BC)

Father of Kore[2]. A Levite who was keeper of the East Gate of the temple.

📖 (31:14)

Miniamin[1], Jeshua[2], Shemaiah[11], Amariah[5], Shekaniah[3] (Shecaniah)
(late C8th BC)

During the revival under Hezekiah[1], they assisted Kore[2] in the distribution of gifts to their fellow priests in the towns.

📖 (31:15)

Maaseiah[5]
(late C7th BC)

Ruler of Jerusalem who was instructed by Josiah[1] to organize the repair the temple.

📖 (34:8–11)

Joah[4]
(late C7th BC)

Son of Joahaz who served as a recorder. He was instructed by Josiah[1] to organize the repair of the temple.

📖 (34:8)

Joahaz
(mid C7th BC)

Father of Joah[4].

📖 (34:8)

Jahath[6], Obadiah[9]
(late C7th BC)

Merarite Levites who directed the temple repair work during the reign of Josiah[1].

📖 (34:12)

Zechariah[16], Meshullam[9]
(late C7th BC)

Kohathite Levites who directed the temple repair work during the reign of Josiah[1].

📖 (34:12)

Abdon[4]
(late C7th BC)

See **Akbor[2]** in 2 Kings, p. 117.

📖 (34:20)

Micah[6]
(mid C7th BC)

See **Micaiah[2]** in 2 Kings, p. 117.

📖 (34:20)

Tokhath
(mid C7th BC)

See **Tikvah** in 2 Kings, p. 117.

📖 (34:22)

Hasrah
(early C7th BC)

See **Harhas** in 2 Kings, p. 117.

📖 (34:22)

Jehiel[6]
(late C7th BC)

An official of the temple in Josiah[1]'s reign who provided the priests with animals for the Passover offerings.

📖 (35:8)

Konaniah[2], Shemaiah[12], Nethanel[7]
(late C7th BC)

Brothers who served as officials in the temple during Josiah[1]'s reign. They provided the priests with animals for the Passover offerings.

📖 (35:9)

Hashabiah[6], Jeiel[8]
(late C7th BC)

Officials of the temple in Josiah[1]'s reign. They provided the priests with animals for the Passover offerings.

📖 (35:9)

Jozabad[6]
(late C7th BC)

Leader of the Levites in Josiah[1]'s reign. He provided the priests with animals for the Passover offerings.

📖 (35:9)

Jeremiah[6]
(c.640–after 586 BC)

Son of Hilkiah[9]. A prophet responsible for the collection of prophecies in the book of Jeremiah. The five poems of lament in the book of Lamentations are also associated with him. Jeremiah needed reassurance when he was called to take up a prophetic role because he was aware of his own weaknesses and was fearful. He wrote laments when Josiah[1] died (609 BC) and when Jerusalem fell to the Babylonians (586 BC). His prophecies bear witness to his own suffering, which included personal rejection by his family and being threatened with death by priests, prophets and people in Jerusalem. He also felt deeply about the suffering and sin of God's people (Jeremiah 8:18 – 9:2). He warned King Zedekiah[2] that the Babylonians would take Jerusalem, but this led to him being imprisoned and then thrown into a cistern to die. He survived but lived in the courtyard of the guard until Jerusalem was captured. Then he was taken in chains into Babylonian exile and later was taken as a hostage to Egypt where it is likely he died. He encouraged the people to repentance and obedience and spoke about a new hope based on a new covenant (Jeremiah 31:31–34).

📖 (35:25; Jeremiah 1; 26–45;
   Lamentations 1–5)

Cyrus
(ruled 559–530 BC)

King of Persia. He conquered the Babylonians and allowed the Jews to return to Jerusalem from exile. The Lord had 'moved the heart of Cyrus' (36:22) and he became actively involved in ensuring that the temple was rebuilt in Jerusalem. Cyrus also returned the temple articles which Nebuchadnezzar had carried away as plunder. In the prophecies of Isaiah he is called the Lord's 'shepherd' and 'anointed', the one whom the Lord would use to fulfil his purposes.

📖 (36:22–23; Ezra 1:1–4, 7–8; 3:7; 4:3;
   5:13–17; 6:14; Isaiah 44:28 – 45:13)

Ezra

Mithredath[1]
(mid C6th BC)

Treasurer to King Cyrus. He counted out the gold and silver items that Nebuchadnezzar had removed when Cyrus restored them to Jerusalem from Babylon.

📖 (1:8)

Sheshbazzar
(mid C6th BC)

Leader in Judah when the exiles returned from Babylon to Jerusalem. He was responsible for the safe return of the exiles and the temple treasures which Cyrus restored to him.

📖 (1:8)

Joshua[3]/Jeshua[3]
(mid C6th BC)

Son of Jozadak. He returned with Zerubbabel and the people from Babylonian exile. He served as high priest in Jerusalem. He was responsible along with Zerubbabel and the priests for the rebuilding of the altar and the re-establishment of worship there.

📖 (2:2; 3:2; Nehemiah 12:1; Haggai 1:1,
   12, 14; 2:2–4; Zechariah 3:1–10;
   6:11–15)

**Nehemiah[1], Seraiah[6]/
Azariah[18], Reelaiah/Raamiah,
Mordecai[1], Bilshan, Mispar/
Mispereth**
(mid C6th BC)

Leaders who returned with
Zerubbabel, Joshua[3] and the people
from Babylonian exile.

📖 (2:2; Nehemiah 7:7; 12:1, 12)

Bigvai[1]
(mid C6th BC)

One of the leaders who returned with
Zerubbabel, Joshua[3] and the people
from Babylonian exile. Possibly to be
identified with Bigvai[2].

📖 (2:2; Nehemiah 7:7)

Rehum[1]/Nehum
(mid C6th BC)

One of the leaders who returned
with Zerubbabel, Joshua[3] and the
people from Babylonian exile.

📖 (2:2; Nehemiah 12:3)

Baanah[3]
(mid C6th BC)

One of the leaders who returned with
Zerubbabel, Joshua[3] and the people
from Babylonian exile. Possibly to be
identified with Baanah[4].

📖 (2:2; Nehemiah 7:7)

Parosh
(? C10th BC)

Father (or ancestor) of Pedaiah[4].
Of his descendants, 2,172 returned
from exile with Zerubbabel,
Joshua[3] and the other leaders. His
name is mentioned in (the book of)
Nehemiah some years later in a list
of families who sealed the agreement
that Nehemiah[2] and the returned
exiles made to serve the Lord.

📖 (2:3; 8:3; 10:25; Nehemiah 3:25; 7:8;
10:14)

Shephatiah[6]
(? C10th BC)

Some 372 of his descendants

returned from exile with Zerubbabel,
Joshua[3] and the other leaders.

📖 (2:4; 8:8; Nehemiah 7:9)

Arah[2]
(? C10th BC)

Of his descendants, 775 (or 652)
returned from exile with Zerubbabel,
Joshua[3] and the other leaders.

📖 (2:5; Nehemiah 7:10)

Pahath-Moab[1]
(? C10th BC)

Of his descendants, 2,812 (or 2,818)
returned from exile with Zerubbabel,
Joshua[3] and the other leaders. His
name is mentioned in (the book of)
Nehemiah some years later in a list
of families who sealed the agreement
that Nehemiah[2] and the returned
exiles made to serve the Lord.

📖 (2:6; 8:4; 10:30; Nehemiah 3:11; 7:11;
10:14)

Jeshua[4], Joab[3]
(? C10th BC)

Descendants of Pahath-Moab.

📖 (2:6; 8:9; Nehemiah 7:11)

Elam[4]
(? C10th BC)

Some 1,254 of his descendants
returned from exile with Zerubbabel,
Joshua[3] and the other leaders. His
name is mentioned in (the book of)
Nehemiah some years later in a list
of families who sealed the agreement
that Nehemiah[2] and the returned
exiles made to serve the Lord.

📖 (2:7; 8:7; 10:2, 26; Nehemiah 7:12;
10:14)

Zattu
(? C10th BC)

Of his descendants, 945 (or 845)
returned from exile with Zerubbabel,
Joshua[3] and the other leaders. His
name is mentioned in (the book of)
Nehemiah some years later in a list
of families who sealed the agreement

that Nehemiah[2] and the returned exiles made to serve the Lord.

📖 (2:8; 8:5; 10:27; Nehemiah 7:13; 10:14)

Zakkai (Zaccai)
(? C10th BC)

Some 760 of his descendants returned from exile with Zerubbabel, Joshua[3] and the other leaders.

📖 (2:9; Nehemiah 7:14)

Bani[3]/Binnui[5]
(? C10th BC)

Of his descendants, 642 (or 648) returned from exile with Zerubbabel, Joshua[3] and the other leaders. His name is mentioned in (the book of) Nehemiah some years later in a list of families who sealed the agreement that Nehemiah[2] and the returned exiles made to serve the Lord.

📖 (2:10; 8:10; 10:29; Nehemiah 7:15; 10:14)

Bebai[1]
(? C10th BC)

Of his descendants, 623 (or 628) returned from exile with Zerubbabel, Joshua[3] and the other leaders. His name is mentioned in (the book of) Nehemiah some years later in a list of families who sealed the agreement that Nehemiah[2] and the returned exiles made to serve the Lord.

📖 (2:11; 8:11; 10:28; Nehemiah 7:16; 10:15)

Azgad[1]
(? C10th BC)

Of his descendants, 1,222 (or 2,322) returned from exile with Zerubbabel, Joshua[3] and the other leaders. His name is mentioned in (the book of) Nehemiah some years later in a list of families who sealed the agreement that Nehemiah[2] and the returned exiles made to serve the Lord.

📖 (2:12; 8:12; Nehemiah 7:17; 10:15)

Adonikam/Adonijah[3]
(? C10th BC)

Of his descendants, 666 (or 667) returned from exile with Zerubbabel, Joshua[3] and the other leaders. His name is mentioned in (the book of) Nehemiah some years later in a list of families who sealed the agreement that Nehemiah[2] and the returned exiles made to serve the Lord.

📖 (2:13; 8:13; Nehemiah 7:18; 10:16)

Bigvai[2]
(? C10th BC)

Of his descendants, 2,056 (or 2,067) returned from exile with Zerubbabel, Joshua[3] and the other leaders. His name is mentioned in (the book of) Nehemiah some years later in a list of families who sealed the agreement that Nehemiah[2] and the returned exiles made to serve the Lord.

📖 (2:14; 8:14; Nehemiah 7:19; 10:16)

Adin
(? C10th BC)

Of his descendants, 454 or (655) returned from exile with Zerubbabel, Joshua[3] and the other leaders. His name is mentioned in (the book of) Nehemiah some years later in a list of families who sealed the agreement that Nehemiah[2] and the returned exiles made to serve the Lord.

📖 (2:15; Nehemiah 7:20; 10:16)

Ater[1]
(? C10th BC)

Some 98 of his descendants returned from exile with Zerubbabel, Joshua[3] and the other leaders. His name is mentioned in (the book of) Nehemiah some years later in a list of families who sealed the agreement that Nehemiah[2] and the returned exiles made to serve the Lord.

📖 (2:16; Nehemiah 7:21; 10:17)

Hezekiah[2]
(? C10th BC)

Head of a family of exiles, the sons of Ater[1], 98 of whose descendants returned from exile with Zerubbabel.

📖 (2:16)

Bezai
(? C10th BC)

Of his descendants, 323 (or 324) returned from exile with Zerubbabel, Joshua[3] and the other leaders. His name is mentioned in (the book of) Nehemiah some years later in a list of families who sealed the agreement that Nehemiah[2] and the returned exiles made to serve the Lord.

📖 (2:17; Nehemiah 7:23; 10:18)

Jorah
(? C10th BC)

Some 112 of his descendants returned from exile with Zerubbabel, Joshua[3] and the other leaders. Possibly to be identified with Hariph (Nehemiah 7:24).

📖 (2:18)

Hashum[1]
(? C10th BC)

Of his descendants, 223 (or 328) returned from exile with Zerubbabel, Joshua[3] and the other leaders. His name is mentioned in (the book of) Nehemiah some years later in a list of families who sealed the agreement that Nehemiah[2] and the returned exiles made to serve the Lord.

📖 (2:19; 10:33; Nehemiah 7:22; 10:18)

Gibbar/Gibeon
(? C10th BC)

Some 95 of his descendants returned from exile with Zerubbabel, Joshua[3] and the other leaders.

📖 (2:20; Nehemiah 7:25)

Elam[5]
(? C10th BC)

Listed among the men of Bethlehem. Some 1,254 of his descendants returned from exile with Zerubbabel, Joshua[3] and the other leaders.

📖 (2:31; Nehemiah 7:34)

Jeshua[5]
(? C10th BC)

A descendant of Jedaiah[3]. Head of a priestly family. Some 973 of his descendants returned from exile with Zerubbabel, Joshua[3] and the other leaders.

📖 (2:36; Nehemiah 7:39)

Immer[3]
(? C10th BC)

Head of a priestly family. Some 1,052 of his descendants returned from exile with Zerubbabel, Joshua[3] and the other leaders.

📖 (2:37; 10:20; Nehemiah 7:40)

Pashhur[2]
(? C10th BC)

Head of a priestly family. Some 1,247 of his descendants returned from exile with Zerubbabel, Joshua[3] and the other leaders.

📖 (2:38; 10:22; Nehemiah 7:41)

Harim[2]
(? C10th BC)

Head of a priestly family. Some 1,052 of his descendants returned from exile with Zerubbabel, Joshua[3] and the other leaders.

📖 (2:39; 10:20; Nehemiah 7:42)

Jeshua[6], Kadmiel[1]
(? C10th BC)

Heads of Levite families. Some 74 members of their families returned from exile with Zerubbabel, Joshua[3] and the other leaders.

📖 (2:40; Nehemiah 7:43)

Hodaviah[4]
(? C10th BC)

A descendant of Jeshua[6] and Kadmiel[1].

📖 (2:40; 3:9; Nehemiah 7:43)

Ater[2], Hatita, Shobai
(? C10th BC)

Their families were temple gatekeepers. Their descendants (along with those of Shallum[7], Talmon and Akkub[2]) numbered 139 (or 138) when they returned from exile with Zerubbabel, Joshua[3] and the other leaders.

📖 (2:42; Nehemiah 7:45)

Ziha[1], Hasupha, Tabbaoth, Keros, Siaha/Sia, Padon, Lebanah/Lebana, Hagabah/Hagaba, Akkub[3], Hagab, Shalmai, Hanan[4], Giddel[1], Gahar, Reaiah[3], Rezin[2], Nekoda[1], Gazzam, Uzza[3], Paseah[2], Besai, Asnah, Meunim, Nephussim, Bakbuk, Hakupha, Harhur, Bazluth, Mehida, Harsha, Barkos, Sisera[2], Temah, Neziah, Hatipha
(? C10th BC)

Their descendants were among the temple servants who returned from exile with Zerubbabel, Joshua[3] and the other leaders.

📖 (2:43–54; Nehemiah 7:46–56)

Sotai, Hassophereth/Sophereth, Peruda/Perida, Jaala, Darkon, Giddel[2], Shephatiah[7], Hattil, Pokereth-Hazzebaim, Ami/Amon[3]
(? C10th BC)

Their descendants, the servants of Solomon, returned from exile with Zerubbabel, Joshua[3] and the other leaders.

📖 (2:55–7; Nehemiah 7:57–59)

Delaiah[3], Tobiah[1], Nekoda[2]
(? C10th BC)

Their descendants, numbering 652, returned with the Israelites from exile even though their family lines could not be established.

📖 (2:60; Nehemiah 7:62)

Hobaiah, Hakkoz[2]
(? C10th BC)

Heads of families of priests whose descendants returned with the Israelites from exile. Because their family lines could not be established they were excluded from the temple priesthood.

📖 (2:61–63; Nehemiah 7:63–65)

Barzillai[3]
(late C11th BC)

Son-in-law of Barzillai[1]. Head of a family of priests whose descendants returned with the Israelites from exile. Because their family line could not be established they were excluded from the temple priesthood.

📖 (2:61–63; Nehemiah 7:63–65)

Henadad
(mid C6th BC)

Head of a family that joined the families of Joshua[3] and Kadmiel to supervise the work on the rebuilding of the temple of Jerusalem following the exile.

📖 (3:9)

Xerxes[1]/Ahasuerus
(ruled Persia 486–465 BC)

Persian king. Son of Darius I. The events of the book of Esther took place during his reign, and the splendour of his royal palace in Susa is described there. He was married to Vashti, and then Esther became his queen. He frequently acted on bad advice, first of all from his nobles and then his second-in-command, Haman. However, when Haman was executed and Mordecai[2] took over, Mordecai and Esther together secured the reversal of Xerxes' edicts and the survival of the Jewish people. Evidence from outside the Bible confirms his wars against the Greeks.

📖 (4:6; Esther 1:1 – 10:3)

Artaxerxes I
(ruled Persia 464–424 BC)

Persian king. He intervened to stop the rebuilding of the temple in Jerusalem after the return from exile, following a letter from Rehum[2] and Shimshai which suggested that the rebuilding of Jerusalem was against his royal interests. Later, he supported Ezra[1] in the rebuilding project and many families returned to Jerusalem during his reign. Nehemiah[2] was his cupbearer and later on Artaxerxes appointed him governor of Judah. In Artaxerxes' thirty-second year Nehemiah returned to him in Susa, although he visited Jerusalem, at least on one occasion, to supervise the community there. (It is possible that the biblical references refer to two [some suggest three] different kings named Artaxerxes.)

📖 (4:7–23; 6:14; 7:1, 11–28; 8:1; Nehemiah 2:1; 5:14; 13:6)

Bishlam, Mithredath[2], Tabeel[1]
(mid C5th BC)

Probably Persian officials. They lodged a complaint against the people of Judah and Jerusalem by writing a letter in Aramaic to Artaxerxes to warn him about the rebuilding of Jerusalem by the returned exiles.

📖 (4:7)

Rehum[2]
(mid C5th BC)

A Persian commanding officer who joined with Shimshai to write a letter to Artaxerxes against the returned exiles. The letter led to a halt in the rebuilding project in Jerusalem.

📖 (4:8–23)

Shimshai
(mid C5th BC)

The Persian secretary who joined with Rehum[2] to write a letter to Artaxerxes against the returned exiles. The letter led to a halt in the rebuilding project in Jerusalem.

📖 (4:8–23)

Ashurbanipal
(ruled Assyria 668–626 BC)

King of Assyria. Son of Esarhaddon and grandson of Sennacherib. He dealt with uprisings in Egypt and Elam (Persia). On defeating Susa, he deported people to Samaria, and Assyria increased its military power.

📖 (4:10)

Haggai
(prophesied 520 BC)

See **Haggai** in *Haggai, p. 215.*

📖 (5:1)

Zechariah[17]
(prophesied c.520–518 BC)

See **Zechariah** in *Zechariah, p. 216.*

📖 (5:1)

Iddo[5]
(late C7th BC)

Father of Berekiah[6]. Grandfather of Zechariah[17].

📖 (5:1; Zechariah 1:1)

Tattenai, Shethar-Bozenai
(late C6th BC)

Governor and official of Trans-Euphrates who reported to Darius[1] that the rebuilding work in Jerusalem had restarted. After Darius confirmed that the building work should be permitted, it picked up pace with practical support from these men and ongoing encouragement from Haggai and Zechariah[17].

📖 (5:3 – 6:15)

Darius[1]
(ruled 521–485 BC)

King of Persia. He allowed the rebuilding work in Jerusalem to proceed and instructed Tattenai and Shethar-Bozenai to give practical help to the returned exiles in the form of finance and animals for burnt offerings. Haggai and Zechariah[17] prophesied during his reign. The temple was completed in the sixth year of Darius's reign.

📖 (5:3 – 6:15; Haggai 1:1; 2:10; Zechariah 1:1, 7; 7:1)

Ezra[1]
(mid C5th BC)

Son of Seraiah[2]. A teacher of the Law and a priest, he returned to Jerusalem from Babylonian exile in the seventh year of King Artaxerxes. God blessed Ezra ('the gracious hand of his God was on him', 7:9) and King Artaxerxes provided him with practical financial help for the rebuilding of the temple as well as animals for offerings. Ezra appointed magistrates, judges and priests, and set out with a large company from the Ahava Canal to return to Jerusalem. Once in Jerusalem, Ezra led his people in prayers of confession concerning their sin of intermarrying while in exile. He organized the family heads to deal with the separation of the men from their foreign wives.

📖 (7:1 – 10:17)

Gershom[2]
(mid C5th BC)

Descendant of Phinehas[1]. One of the family heads who returned to Jerusalem with Ezra[1].

📖 (8:2)

Daniel[2]
(mid C5th BC)

Descendant of Ithamar. One of the family heads who returned to Jerusalem with Ezra[1]. This is probably the same Daniel as the one who sealed the covenant of recommitment to the Lord with Nehemiah[2] (Nehemiah 10:6).

📖 (8:2)

Shekaniah[4] (Shecaniah)
(mid C5th BC)

One of the family heads who returned to Jerusalem with Ezra[1].

📖 (8:3)

Zechariah[18]
(mid C5th BC)

Descendant of Parosh. One of the family heads who returned to Jerusalem with Ezra[1]; 150 men came with him.

📖 (8:2)

Eliehoenai[2]
(mid C5th BC)

Son of Zerahiah[2]. Descendant of Pahath-Moab. One of the family heads who returned to Jerusalem with Ezra[1]; 200 men came with him.

📖 (8:4)

Zerahiah[2]
(early C5th BC)

Father of Eliehoenai[2].

📖 (8:4)

Shekaniah[5] (Shecaniah)
(mid C5th BC)

Son of Jahaziel[5]. Descendant of Zattu. One of the family heads who returned to Jerusalem with Ezra[1]; 300 men came with him.

📖 (8:5)

Jahaziel[5]
(early C5th BC)

Father of Shekaniah[5].

📖 (8:5)

Ebed[2]
(mid C5th BC)

Son of Jonathan[9]. Descendant of Adin. One of the family heads who returned to Jerusalem with Ezra[1]; 50 men came with him.

📖 (8:6)

Jonathan[9]
(early C5th BC)
Father of Ebed[2].
📖 (8:6)

Jeshaiah[4]
(mid C5th BC)
Son of Athaliah[3]. Descendant of Elam[4]. One of the family heads who returned to Jerusalem with Ezra[1]; 70 men came with him.
📖 (8:7)

Athaliah[3]
(early C5th BC)
Father of Jeshaiah[4].
📖 (8:7)

Zebadiah[8]
(mid C5th BC)
Son of Michael[10]. Descendant of Shephatiah[6]. One of the family heads who returned to Jerusalem with Ezra[1]; 80 men came with him.
📖 (8:8)

Michael[10]
(early C5th BC)
Father of Zebadiah[8].
📖 (8:8)

Obadiah[10]
(mid C5th BC)
Son of Jehiel[7]. Descendant of Joab[3]. One of the family heads who returned to Jerusalem with Ezra[1]; 218 men came with him.
📖 (8:9)

Jehiel[7]
(early C5th BC)
Father of Obadiah[10].
📖 (8:9)

Shelomith[6]
(mid C5th BC)
Son of Josiphiah. Descendant of Bani[3]. One of the family heads who returned to Jerusalem with Ezra[1]; 160 men came with him.
📖 (8:10)

Josiphiah
(early C5th BC)
Father of Shelomith[6].
📖 (8:10)

Zechariah[19]
(mid C5th BC)
Son of Bebai[2]. Descendant of Bebai[1]. One of the family heads who returned to Jerusalem with Ezra[1]; 28 men came with him.
📖 (8:11)

Bebai[2]
(early C5th BC)
Father of Zechariah[19].
📖 (8:11)

Johanan[7]
(mid C5th BC)
Son of Hakkatan. Descendant of Azgad. One of the family heads who returned to Jerusalem with Ezra[1]; 110 men came with him.
📖 (8:12)

Hakkatan
(early C5th BC)
Father of Johanan[7].
📖 (8:12)

Eliphelet[5], Jeuel[2], Shemaiah[13]
(mid C5th BC)
Descendants of Adonikam. Heads of families who returned to Jerusalem with Ezra[1]. The men who came with them numbered 60.
📖 (8:13)

Uthai[2], Zakkur[5]
(mid C5th BC)
Descendants of Bigvai[2]. Heads of families who returned to Jerusalem with Ezra[1]. The men who came with them numbered 70.
📖 (8:14)

Eliezer[7], Ariel, Shemaiah[14], Elnathan[2], Jarib[2], Elnathan[3], Nathan[7], Zechariah[20], Meshullam[10]
(mid C5th BC)

Leaders of the people who were brought together by Ezra[1] at the Ahava Canal. They were sent to Iddo[6] at Kasiphia to ask him for some Levites to serve the returning exiles by looking after the dedicated items and serving in the temple.

📖 (8:16)

Joiarib[1], Elnathan[4]
(mid C5th BC)

Men of learning who were sent by Ezra[1], with the nine leaders of the people, to Iddo[6] at Kasiphia to ask him for some Levites to serve the returning exiles by looking after the dedicated items and serving in the temple.

📖 (8:16)

Iddo[6]
(mid C5th BC)

A temple servant in Kasiphia, Persia, to whom Ezra[1] sent a delegation requesting some Levites to serve the returning exiles. Iddo sent 38 Levites with a company of 220 temple servants to help them.

📖 (8:17–20)

Sherebiah[1]
(mid C5th BC)

A Levite and descendant of Mahli[1] who was sent by Iddo[6] to Ezra[1] at the Ahava Canal. He is described as 'a capable man'. Along with Hashabiah[7] and 10 others he was put in charge of the temple treasures.

📖 (8:18, 24)

Hashabiah[7]
(mid C5th BC)

A Levite and descendant of Merari who was sent by Iddo[6] to Ezra[1] at the Ahava Canal. Along with

Sherebiah[1] and 10 others he was put in charge of the temple treasures.

📖 (8:19, 24)

Jeshaiah[5]
(mid C5th BC)

A Levite and descendant of Merari who was sent by Iddo[6] to Ezra[1] at the Ahava Canal.

📖 (8:19)

Meremoth[1]
(mid C5th BC)

Son of Uriah[3]. Ezra[1] and the Levites with him weighed out the temple treasures into his hands when they arrived in Jerusalem. He was among the priests who joined Nehemiah[2] in sealing the agreement that the people made to obey the Book of the Law.

📖 (8:33; Nehemiah 3:4, 21; 10:5)

Uriah[3]
(early C5th BC)

Father of Meremoth[1]. Son of Hakkoz[3]. A priest.

📖 (8:33; Nehemiah 3:4)

Eleazar[5]
(mid C5th BC)

Son of Phinehas[3]. When Ezra[1] reached Jerusalem, Eleazar assisted him in weighing out the gold, silver and sacred items and recording the weight.

📖 (8:33–34)

Phinehas[3]
(early C5th BC)

Father of Eleazar[5].

📖 (8:33)

Jozabad[7]
(mid C5th BC)

Son of Jeshua[7]. A Levite. When Ezra[1] reached Jerusalem, Jozabad assisted him in weighing out the gold, silver and sacred items and recording the weight. He assumed charge of the outside work of the temple in Jerusalem.

📖 (8:33; Nehemiah 11:16)

Jeshua[7]
(early C5th BC)

Father of Jozabad[7].

📖 (8:33)

Noadiah[1]
(mid C5th BC)

Son of Binnui[1]. When Ezra[1] reached Jerusalem, Noadiah assisted him in weighing out the gold, silver and sacred items and recording the weight.

📖 (8:33)

Binnui[1]
(early C5th BC)

Father of Noadiah[1].

📖 (8:33)

Shekaniah[6] (Shecaniah)
(mid C5th BC)

Son of Jehiel[8]. A descendant of Elam[4]. He alerted Ezra[1] to the unfaithfulness of the people who had married foreign women in exile. He suggested that Ezra lead the people in covenant renewal.

📖 (10:1–4)

Jehiel[8]
(early C5th BC)

Father of Shekaniah[6].

📖 (10:2)

Jehohanan[5]
(mid C5th BC)

Son of Eliashib[3]. Owner of a room where Ezra[1] mourned following Shekaniah[6]'s confession that the people had sinned by marrying foreign women in exile.

📖 (10:6)

Eliashib[3]
(early C5th BC)

Father of Jehohanan[5] and Joiada[2]. Son of Joiakim. As high priest in Jerusalem he took charge of the rebuilding of the Sheep Gate in the city wall and was in charge of the temple store rooms. Nehemiah[2] criticized Eliashib for providing a room for Tobiah[2] in the temple courts.

📖 (10:6; Nehemiah 3:1, 20–21; 12:10, 22–23; 13:4–7, 28)

Jonathan[10]
(mid C5th BC)

Son of Asahel[4]. One of four men who opposed Ezra[1]'s instruction that the exiles who had married foreign wives should separate themselves from them.

📖 (10:15)

Asahel[4]
(early C5th BC)

Father of Jonathan[10].

📖 (10:15)

Jahzeiah
(mid C5th BC)

Son of Tikvah[2]. One of four men who opposed Ezra[1]'s instruction that the exiles who had married foreign wives should separate themselves from them.

📖 (10:15)

Tikvah[2]
(early C5th BC)

Father of Jahzeiah.

📖 (10:15)

Meshullam[11]
(mid C5th BC)

One of four men who opposed Ezra[1]'s instruction that the exiles who had married foreign wives should separate themselves from them.

📖 (10:15)

Shabbethai[1]
(mid C5th BC)

A Levite. One of four men who opposed Ezra[1]'s instruction that the exiles who had married foreign wives should separate themselves from them.

📖 (10:15)

Maaseiah[6], Eliezer[8], Jarib[3], Gedaliah[3]
(mid C5th BC)

Descendants of Joshua[3]. They had taken foreign wives during the exile. Following Ezra[1]'s instructions, they separated from their wives and presented guilt offerings.

📖 (10:18–19)

Hanani[4], Zebadiah[9]
(mid C5th BC)

Descendants of Immer[3]. They separated from their foreign wives following Ezra[1]'s instructions.

📖 (10:20)

Maaseiah[7], Elijah[3], Shemaiah[15], Jehiel[9], Uzziah[4]
(mid C5th BC)

Descendants of Harim[2] who separated from their foreign wives following Ezra[1]'s instructions.

📖 (10:21)

Elioenai[4], Maaseiah[8], Ishmael[6], Nethanel[8], Jozabad[8], Elasah[1]
(mid C5th BC)

Descendants of Pashhur[2] who separated from their foreign wives following Ezra[1]'s instructions.

📖 (10:22)

Jozabad[9], Shimei[17], Kelaiah/Kelita[1], Pethahiah[2], Judah[2], Eliezer[9]
(mid C5th BC)

Levites who separated from their foreign wives following Ezra[1]'s instructions.

📖 (10:23)

Eliashib[4]
(mid C5th BC)

A musician who separated from his foreign wife following Ezra[1]'s instructions.

📖 (10:24)

Shallum[11]
(mid C5th BC)

A gatekeeper who separated from his foreign wife following Ezra[1]'s instructions. (Possibly to be identified with Shallum[7].)

📖 (10:24)

Telem, Uri[3]
(mid C5th BC)

Gatekeepers who separated from their foreign wives following Ezra[1]'s instructions.

📖 (10:24)

Ramiah, Izziah, Malkijah[4], Mijamin[2], Eleazar[6], Malkijah[5], Benaiah[8]
(mid C5th BC)

Descendants of Parosh who separated from their foreign wives following Ezra[1]'s instructions.

📖 (10:25)

Mattaniah[5], Zechariah[21]
(mid C5th BC)

Descendants of Elam[4] who separated from their foreign wives following Ezra[1]'s instructions.

📖 (10:26)

Jehiel[10]
(mid C5th BC)

A descendant of Elam[4] who separated from his foreign wife following Ezra[1]'s instructions. Possibly to be identified with Jehiel[8], father of Shekaniah[6].

📖 (10:26)

Abdi[3], Jeremoth[3], Elijah[4]
(mid C5th BC)

Descendants of Elam[4] who separated from their foreign wives following Ezra[1]'s instructions.

📖 (10:26)

Elioenai[5], Eliashib[5], Mattaniah[6], Jeremoth[4], Zabad[5], Aziza
(mid C5th BC)

Descendants of Zattu who separated from their foreign wives following Ezra[1]'s instructions.

📖 (10:27)

Jehohanan[6], Hananiah[5], Zabbai[1], Athlai
(mid C5th BC)

Descendants of Bebai[1] who separated from their foreign wives following Ezra[1]'s instructions.

📖 (10:28)

Meshullam[12], Malluk[2] (Malluch), Adaiah[6], Jashub[2], Sheal, Jeremoth[5]
(mid C5th BC)

Descendants of Bani[3] who separated from their foreign wives following Ezra[1]'s instructions.

📖 (10:29)

Adna[1], Kelal, Benaiah[9], Maaseiah[9], Mattaniah[7], Bezalel[2], Binnui[2], Manasseh[3]
(mid C5th BC)

Descendants of Pahath-Moab who separated from their foreign wives following Ezra[1]'s instructions.

📖 (10:30)

Eliezer[10], Ishijah, Malkijah[6], Shemaiah[16], Shimeon, Benjamin[3], Malluk[3], Shemariah[3]
(mid C5th BC)

Descendants of Harim[2] who separated from their foreign wives

following Ezra[1]'s instructions.

📖 (10:32)

Mattenai[1], Mattattah, Zabad[6], Eliphelet[6], Jeremai, Manasseh[4], Shimei[18]
(mid C5th BC)

Descendants of Hashum[1] who separated from their foreign wives following Ezra[1]'s instructions.

📖 (10:33)

Maadai, Amram[2], Uel, Benaiah[10], Bedeiah, Keluhi, Vaniah, Meremoth[2], Eliashib[6], Mattaniah[8], Mattenai[2], Jaasu
(mid C5th BC)

Descendants of Bani[5] who separated from their foreign wives following Ezra[1]'s instructions.

📖 (10:34–37)

Binnui[3]
(unknown)

Ancestor of some of those who separated from their foreign wives.

📖 (10:38)

Shimei[19], Shelemiah[2], Nathan[8], Adaiah[7], Maknadebai (Macnadebai), Shashai, Sharai, Azarel[4], Shelemiah[3], Shemariah[4], Shallum[12], Amariah[6], Joseph[4]
(mid C5th BC)

Descendants of Binnui[3] who separated from their foreign wives following Ezra[1]'s instructions.

📖 (10:38–42)

Nebo
(unknown)

An ancestor of seven men who separated from their foreign wives following the instructions of Ezra[1].

📖 (10:43)

Jeiel[9], Mattithiah[4], Zabad[7], Zebina, Jaddai, Joel[11], Benaiah[11]
(mid C5th BC)

Descendants of Nebo who separated from their foreign wives following Ezra[1]'s instructions.

📖 (10:43)

Nehemiah

Nehemiah[2]
(mid C5th BC)

Son of Hakaliah. Brother of Hanani[5]. Cupbearer to King Artaxerxes of Persia. When he heard about the broken walls of Jerusalem, Nehemiah wept and prayed and returned to Jerusalem to supervise the rebuilding of the walls. The project faced many setbacks and some opposition, but Nehemiah proved resilient. He was appointed governor of Judah. On the completion of the walls, Nehemiah linked up with Ezra[1] to lead the people in religious reform through the renewal of their covenant commitment to the Lord. Nehemiah organized a joyful celebration to mark the dedication of the rebuilt wall of Jerusalem. He returned to Artaxerxes in Babylon but kept a close watch on Jerusalem, as is shown by his return and subsequent involvement in setting the people right when they further erred from the ways of the Lord.

📖 (1:1 – 13:31)

Hakaliah (Hacaliah)
(early C5th BC)

Father of Nehemiah[2].

📖 (1:1; 10:1)

Hanani[5]
(mid C5th BC)

Brother of Nehemiah[2]. He resided in Judah and brought Nehemiah a depressing report about the situation facing the returned exiles there. Once the walls were rebuilt, Nehemiah put Hanani in charge of the security of Jerusalem.

📖 (1:2–3; 7:2–3)

Asaph[4]
(mid C5th BC)

Keeper of the royal park. Artaxerxes provided Nehemiah[2] with a letter to Asaph granting him timber from the park for his building project.

📖 (2:8)

Sanballat
(mid C5th BC)

A Horonite official in Jerusalem who, with Tobiah[2], was disturbed by Nehemiah[2]'s appearance in Jerusalem. He opposed the rebuilding of the walls at every point and became an enemy of Nehemiah and the Jews. He became father-in-law of one of Joiada[2]'s sons.

📖 (2:10; 4:1–9; 6:1–14; 13:28)

Tobiah[2]
(mid C5th BC)

An Ammonite official in Jerusalem who, with Sanballat, was disturbed by Nehemiah[2]'s appearance in Jerusalem. He opposed the rebuilding of the walls at every point and became an enemy of Nehemiah and the Jews. He won favours from Eliashib[3] the priest, in terms of a room in the temple courts, but Nehemiah ensured that Tobiah was turned out.

📖 (2:10; 4:1–9; 6:1–14; 13:4–9)

Geshem
(mid C5th BC)

An Arab who joined with Tobiah[2] and Sanballat in opposing Nehemiah[2]'s rebuilding of the wall of Jerusalem.

📖 (2:19; 6:1–7)

Zakkur[6] (Zaccur)
(mid C5th BC)

Son of Imri[2]. He worked on the rebuilding of the wall of Jerusalem under Nehemiah[2]. He worked on the section next to where the men of Jericho worked.

📖 (3:2)

Imri[2]
(early C5th BC)

Father of Zakkur[6].

📖 (3:2)

Hassenaah
(early C5th BC)

His sons rebuilt the Fish Gate in the wall of Jerusalem.

📖 (3:3)

Hakkoz[3]
(late C6th BC)

Father of Uriah[3] and grandfather of Meremoth[1]. His descendants rebuilt the sections of the wall of Jerusalem near the Fish Gate and near Eliashib[3]'s house.

📖 (3:4, 21)

Meshullam[13]
(mid C5th BC)

Son of Berekiah[6]. He repaired a section of the wall of Jerusalem near the Fish Gate.

📖 (3:4, 30)

Berekiah[6]
(early C5th BC)

Father of Meshullam[13].

📖 (3:4, 30)

Meshezabel[1]
(late C6th BC)

Father of Berekiah[6].

📖 (3:4)

Zadok[6]
(mid C5th BC)

Son of Baana[3]. He repaired a section of the wall of Jerusalem next to where Meshullam[13] worked.

📖 (3:4)

Baana[3]
(early C5th BC)

Father of Zadok[6].

📖 (3:4)

Joiada[1]
(mid C5th BC)

Son of Paseah[3]. With Meshullam[14], he repaired the Jeshanah Gate in the wall of Jerusalem.

📖 (3:6)

Paseah[3]
(early C5th BC)

Father of Joiada[1].

📖 (3:6)

Meshullam[14]
(mid C5th BC)

Son of Besodeiah. With Joiada[1], he repaired the Jeshanah Gate in the wall of Jerusalem.

📖 (3:6)

Besodeiah
(early C5th BC)

Father of Meshullam[14].

📖 (3:6)

Melatiah
(mid C5th BC)

A Gibeonite. He worked with Jadon on the section of the wall of Jerusalem next to the Jeshanah Gate.

📖 (3:7)

Jadon
(mid C5th BC)

A Meronothite. He worked with Melatiah on the section of the wall of Jerusalem next to the Jeshanah Gate.

📖 (3:7)

Uzziel[6]
(mid C5th BC)

Son of Harhaiah. A goldsmith. He worked next to Melatiah and Jadon on the next section of the wall of Jerusalem.

(3:8)

Harhaiah
(early C5th BC)

Father of Uzziel[6].

(3:8)

Hananiah[6]
(mid C5th BC)

Son of Harhaiah. A perfume-maker. He worked next to Uzziel[6] on the next section of the wall of Jerusalem as far as the Broad Wall.

(3:8)

Rephaiah[5]
(mid C5th BC)

Son of Hur[4]. One of the rulers of a half-district of Jerusalem. He worked next to Hananiah[6] on the next section of the wall of Jerusalem.

(3:9)

Hur[4]
(early C5th BC)

Father of Rephaiah[5].

(3:9)

Jedaiah[4]
(mid C5th BC)

Son of Harumaph. He worked next to Rephaiah[5] on the next section of the wall of Jerusalem opposite his house.

(3:10)

Harumaph
(early C5th BC)

Father of Jedaiah[4].

(3:10)

Hattush[2]
(mid C5th BC)

Son of Hashabneiah[1]. He worked next to Jedaiah[4] on the next section of the wall of Jerusalem.

(3:10)

Hashabneiah[1]
(early C5th BC)

Father of Hattush[2].

(3:10)

Hasshub[2]
(mid C5th BC)

Son of Pahath-Moab[2]. He worked next to Hattush[2] on the next section of the wall of Jerusalem and repaired the Tower of the Ovens.

(3:11)

Pahath-Moab[2]
(early C5th BC)

Father of Hasshub[2].

(3:11; 10:14)

Shallum[13]
(mid C5th BC)

Son of Hallohesh[1]. One of the rulers of a half-district of Jerusalem. He worked with his daughters next to Hasshub[2] on the next section of the wall of Jerusalem.

(3:12)

Hallohesh[1]
(early C5th BC)

Father of Shallum[13].

(3:12)

Hanun[2]
(mid C5th BC)

He repaired the Valley Gate and about 450 metres of the wall of Jerusalem as far as the Dung Gate with the help of the residents of Zanoah.

(3:13)

Malkijah[7]
(mid C5th BC)

Son of Rekab[3]. Ruler of the district of Beth Hakkerem. He repaired the Dung Gate.

📖 (3:14)

Rekab[3] (Recab)
(early C5th BC)

Father of Malkijah[7].

📖 (3:14)

Shallun
(mid C5th BC)

Son of Kol-Hezeh[1]. Ruler of the district of Mizpah. He repaired the Fountain Gate and the wall of the Pool of Siloam.

📖 (3:15)

Kol-Hozeh[1] (Col-Hozeh)
(early C5th BC)

Father of Shallun.

📖 (3:15)

Nehemiah[3]
(mid C5th BC)

Son of Azbuk. Ruler of the half-district of Beth Zur. He worked next to Shallun on the next section of the wall of Jerusalem up to the point opposite the tombs of David.

📖 (3:16)

Azbuk
(early C5th BC)

Father of Nehemiah[3].

📖 (3:16)

Rehum[3]
(mid C5th BC)

Son of Bani[4]. A Levite. He worked next to Nehemiah[3] on the next section of the wall of Jerusalem.

📖 (3:17)

Bani[4]
(early C5th BC)

Father of Rehum[3].

📖 (3:17)

Hashabiah[8]
(mid C5th BC)

Ruler of the half-district of Keilah. He worked next to Rehum[3] on the next section of the wall of Jerusalem.

📖 (3:17)

Binnui[4]/Bavvai
(mid C5th BC)

Son of Henadad. Ruler of the other half-district of Keilah. He worked next to Hashabiah[8] on the next section of the wall of Jerusalem. He also repaired the section from Azariah[19]'s house to the angle and the corner.

📖 (3:18, 24)

Ezer[5]
(mid C5th BC)

Son of Jeshua[8]. Ruler of Mizpah. He worked next to Binnui[4] on the next section of the wall of Jerusalem from the point facing the armoury to the angle of the wall.

📖 (3:19)

Jeshua[8]
(early C5th BC)

Father of Ezer[5].

📖 (3:19)

Baruch[1]
(mid C5th BC)

Son of Zabbai[2]. Ruler of Mizpah. He worked zealously next to Ezer[5] on the next section of the wall of Jerusalem from the angle of the wall to the entrance of the house of Eliashib[3] the high priest.

📖 (3:20)

Zabbai[2]
(early C5th BC)

Father of Baruch[1].

📖 (3:20)

Benjamin[4]
(mid C5th BC)

Possibly to be identified with Benjamin[3]. He and Hasshub[3] repaired a section of the wall of Jerusalem in front of their houses.

(3:23; 12:34)

Hasshub[3]
(mid C5th BC)

He repaired a section of the wall of Jerusalem in front of his house.

(3:23)

Azariah[19]
(mid C5th BC)

Son of Maaseiah[10]. He repaired a section of the wall of Jerusalem in front of his house.

(3:23)

Maaseiah[10]
(early C5th BC)

Father of Azariah[19]. Son of Ananiah.

(3:23)

Ananiah
(late C6th BC)

Father of Maaseiah[10].

(3:23)

Palal
(mid C5th BC)

Son of Uzai. He worked on the section of the wall of Jerusalem opposite the angle and the tower of the upper palace near the court of the guard.

(3:25)

Uzai
(early C5th BC)

Father of Palal.

(3:25)

Pedaiah[4]
(mid C5th BC)

Son of Parosh. He worked with the temple servants who lived on the hill of Ophel next to Palal on the next section of the wall of Jerusalem up to the point of the Water Gate.

(3:25)

Zadok[7]
(mid C5th BC)

Son of Immer[4]. He repaired a section of the wall of Jerusalem opposite his house.

(3:29)

Immer[4]
(early C5th BC)

Father of Zadok[7].

(3:29)

Shemaiah[17]
(mid C5th BC)

Son of Shekaniah[7], the guard at the East Gate.

(3:29)

Shekaniah[7] (Shecaniah)
(early C5th BC)

Father of Shemaiah[17].

(3:29)

Hananiah[7]
(mid C5th BC)

Son of Shelemiah[4]. He worked next to Shemaiah[17] on the next section of the wall of Jerusalem.

(3:30)

Shelemiah[4]
(early C5th BC)

Father of Hananiah[7].

(3:30)

Hanun[3]
(mid C5th BC)

Sixth son of Zalaph. He worked next to Hananiah[7] on the next section of the wall of Jerusalem.

(3:30)

Zalaph
(early C5th BC)

Father of Hanun[3] and at least five other sons.

(3:30)

Malkijah[8]
(mid C5th BC)

A goldsmith. He made repairs on the wall of Jerusalem as far as the house of the temple servants and merchants, opposite the Inspection Gate up to the room above the corner.

📖 (3:31)

Shemaiah[18]
(mid C5th BC)

Son of Delaiah[4]. When Nehemiah[2] visited him, Shemaiah gave Nehemiah bad advice, because he had been hired by Tobiah[2] and Sanballat to intimidate Nehemiah.

📖 (6:10–13)

Delaiah[4]
(early C5th BC)

Father of Shemaiah[18]. Son of Mehetabel[2].

📖 (6:10)

Mehetabel[2]
(late C6th BC)

Father of Delaiah[4].

📖 (6:10)

Noadiah[2]
(mid C5th BC)

A prophetess who tried to intimidate Nehemiah[2] and frustrate the process of rebuilding the wall of Jerusalem.

📖 (6:14)

Shekaniah[8] (Shecaniah)
(early C5th BC)

Father-in-law of Tobiah[2]. Son of Arah[3].

📖 (6:18)

Arah[3]
(late C6th BC)

Father of Shekaniah[8].

📖 (6:18)

Jehohanan[7]
(mid C5th BC)

Son of Tobiah[2]. Husband of Meshullam[13]'s daughter.

📖 (6:18)

Hananiah[8]
(mid C5th BC)

Commander of the citadel. After the wall of Jerusalem was rebuilt he was put in charge of Jerusalem by Nehemiah[2] to work alongside Hanani[5]. He is described as a trustworthy man who feared God more than most people.

📖 (7:2)

Azariah[20]
(mid C6th BC)

See **Seraiah[6]** *in Ezra, p. 168.*

📖 (7:7)

Raamiah
(mid C6th BC)

See **Reelaiah** *in Ezra, p. 168.*

📖 (7:7)

Nahamani
(mid C6th BC)

One of the leaders who returned with Zerubbabel, Joshua[3] and the people from Babylonian exile.

📖 (7:7)

Nehum
(mid C6th BC)

See **Rehum[1]** *in Ezra, p. 168.*

📖 (7:7)

Binnui[5]
(? C10th BC)

See **Bani[3]** *in Ezra, p. 169.*

📖 (7:15)

Hariph
(? C10th BC)

See **Jorah** *in Ezra, p. 170.*

📖 (7:24)

Gibeon
(? C10th BC)
See **Gibbar** *in Ezra, p. 170.*
📖 (7:25)

Sia
(? C10th BC)
See **Siaha** *in Ezra, p. 171.*
📖 (7:47)

Lebana
(? C10th BC)
See **Lebanah** *in Ezra, p. 171.*
📖 (7:48)

Hagaba
(? C10th BC)
See **Hagabah** *in Ezra, p. 171.*
📖 (7:48)

Sophereth
(? C10th BC)
See **Hassophereth** *in Ezra, p. 171.*
📖 (7:57)

Perida
(? C10th BC)
See **Peruda** *in Ezra, p. 171.*
📖 (7:57)

Amon[3]
(? C10th BC)
See **Ami** *in Ezra, p. 171.*
📖 (7:59)

Mattithiah[5], Shema[4], Anaiah[1], Uriah[4], Hilkiah[6], Maaseiah[11]
(mid C5th BC)

These men stood on the right of Ezra[1] when he stood on a raised wooden platform in the square before the Water Gate to read the Book of the Law to the returned exiles.
📖 (8:4)

Pedaiah[5], Mishael[2], Malkijah[9], Hashum[2], Hashbaddanah
(mid C5th BC)

These men stood on the left of Ezra[1] when he stood on a raised wooden platform in the square before the Water Gate to read the Book of the Law to the returned exiles.
📖 (8:4)

Zechariah[22]
(mid C5th BC)

Possibly to be identified with Zechariah[20]. Stood on the left of Ezra[1] when he stood on a raised wooden platform in the square before the Water Gate to read the Book of the Law to the returned exiles.
📖 (8:4)

Meshullam[15]
(mid C5th BC)

He stood on the left of Ezra[1] when he stood on a raised wooden platform in the square before the Water Gate to read the Book of the Law to the returned exiles.
📖 (8:4)

Jeshua[9], Bani[5]
(mid C5th BC)

Levites who read from the Book of the Law and clarified its meaning for the people after they worshipped God following Ezra[1] reading the Book of the Law in the square before the Water Gate.
📖 (8:7)

Sherebiah[2]
(mid C5th BC)

Possibly to be identified with Sherebiah[1] (Ezra 8:18). One of the Levites who read from the Book of the Law and clarified its meaning for the people after they worshipped God following Ezra[1] reading the Book of the Law in the square before the Water Gate.
📖 (8:7; 9:4–5; 10:12; 12:8, 24)

Jamin[3]
(mid C5th BC)

One of the Levites who read from the Book of the Law and clarified its meaning for the people after they worshipped God following Ezra[1] reading the Book of the Law in the square before the Water Gate.

📖 (8:7)

Akkub[4]
(mid C5th BC)

Possibly to be identified with Akkub[2]. One of the Levites who read from the Book of the Law and clarified its meaning for the people after they worshipped God following Ezra[1] reading the Book of the Law in the square before the Water Gate.

📖 (8:7)

Shabbethai[2]
(mid C5th BC)

Possibly to be identified with Shabbethai[1].One of the Levites who read from the Book of the Law and clarified its meaning for the people after they worshipped God following Ezra[1] reading the Book of the Law in the square before the Water Gate.

📖 (8:7)

Hodiah[2]
(mid C5th BC)

One of the Levites who read from the Book of the Law and clarified its meaning for the people after they worshipped God following Ezra[1] reading the Book of the Law in the square before the Water Gate.

📖 (8:7; 10:10)

Maaseiah[12]
(mid C5th BC)

Possibly to be identified with Maaseiah[11]. One of the Levites who read from the Book of the Law and clarified its meaning for the people after they worshipped God following Ezra[1] reading the Book

of the Law in the square before the Water Gate.

📖 (8:7)

Kelita[2]
(mid C5th BC)

Possibly to be identified with Kelita[1]. One of the Levites who read from the Book of the Law and clarified its meaning for the people after they worshipped God following Ezra[1] reading the Book of the Law in the square before the Water Gate.

📖 (8:7; 10:10)

Azariah[21]
(mid C5th BC)

Possibly to be identified with Azariah[20]. One of the Levites who read from the Book of the Law and clarified its meaning for the people after they worshipped God following Ezra[1] reading the Book of the Law in the square before the Water Gate.

📖 (8:7)

Jozabad[10], Hanan[5], Pelaiah[2]
(mid C5th BC)

Levites who read from the Book of the Law and clarified its meaning for the people after they worshipped God following Ezra[1] reading the Book of the Law in the square before the Water Gate.

📖 (8:7)

Bani[6], Bunni[1], Bani[7], Kenani
(mid C5th BC)

Levites who stood on the stairs of the Levites and cried out to the Lord following the prayers of confession offered by the returned exiles and the reading of the Book of the Law.

📖 (9:4)

Kadmiel[2]
(mid C5th BC)

A Levite who stood on the stairs of the Levites and offered praise to the Lord following the prayers of confession offered by the returned exiles and the reading of the Book of the Law. He also joined Nehemiah[2] to seal the covenant agreement to obey the Lord. Possibly to be identified with Kadmiel[1].

(9:4–5; 10:9; 12:8, 24)

Hashabneiah[2], Shebaniah[2]
(mid C5th BC)

Levites who offered praise to the Lord following the prayers of confession offered by the returned exiles and the reading of the Book of the Law.

(9:5)

Zedekiah[4], Seraiah[7], Azariah[22], Jeremiah[7], Pashhur[3], Amariah[7], Malkijah[10], Hattush[3], Shebaniah[3], Malluk[4], Harim[3], Meremoth[3], Obadiah[11], Daniel[3], Ginnethon[1], Baruch[2], Meshullam[16], Abijah[8], Mijamin[3], Maaziah[2], Bilgai, Shemaiah[19]
(mid C5th BC)

Priests who joined Nehemiah[2] in sealing the agreement that the people made to obey the Book of the Law. (See also Nehemiah 12:1–7.)

(10:1–8)

Jeshua[10]
(mid C5th BC)

Son of Azaniah. One of the Levites who joined Nehemiah[2] to seal the covenant agreement to obey the Lord. Possibly to be identified with Jeshua[8].

(10:9; 12:8)

Azaniah
(early C5th BC)

Father of Jeshua[10].

(10:9)

Mika[3] (Mica), Rehob[2], Hashabiah[9], Zakkur[7], Shebaniah[4], Hodiah[3], Beninu
(mid C5th BC)

Levites who joined Nehemiah[2] to seal the covenant agreement to obey the Lord.

(10:11–13)

Bunni[2], Adonijah[4], Azzur[1], Hodiah[4], Anathoth[2], Nebai, Magpiash, Meshullam[17], Hezir[2], Meshezabel[2], Zadok[8], Jaddua[1], Pelatiah[3], Hanan[6], Anaiah[2], Hoshea[4], Hananiah[9], Hasshub[4], Hallohesh[2], Pilha, Shobek, Rehum[4], Hashabnah, Maaseiah[13], Ahiah, Hanan[7], Anan, Malluk[5], Harim[4]
(mid C5th BC)

Leaders of the people who joined Nehemiah[2] to seal the covenant agreement to obey the Lord.

(10:15–27)

Baanah[4]
(mid C5th BC)

Possibly to be identified with Baanah[3]. One of the leaders of the people who joined Nehemiah[2] to seal the covenant agreement to obey the Lord.

(10:27)

Athaiah
(mid C5th BC)

Son of Uzziah[5]. A provincial leader from the descendants of Judah who settled in Jerusalem after the walls were rebuilt.

(11:4)

Uzziah[5]
(early C5th BC)
Father of Athaiah. Son of
Zechariah[23].
📖 (11:4)

Zechariah[23]
(late C6th BC)
Father of Uzziah[5]. Son of
Amariah[8].
📖 (11:4)

Amariah[8]
(mid C6th BC)
Father of Zechariah[23]. Son of
Shephatiah[8].
📖 (11:4)

Shephatiah[8]
(early C6th BC)
Father of Amariah[8]. Son of
Mahalalel[2].
📖 (11:4)

Mahalalel[2]
(late C7th BC)
Father of Shephatiah[8]. Descendant
of Perez.
📖 (11:4)

Maaseiah[14]
(mid C5th BC)
Son of Baruch[3]. A provincial leader
from the descendants of Judah who
settled in Jerusalem after the walls
were rebuilt.
📖 (11:5)

Baruch[3]
(early C5th BC)
Father of Maaseiah[14]. Son of Kol-
Hezeh[2].
📖 (11:5)

Kol-Hozeh[2] (Col-Hozeh)
(late C6th BC)
Father of Baruch[3]. Son of Hazaiah.
📖 (11:5)

Hazaiah
(mid C6th BC)
Father of Kol-Hezeh[2]. Son of
Adaiah[8].
📖 (11:5)

Adaiah[8]
(early C6th BC)
Father of Hazaiah. Son of Joiarib[2].
📖 (11:5)

Joiarib[2]
(late C7th BC)
Father of Adaiah[8]. Son of
Zechariah[24].
📖 (11:5)

Zechariah[24]
(mid C7th BC)
Father of Joiarib[2]. Descendant of
Shelah[2].
📖 (11:5)

Joed
(mid C5th BC)
Father of Meshullam[5]. Son of
Pedaiah[6]. An ancestor of Sallu[1]
the Benjamite who settled in
Jerusalem after the walls were rebuilt.
📖 (11:7)

Pedaiah[6]
(early C5th BC)
Father of Joed. Son of Kolaiah[1].
📖 (11:7)

Kolaiah[1]
(late C6th BC)
Father of Pedaiah[6]. Son of
Maaseiah[15].
📖 (11:7)

Maaseiah[15]
(mid C6th BC)
Father of Kolaiah[1]. Son of Ithiel[1].
📖 (11:7)

Ithiel[1]
(early C6th BC)

Father of Maaseiah[15]. Son of Jeshaiah[6].

📖 (11:7)

Jeshaiah[6]
(late C7th BC)

Father of Ithiel[1].

📖 (11:7)

Gabbai, Sallai
(mid C5th BC)

Followers of Sallu[1] who settled in Jerusalem after the walls were rebuilt.

📖 (11:8)

Joel[12]
(mid C5th BC)

Son of Zikri[11] and chief officer of the descendants of Benjamin[1] who settled in Jerusalem after the walls were rebuilt.

📖 (11:9)

Zikri[11] (Zicri)
(early C5th BC)

Father of Joel[12].

📖 (11:9)

Judah[3]
(mid C5th BC)

Son of Hassenuah[2]. Among the descendants of Benjamin[1] who settled in Jerusalem after the walls were rebuilt. He was in charge of the New Quarter of the city.

📖 (11:9)

Hassenuah[2]
(early C5th BC)

Father of Judah[3].

📖 (11:9)

Jedaiah[5]
(mid C5th BC)

Son of Joiarib[3]. One of the priests who settled in Jerusalem after the walls were rebuilt.

📖 (11:10)

Joiarib[3]
(early C5th BC)

Father of Jedaiah[5]. His son was one of the priests who settled in Jerusalem after the walls were rebuilt.

📖 (11:10)

Jakin[4]
(mid C5th BC)

One of the priests who settled in Jerusalem after the walls were rebuilt.

📖 (11:10)

Seraiah[8]
(mid C5th BC)

Possibly to be identified with Seraiah[7]. Son of Hilkiah[7]. One of the priests who settled in Jerusalem after the walls were rebuilt.

📖 (11:11)

Hilkiah[7]
(early C5th BC)

Possibly to be identified with Hilkiah[6]. Father of Seraiah[8]. Son of Meshullam[7].

📖 (11:11)

Adaiah[9]
(mid C5th BC)

Son of Jeroham[8] (or possibly Jeroham[4]). One of the priests who settled in Jerusalem after the walls were rebuilt. *Possibly to be identified with* **Adaiah[4]** *in 1 Chronicles, p. 145.*

📖 (11:12)

Pelaliah
(late C6th BC)

Father of Jeroham[8] (or possibly Jeroham[4], see 1 Chronicles 9:12). Son of Amzi[2]. Mentioned among the ancestors of Adaiah[4], one of the priests who settled in Jerusalem after the walls were rebuilt.

📖 (11:12)

Amzi[2]
(mid C6th BC)
Father of Pelaliah. Son of
Zechariah[25].
📖 (11:12)

Zechariah[25]
(early C6th BC)
Father of Amzi[2]. Son of Pashhur[2].
📖 (11:12)

Amashsai
(mid C5th BC)
Son of Azarel[4]. One of the priests
who settled in Jerusalem after the
walls were rebuilt.
📖 (11:13)

Azarel[5]
(early C5th BC)
Father of Amashsai. Son of Ahzai.
📖 (11:13)

Ahzai
(late C6th BC)
Father of Azarel[5]. Descendant of
Meshillemoth[2].
📖 (11:13)

Meshillemoth[2]
(early C7th BC)
Ancestor of Ahzai. Son of Immer[1].
Probably to be identified with
Meshillemith *in 1 Chronicles,*
p. 146.
📖 (11:13)

Zabdiel[2]
(mid C5th BC)
Son of Haggedolim. Chief officer of
the priests who settled in Jerusalem
after the walls were rebuilt.
📖 (11:14)

Haggedolim
(early C5th BC)
Father of Zabdiel[2].
📖 (11:14)

Bunni[3]
(late C8th BC)
Father of Hashabiah[2]. Mentioned
among the ancestors of Shemaiah[5],
one of the Levites who settled in
Jerusalem after the walls were rebuilt.
📖 (11:15)

Zabdi[3]
(mid C7th BC)
Father of Mika[2]. Son of Asaph[3].
Mentioned among the ancestors of
Mattaniah[2], one of the Levites who
settled in Jerusalem after the walls
were rebuilt.
Probably to be identified with **Zikri[5]**
in 1 Chronicles, p. 146.
📖 (11:17)

Bakbukiah[1]
(mid C5th BC)
One of the Levites who settled in
Jerusalem after the walls were rebuilt.
📖 (11:17)

Abda[2]
(mid C5th BC)
Son of Shammua[3]. One of the
Levites who settled in Jerusalem after
the walls were rebuilt.
📖 (11:17)

Shammua[3]
(early C5th BC)
Father of Abda[2]. Son of Galal[3].
📖 (11:17)

Galal[3]
(late C6th BC)
Father of Shammua[3]. Descendant
of Jeduthun.
📖 (11:17)

Ziha[2], Gishpa
(mid C5th BC)
These men were placed in charge
of the temple servants who lived
on the hill of Ophel following the
repopulation of Jerusalem.
📖 (11:21)

Uzzi[5]
(mid C5th BC)

Son of Bani[8]. Chief officer of the Levites who lived in Jerusalem.

📖 (11:22)

Bani[8]
(early C6th BC)

Father of Uzzi[5]. Son of Hashabiah[10].

📖 (11:22)

Hashabiah[10]
(mid C6th BC)

Father of Bani[8]. Son of Mattaniah[2].

📖 (11:22)

Pethahiah[3]
(mid C5th BC)

Son of Meshezabel[3]. A descendant of Zerah[3]. Acted as the king's agents in the people's affairs following the repopulation of Jerusalem.

📖 (11:24)

Meshezabel[3]
(early C5th BC)

Father of Pethahiah[3].

📖 (11:24)

Ezra[2], Amariah[9], Shekaniah[9] (Shecaniah), Rehum[5], Iddo[7], Ginnethon[2], Moadiah, Bilgah[2], Sallu[2], Amok, Hilkiah[8], Jedaiah[6]
(mid C6th BC)

Leaders of the priests who returned from exile with Zerubbabel and Joshua[3].

📖 (12:1–7, 12–21)

Judah[4], Mattaniah[9]
(mid C6th BC)

Levites who returned from exile with Zerubbabel and Joshua[3].

📖 (12:8)

Unni[2]
(mid C6th BC)

One of the associates of the Levites who returned from exile with Zerubbabel and Joshua[3].

📖 (12:9)

Joiakim
(early C5th BC)

Son of Joshua[3]. Father of Eliashib[3]. He served as high priest during the days of Nehemiah[2] and Ezra[1].

📖 (12:10, 12, 26)

Joiada[2]
(late C5th BC)

Son of Eliashib[3]. Father of Jonathan[11].

📖 (12:10–11, 22)

Jonathan[11]
(early C4th BC)

Son of Joiada[2]. Father of Jaddua[2].

📖 (12:11)

Jaddua[2]
(mid C4th BC)

Son of Jonathan[11].

📖 (12:11, 22)

Meraiah
(early C5th BC)

Head of the priestly family of Seraiah[7] when Joiakim was high priest.

📖 (12:12)

Hananiah[10]
(early C5th BC)

Head of the priestly family of Jeremiah[7] when Joiakim was high priest.

📖 (12:12)

Meshullam[18]
(early C5th BC)

Head of the priestly family of Ezra[2] when Joiakim was high priest.

📖 (12:13)

Jehohanan[8]
(early C5th BC)

Head of the priestly family of
Amariah[7] when Joiakim was high
priest.

📖 (12:13)

Jonathan[12]
(early C5th BC)

Head of the priestly family of
Malluk[4] when Joiakim was high
priest.

📖 (12:14)

Joseph[5]
(early C5th BC)

Head of the priestly family of
Shekaniah[9] when Joiakim was high
priest.

📖 (12:14)

Adna[2]
(early C5th BC)

Head of the priestly family of
Harim[3] when Joiakim was high
priest.

📖 (12:15)

Helkai
(early C5th BC)

Head of the priestly family of
Meremoth[3] when Joiakim was high
priest.

📖 (12:15)

Zechariah[26]
(early C5th BC)

Head of the priestly family of Iddo[7]
when Joiakim was high priest.

📖 (12:16)

Meshullam[19]
(early C5th BC)

Head of the priestly family of
Ginnethon[1] when Joiakim was
high priest.

📖 (12:16)

Zikri[12] (Zicri)
(early C5th BC)

Head of the priestly family of
Abijah[8] when Joiakim was high
priest.

📖 (12:17)

Miniamin[2]
(mid C5th BC)

A priestly family in the days of
Nehemiah[2].

📖 (12:17)

Piltai
(early C5th BC)

Head of the priestly family of
Miniamin[2] and Moadiah when
Joiakim was high priest.

📖 (12:17)

Shammua[4]
(early C5th BC)

Head of the priestly family of
Bilgah[2] when Joiakim was high
priest.

📖 (12:18)

Jehonathan[2]
(early C5th BC)

Head of the priestly family of
Shemaiah[19] when Joiakim was
high priest.

📖 (12:18)

Mattenai[3]
(early C5th BC)

Head of the priestly family of
Joiarib[3] when Joiakim was high
priest.

📖 (12:19)

Uzzi[6]
(early C5th BC)

Head of the priestly family of
Jedaiah[6] when Joiakim was high
priest.

📖 (12:19)

Kallai
(early C5th BC)
Head of the priestly family of Sallu[2] when Joiakim was high priest.
(12:20)

Eber[5]
(early C5th BC)
Head of the priestly family of Amok when Joiakim was high priest.
(12:20)

Hashabiah[11]
(early C5th BC)
Head of the priestly family of Hilkiah[8] when Joiakim was high priest.
(12:21)

Nethanel[9]
(early C5th BC)
Head of the priestly family of Jedaiah[6] when Joiakim was high priest.
(12:21)

Johanan[8]
(mid C5th BC)
Son of Eliashib[3].
(12:22–23)

Jeshua[11]
(mid C5th BC)
Son of Kadmiel[2].
(12:24)

Bakbukiah[2], Obadiah[12], Meshullam[20]
(early C5th BC)
Temple gatekeepers who guarded the storehouses during the high priesthood of Joiakim.
(12:25)

Hoshaiah[1]
(mid C5th BC)
He participated in the celebrations when the rebuilt wall of Jerusalem was dedicated. He followed the choir that led the procession on top of the wall toward the Dung Gate, along with half the leaders of Judah.
(12:32)

Azariah[23], Ezra[3], Meshullam[21]
(mid C5th BC)
These men accompanied Hoshaiah[1] in the procession to celebrate the dedication of the rebuilt wall of Jerusalem.
(12:33)

Judah[5]
(mid C5th BC)
Possibly to be identified with Judah[4]. He accompanied Hoshaiah[1] in the procession to celebrate the dedication of the rebuilt wall of Jerusalem.
(12:34)

Benjamin[5], Shemaiah[20], Jeremiah[8]
(mid C5th BC)
These men accompanied Hoshaiah[1] in the procession to celebrate the dedication of the rebuilt wall of Jerusalem.
(12:34)

Zechariah[27]
(mid C5th BC)
Son of Jonathan[13]. Accompanied Hoshaiah[1] in the procession to celebrate the dedication of the rebuilt wall of Jerusalem.
(12:35)

Jonathan[13]
(early C5th BC)
Father of Zechariah[27]. Son of Shemaiah[21].
(12:35)

Shemaiah[21]
(late C6th BC)
Father of Jonathan[13]. Son of Mattaniah[10].
(12:35)

Mattaniah[10]
(mid C6th BC)

Father of Shemaiah[21]. Son of Micaiah[4].

📖 (12:35)

Micaiah[4]
(early C6th BC)

Father of Mattaniah[10]. Descendant of Zakkur[3].

📖 (12:35)

Shemaiah[22]
(mid C5th BC)

An associate of Zechariah[27] who accompanied Hoshaiah[1] in the procession to celebrate the dedication of the rebuilt wall of Jerusalem.

📖 (12:36)

Azarel[6]
(mid C5th BC)

An associate of Zechariah[27] who accompanied Hoshaiah[1] in the procession to celebrate the dedication of the rebuilt wall of Jerusalem.

📖 (12:36)

Milalai, Gilalai, Maai, Nethanel[10]
(mid C5th BC)

Associates of Zechariah[27] who accompanied Hoshaiah[1] in the procession to celebrate the dedication of the rebuilt wall of Jerusalem.

📖 (12:36)

Judah[6]
(mid C5th BC)

Possibly to be identified with Judah[4]. An associate of Zechariah[27] who accompanied Hoshaiah[1] in the procession to celebrate the dedication of the rebuilt wall of Jerusalem.

📖 (12:36)

Hanani[6]
(mid C5th BC)

An associate of Zechariah[27] who accompanied Hoshaiah[1] in the procession to celebrate the dedication of the rebuilt wall of Jerusalem.

📖 (12:36)

Eliakim[3], Maaseiah[16]
(mid C5th BC)

Priests with trumpets who joined the choirs and Nehemiah[2] to give joyful thanks to God when they took their places in the temple at the service to dedicate the rebuilt wall of Jerusalem.

📖 (12:41)

Miniamin[3]
(mid C5th BC)

Possibly to be identified with Miniamin[2]. One of the priests with trumpets who joined the choirs and Nehemiah[2] to give joyful thanks to God when they took their places in the temple at the service to dedicate the rebuilt wall of Jerusalem.

📖 (12:41)

Micaiah[5]
(mid C5th BC)

Possibly to be identified with Micaiah[4]. One of the priests with trumpets who joined the choirs and Nehemiah[2] to give joyful thanks to God when they took their places in the temple at the service to dedicate the rebuilt wall of Jerusalem.

📖 (12:41)

Elioenai[6], Zechariah[28]
(mid C5th BC)

Priests with trumpets who joined the choirs and Nehemiah[2] to give joyful thanks to God when they took their places in the temple at the service to dedicate the rebuilt wall of Jerusalem.

📖 (12:41)

Hananiah[11]
(mid C5th BC)

Possibly to be identified with
Hananiah[10]. One of the priests
with trumpets who joined with the
choirs and Nehemiah[2] to give joyful
thanks to God when they took their
places in the temple at the service to
dedicate the rebuilt wall of Jerusalem.

📖 (12:41)

**Maaseiah[17], Shemaiah[23],
Eleazar[7], Uzzi[7],
Jehonanan[9], Malkijah[11],
Elam[6]**
(mid C5th BC)

These men joined with the choirs
and Nehemiah[2] to give joyful
thanks to God when they took
their places in the temple at the
service to dedicate the rebuilt wall of
Jerusalem.

📖 (12:42)

Ezer[6]
(mid C5th BC)

Possibly to be identified with Ezer[5].
He joined with the choirs and
Nehemiah[2] to give joyful thanks to
God when they took their places in
the temple at the service to dedicate
the rebuilt wall of Jerusalem.

📖 (12:42)

Jezrahiah
(mid C5th BC)

Choirmaster of the two great choirs
that led the joyful celebrations when
the rebuilt wall of Jerusalem was
dedicated.

📖 (12:42)

Shelemiah[5]
(mid C5th BC)

A priest who, along with Zadok[9]
and Pedaiah[7], was put in charge
of the storehouses by Nehemiah[2]
because he was considered
trustworthy.

📖 (13:13)

Zadok[9]
(mid C5th BC)

A scribe who, along with
Shelemiah[5] and Pedaiah[7], was
put in charge of the storehouses
by Nehemiah[2] because he was
considered trustworthy.

📖 (13:13)

Pedaiah[7]
(mid C5th BC)

A Levite who, along with
Shelemiah[5] and Zadok[9], was
put in charge of the storehouses
by Nehemiah[2] because he was
considered trustworthy.

📖 (13:13)

Hanan[8]
(mid C5th BC)

Son of Zakkur[8]. He was appointed
by Nehemiah[2] as an assistant
to Shelemiah[5], Zadok[9] and
Pedaiah[7].

📖 (13:13)

Zakkur[8]
(early C5th BC)

Father of Hanan[8]. Son of
Mattaniah[11].

📖 (13:13)

Mattaniah[11]
(late C6th BC)

Father of Zakkur[8].

📖 (13:13)

Esther

Xerxes
(ruled Persia 486–465 BC)

See **Xerxes[1]** *in Ezra, p. 171.*

📖 (1:1)

Vashti
(early C5th BC)

Queen and wife of King Xerxes[1].
She was deposed from her royal

position by means of a royal decree when she refused to obey Xerxes' command to parade her beauty before the people. Esther was selected as her successor.

📖 (1:9 – 2:1)

Mehuman, Biztha
(early C5th BC)

Among the seven eunuchs who served King Xerxes[1] in his royal palace. They were sent to bring Queen Vashti to him, but she refused to come.

📖 (1:10)

Harbona
(early C5th BC)

One of seven eunuchs who served King Xerxes[1] in his royal palace. They were sent to bring Queen Vashti to him, but she refused to come. He told Xerxes about the gallows Haman had set up on which he planned to hang Mordecai.

📖 (1:10; 7:9)

Bigtha, Abagtha, Zethar, Karkas (Carcas)
(early C5th BC)

Among the seven eunuchs who served King Xerxes[1] in his royal palace. They were sent to bring Queen Vashti to him, but she refused to come.

📖 (1:10)

Karshena (Carshena), Shethar, Admatha, Tarshish[3], Meres, Marsena
(early C5th BC)

Among the seven close advisers and nobles of King Xerxes[1]. They were considered experts in the law and justice and 'understood the times'. Xerxes consulted them about what he should do about Vashti's disobedience.

📖 (1:13–14, 21)

Memukan (Memucan)
(early C5th BC)

The spokesman of the seven close advisers and nobles of King Xerxes[1]. They were considered experts in the law and justice and 'understood the times'. Xerxes consulted them about what he should do about Vashti's disobedience. Memukan acted as their spokesman and advised Xerxes to depose Vashti for fear that her example would lead other women to disobey their husbands.

📖 (1:13–14, 21)

Mordecai[2]
(early C5th BC)

Son of Jair[4]. A Benjamite who had taken up residence in Susa. He brought up his cousin Esther following the death of her parents. When Esther was taken to the king's harem, he continued to watch out for her and give her advice. He uncovered a plot to assassinate Xerxes[1] and through Esther the king was informed. He was unwilling to give Xerxes' second-in-command, Haman, respect and this led to enmity between them. Haman was determined to kill Mordecai and all his people. When Mordecai found out Haman's intentions, he enlisted Esther's help. Together they achieved Haman's downfall and Haman was hanged on the gallows that he had erected for Mordecai. Mordecai was honoured for his loyalty to the king, especially in thwarting the assassination attempt. He assumed the signet ring of authority previously owned by Haman. At his command a new edict was circulated allowing the Jews to protect themselves against their enemies. Mordecai became powerful and he led the Jewish people in the first celebration to commemorate their survival. Mordecai continued to act for his people's welfare and was highly esteemed.

📖 (2:5–10, 15, 19–23; 3:2–6; 4:1–17; 5:9 – 6:14; 8:1–2, 7–10, 15; 9:3–4, 20–23, 29–31; 10:1–3)

Jair[4]
(late C6th BC)

Father of Mordecai[2] and son of Shimei[20].

📖 (2:5)

Shimei[20]
(mid C6th BC)

Father of Jair[4]. Son of Kish[5].

📖 (2:5)

Kish[5]
(early C6th BC)

Father of Shimei[20]. Benjamite who had been taken into exile by Nebuchadnezzar.

📖 (2:5)

Hadassah
(born c.500 BC)

Alternative name for Esther (see below).

📖 (2:7)

Esther
(born c.500 BC)

Also called Hadassah. Daughter of Abihail[5]. A young Jewish orphan girl brought up in Susa by her cousin Mordecai[2]. She was very beautiful and following the demise of Vashti she was taken into Xerxes[1]'s harem. She quickly gained favour with those in charge of the harem, although she was still guided by Mordecai in her decisions. She won Xerxes' favour and he made her his queen. She informed Xerxes of a plot to kill him following information from Mordecai. When she discovered Mordecai was in mourning over Haman's plot to wipe out her people, she was initially unsure that she could help. However, Mordecai told her that her royal position gave

her unique responsibilities to help her people and she responded with resolute determination. She lured Xerxes and Haman to her banquets in a carefully planned operation. There she publicly uncovered Haman as the enemy of her people. Xerxes put Haman to death and gave Esther his estate. She then ensured that a new edict was distributed so her people could be saved. She asked Xerxes for permission for Haman's sons to be put to death. The Jews celebrated their victory and Esther wrote letters to all the provinces of the Jews confirming the celebration of Purim in memory of their survival.

📖 (2:7–22; 4:4 – 5:14; 7:1–8; 9:12–13, 29–32)

Hegai
(early C5th BC)

Official of Xerxes[1] who was in charge of his harem. He treated Esther favourably, giving her beauty treatments and special food and attendants. He put Esther in the best place in the harem.

📖 (2:8–9, 15)

Shaashgaz
(early C5th BC)

Eunuch and official of Xerxes[1] who was in charge of the concubines in another section of the harem. When Esther returned from the king she would be returned to Shaashgaz's care.

📖 (2:14)

Abihail[5]
(late C6th BC)

Father of Esther. Uncle of Mordecai[2].

📖 (2:15; 9:29)

Bigthana, Teresh
(early C5th BC)

Officials of Xerxes[1] who guarded his door. They conspired to assassinate Xerxes. However,

Mordecai[2] found out about the plot and told Esther, who warned Xerxes. They were impaled for their treachery.

📖 (2:21–23; 6:2)

Haman
(early C5th BC)

Son of Hammedatha. An Agagite whose family line was the traditional enemy of the Jews. Husband of Zeresh. Second in command to King Xerxes[1], but riddled with anger because Mordecai[2] would not recognize his authority, Haman plotted to annihilate the Jews. He erected a gallows to hang Mordecai but his plans were thwarted because Xerxes decided to honour Mordecai instead. Haman was denounced by Esther before Xerxes as the enemy of her people. Xerxes gave the order for Haman to be hanged.

📖 (3:1–15; 4:7–8; 5:4–14; 6:4 – 7:1, 6–10; 8:1–8; 9:11–15, 24–25)

Hammedatha
(late C6th BC)

Father of Haman. An Agagite.

📖 (3:1, 10; 8:5; 9:24)

Hathak (Hathach)
(early C5th BC)

One of the eunuchs whom Xerxes[1] assigned to attend Esther. When Mordecai[2] was in mourning following Haman's edict, Esther sent Hathak to find out what was wrong and he acted as a go-between for them.

📖 (4:5–17)

Zeresh
(early C5th BC)

Wife of Haman. She suggested to Haman that he should build the gallows to hang Mordecai[2] because he was causing Haman so much distress. However, when Mordecai was honoured by King Xerexes[1] she told Haman that he would come to ruin because Mordecai was a Jew.

📖 (5:10–14; 6:12–13)

Parshandatha, Dalphon, Aspatha, Poratha, Adalia, Aridatha, Parmashta, Arisai, Aridai, Vaizatha
(early C5th BC)

Haman's 10 sons who were killed by the Jews following Haman's defeat and Mordecai[2]'s rise to power.

📖 (9:7–9)

3 The Books of Poetry and Wisdom

The poetry and wisdom books of the Old Testament are varied in theme, style and origin. Sometimes Job is identified as the oldest book in the Bible, but its dating is uncertain. The book of Psalms is a compilation of poems, songs and reflections, and came together over a long period of time, reflecting Israel's worship over a long period of its history. Job and some of Psalms, along with Proverbs, Song of Songs and Ecclesiastes, are sometimes called wisdom texts. They reflect on the nature and order in the world in the context of honest, questioning faith. Their dominant theme is that the fear of the Lord is the key to true wisdom and a successful, purposeful life.

Job

Job
(? early 2nd millennium BC)

In the story in the book that bears his name, Job is a God-fearing man who lived in Uz and was blessed by God with family and possessions. However, God allowed all he had, including his health, to be stripped away from him. In this desperate sorrow Job did not waver in his commitment to God and even in his agony declared, 'I know that my redeemer lives' (19:25). His friends offered him various ways of understanding his predicament. The Lord himself talked with Job and Job recognized that God's ways are incomprehensible. Job realized he had been wrong to question God's ways and acknowledged that through this time of trial his understanding of God had developed (42:5). At the end of the story Job interceded for his friends, and the Lord brought more blessing in the latter part of Job's life than he had known in the period before his trial. In Ezekiel, Job is mentioned along with Noah[1] and Daniel[2] as examples of righteousness. The letter of James refers to Job's perseverance in suffering.

📖 (1:1 – 42:17; Ezekiel 14:14, 20; James 5:11)

Eliphaz[2], Bildad, Zophar
(? early 2nd millennium BC)

Three friends of Job who wept and mourned with him in silence when they witnessed the severity of his suffering. When they did speak, they offered Job little help because they simply reaffirmed traditional views about suffering being caused by sin. Job referred to them as 'miserable comforters'. The Lord rebuked them for not speaking about him in right ways, but Job prayed for them and they were not judged for their folly. Instead their friendship with Job was restored.

📖 (2:11–13; 4:1 – 5:27; 8:1–22; 11:1–20; 15:1–35; 18:1–21; 20:1–29; 22:1–30; 25:1–6; 42:7–9)

Elihu[5]
(? early 2nd millennium BC)

Son of Barakel. A Buzite. He was younger than Job's three other friends and waited until they had finished before he spoke to Job. Angry that the older men had been unable to refute Job, he embarked on a long discourse justifying his intervention and claiming that he was able to bring Job to a place of wisdom. His speech extolled God for his wisdom and glory, and criticized Job for his lack of reverence, humility and understanding. The critical tone of his speech preceded the Lord's own words to Job.

📖 (32:2 – 37:24)

Barakel
(? early 2nd millennium BC)

Father of Elihu[5]. From the family of Ram[3].

📖 (32:2, 6)

Ram[3]
(? early 2nd millennium BC)

The head of the family to which Elihu[5] belonged.

📖 (32:2)

Jemimah, Keziah, Keren-Happuch
(? early 2nd millennium BC)

The three beautiful daughters of Job who were born to him after he was restored. They received a share of their father's inheritance along with their brothers.

📖 (42:13–15)

Psalms

Cush[2]
(late C11th BC)

A Benjamite enemy of David about whom Psalm 7 was written.

📖 (7 title)

Abimelek[4] (Abimelech)
(late C11th BC)

Mentioned in the title of Psalm 34, which describes the occasion when David wrote this psalm. Possibly to be identified with Achish, the Philistine king of Gath (see 2 Samuel 27:2).

📖 (34 title)

Asaph[2]
(early C10th BC)

See **Asaph[2]** in 1 Chronicles, p. 137.

📖 (50; 73–83 titles)

Proverbs

Solomon
(c.990–930 BC; reigned 970–930 BC)

See **Solomon** in 2 Samuel, p. 81.

📖 (1:1; 10:1; 25:1)

Agur
(unknown)

Son of Jakeh. A wise man who spoke the words of wisdom recorded in Proverbs 30.

📖 (30:1–33)

Jakeh
(unknown)

Father of Agur.

📖 (30:1)

Ithiel[2]
(unknown)

Although the Hebrew could be understood in a number of ways it is possible that Agur's words of wisdom were addressed to an otherwise unknown man called Ithiel.

📖 (30:1)

Lemuel
(unknown)

A king whose inspired words recorded in Proverbs 31:1–9 were taught to him by his mother.

📖 (31:1)

Ecclesiastes

David
(1040–970 BC)
See **David** *in 1 Samuel, p. 73.*
📖 (1:1)

Song of Songs

Solomon
(c.990–930 BC; reigned 970–930 BC)
See **Solomon** *in 2 Samuel, p. 81.*
📖 (1:1)

4 The Prophets

The Old Testament prophets were primarily orators. Their words are recorded in the books that bear their names. Their messages were powerful and often delivered in dramatic ways. The prophets understood themselves to be God's messengers and they used poetry, rhetoric, imagery and passion to ensure their messages were heard and understood. The Old Testament prophetic literature is frequently quoted from in the New Testament, especially as a way of confirming the message and ministry of Jesus.

Isaiah

Isaiah
(late C8th BC)
See **Isaiah** in 2 Kings, p. 115.
📖 (1:1)

Shear-Jashub
(late C8th BC)
Son of Isaiah. His name is symbolic, meaning 'a remnant will return'. Isaiah was instructed to take him with him to meet Ahaz[1].
📖 (7:3)

Tabeel[2]
(early C8th BC)
Father of the man whom Pekah and Rezin[1] planned to set up as king of Judah once they had conquered Judah.
📖 (7:6)

Immanuel
This symbolic name, meaning 'God with us', was given to the son whom Isaiah predicted would be born to a young woman as a sign to Ahaz[1]. Matthew's Gospel states that these words of prophecy are fulfilled in the birth of Jesus.
📖 (7:14–17; 8:8, 10; Matthew 1:22–23)

Maher-Shalal-Hash-Baz
(born c.736 BC)
This symbolic name, meaning 'quick to the plunder, swift to the spoil', was given by Isaiah to one of his sons following the command of the Lord. It indicated the quick demise of Pekah and Rezin[1].
📖 (8:1–4)

Zechariah[29]
(late C8th BC)
Son of Jeberekiah. Alongside Uriah[2] he acted as a witness when Isaiah recorded the name Maher-Shalal-Hash-Baz, which the Lord had given him for his son.
📖 (8:2)

Jeberekiah
(mid C8th BC)
Father of Zechariah[29].
📖 (8:2)

Sargon
(ruled Assyria 722–705 BC)
Son of Tiglath-Pileser III. Under his command Ashdod fell to the Assyrians, and Isaiah warned the people of Assyria's strength. Sargon was king of Assyria when Samaria fell.
📖 (20:1)

Timeline of the prophets

This timeline shows the relationship between Judah's history and the prophets' ministry.

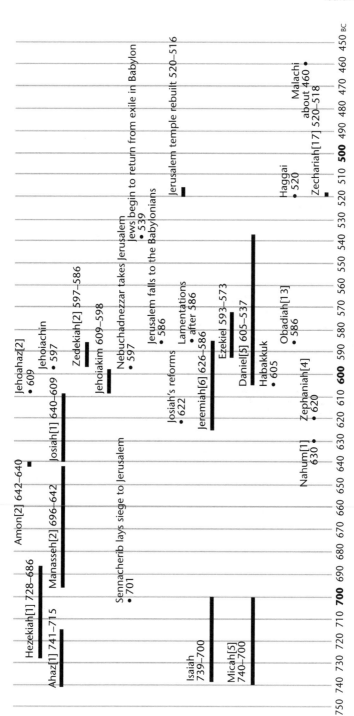

Ahaz[1] 741–715

Hezekiah[1] 728–686

Manasseh[2] 696–642

Amon[2] 642–640

Josiah[1] 640–609

Jehoahaz[2]
• 609

Jehoiachin

Jehoiakim 609–598

Zedekiah[2] 597–586

Isaiah
739–700

Micah[5]
740–700

Sennacherib lays siege to Jerusalem
• 701

Nahum[1]
630 •

Zephaniah[4]
• 620

Josiah's reforms
• 622

Jeremiah[6] 626–586

Nebuchadnezzar takes Jerusalem
• 597

Jerusalem falls to the Babylonians
• 586

Lamentations
• after 586

Ezekiel 593–573

Daniel[5] 605–537

Habakkuk
• 605

Obadiah[13]
• 586

Jews begin to return from exile in Babylon
• 539

Jerusalem temple rebuilt 520–516

Haggai
• 520

Malachi
about 460 •

Zechariah[17] 520–518

750 740 730 720 710 **700** 690 680 670 660 650 640 630 620 610 **600** 590 580 570 560 550 540 530 520 510 **500** 490 480 470 460 450 BC

Hezekiah
(c.740–686 BC; reigned 728–686 BC)
See **Hezekiah[1]** *in 2 Kings, p. 111.*
📖 (36:1)

Jeremiah

Jeremiah
(c.640–after 586 BC)
See **Jeremiah[6]** *in 2 Chronicles, p. 167.*
📖 (1:1)

Hilkiah[9]
(early C7th BC)
Father of Jeremiah[6].
📖 (1:1)

Zephaniah[3]
(early C6th BC)
Son of Maaseiah[18]. A priest who acted as an intermediary between Zedekiah[2] and Jeremiah[6]. Zedekiah sent him with Pashhur[1] to Jeremiah[6] in the hope that Jeremiah would confirm that Nebuchadnezzar would not attack Judah. However, the message they received confirmed that the Lord would deliver Judah into the hands of Nebuchadnezzar. Later Zedekiah sent him with Jehukal to ask Jeremiah to pray for Judah.
📖 (21:1–7; 29:25–29; 37:3)

Maaseiah[18]
(late C7th BC)
Father of Zephaniah[3]. Son of Shallum[14].
📖 (21:1; 29:25; 35:4; 37:3)

Micah[5]
(prophesied c.740–700 BC)
See **Micah[5]** *the prophet in Micah, p. 214.*
📖 (26:18)

Uriah[5]
(prophesied late C7th BC)
Son of Shemaiah[24]. A prophet from Kiriath Jearim. His message to Jerusalem echoed that of Jeremiah[6], which angered King Jehoiakim. Although he fled to Egypt, Elnathan[5] and some other men sent by Jehoiakim pursued him there. He was brought back to Jehoiakim and was killed and buried in a common grave. His death demonstrated the danger of Jeremiah's own position.
📖 (26:20–24)

Shemaiah[24]
(mid C7th BC)
Father of Uriah[5].
📖 (26:20)

Elnathan[5]
(late C7th BC)
Son of Akbor[3]. One of the officials of King Jehoiakim. He went to Egypt to pursue Uriah[5]. Later these officials advised Baruch[4] and Jeremiah[6] to go into hiding when the king was about to learn of the contents of the scroll containing Jeremiah's prophecy against Jerusalem. Elnathan was among those who urged the king not to burn this scroll, but his advice was ignored.
📖 (26:22; 36:11–26)

Hananiah[12]
(prophesied c.593 BC)
Son of Azzur[2]. A prophet from Gibeon whom Jeremiah[6] exposed as a false prophet who only delivered the lies the people wanted to hear. Jeremiah told him that God would bring about his death and he died that same year.
📖 (28:1–17)

Azzur[2]
(late C7th BC)
Father of Hananiah[12].
📖 (28:1)

Elasah[2]
(early C6th BC)

Son of Shaphan[1]. Along with Gemariah[1], he took Jeremiah[6]'s letter from Jerusalem to the exiles in Babylon.

📖 (29:3)

Gemariah[1]
(early C6th BC)

Son of Hilkiah[10]. Along with Elasah[2], he took Jeremiah[6]'s letter from Jerusalem to the exiles in Babylon.

📖 (29:3)

Hilkiah[10]
(late C7th BC)

Father of Gemariah[1]. Possibly to be identified with Hilkiah[6] or Hilkiah[7].

📖 (29:3)

Ahab[2]
(early C6th BC)

Son of Kolaiah[2]. A false prophet. In his letter to the Jews in exile, Jeremiah[6] announced that the Lord would put Ahab to death at the hands of Nebuchadnezzar because of his lies and immorality.

📖 (29:20–23)

Kolaiah[2]
(late C7th BC)

Father of Ahab[2].

📖 (29:21)

Zedekiah[5]
(early C6th BC)

Son of Maaseiah[19]. A false prophet. In his letter to the Jews in exile Jeremiah[6] announced that the Lord would put Zedekiah to death at the hands of Nebuchadnezzar because of his lies and immorality.

📖 (29:20–23)

Maaseiah[19]
(late C7th BC)

Father of Zedekiah[5].

📖 (29:21)

Shemaiah[25]
(early C6th BC)

A Nehelamite. A false prophet who told lies and stirred up trouble for Jeremiah[6]. Jeremiah prophesied that the Lord would bring an end to his descendants.

📖 (29:24–32)

Jehoiada[4]
(early C6th BC)

A priest in Jeremiah[6]'s time who was succeeded by Zephaniah[3]. *Possibly the same person as* **Jehoiada[2]** *in 2 Kings, p. 107.*

📖 (29:26)

Hanamel
(early C6th BC)

Cousin of Jeremiah[6] who owned a field that Jeremiah bought for 17 shekels of silver. It was a symbolic act to illustrate the message that despite Jerusalem being besieged by Babylon, its prosperity would one day be restored by the Lord.

📖 (32:9, 12)

Baruch[4]
(late C7th BC)

Son of Neriah. Jeremiah[6]'s scribe and assistant. He witnessed the symbolic actions that accompanied Jeremiah's prophetic words. He was responsible for the writing down and the reading of the scroll which Jehoiakim burnt. He went into hiding with Jeremiah and wrote down all Jeremiah's words again on the replacement scroll. On another occasion Jeremiah dictated words that Baruch wrote down which assured Baruch himself that God would protect his life.

📖 (32:12–13; 36:4–32; 43:3, 6; 45:1–5)

Neriah
(mid C7th BC)

Son of Mahseiah. Father of Baruch[4] and Seraiah[10].

📖 (32:12; 36:4, 8, 14, 32; 43:3, 6; 45:1; 51:59)

Mahseiah
(early C7th BC)

Father of Neriah.

📖 (32:12; 51:59)

Jaazaniah[2]
(late C7th BC)

Son of Jeremiah[9]. A Rekabite and descendant of Jehonadab. This family line had been faithful to the instructions given to them by their ancestor for many generations. Jeremiah[6] contrasted their faithfulness with the unfaithfulness of the people of Judah and the inhabitants of Jerusalem.

📖 (35:1–19)

Jeremiah[9]
(mid C7th BC)

Father of Jaazaniah[2]. Son of Habazziniah. A Rekabite and descendant of Jehonadab.

📖 (35:3)

Habazziniah
(early C7th BC)

Father of Jeremiah[9]. A Rekabite and descendant of Jehonadab.

📖 (35:3)

Hanan[9]
(late C7th BC)

Son of Igdaliah. A man of God whose sons had a room assigned for their use in the house of God next to the room of the officials. It was to this room that Jeremiah[6] took the Rekabite family.

📖 (35:4)

Igdaliah
(mid C7th BC)

Father of Hanan[9].

📖 (35:4)

Shallum[14]
(mid C7th BC)

Father of Maaseiah[18].

📖 (35:4)

Gemariah[2]
(late C7th BC)

Son of Shaphan[1]. Father of Micaiah[6]. He had a room in the upper courtyard at the entrance of the New Gate of the temple. It was here that Baruch[4] read the contents of the scroll containing the words of Jeremiah[6]. Gemariah was among those who urged the king not to burn this scroll but his advice was ignored.

📖 (36:10–11, 25)

Micaiah[6]
(late C7th BC)

Son of Gemariah[2]. He listened to the words that Baruch[4] read from the scroll Jeremiah[6] had dictated and reported the contents of the scroll to the royal officials.

📖 (36:11, 13)

Elishama[6]
(late C7th BC)

An official of Jehoiakim who served as secretary. He was among those who heard Micaiah[6]'s report about the content of the scroll dictated by Jeremiah[6] to Baruch[4].

📖 (36:12, 20)

Delaiah[5]
(late C7th BC)

Son of Shemaiah[26]. He was among those who heard Micaiah[6]'s report about the content of the scroll dictated by Jeremiah[6] to Baruch[4]. He was among those who urged the king not to burn this scroll but his advice was ignored.

📖 (36:12, 25)

Shemaiah[26]
(mid C7th BC)

Father of Delaiah[5].

📖 (36:12)

Zedekiah[6]
(late C7th BC)

Son of Hananiah[13]. He was among those who heard Micaiah[6]'s report about the content of the scroll dictated by Jeremiah[6] to Baruch[4].

📖 (36:12)

Hananiah[13]
(mid C7th BC)

Father of Zedekiah[6].

📖 (36:12)

Jehudi
(late C7th BC)

Son of Nethaniah[4]. He was sent by the officials of Zedekiah[6] to find Baruch[4] and his scroll so he could read it to them.

📖 (36:14, 20–24)

Nethaniah[4]
(mid C7th BC)

Father of Jehudi. Son of Shelemiah[6].

📖 (36:14)

Shelemiah[6]
(early C7th BC)

Father of Nethaniah[4]. Son of Cushi[1].

📖 (36:14)

Cushi[1]
(late C8th BC)

Father of Shelemiah[6].

📖 (36:14)

Jerahmeel[3]
(late C7th BC)

Son of Jehoiakim (or possibly a more distant relative). Jehoiakim sent him with Seraiah[9] and Shelemiah[7] to arrest Jeremiah[6] and Baruch[4] on account of the scroll they were responsible for, but Jeremiah and Baruch could not be found.

📖 (36:26)

Seraiah[9]
(late C7th BC)

Son of Azriel[3]. Jehoiakim sent him with Jerahmeel[3] and Shelemiah[7] to arrest Jeremiah[6] and Baruch[4] on account of the scroll they were responsible for, but Jeremiah and Baruch could not be found.

📖 (36:26)

Azriel[3]
(mid C7th BC)

Father of Seraiah[9].

📖 (36:26)

Shelemiah[7]
(late C7th BC)

Son of Abdeel. Jehoiakim sent him with Jerahmeel[3] and Seraiah[9] to arrest Jeremiah[6] and Baruch[4] on account of the scroll they were responsible for, but Jeremiah and Baruch could not be found.

📖 (36:26)

Abdeel
(mid C7th BC)

The father of Shelemiah[7].

📖 (36:26)

Jehukal (Jehucal)
(early C6th BC)

Son of Shelemiah[8]. After Nebuchadnezzar had made Zedekiah[2] king of Judah, Zedekiah sent Jehukal to Jeremiah[6] to ask him to pray for him. Along with other royal officials he became responsible for putting Jeremiah in a cistern to die.

📖 (37:3; 38:1–6)

Shelemiah[8]
(late C7th BC)

Father of Jehukal.

📖 (37:3; 38:1)

Irijah
(early C6th BC)

Son of Shelemiah[9]. The captain of the guard who challenged

Jeremiah[6] when he attempted to leave Jerusalem by the Benjamin Gate. He accused Jeremiah of deserting to the Babylonians. Jeremiah protested his innocence but Irijah would not listen to him and arrested him: this resulted in Jeremiah being beaten and imprisoned.

📖 (37:13–14)

Shelemiah[9]
(late C7th BC)

Father of Irijah. Son of Hananiah[14].

📖 (37:13)

Hananiah[14]
(mid C7th BC)

Father of Shelemiah[9]. Grandfather of Irijah.

📖 (37:13)

Shephatiah[9]
(early C6th BC)

Son of Mattan[2]. Along with other royal officials he became responsible for putting Jeremiah[6] in a cistern to die.

📖 (38:1–6)

Mattan[2]
(late C7th BC)

Father of Shephatiah[9].

📖 (38:1)

Gedaliah[4]
(early C6th BC)

Son of Pashhur[4]. Along with other royal officials he became responsible for putting Jeremiah[6] in a cistern to die.

📖 (38:1–6)

Pashhur[4]
(late C7th BC)

Father of Gedaliah[4].

📖 (38:1)

Malkijah[12]
(early C6th BC)

King Zedekiah[2]'s son who owned the cistern into which Jeremiah was lowered.

📖 (38:6)

Ebed-Melek (Ebed-Melech)
(early C6th BC)

A Cushite official in the royal palace of Zedekiah[2]. He pleaded with Zedekiah for Jeremiah[6]'s life and lifted Jeremiah up out of the cistern.

📖 (38:7–12)

Jonathan[14]
(early C6th BC)

Owner of a house known to Jeremiah[6] and Zedekiah[2].

📖 (38:26)

Nergal-Sharezer[1], Nebo-Sarsekim, Nergal-Sharezer[2]
(early C6th BC)

High-ranking Babylonian officials mentioned in Jeremiah[6]'s account of the fall of Jerusalem. When Zedekiah[2] and his army saw them taking their seats in the Middle Gate when the wall of Jerusalem was breached, Zedekiah's army fled in fear. They arranged for Jeremiah's release from the courtyard of the guard.

📖 (39:3, 13)

Nebushazban
(early C6th BC)

A high-ranking Babylonian official involved in Jeremiah[6]'s release from the courtyard of the guard.

📖 (39:13)

Jonathan[15]
(early C6th BC)

Son of Kareah. He was among the army officials who went to Gedaliah[1] at Mizpah to seek reassurance.

📖 (40:8)

Ephai
(early C6th BC)

A Netophathite. His sons were among the army officials who went to Gedaliah[1] at Mizpah to seek reassurance.

📖 (40:8)

Baalis
(early C6th BC)

King of the Ammonites. Johanan[1] warned Gedaliah[1] that Baalis had commissioned Ishmael[2] to kill him.

📖 (40:14)

Jezaniah/Azariah[24]
(early C6th BC)

Son of Hoshaiah[2]. One of the army officers who led the people of Mizpah into Egypt to escape the Babylonians. They asked Jeremiah[6] to pray for them so they would know God's will. But when Jeremiah told them not to go down to Egypt but to stay in Judah, they disobeyed the word of the Lord.

📖 (42:1 – 43:7)

Hoshaiah[2]
(late C7th BC)

Father of Jezaniah.

📖 (42:1)

Azariah[24]
(early C6th BC)

See **Jezaniah** above.

📖 (42:1 – 43:7)

Seraiah[10]
(early C6th BC)

Son of Neriah. Zedekiah[2]'s staff officer who accompanied him to Babylon in the fourth year of his reign. Jeremiah[6] sent him with a scroll that spoke of the disaster that would befall Babylon. Seraiah was instructed to read it aloud and then throw the scroll into the Euphrates as a sign that Babylon would fall and never rise again.

📖 (51:59–64)

Lamentations

The names mentioned in this book have already been listed under an earlier book.

Ezekiel

Ezekiel
(c.622–after 573 BC)

Son of Buzi. From a priestly family, he served as a prophet to the exiles in Babylon. His prophecies are recorded in the book of Ezekiel. The first three chapters of the book of Ezekiel bear witness to his call to his prophetic role which came in the form of a vision in which God told Ezekiel to eat a scroll. The initial messages he received related to the people's rebellion and the Lord warned him that his words would not be heeded. Ezekiel was depressed by his task. As his ministry progressed, his message was more readily received. His messages were sometimes delivered through dramatic and symbolic actions. His prophecies called God's people to repentance but also reassured them that God was with them in exile and that he would take the initiative to restore them to a new Jerusalem. His life was not always easy and when his own wife died he was not permitted to mourn for her. This is one example of how Ezekiel's life and message were often intertwined because God's word to his people at this time concerned the fact that they would not mourn when the temple in Jerusalem was desecrated. The Lord refers to Ezekiel as 'the son of man', which indicates his role as God's messenger.

📖 (1:1 – 48:35)

Buzi
(mid C7th BC)

Father of Ezekiel.

📖 (1:3)

Jaazaniah[3]
(early C6th BC)

Son of Shaphan[2]. Stood among the 70 elders of Israel in Ezekiel's vision.

📖 (8:11)

Shaphan[2]
(late C7th BC) .

Father of Jaazaniah[3].

📖 (8:11)

Jaazaniah[4]
(early C6th BC)

Son of Azzur[3]. A leader of the people who stood among the 25 men at the gate of the house of the Lord in Ezekiel's vision.

📖 (11:1)

Azzur[3]
(late C7th BC)

Father of Jaazaniah[4].

📖 (11:1)

Pelatiah[4]
(early C6th BC)

Son of Benaiah[12]. A leader of the people who stood among the 25 men at the gate of the house of the Lord in Ezekiel's vision.

📖 (11:1)

Benaiah[12]
(late C7th BC)

Father of Pelatiah[4].

📖 (11:1)

Daniel[4]
(unknown)

Mentioned in Ezekiel's prophecy alongside Noah[1] and Job. Presumably a man known from antiquity for his righteousness.

📖 (14:14, 20)

Oholah (symbolic)
The older of two prostitute sisters named in a divine speech received by Ezekiel. She was symbolic of Samaria, who lusted after the Assyrians, who in turn abused her and killed her.

📖 (23:1–49)

Oholibah (symbolic)
The younger of two prostitute sisters named in a divine speech received by Ezekiel. She was symbolic of Jerusalem. Although she saw the fate of Oholah, she acted with more depravity and she lusted after the Babylonians. All her lovers would abuse, mutilate and destroy her.

📖 (23:1–49)

Gog[2] (symbolic)
A chief prince of Meshek and Tubal, in the land of Magog. Ezekiel prophesied against him that when he attacked the land of Israel, God would respond with fierce anger and would purify the land by wiping out Gog and all the nations that side with him. Used symbolically in Revelation.

📖 (38:2 – 39:16; Revelation 20:8)

Daniel

Nebuchadnezzar
(ruled Babylon 605–562 BC)

See **Nebuchadnezzar** *in 2 Kings, p. 119.*

📖 (1:1)

Ashpenaz
(late C7th BC)

Chief court official of Nebuchadnezzar. He brought Daniel[5] and his companions into the king's service and gave them their Babylonian names.

📖 (1:3–7)

Daniel[5]
(c.620–after 537 BC)

Also known by his Babylonian name Belteshazzar, which was assigned to him by Ashpenaz. Chosen because of his handsome appearance and aptitude for learning, he was brought into the service of Nebuchadnezzar. During his three-year training programme he refused to eat meat or drink wine because he wanted to retain ritual purity. God blessed Daniel with great learning and also the ability to interpret dreams and visions. He interpreted the dream of Nebuchadnezzar, so preserving his life and the lives of all the wise men in Babylon. Nebuchadnezzar recognized the greatness of Daniel's God, and Daniel himself was promoted in the royal court and given charge over all the wise men. He interpreted Nebuchadnezzar's second dream as well as the writing on the wall, which his son Belshazzar needed to be interpreted, and this brought him further honour. However, when Darius[2] the Mede took over the kingdom, his officials were jealous of Daniel's popularity and they conspired against him. They advised Darius to decree that for 30 days everyone in his kingdom should worship him alone. Daniel continued to pray publicly to God three times every day and was thrown into the lions' den. To Darius's delight Daniel was protected by his God and was released from the den of lions the following morning. Daniel received a series of dreams and visions that highlighted God's protection for his people despite the strength of the nations around them. They anticipate the final victory of God whose kingdom is eternal, not temporary like earthly kingdoms. Daniel remained in Babylonian exile for over 60 years. Jesus referred to Daniel's prophecies when he spoke about the destruction of the temple and the end times.

📖 (1:1 – 12:13; Matthew 24:15)

Hananiah[15], Mishael[3], Azariah[25]
(born late C7th BC)

Also known respectively by the Babylonian names Shadrach, Meshach and Abednego. These men from Judah accompanied Daniel[5] when he was brought into the service of Nebuchadnezzar. Like Daniel they were handsome, with an aptitude for learning, and embarked on three years' training, which included privileges that they refused such as being given food and wine from the king's table. God blessed these men with great understanding and insight, which was duly recognized by Nebuchadnezzar, who welcomed them into his service. When their lives were threatened by the king's decree that all the wise men should be put to death, Daniel went straight to these friends to ask them to plead to God for mercy. Following Daniel's successful interpretation of the king's dream, they became administrators over the whole province of Babylon. However, when Nebuchadnezzar made his gold image and demanded that all his subjects bow down and worship it, these men refused to do so. Their refusal to commit idolatry meant they were thrown into a blazing furnace. God protected them in the furnace and the flames did not hurt them. Nebuchadnezzar led the praise to the Most High God that these men served and who had delivered them by his angel.

📖 (1:3–20; 2:17, 49; 3:12–30)

Belteshazzar, Shadrach, Meshach, Abednego
(born late C7th BC)

The Babylonian names assigned to Daniel[5], Hananiah[15], Mishael[3] and Azariah[25] by Ashpenaz.

📖 (1:6)

Arioch[2]
(late C7th BC)

The commander of Nebuchadnezzar's guard. He was sent out by the king to put to death all the wise men of Babylon because none had been able to explain the king's dream. When he met Daniel[5], he explained why the king was so angry and Daniel was able to intervene.

📖 (2:14–15)

Belshazzar
(acting king 553–539 BC)

Son of Nabonidus. When he became king of Babylonia, he held a banquet for his nobles, during which he was overcome with fear when a hand appeared and wrote on the wall of the royal palace. None of his advisors were able to interpret the writing but his wife recommended Daniel[5]'s services. Daniel interpreted the dream, indicating that God would take away his kingdom and divide it between the Medes and the Persians. This punishment was a result of his lack of humility because he had set himself up against the Lord.

Belshazzar promoted Daniel as third in the kingdom but that very night he was killed and Darius took over his kingdom.

📖 (5:1–30; 7:1)

Darius[2]
(born c.600 BC)

Son of Xerxes[2]. Nothing more is known about a king with this name, so he has been variously identified with other known rulers, including Cyrus. A Mede who at the age of 62 took over the Babylonian kingdom upon Belshazzar's death.

📖 (5:30 – 6:28; 9:1; 11:1)

Angels

The Bible contains about 300 references to angels. Two angels are named:

• the archangel Gabriel, who appeared to Daniel[5] to interpret the vision of the end times and give him insight and understanding (Daniel 8:16; 9:21). In Jewish literature of the period between the Old Testament and the New Testament, he is one of the angels that were viewed as standing before God presenting the prayers of the saints. In the New Testament, he appeared to Zechariah[30] to prophesy the birth of John[1] the Baptist (Luke 1:19), and then to Mary to prophesy the birth of Jesus (Luke 1:26).

• the archangel Michael[11], the 'great ruler who protects the people of God' (Daniel 10:13, 21; 12:1), the one who disputed with Satan about Moses' body (Jude 9), and who defeats Satan and his forces (Revelation 12:7).

The Apocrypha also mentions Raphael (Tobit 3:17; 8:3; 12:6–21).

Gabriel (angel)
See panel above.

Xerxes[2]
(unknown)

Father of Darius[2], the Mede.

📖 (9:1)

Michael[11] (angel)
See panel above.

Hosea

Hosea
(prophesied c.755–725 BC)

Son of Beeri[2]. A prophet during the reigns of Uzziah[1], Jotham[2], Ahaz[1], Hezekiah[1] and Jeroboam[2] whose prophecies are recorded in the book that bears his name. His ministry took place in the northern kingdom and emphasized God's remarkable love for his people and his capacity to forgive them despite their sin. His message was reinforced by his own family life: his wife, Gomer[2], was a prostitute and an adulteress but the Lord told

Hosea to love her. His children were given names which pointed to the fact that Israel had broken her covenant with God. Hosea's message culminates in his plea that Israel turn back to the Lord and experience his loving forgiveness. Paul refers to Hosea's prophecy to demonstrate how God has made his glory known to his people, who are the objects of his mercy.

📖 (1:1 – 14:9; Romans 9:25–26)

Beeri[2]
(early C8th BC)

Father of Hosea.

📖 (1:1)

Gomer[2]
(mid C8th BC)

Daughter of Diblaim. A prostitute. Hosea married her at the Lord's instruction. She continued in her promiscuous ways after their marriage, but Hosea was instructed to show his love to her again. She bore him three children, who were given symbolic names. Her unfaithfulness symbolized the unfaithfulness of Israel, while Hosea's persistent love for her symbolized God's undying love for his people.

📖 (1:3–8; 3:1–3)

Diblaim
(early C8th BC)

Father of Gomer[2].

📖 (1:3)

Jezreel[2]
(born mid C8th BC)

First son of Hosea and Gomer[2]. His name symbolized that God would act to punish Israel for the great evil that Jehu had committed when he wiped out the family of Ahab in Jezreel (2 Kings 10).

📖 (1:3–5)

Lo-Ruhamah
(born mid C8th BC)

Daughter of Hosea and Gomer[2],

born after Jezreel[2]. Her name means 'not loved' and symbolized the broken relationship between God and Israel.

📖 (1:6–7)

Lo-Ammi
(born mid C8th BC)

Son of Hosea and Gomer[2], born after Lo-Ruhamah. His name means 'not my people' and symbolized the broken relationship between God and Israel.

📖 (1:8–9)

Shalman
(unknown)

Mentioned in Hosea's prophecy as being responsible for the destruction of Beth Arbel, including the violent deaths of women and children. Possibly an Assyrian king.

📖 (10:14)

Joel

Joel[13]
(uncertain; perhaps C5th BC)

Son of Pethuel. Nothing else is known about this prophet except his prophecies, recorded in the book that bears his name, which point to coming judgment and then blessing for God's people who turn away from their sin. They anticipate 'the Day of the Lord' when God will intervene decisively on behalf of his people. There are some allusions to his prophecies in the book of Revelation. Peter indicated that the words of Joel 2:28–29, regarding the pouring out of the Holy Spirit, were fulfilled on the Day of Pentecost.

📖 (1:1 – 3:21; Acts 2:16–21)

Pethuel
(unknown)

Father of Joel[13].

📖 (1:1)

Amos

Amos[1]
(prophesied c.765–755 BC)

A shepherd and tender of fig trees from Tekoa. He prophesied during the days of Uzziah[1] and Jeroboam[2] and he addressed the northern kingdom of Israel. His message, recorded in the book that bears his name, was that Israel had not repented of her sins despite the warnings they had received. Amos advised that repentance was required and that faith should be seen practically in social justice. Amos predicted that the people would suffer in exile but God would restore them to their land.

📖 (1:1 – 9:15)

Amaziah[4]
(mid C8th BC)

Priest of Bethel. He reported Amos[1] to Jeroboam[2] for his message that Israel would go into exile. He told Amos to go back to Judah and stop his ministry at Bethel. Amos responded that God had given him his message and he repeated it, declaring that Amaziah himself would die in exile.

📖 (7:10–17)

Obadiah

Obadiah[13]
(prophesied c.585 BC)

A prophet whose vision is recorded in the book that bears his name. It relates to the early days of the exile and concerns God's judgment on Edom and the coming Day of the Lord when God's people would be delivered and his kingdom would be established.

📖 (1–21)

Jonah

Jonah[1]
(prophesied c.760 BC)

Son of Amittai. A prophet from Gath Hepher, a village north of Nazareth. He was instrumental in Jeroboam[2]'s decisions to restore the boundaries of Israel to what they were before Aram took territory. The book of Jonah tells the story of Jonah running away from God following God's instruction to him to preach in the city of Nineveh. He took a ship heading for Tarshish but a storm broke out. Jonah was thrown overboard and found himself in the belly of a great fish. Jonah offered a prayer of contrition from inside the fish. He was spat up onto dry land and the Lord instructed him again to go to Nineveh, and this time he obeyed. The people there repented and turned to the Lord. Jonah had another lesson to learn: God is compassionate to those who repent. Jesus referred to the story of Jonah when he spoke about his own burial in the tomb for three days and nights. He suggested that Nineveh's repentance compared favourably with the stubborn responses to his own ministry.

📖 (1:1 – 4:11; 2 Kings 14:25; Matthew 12:39–41; 16:4; Luke 11:29–32)

Micah

Micah[5]
(prophesied c.740–700 BC)

From Moresheth. A prophet whose ministry spanned the reigns of Jotham[2], Ahaz[1] and Hezekiah[1]. He was particularly concerned with righting injustice and rebuking the leadership of God's people. At the same time he was mindful of future hope and salvation because of God's merciful and compassionate nature. His prophecies, and the way they were heeded by Hezekiah, were remembered by the elders who spoke up to protect Jeremiah[6] from the growing opposition he faced in the light of his prophecies announcing defeat for Judah. His prophecy is referred to in Matthew's Gospel, as it relates to Bethlehem as the place of the Messiah's birth.

📖 (1:1 – 7:20; Jeremiah 26:18; Matthew 2:3–6)

Nahum

Nahum[1]
(prophesied c.630 BC)

From a town called Elkosh, an unknown location. His prophecy, recorded in the book that bears his name, emphasizes God's sovereignty over the nations and his care for those who trust him. In contrast, Nahum predicted the fatal fall of Nineveh, the capital of the Assyrian Empire, because of her idolatry and wickedness.

📖 (1:1 – 3:19)

Habakkuk

Habakkuk
(prophesied c.605 BC)

A prophet living at the time when the Babylonians were assuming power and whose prophecies are recorded in the book that bears his name. He questioned God about why he allowed injustice to thrive and how the Babylonians could be used to execute judgment on Judah. Despite his questions, he reaffirmed in song his personal confidence in God's sovereignty, finding his strength in God's saving mercy.

📖 (1:1 – 3:19)

Zephaniah

Zephaniah[4]
(prophesied c.620 BC)

Son of Cushi[2]. A prophet during the reign of Josiah[1] whose prophecies are recorded in the book that bears his name. He describes a forthcoming day of the Lord which demonstrates God's just judgment alongside his love and restoration for the faithful. Like Amos[1], he was concerned with social injustice and calls God's people to repentance.

📖 (1:1 – 3:20)

Cushi[2]
(mid C7th BC)

Father of Zephaniah[4]. Son of Gedaliah[5].

📖 (1:1)

Gedaliah[5]
(early C7th BC)

Father of Cushi[2]. Son of Amariah[10].

📖 (1:1)

Amariah[10]
(late C8th BC)

Father of Gedaliah[5]. Son of Hezekiah[3].

📖 (1:1)

Hezekiah[3]
(mid C8th BC)

Father of Amariah[10]. Some suggest the reference here is to Hezekiah[1] king of Judah, suggesting that Zephaniah[4] was of royal descent.

📖 (1:1)

Haggai

Haggai
(prophesied 520 BC)

Prophet who encouraged God's people to rebuild the temple in Jerusalem. His prophecies are recorded in the book that bears his name and are all delivered in Darius[1]'s reign during a four-month period in 520 BC. His prophecies anticipate a messianic age when the earthly temple in Jerusalem would be surpassed.

📖 (1:1 – 2:23; Ezra 5:1; 6:14–15)

Zechariah

Zechariah[17]
(prophesied c.520–518 BC)

Son of Berekiah[7]. Grandson of Iddo[5]. Prophet and priest who returned with the exiles from Babylon and encouraged God's people to rebuild the temple in Jerusalem. His prophecies are recorded in the book that bears his name and are delivered during Darius[1]'s reign in a two-year period spanning 520–518 BC. His prophecies consist of visions and oracles which anticipate the time when the Messiah would come. These oracles have 'apocalyptic' qualities (i.e. they uncover truths about a future time through symbolic descriptions and language). Zechariah's prophecies are frequently quoted in the New Testament.

📖 (1:1 – 14:21; Ezra 5:1; 6:14–15; see Matthew 21:5; 26:15, 28, 31; 27:9; Mark 14:27; Luke 22:20; John 12:15; 19:37; 1 Corinthians 11:25; Hebrews 13:20)

Berekiah[7]
(early C6th BC)

Father of Zechariah[17].

📖 (1:1)

Heldai[2] (Helem[2], NIV 2011 footnote), Tobijah[2], Jedaiah[7]
(late C6th BC)

Men who had returned from exile in Babylon. They provided gold and silver for the crown that Zechariah[17] placed on the head of Josiah[2] the high priest. Their names became associated with the crown, which served as a memorial in the temple.

📖 (6:9–14)

Josiah[2]
(late C6th BC)

Son of Zephaniah[5]. He owned the house where Zechariah[17] went to crown Joshua[3] as high priest. His name became associated with the crown, which served as a memorial in the temple. He is also called 'Hen', which means 'the gracious one'.

📖 (6:10, 14)

Zephaniah[5]
(mid C6th BC)

Father of Josiah[2].

📖 (6:10)

Hen
(late C6th BC)

See **Josiah[2]** *in Zechariah, p. 216 (above).*

📖 (6:14)

Sharezer[2], Regem-Melek (Regem-Melech)
(late C6th BC)

Envoys sent from Bethel to Jerusalem to ask about whether they should keep the fast in the fifth month as their ancestors had done. Zechariah[17] challenged them instead about the importance of true justice and devotion towards God.

📖 (7:2–3)

Malachi

Malachi
(prophesied c.460 BC)

A prophet whose words are recorded in the last book of the Old Testament. The book is designed around a series of rhetorical questions which raise issues relating to God's loyalty to his people and their responding lack of faithfulness.

The prophet rebuked the people for their inconsistent lifestyles. He rebuked unfaithful and dishonest priests and called the people to be faithful in their offerings. However, he looked forward to 'the Day of the Lord' when evildoers would be consumed by fire but the faithful remnant of his people would be preserved as God's treasured possession.

📖 (1:1 – 4:6)

5 The Gospels and Acts

The New Testament opens with four accounts of the life and ministry of Jesus Christ. These accounts are followed by a record of what happened after Jesus' death, resurrection and ascension. From these records we learn about the great impact of Jesus throughout his lifetime and in the immediate subsequent years. We are introduced to his followers, who were so inspired by Jesus' life among them that they continued to spread his message even when faced with persecution and martyrdom. They, along with other notable converts like Paul, travelled to spread the good news and founded churches that safeguarded the Christian message. This was achieved through the presence of the Holy Spirit among them.

Matthew

Jesus
(c.5 BC–AD 33)

Son of Mary[1] and Joseph[6]. Born in Bethlehem in Judea during a census but grew up in Nazareth. His siblings included unnamed sisters, and brothers called James[3], Joseph[8], Simon[3] and Judas[2]. Jesus was circumcised on the eighth day and later presented in the temple, where Simeon[2] and Anna delivered a prophetic message about Jesus' messianic ministry. When Jesus was about two years old, Magi (wise men from the East) came to worship him. At 12 years old, he went to Jerusalem for the Passover celebrations. He became separated from his parents when they began their journey home but he remained in the temple listening to the teachers there. He was baptized in the Jordan by John[1] the Baptist and then spent 40 days in the wilderness alone. He began a teaching and healing ministry around Galilee, initially in the synagogues, drawing a group of disciples around him. He

spoke to his disciples using parables to aid their understanding, especially when talking about the nature of the kingdom of God. His miracles were more than demonstrations of his power: they met the needs people had, whether for food (the feeding of the 5,000), healing (the blind man, lepers, mental illness) or for safety (the calming of the storm on Lake Galilee). His efforts were particularly geared towards the outcasts of society. After about three years, Jesus' ministry extended towards Jerusalem, where he arrived riding on a donkey. His popularity, and his claims about his own identity and God's kingdom, meant that he quickly faced opposition from religious leaders. He was betrayed by Judas Iscariot and tried by Jewish leaders before being handed over to Roman officials and finally condemned to death by Pontius Pilate. He suffered death by crucifixion on a hill outside Jerusalem. He was buried in a tomb but his followers testified to his resurrection because he appeared to them before he ascended into heaven. His followers believed that Jesus was fully human but also fully divine. They believed he was the Son of God who came to make God known and salvation available to the human race. Their faith in him grew, and the Christian church was formed to nurture the faith of Jesus' followers. The church believed that Jesus had ascended from earth to a position of authority in heaven. The Christian hope is based on the belief that Jesus will one day return to this world as Lord of all.

📖 (Matthew, Mark, Luke, John's Gospels; Revelation 22:16, 20–21)

Jesus Christ

The Son of God, who became a human being to come into this world. The Bible emphasizes both Jesus' full divinity and his full humanity. He came to earth to make God known and to secure salvation for the human race. Through his resurrection and ascension, he is now in a position of authority in heaven and will return to this world at the end of human history. *See also God, p. 15; Holy Spirit, p. 234.*

Names, titles and descriptions of Jesus Christ

Alpha and Omega	Revelation 1:8; 22:13
Bread of life	John 6:35
Bright Morning Star	Revelation 22:16
Chief Shepherd	1 Peter 5:4
Christ/Messiah	Matthew 16:16; John 1:41; Mark 1:1
Gate	John 10:7
Good shepherd	John 10:11, 14
Head	Ephesians 1:22
Head of the church	Colossians 1:18
High priest	Hebrews 3:1
Holy and Righteous One	Acts 3:14
Holy One of God	Mark 1:24
I am	John 8:58
Immanuel	Isaiah 7:14; Matthew 1:23
King of kings	Revelation 17:14
King of the Jews	Matthew 27:37
Lamb	Revelation 5:6–14
Lamb of God	John 1:29
Last Adam	1 Corinthians 15:45
Light of the world	John 8:12
Lion of Judah	Revelation 5:5
Living One	Revelation 1:18
Lord	Matthew 8:25; Acts 2:36
Lord of lords	Revelation 17:14
Mediator	1 Timothy 2:5; Hebrews 8:6; 9:15; 12:24
Prince	Acts 5:31
Rabbi (Teacher)	John 1:38

Resurrection and the life	John 11:25
Rock	1 Corinthians 10:4
Root and Offspring of David	Revelation 22:16
Saviour	Luke 2:11; Titus 1:4
Son of David	Matthew 1:1; 20:30
Son of God	Romans 1:4
Son of Man	Matthew 8:20; Mark 10:45; Luke 19:10
Son of the Most High	Luke 1:32
True vine	John 15:1
Way, the truth and the life	John 14:6
Word of God	John 1:1

Abiud
(early C5th BC)

Son of Zerubbabel. Father of Eliakim[4]. Mentioned in the genealogy of Jesus' father, Joseph[6].

(1:13)

Eliakim[4]
(mid C5th BC)

Son of Abiud. Father of Azor. Mentioned in the genealogy of Jesus' father, Joseph[6].

(1:13)

Azor
(early C4th BC)

Son of Eliakim[4]. Father of Zadok[10]. Mentioned in the genealogy of Jesus' father, Joseph[6].

(1:13–14)

Zadok[10]
(mid C4th BC)

Son of Azor. Father of Akim. Mentioned in the genealogy of Jesus' father, Joseph[6].

(1:14)

Akim
(early C3rd BC)

Son of Zadok[10]. Father of Eliud. Mentioned in the genealogy of Jesus' father, Joseph[6].

(1:14)

Eliud
(mid C3rd BC)

Son of Akim. Father of Eleazar[8]. Mentioned in the genealogy of Jesus' father, Joseph[6].

(1:14–15)

Eleazar[8]
(early C2nd BC)

Son of Eliud. Father of Matthan. Mentioned in the genealogy of Jesus' father, Joseph[6].

(1:15)

Matthan
(mid C2nd BC)

Son of Eleazar[8]. Father of Jacob[2]. Mentioned in the genealogy of Jesus' father, Joseph[6].

(1:15)

Jacob[2]
(early C1st BC)

Son of Matthan. Father of Joseph[6]. Mentioned in the genealogy of Jesus' father, Joseph[6].

(1:15–16)

Joseph[6]
(mid C1st BC)

Son of Jacob[2]. He became the husband of Jesus' mother Mary[1] after Jesus had been 'conceived of the Holy Spirit'. He is described as devout. In a dream the angel of the Lord appeared to Joseph and instructed him to take Mary[1] as his wife. He led his pregnant wife to Bethlehem for the census and Jesus was born there. Following another dream, they returned via Egypt and waited there until the threat on Jesus' life was diminished by Herod[1]'s death. Joseph followed the Jewish practice and had Jesus circumcised, taking him to the temple for purification. He took the family each year to Jerusalem for the Passover. In Nazareth he was a carpenter by trade, which probably involved both woodwork and stonemasonry. He may have died before Jesus' public ministry began, as there is no mention of him outside the texts that deal with Jesus' early life. In Matthew's Gospel, Joseph's genealogy is traced back to the royal line of David; in Luke's Gospel, Joseph's family line is traced back to Adam.

📖 (1:16, 18–24; 2:13–23; Luke 1:27; 2:4–5, 16, 22–33, 39, 41–52; 3:23–38; 4:22)

Mary[1]
(c.20 BC–after AD 60)

Virgin mother of Jesus who conceived him 'from the Holy Spirit'. The Protestant Church believes that later she bore other sons and daughters. However, because the Roman Catholic Church believes that Mary remained a virgin throughout her life, it maintains these were only half-siblings of Jesus through Joseph[6]'s line. She was betrothed at the time to Joseph, who married her despite her pregnancy. She received a visit from the angel Gabriel before her son was born, which confirmed her place in God's plan as mother of a Saviour. She shared her joy with Elizabeth, her relative, who described Mary and her unborn son as blessed. Mary's faith is seen in the way she responded to the call of God in her song of praise (the Magnificat). She gave birth to Jesus in an animal shed attached to an inn in Bethlehem.

She was present when the Magi came to visit Jesus and marvelled at the words spoken by Simeon[2] and Anna in the temple courts in Jerusalem when Jesus was presented there. She took the initiative in asking Jesus to provide some wine for the wedding in Cana. Mary witnessed the crucifixion of Jesus, where Jesus showed his concern for her by asking his beloved disciple to consider her as his mother, and himself as her son. Mary was among those praying with the disciples after the resurrection in the upper room.

📖 (1:18 – 2:23; Luke 1:26–56; 2:1–20, 22, 33–39, 41–52; John 2:1–12; 19:25–27; Acts 1:14)

Herod[1] (Herod the Great)
(ruled 37–4 BC)

Roman king in Israel, following the Roman conquest of Israel. He was known for his heavy-handed rule, which included putting to death anyone he suspected of being a possible usurper, even members of his own family. When Herod heard from the Magi that a new king had been born, he tried to trick them into giving him details of the location of this child. When the Magi did not return with the information he needed, he ordered a massacre of all the boys in Bethlehem under the age of two. This became known as the Massacre of the Innocents. Jesus avoided the massacre because Mary[1] and Joseph[6] had taken him to Egypt.

📖 (2:1–19, 22; Luke 1:5)

Archelaus
(ruled Judea 4 BC–AD 6)

Son of Herod[1]. Herod's kingdom was divided up between his three sons, and Archelaus succeeded his father as ruler of Judea. It seems that his reputation of following in his father's murderous footsteps was quickly realized by Joseph[6].

📖 (2:22)

Herod Family Tree

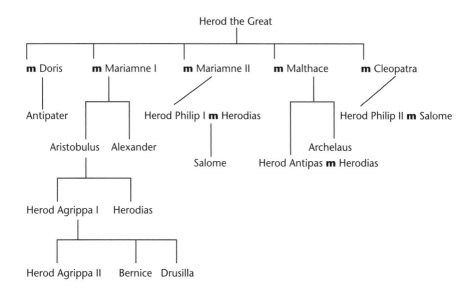

Herod Agrippa I	Herod [3]	Herodias	daughter of Aristobulus	
Herod Agrippa II	Herod [4]		wife of Herod Philip I	
Herod Antipas	Herod [2]		Herod Antipas divorces his wife to	
Herod the Great	Herod [1]		marry Herodias	
Herod Philip I	Philip [2]	Salome	Salome[2]	
Herod Philip II	Philip [3]		daughter of Herod Philip I by Herodias	
			wife of Herod Philip II	

John[1]/John the Baptist
(c.5 BC–c. AD 32)

Son of Zechariah[30] and Elizabeth. Born in his parents' old age, following a promise given by an angel, approximately six months before Jesus was born. As an unborn baby, John leaped in his mother's womb when Mary[1] shared the news of her own pregnancy. John was circumcised on the eighth day and was named as the angel had instructed. John wore clothes of camel hair, ate locusts and wild honey and led an ascetic lifestyle. His ministry called people to repentance and baptism in water. He baptized Jesus in the River Jordan. Jesus referred to him as a prophet, a second Elijah[1]. John referred to Jesus as the Lamb of God, the one who followed him but was greater than he was. He was imprisoned and then beheaded when Salome[2], the daughter of Herodias, gave Herod[2] the opportunity to get rid of John, who had often criticized him for his marriage to his brother's wife.

📖 (3:1–17; 11:2–14; 14:1–12; Mark 1:4–8, 14; 6:14–29; 8:28; Luke 1:11–25, 39–45, 57–63; 3:1–21; 7:18–35; 9:7–9; 20:4; John 1:6, 15, 19–35, 40; 3:22–36; 5:33–36; Acts 1:5; 11:16; 13:24–25)

Simon[1]/Simon Peter/Peter/ Cephas
(died c. AD 65)

Son of John[3]. A fisherman from Bethsaida who became a disciple of Jesus. Brother of Andrew. He was married and his mother-in-law was healed by Jesus early on in Jesus' ministry. Jesus gave him the name Peter (Greek form of the Aramaic name Cephas, meaning 'the rock') when he declared Jesus to be the Christ (Messiah). He often acted as the spokesperson for the other disciples and was eager to participate in the miraculous deeds of Jesus, like walking on water. He was also aware of his own sinfulness when Jesus' divine authority was displayed. Along with James[1] and John[2], he witnessed the transfiguration of Jesus and the raising of Jairus's daughter and accompanied Jesus in the Garden of Gethsemane. He initially refused to allow Jesus to wash his feet. After Jesus was arrested, he denied knowing Jesus three times. However, after his resurrection Jesus appeared to Simon Peter and other disciples who were fishing in the Sea of Galilee. Jesus asked Peter to confirm three times that he loved him and appointed him to look after his followers. On the Day of Pentecost about 3,000 people responded to his preaching and became Christians. He took the Christian message to the Gentiles and baptized the first Gentile converts (Cornelius and his family). Sometimes his ministry resulted in healing miracles but he was imprisoned too. He travelled with John[2] and visited Samaria and Samaritan villages. He became leader of the church in Jerusalem and wrote 1 and 2 Peter. He was associated with the churches at Antioch and Rome. From the second century onwards the leader of the church at Rome traced his authority back to Peter.

📖 (4:18–20; 8:14–16; 14:28–31; 15:15; 16:13–20, 23; Mark 1:16–18, 29–30, 36; 3:16; 5:37–43; 8:27–33; 9:2–13; 10:28; 11:21; 14:27–42, 54, 66–72; Luke 4:38; 5:4–11; 6:14; 9:28–36; 12:41; 18:28; 22:8, 31–34, 54–62; 24:12, 34; John 1:40–42, 44; 6:68–69; 13:6–9, 24, 36–38; 20:2–10; 21:1–23; Acts 1:13, 15–22; 2:14–41; 3:1 – 5:42; 8:14–25; 10:1 – 11:18; 12:1–18; 1 Corinthians 1:12; 9:5; Galatians 1:18; 2:9, 11, 14; 1 Peter, 2 Peter)

Andrew
(C1st AD)

Son of John[3]. A fisherman from Bethsaida, brother of Simon[1] Peter, who became a disciple of Jesus. He originally followed John[1] the Baptist. He was present with Simon Peter, James[1] and John[2] when they questioned Jesus about the end times. He was active alongside the other disciples in the early church.

📖 (4:18–20; 10:2; Mark 1:16–18, 29; 3:18; 13:3; John 1:35–41; 6:8–9; 12:22; Acts 1:13–14)

James[1]
(died AD 43)

A fisherman who became a disciple of Jesus. Brother of John[2]. Son of Zebedee and Mary[3] (or possibly Salome[1]). Jesus gave him and John[2] the name Boanerges, meaning 'sons of thunder', probably indicating their personality type. He became one of Jesus' closest friends and with Simon[1] Peter and John[2] witnessed the transfiguration of Jesus and the raising of Jairus's daughter, and accompanied Jesus in the Garden of Gethsemane. He was martyred for his faith at the hands of Herod[3].

📖 (4:21–22; 27:56; Mark 1:19–20, 29; 3:17; 5:37–43; 9:2–13; 10:35, 41; 14:33; 16:1; Luke 5:10; 6:14; 9:28–35, 54; John 21:2; Acts 1:13; 12:2)

Zebedee
(late C1st BC)

Father of James[1] and John[2]. A fisherman. Married to Mary[3] (or possibly Salome[1]).

📖 (4:21–22; 10:2; 26:37; 27:56; Mark 1:19–20; 3:17; 10:35; Luke 5:10; John 21:2)

John[2]/Joseph[7]/Joses
(C1st AD)

A fisherman who became a disciple of Jesus. Brother of James[1]. Son of Zebedee and Mary[3] (or possibly Salome[1]) who stood alongside the women at Jesus' crucifixion. Jesus gave him and James[1] the name Boanerges, meaning 'sons of thunder', probably indicating their personality. He became one of Jesus' closest friends and with Simon[1] Peter and James[1] witnessed the transfiguration of Jesus and the raising of Jairus's daughter, and accompanied Jesus in the Garden of Gethsemane. He is probably the disciple referred to in John's Gospel as 'the disciple whom Jesus loved' and may have been the author of the fourth Gospel and also, though more debated, the three letters of John and the book of Revelation. He supported Peter in his early ministry and later became a leader in the churches at Jerusalem and Ephesus.

📖 (4:21–22; 27:56; Mark 1:19–20, 29; 3:17; 5:37–43; 9:2–13, 38; 10:35, 41; 14:33; Luke 5:10; 6:14; 9:28–35, 49, 54; John 13:23; 21:2, 20–24; Acts 1:13; 3:1–5, 11; 4:13, 19; 8:14–25; Galatians 2:9; 1–3 John; Revelation 1:1, 4, 9; 22:8)

Matthew/Levi[2]
(C1st AD)

Son of Alphaeus[2]. A tax collector who followed Jesus. He hosted a meal for Jesus and other tax collectors, but the Pharisees took offence that Jesus ate with people they classed as sinners. Author of Matthew's Gospel.

📖 (9:9–13; 10:3; Mark 2:14; 3:18; Luke 5:27–32; 6:15; Acts 1:13)

Philip[1]
(C1st AD)

A disciple of Jesus from Bethsaida in Galilee. He introduced his friend Bartholomew (Nathanael) to Jesus. Before Jesus fed the 5,000 men, he asked Philip where they could buy enough bread for all these people.

Philip responded by calculating how much money that would cost. Philip appears to have been a particularly close friend of Andrew.

📖 (10:3; Mark 3:18; Luke 6:14; John 1:43–51; 6:5–7; 12:21–22; Acts 1:13)

Bartholomew/Nathanael
(C1st AD)

A disciple of Jesus, whom Philip[1] introduced to Jesus. Jesus commended him as a 'true Israelite'. He recognized Jesus to be the Son of God.

📖 (10:3; Mark 3:18; Luke 6:14; John 1:43–51; 21:2; Acts 1:13)

Thomas/Didymus ('the twin')
(C1st AD)

Often caricatured as 'the doubter' because he would not believe Jesus had risen until he could touch Jesus' wounded side and see the nail prints in his hands, but when he did so he made a bold declaration of faith.

📖 (10:3; Mark 3:18; Luke 6:15; John 11:16; 14:5; 20:24–29; 21:2; Acts 1:13)

James[2]
(C1st AD)

A disciple of Jesus and son of Alphaeus[1].

📖 (10:3; Mark 3:18; Luke 6:15; Acts 1:13)

Alphaeus[1]
(late C1st BC)

Father of James[2].

📖 (10:3; Mark 3:18; Luke 6:15; Acts 1:13)

Thaddaeus/Judas[3]
(C1st AD)

A disciple of Jesus. He questioned Jesus when he was speaking about the coming Holy Spirit. Luke refers to him as the son of James[4].

📖 (10:3; Mark 3:18; Luke 6:16; John 14:22; Acts 1:13)

Simon[2] ('the Zealot')
(C1st AD)

A disciple of Jesus. 'Zealot' might indicate he was a member of a religious group bearing that name, or it might have been a nickname to indicate his zealous commitment to the history and preservation of true Israelite faith.

📖 (10:4; Mark 3:18; Luke 6:15; Acts 1:13)

Judas[1]/Judas Iscariot
(died AD 33)

Son of Simon[7] Iscariot. A disciple of Jesus. He betrayed Jesus to the Jewish authorities for 30 pieces of silver. His reasons for betraying Jesus are the subject of much speculation and are sometimes identified with his love of money, personal weakness and fear, or his rejection of Jesus' claim to be Messiah. Matthew's Gospel tells us that Judas committed suicide after Jesus' death. The early church appointed Matthias to fill his place.

📖 (10:4; 26:14–16, 47–51; 27:3–10; Mark 3:19; 14:10–11, 43–47; Luke 6:16; John 6:70–71; 12:1–8; 13:2, 21–30; 18:2–3, 5; Acts 1:15–26)

James[3], Joseph[8], Simon[3], Judas[2]
(C1st AD; James[3] died AD 62)

Listed as the brothers of Jesus. The Roman Catholic Church, in adherence to the doctrine of the perpetual virginity of Mary, suggests these were Jesus' cousins or half-brothers. James[3] became leader of the church in Jerusalem and the letter of James is traditionally credited to him.

📖 (13:55; Mark 3:31–32; 6:3; Luke 8:19–20; Acts 12:17; 15:13–21; 21:17; Galatians 2:9; James 1:1; Jude 1)

Herod[2] Antipas (tetrarch of Galilee)
(ruled 4 BC–AD 39)

Son of Herod[1]. Along with his brothers Archelaus and Philip[2] he received a third of Herod[1]'s territory upon his death. John[1] the Baptist criticized him for taking his brother Philip's wife, Herodias. Herod[2] was responsible for beheading John the Baptist in response to an unusual birthday request from Salome[2], the daughter of Herodias. The Jewish historian Josephus identifies Herodias' daughter as Salome, although this name does not appear in the biblical text. Pilate involved Herod in assessing whether Jesus deserved to be put to death because Herod's jurisdiction included Galilee and Perea, where Jesus had lived.

📖 (14:1–12; Mark 6:14–29; Luke 3:1, 19–20; 9:7–9; 13:31; 23:7–12, 15; Acts 4:27; 13:1)

Herodias
(born c.8 BC)

Wife of Philip[2], who was probably taken away from him to become Herod[2]'s wife. She encouraged her daughter Salome[2] to ask for John[1] the Baptist's head on a platter as a birthday gift from Herod[2].

📖 (14:1–12; Mark 6:17–29; Luke 3:19)

Philip[2]
(C1st AD)

Husband of Herodias. One of the sons of Herod[1], who lived a private life in Rome.

📖 (14:3; Mark 6:17; Luke 3:1, 19)

Jonah[2]/John[3]
(late C1st BC)

Father of Simon[1] Peter and Andrew.

📖 (16:17; John 1:42; 21:15–17)

Caiaphas
(high priest AD 18–36)

Son-in-law of the high priest Annas, whom he succeeded. Caiaphas was high priest for nearly 18 years, including the time when John[1] began his ministry and when Jesus died. He was in charge of the Sanhedrin when Jesus was brought before this Jewish council. He asked Jesus directly if he was Christ and charged him with blasphemy when he responded. In John's Gospel Caiaphas delivers a word of prophecy about Jesus dying for the salvation of the Jewish nation. He was at the Sanhedrin Council when Simon[1] Peter and John[2] were brought before it.

📖 (26:3, 57–67; Luke 3:2; John 11:49–53; 18:13–14, 24, 28; Acts 4:6)

Pilate/Pontius Pilate
(governor AD 26–36)

The Roman governor in Judea. Jesus was brought before Pilate, who questioned him about whether he claimed to be the king of the Jews. Jesus' minimal responses amazed Pilate and he was suspicious about why the Jews wanted Jesus condemned. He decided to offer a choice between Barabbas and Jesus. The crowd asked for Barabbas to be released and demanded that Jesus be crucified. Pilate's wife warned him not to be responsible for the death of an innocent man. Pilate washed his hands and announced that Jesus' blood was on the people's hands, before handing Jesus over to be flogged and crucified. Pilate is seen as a weak leader who was eager to please the crowd rather than committed to justice. In Luke's Gospel he involved Herod[2] in the task of assessing Jesus' culpability in an attempt to pass on the responsibility. Pilate penned the words fastened to Jesus' cross, 'Jesus of Nazareth. King of the Jews'. Pilate gave permission to Joseph[9] of Arimathea to take Jesus' body away. He ordered that a seal be placed over Jesus' tomb and a guard keep watch.

📖 (27:2, 11–26, 57–58, 62–66; Mark 15:1–15; Luke 3:1; 13:1; 23:1–25, 52; John 18:28 – 19:22; Acts 4:27; 13:28)

Simon[4]
(met Jesus AD 33)

A leper who lived in Bethany. Jesus went to his house and while he was having a meal there a woman poured expensive perfume on his head.

📖 (26:6–7; Mark 14:3)

Barabbas/Jesus Barabbas
(released AD 33)

A well-known criminal and prisoner who was released by Pilate in preference to Jesus, following the crowd's request. He was guilty of insurrection and murder.

📖 (27:15–22; Mark 15:6–15; Luke 23:18–25; John 18:39–40)

Simon[5] (of Cyrene)
(carried Jesus' cross AD 33)

Father of Alexander[1] and Rufus[1]. He was forced to carry Jesus' cross to Golgotha, presumably because Jesus was too weak from the flogging he endured.

📖 (27:32; Mark 15:21; Luke 23:26)

Mary[2]/Mary Magdalene
(travelled with Jesus c. AD 30–33)

One of the women who travelled with Jesus and his disciples and supported them. She had been healed of demon possession. She was among the women who witnessed Jesus' death on the cross. On the day after his crucifixion, she visited Jesus' tomb and saw that the stone had been removed. She saw an angel and met with Jesus after his resurrection; he addressed her personally by name. She reported to the other disciples, 'I have seen the Lord.'

📖 (27:55–56; 28:1–10; Mark 15:40–41, 47; 16:1–8; Luke 8:2; 23:49; 24:1–10; John 19:25; 20:1–18)

Mary[3]
(born late C1st BC)

Mother of James[1] and John[2] (Joseph/Joses). Wife of Zebedee. Possibly sister of Mary[1]. She was among the women who had tended his needs during his lifetime and then witnessed Jesus' death and resurrection.

📖 (27:55–56; 28:1–10; Mark 15:40–41, 47; 16:1–8; Luke 24:1–12; John 19:25)

Joseph[9] (of Arimathea)
(early–mid C1st AD)

A member of the Jewish Sanhedrin Council who is described as 'good and upright'. After Jesus was crucified he summoned the courage to ask

Pilate for Jesus' body. With support from Nicodemus, he wrapped Jesus' body in linen cloths and placed it in a tomb which he had cut out from the rock.

📖 (27:57–60; Mark 15:42–46; Luke 23:50–55; John 19:38–42)

Mark

Mark
(C1st AD)
See **John[5] Mark** *in Acts, p. 237.*

Simon
(died c. AD 65)
See **Simon[1]/Simon Peter/ Peter/Cephas** *in Matthew, p. 223.*
📖 (1:16–18, 29–30)

Alphaeus[2]
(late C1st BC)
Father of Matthew (Levi[2]).
📖 (2:14)

Boanerges
(C1st AD)
See **James[1]** *and* **John[2]** *in Matthew, p. 223 and 224.*
📖 (3:17)

Legion
(met Jesus c. AD 31)
A name associated with the man in the region of the Gerasenes who was possessed by many demons. Jesus cured this man by sending the demons into a herd of pigs. His mental health was restored and the people were amazed. He wanted to follow Jesus but Jesus told him to go home and tell everyone what Jesus had done for him.
📖 (5:1–19; Luke 8:26–39)

Jairus
(met Jesus c. AD 31)
A synagogue leader who pleaded with Jesus to heal his 12-year-old daughter when she was dying. He received a message that his daughter had died before Jesus reached his house. However, Jesus went into the house and told the little girl to get up. Her life was restored to her, to the amazement of those who had been mourning her death.
📖 (5:21–24, 35–43; Matthew 9:18–19, 23–26; Luke 8:40–42, 49–56)

Bartimaeus
(met Jesus c. AD 33)
His name means 'Son of Timaeus'. A blind beggar sitting on the roadside as Jesus was leaving Jericho. He cried out to Jesus for mercy and Jesus restored his sight. He then joined the crowds following Jesus.
📖 (10:46–52; Luke 18:35–43)

Timaeus
(late C1st BC)
Father of Bartimaeus.
See **Bartimaeus** *in Mark, p. 227 (above).*
📖 (10:46)

Alexander[1], Rufus[1]
(mid C1st AD)
Sons of Simon[5] of Cyrene. Possibly mentioned by Mark because they were known in their own right in the early church.
📖 (15:21)

Salome[1]
(at Jesus' crucifixion AD 33)
Present with Mary[2] and Mary[3] when Jesus died. She also went with them to the tomb to anoint Jesus' body with spices and found the stone rolled away and an angel declaring that Jesus was risen.
📖 (15:40–41; 16:1–8)

Luke

Luke
(C1st AD)
See **Luke** *in Colossians, p. 247.*

Theophilus
(late C1st AD)

The person for whom the records contained in Luke's Gospel and the Acts of the Apostle were written. He is called 'most excellent', suggesting he was a man of high standing in New Testament times. Alternatively his name, which means 'lover of God', may have been attached to Luke's records to indicate that the contents were relevant for all those who loved God.

(1:3; Acts 1:1)

Zechariah[30]
(C1st BC)

Father of John[1] the Baptist. Husband of Elizabeth. A priest of Abijah[7]'s division who is described as 'righteous and obedient to the Lord's decrees'. He was chosen to go into the temple in Jerusalem to burn incense, and on this occasion the angel Gabriel appeared to him and promised him a son who would be filled with the Holy Spirit before he was born. Zechariah expressed his disbelief that this would happen to him in his old age and he was struck dumb. It was on the eighth day after his son's birth, on the occasion of his circumcision, that Zechariah confirmed that his son was to be called John, and his speech

was restored to him. He immediately praised God and, filled with the Holy Spirit himself, he prophesied that his son would prepare the way of the Lord.

(1:5–22, 40, 57–79)

Elizabeth
(C1st BC)

Mother of John[1] the Baptist. Wife of Zechariah[30]. She was a descendant of Aaron and is described along with her husband as 'righteous and obedient to the Lord'. She was old and unable to have children when the angel appeared to her husband, promising him that she would give him a son. She was six months pregnant when Mary[1] received her visit from Gabriel, indicating that she too would have a son. Elizabeth expressed her joy with her relative and declared that Mary and her son were blessed. When Elizabeth's son was born her relatives and friends shared in her joy and she gave her son the name John.

(1:5–26, 36–45, 57–66)

Quirinius
(c.51 BC–AD 21)

Governor of Syria when Caesar Augustus ordered a census of the entire Roman world.

(2:2)

Caesars

Name	Birth and death	Reigned	
Julius Caesar	100–44 BC	49–44 BC	
Augustus	63 BC–AD 14	27 BC–AD 14	Luke 2:1
Tiberius	42 BC–AD 37	AD 14–37	Luke 3:1; John 19:12
Caligula	AD 12–41	AD 37–41	
Claudius	10 BC–AD 54	AD 41–54	Acts 11:28; 17:7; 18:2
Nero	AD 37–68	AD 54–68	Acts 25:11; 27:24

Simeon[2]
(C1st BC)

A righteous and devout man on whom the Holy Spirit rested. He was in the temple courts in Jerusalem when Jesus' parents presented him there to fulfil the requirements of the Law. He recognized Jesus as the promised Messiah and blessed him and his family and praised God.

📖 (2:25–35)

Anna
(C1st BC)

Daughter of Phanuel, from the tribe of Asher. She was very old and had been a widow for many years when Mary[1] and Joseph[6] brought Jesus to the temple. She worshipped continuously in the temple and when she saw Jesus she praised God and spoke about the redemption he would bring.

📖 (2:36–38)

Phanuel
(late C2nd BC)

Father of Anna.

📖 (2:36)

Lysanias
(early–mid C1st AD)

Tetrarch of Abilene, a region north-west of Damascus, at the time when John[1] the Baptist began his ministry.

📖 (3:1)

Philip[3]
(tetrarch of Iturea and Traconitis 4 BC–AD 34).

Son of Herod[1]. Along with his brothers, Archelaus and Herod[2], he received a third of Herod[1]'s territory upon his death.

📖 (3:1)

Annas
(high priest AD 7–15)

High priest who was succeeded by his son Caiaphas. It appears that there was a transition period, which explains why Luke identifies both Annas and Caiaphas as high priests in the fifteenth year of Tiberius Caesar. When Jesus was arrested he came first before Annas and then was sent on to Caiaphas. Annas was still active in the Sanhedrin Council when Simon[1] Peter and John[2] were brought before its leaders.

📖 (3:2; John 18:13, 24; Acts 4:6; 5:17, 21)

Heli
(mid C1st BC)

Father of Joseph[6]. Son of Matthat[1].

📖 (3:24)

Matthat[1]
(early C1st BC)

Father of Heli. Son of Levi[3].

📖 (3:24)

Levi[3]
(late C2nd BC)

Father of Matthat[1]. Son of Melki[1].

📖 (3:24)

Melki[1]
(mid C2nd BC)

Father of Levi[3]. Son of Jannai.

📖 (3:24)

Jannai
(mid C2nd BC)

Father of Melki[1]. Son of Joseph[10].

📖 (3:24)

Joseph[10]
(early C2nd BC)

Father of Jannai. Son of Mattathias[1].

📖 (3:24)

Mattathias[1]
(late C3rd BC)

Father of Joseph[10]. Son of Amos[2].

📖 (3:25)

Amos[2]
(mid C3rd BC)
Father of Mattathias[1]. Son of
Nahum[2].
📖 (3:25)

Nahum[2]
(early C3rd BC)
Father of Amos[2]. Son of Esli.
📖 (3:25)

Esli
(late C4th BC)
Father of Nahum[2]. Son of Naggai.
📖 (3:25)

Naggai
(mid C4th BC)
Father of Esli. Son of Maath.
📖 (3:25)

Maath
(mid C4th BC)
Father of Naggai. Son of
Mattathias[2].
📖 (3:26)

Mattathias[2]
(early C4th BC)
Father of Maath. Son of Semein.
📖 (3:26)

Semein
(late C5th BC)
Father of Mattathias[2]. Son of Josek.
📖 (3:26)

Josek (Josech)
(mid C5th BC)
Father of Semein. Son of Joda.
📖 (3:26)

Joda
(early C5th BC)
Father of Josek. Son of Joanan.
📖 (3:26)

Joanan
(late C6th BC)
Father of Joda. Son of Rhesa
📖 (3:27)

Rhesa
(mid C6th BC)
Father of Joanan. Son of Zerubbabel.
📖 (3:27)

Neri
(late C7th BC)
Father of Shealtiel. Son of Melki[2].
📖 (3:27)

Melki[2]
(mid C7th BC)
Father of Neri. Son of Addi.
📖 (3:28)

Addi
(mid C7th BC)
Father of Melki[2]. Son of Cosam.
📖 (3:28)

Cosam
(early C7th BC)
Father of Addi. Son of Elmadam.
📖 (3:28)

Elmadam
(early C7th BC)
Father of Cosam. Son of Er[3].
📖 (3:28)

Er[3]
(late C8th BC)
Father of Elmadam. Son of Joshua[4].
📖 (3:28)

Joshua[4]
(mid C8th BC)
Father of Er[3]. Son of Eliezer[11].
📖 (3:29)

Eliezer[11]
(mid C8th BC)
Father of Joshua[4]. Son of Jorim.
📖 (3:29)

Jorim
(early C8th BC)
Father of Eliezer[11]. Son of Matthat[2].
📖 (3:29)

Matthat[2]
(early C8th BC)
Father of Jorim. Son of Levi[4].
📖 (3:29)

Levi[4]
(late C9th BC)
Father of Matthat[2]. Son of Simeon[3].
📖 (3:29)

Simeon[3]
(mid C9th BC)
Father of Levi[4]. Son of Judah[7].
📖 (3:30)

Judah[7]
(mid C9th BC)
Father of Simeon[3]. Son of Joseph[11].
📖 (3:30)

Joseph[11]
(early C9th BC)
Father of Judah[7]. Son of Jonam.
📖 (3:30)

Jonam
(early C9th BC)
Father of Joseph[11]. Son of Eliakim[5].
📖 (3:30)

Eliakim[5]
(late C10th BC)
Father of Jonam. Son of Melea.
📖 (3:30)

Melea
(mid C10th BC)
Father of Eliakim[5]. Son of Menna.
📖 (3:31)

Menna
(mid C10th BC)
Father of Melea. Son of Mattatha.
📖 (3:31)

Mattatha
(early C10th BC)
Father of Menna. Son of Nathan[1].
📖 (3:31)

Cainan
(?C17th AM)
Father of Shelah[1]. Son of Arphaxad.
📖 (3:36)

Simon
(died c. AD 65)
See **Simon[1]/Simon Peter/Peter/Cephas** *in Matthew, p. 223.*
📖 (4:38, 5:4–11)

James[4]
(late C1st BC)
Father of Judas[3].
📖 (6:16; Acts 1:13)

Simon[6]
(met Jesus c. AD 31)
A Pharisee who invited Jesus to dinner. At the meal in his house a woman poured perfume on Jesus' feet. Simon objected on account of the woman's sinful past but Jesus told him that the woman's love was great because she had been forgiven so much.
📖 (7:36–50)

Joanna
(travelled with Jesus c. AD 30–33)
Wife of Chuza. She joined other women, including Mary[2] Magdalene and Susanna, in travelling with Jesus and caring for his needs from their own resources. She was among the women who took spices to his tomb to anoint Jesus' body and found that the body was missing. Instead they encountered two men who looked like angels.

With the other women, Joanna reported all this to the apostles.

📖 (8:3; 24:1–11)

Chuza (Cuza)
(early C1st AD)

Husband of Joanna. He served as manager in Herod[2]'s house.

📖 (8:3)

Susanna
(travelled with Jesus c. AD 30–33)

She joined other women, including Mary[2] Magdalene and Joanna, in travelling with Jesus and caring for his needs from their own resources.

📖 (8:3)

Martha
(met Jesus c. AD 32–33)

Sister of Lazarus[2] and Mary[4]. The family lived in Bethany. On one occasion when Jesus came to their house, she was busy with practical tasks and complained to Jesus that Mary sat at his feet listening to him while she did all the work. Jesus responded to her, recognizing her tendency towards worry but at the same time reaffirming Mary. When Lazarus was taken ill, the sisters sent word to Jesus but by the time he reached their house he had already died and was in the tomb. Martha went to meet Jesus and declared her faith in Jesus as the Messiah. When they took Jesus to Lazarus's tomb, Jesus wept but ordered the stone to be removed and he raised Lazarus to life. John's Gospel records another occasion when Jesus went to their house and Martha served a meal in Jesus' honour.

📖 (10:38–42; John 11:1–44; 12:1–2)

Mary[4]
(met Jesus c. AD 32–33)

Sister of Lazarus[2] and Martha. When Jesus came to their house she sat at Jesus' feet listening to him. Jesus commended her for choosing to attend to his words. When Lazarus was taken ill, the sisters sent word

to Jesus but by the time he reached their house he had already died and was in the tomb. Jesus wept with the sisters but then ordered the stone to be removed and Lazarus was raised to life. John's Gospel records another occasion when Jesus went to their house and Mary poured pure nard perfume over Jesus' feet.

📖 (10:38–42; John 11:1–44; 12:1–8)

Lazarus[1]
(fictional)

The name of a beggar in one of the parables Jesus told his disciples. This beggar was hungry and disease-ridden in his lifetime but in heaven he received a place next to Abraham.

📖 (16:20–31)

Zacchaeus
(met Jesus AD 33)

The name of a tax collector in Jericho who climbed a sycamore-fig tree to see Jesus. Jesus called him down from the tree and went to his house. While the people complained that Jesus had gone to a sinner's house, Zacchaeus repented and vowed to recompense those he had cheated out of money. He gave half of his possessions to the poor. Jesus declared that Zacchaeus was a recipient of salvation and a son of Abraham.

📖 (19:1–10)

Cleopas
(met the risen Jesus AD 33)

One of the men who were walking on the road to Emmaus after Jesus' resurrection. The men were talking about the recent events in Jerusalem when Jesus himself joined with them but they did not recognize him. Jesus discussed the Scriptures with them. It was only after he broke bread with them, in a re-enactment of the last supper, that they recognized him. They returned to Jerusalem and told the 11 disciples that Jesus had risen from the dead.

📖 (24:13–35)

John

John[2]
(C1st AD)
See **John[2]** in *Matthew, p. 224.*

John[3]
(late C1st BC)
See **Jonah[2]/John[3]** in *Matthew, p. 225.*
📖 (1:42)

Cephas
(died c. AD 65)
See **Simon[1]/Simon Peter/ Peter/Cephas** in *Matthew, p. 223.*
📖 (1:42)

Nathanael
(C1st AD)
See **Bartholomew** in *Matthew, p. 224.*
📖 (1:45–51)

Nicodemus
(met Jesus c. AD 30)
A Pharisee and member of the Sanhedrin Council. He came to Jesus during the night and Jesus explained to him what it meant to be 'born again' by the Spirit of God. On another occasion when Jesus was in Jerusalem, Nicodemus challenged his fellow Jewish leaders about their antagonism towards Jesus. In return Nicodemus received a sharp rebuttal. Nicodemus supported Joseph[8] of Arimathea when he took Jesus' body for burial. Nicodemus provided a mixture of myrrh and aloes, and assisted Joseph in wrapping the body in linen and laying it in the tomb.
📖 (3:1–21; 7:50–52; 19:39–40)

Lazarus[2]
(met Jesus c. AD 32–33)
From Bethany and brother of Mary[4] and Martha. Jesus wept when this friend whom he loved died. He then raised him to life by summoning him out of the tomb where his linen-wrapped body had laid for four days. Jesus declared that this miraculous deed would show the glory of God and induce belief in him. Those who had witnessed this miracle, or had heard about it, flocked to welcome Jesus to Jerusalem waving palm branches and shouting hosanna.
📖 (11:1–44; 12:17)

Didymus
(C1st AD)
See **Thomas/Didymus** in *Matthew, p. 224.*
📖 (11:16)

Simon[7] Iscariot
(late C1st BC)
Father of Judas[1] Iscariot, the betrayer.
📖 (13:2, 26)

Malchus
(met Jesus AD 33)
Servant of Caiaphas, the high priest. He was present when Jesus was arrested. Simon[1] Peter cut off his right ear with a sword.
📖 (18:10)

Clopas
(early C1st AD)
John's Gospel is alone in identifying this man as the husband of Mary[3] (or another Mary) who stood near the cross of Jesus.
📖 (19:25)

Acts

Luke
(C1st AD)
See **Luke** in *Colossians, p. 247.*

Theophilus
(late C1st AD)
See **Theophilus** in *Luke, p. 228.*
📖 (1:1)

The Holy Spirit

The third person of the Trinity, who is equal to God the Father and Jesus Christ in eternity, nature and status. *See also God, p. 15; Jesus Christ, p. 219.*

Names, titles and descriptions of the Holy Spirit

Advocate (Counsellor)	John 14:26; 15:26
Deposit	2 Corinthians 1:21–22; Ephesians 1:14
Dove	Matthew 3:16; John 1:32
Eternal Spirit	Hebrews 9:14
Fire	Acts 2:3–4
Oil of anointing	Isaiah 61:1; Acts 10:38
Seal	Ephesians 1:13; 4:30
Spirit of adoption to sonship	Romans 8:15
Spirit of Christ	Romans 8:9
Spirit of glory	1 Peter 4:14
Spirit of God	Genesis 1:2; Romans 8:9
Spirit of grace and supplication	Zechariah 12:10fn
Spirit of him who raised Jesus from the dead	Romans 8:11
Spirit of holiness	Romans 1:4
Spirit of judgment and fire	Isaiah 4:4fn
Spirit of life	Romans 8:2
Spirit of the Father	Matthew 10:20
Spirit of the Lord	Judges 3:10; 1 Samuel 16:13
Spirit of the Son	Galatians 4:6
Spirit of truth	John 14:17; 16:13
Spirit of wisdom and understanding	Isaiah 11:2
Water	John 7:37–39; Isaiah 44:3
Wind or breath	Acts 2:2; Ezekiel 37:9–14; John 3:8; 20:22

Peter
(died c. AD 65)

See **Simon[1]/Simon Peter/ Peter/Cephas** *in Matthew, p. 223.*

📖 (1:13, 15–22; 2:14–41)

Judas[3]
(C1st AD)

See **Thaddaeus** *in Matthew, p. 224.*

📖 (1:13)

Joseph[12] (Barsabbas)/Justus
(mid C1st AD)

One of two men proposed by the believers gathered in Jerusalem after Jesus' ascension to take the place of Judas[1] as an apostle. He was not appointed but his credentials included being an eyewitness to the life and ministry of Jesus.

📖 (1:23–26)

Matthias
(mid C1st AD)

Proposed by the early church alongside Joseph[12] to replace Judas as an apostle. He was duly elected to the role after prayer and the casting of lots. He had been an eyewitness to the life and ministry of Jesus.

📖 (1:23–26)

John[4], Alexander[2]
(met Peter and John c. AD 33)

Two members of the family of Annas, the high priest, who were present at the Sanhedrin Council when Peter and John[2] were brought before them.

📖 (4:6)

Joseph[13]/Barnabas
(associate of Saul[2]/Paul c. AD 45–50)

A Levite from Cyprus who became Paul's friend and colleague. He is described as being full of the Holy Spirit and faith. He persuaded the church in Jerusalem that they should accept Paul as a Christian believer following his conversion. He was given the name Barnabas (meaning 'son of encouragement') by the apostles, who recognized the value of his ministry of encouragement. He worked in the church at Antioch with Paul for a year. He was then sent out with Paul on his first mission trip, starting in Cyprus. He disagreed with Paul about John[5] Mark's involvement in Paul's second mission trip and then separated from Paul to take John Mark to Cyprus.

📖 (4:36; 9:26–27; 11:22–26, 30; 12:25 – 13:8; 13:42 – 15:39; 1 Corinthians 9:6; Galatians 2:1, 9, 13; Colossians 4:10)

Ananias[1], Sapphira
(died c. AD 33)

Husband and wife who attempted to deceive the apostles about the amount of money they had donated to the church from the sale of a field. When their deception was uncovered they both died suddenly.

📖 (5:1–11)

Gamaliel[2]
(died AD 50)

Respected Pharisee and teacher of the Law. He addressed the Sanhedrin and persuaded its members that Peter and the other apostles should not be put to death. His argument was that if their teaching was of human origin it would fail and if it was from God then God would give them success. It is probable that Saul[2]/Paul studied under this same Gamaliel when he was trained in Judaism.

📖 (5:33; 22:3)

Theudas
(early C1st AD)

An example of someone whose uprising failed; mentioned by Gamaliel[2] in his speech to the Sanhedrin.

📖 (5:36)

Judas[4]
(early C1st AD)

A Galilean mentioned in Gamaliel[2]'s speech to the Sanhedrin as an example of someone whose uprising failed.

📖 (5:37)

Stephen
(died c. AD 33)

An early Christian known for his faith, grace and power inspired by the Holy Spirit. He was one of the seven men set apart to help the apostles. He was opposed by the Jewish leaders but with a face 'like the face of an angel' he delivered a powerful sermon to the Sanhedrin Council. With the unconverted Saul[2]/Paul watching, he was stoned to death as the first Christian martyr. Upon his martyrdom persecution against the Christian church broke out.

📖 (6:5, 8–15; 7:1 – 8:2; 11:19; 22:20)

Philip[4]
(mid C1st AD)

An early Christian evangelist from Caesarea. During his ministry in Samaria, Simon[8] the sorcerer was converted. His conversation with an Ethiopian official led to the Ethiopian's conversion and baptism. He was one of the seven men set apart to help the apostles.

📖 (6:5; 8:5–13, 26–40; 21:8)

Procorus, Nicanor, Timon, Parmenas, Nicolas
(mid C1st AD)

Along with Stephen and Philip[3] these five men were set apart by prayer and the laying on of hands to assist the apostles, particularly in the practical task of food distribution. Nicolas was a Jewish convert from Antioch.

📖 (6:1–6)

Saul[2]/Paul
(died c. AD 65)

A Roman citizen, Pharisee and persecutor of the church who was present encouraging Stephen's martyrdom. However, he had a significant conversion experience on the road to Damascus, where he saw a vision of the risen Christ and was struck blind. He began preaching in Galatia, Damascus and Jerusalem before embarking on a series of mission trips. He worked as a tentmaker to support himself. He founded many churches along the Mediterranean coast and wrote numerous letters (Romans–Philemon) to stay in contact with churches he had founded and individuals to whom he had given responsibility. He identified a special calling to ministry among the Gentiles. He was imprisoned in Caesarea and sent to Rome for trial, where he endured further imprisonment and house arrest. It is likely that he was martyred during the reign of Nero.

📖 (7:58 – 8:3; 9:1–30; 11:25–26, 30; 12:25 – 26:31; Romans 11:13; 15:23–32; 1 Corinthians 4:12–13; 15:30–32; 2 Corinthians 1:8 – 2:4; Galatians 2:7–21; 1 Thessalonians 2:17 – 3:5; 2 Thessalonians 3:7–10)

Simon[8] (the sorcerer)
(met Philip c. AD 33)

Capable of amazing deeds of sorcery, he was well known in Samaria. He was converted and baptized under Philip[4]'s ministry. When he encountered Simon[1] Peter and John[2], he offered them money in the mistaken belief that he could buy from them the ability to confer the gift of the Holy Spirit on others. They challenged him about his attitude and Simon asked them to pray for him.

📖 (8:9–24)

Ananias[2]
(met Saul[2]/Paul c. AD 34)

A Jewish Christian in Damascus who was highly respected. In a vision he was instructed to go to the house of Judas[5] to find Saul, following his experience on the Damascus Road. He was fearful, because of Saul's reputation as a persecutor of Christians, but he obeyed and laid his hands on Saul. Saul's sight was restored and he received the Holy Spirit.

📖 (9:10–19; 22:12–16)

Judas[5]
(met Saul[2]/Paul c. AD 34)

Owner of the house in Straight Street to which Saul went after his experience on the road to Damascus and where Ananias[2] visited him.

📖 (9:11)

Aeneas
(healed c. AD 40)

A paralysed man in Lydda who was healed through the ministry of Peter. His healing resulted in many other conversions in Lydda and Sharon.

📖 (9:33–35)

Tabitha/Dorcas
(raised c. AD 40)

A disciple in Joppa who was known for works of charity. She became sick and died but Peter raised her to life again.

📖 (9:36–42)

Simon[9] (the tanner)
(met Peter c. AD 40)

Peter stayed in this man's house, by the sea, in Joppa.

📖 (9:43; 10:6, 17–20, 32)

Cornelius
(converted c. AD 40)

A God-fearing Gentile centurion in the Italian Regiment based in Caesarea. In a vision he was instructed to send men to collect Peter from Simon[9]'s house. When Peter arrived at Cornelius's house, he declared to all the people gathered there that the Christian message was for Gentiles as well as Jews. Many were baptized with the Holy Spirit and with water.

📖 (10:1–8, 17, 22, 24–48)

Agabus
(prophesied c. AD 45–57)

A prophet from Jerusalem who arrived in Antioch when Barnabas and Saul[2]/Paul were teaching there. He prophesied that there would be a severe famine across the Roman Empire. Later on he encountered Paul again at Caesarea and warned him that he would be bound for his faith by the Jewish leaders in Jerusalem.

📖 (11:27–28; 21:10–11)

Claudius[1]
(emperor AD 41–54)

Roman emperor under whose reign the empire experienced famine. He ordered all Jews to leave Rome. *See panel, p. 228.*

📖 (11:28; 18:2)

Herod[3]/Agrippa[1]
(10 BC–AD 44)

Grandson of Herod[1], he ruled in Galilee from AD 39 to 44. He persecuted the first Christians, and put James[1] to death by the sword and imprisoned Peter. When Peter was delivered from the prison by the intervention of an angel, Herod executed the prison guards. He was struck down by an angel of the Lord in Caesarea because he accepted acclaim as a god and his body was eaten by worms.

📖 (12:1, 4, 6, 11, 19–23)

Mary[5]
(C1st AD)

Mother of John[5] Mark. She was wealthy enough to have her own house and a servant. She invited many people into her house to pray, and Peter went to her house when he escaped from prison.

📖 (12:12)

John[5] Mark
(mid C1st AD)

Cousin of Barnabas who accompanied him and Saul[2]/Paul on their first mission trip. However, he left them early and returned to Jerusalem. This made Paul reluctant to take him on further trips but he accompanied Barnabas from then on. When Paul was imprisoned in Rome he asked John Mark to help him. He was a friend of Peter and probably the author of Mark's Gospel.

📖 (12:12, 25; 13:13; 15:36–40; Colossians 4:10; 2 Timothy 4:11; Philemon 24)

Rhoda
(servant c. AD 43)

Servant in Mary[5]'s house who heard Peter when he knocked at the door when he was released from prison during the night. Overjoyed, she left him on the doorstep and ran back to tell the praying guests, who were too astounded to believe her until they saw Peter for themselves.

📖 (12:13–15)

Blastus
(mid C1st AD)

A trusted personal servant of King Herod[3] who assisted the people of

Tyre and Sidon in their quarrel with the king.

📖 (12:20)

Simeon[4] (Niger), Lucius[1] (of Cyrene), Manaen
(leaders c. AD 48)

Prophets and teachers in Antioch who fasted, prayed and placed their hands on Saul[2]/Paul and Barnabas before they left for Cyprus on their first mission trip.

📖 (13:1)

Bar-Jesus/Elymas
(met Saul[2]/Paul AD 48)

A Jewish sorcerer, false prophet and attendant of Sergius Paulus who opposed Paul and Barnabas in Paphos on the island of Cyprus. He attempted to keep Sergius Paulus from faith. Paul called him 'a child of the devil' and he was struck blind.

📖 (13:6–12)

Sergius Paulus
(proconsul AD 47/48)

Proconsul in Paphos who sent for Saul[2]/Paul and Barnabas so he could hear God's word. Despite an attempt by Elymas to keep him away from faith, he believed and was amazed at their teaching.

📖 (13:7–12)

Judas[6] (Barsabbas)
(leader c. AD 49)

Prophet and leader of the believers in Jerusalem, he was chosen with Silas by the apostles and elders there to accompany Paul and Barnabas to Antioch. He encouraged the believers there before returning with Silas to Jerusalem.

📖 (15:22, 27, 32–34)

Silas/Silvanus
(associate of Paul AD 49–65)

Roman citizen, prophet and leader of the believers in Jerusalem, he was chosen with Judas[6] by the apostles and elders there to accompany Paul and Barnabas to Antioch. He encouraged the believers there before returning with Judas to Jerusalem. When Barnabas parted company with Paul, Paul chose Silas to accompany him on his next mission trip. He was in prison with Paul, praying and singing hymns, when an earthquake shook the prison and the doors were released. He accompanied Paul to Thessalonica and Berea, and later with Timothy met Paul again in Athens. Silas assisted Paul in the writing of the letter of 1 Peter.

📖 (15:22, 27, 32–34, 40; 16:19–40; 17:4–15; 18:5; 2 Corinthians 1:19; 1 Peter 5:12)

Timothy
(associate of Paul AD 50–65)

See **Timothy** *in 1 Timothy, p. 247.*

📖 (16:1–3)

Lydia[2]
(met Paul c. AD 50)

A seller of purple cloth from Thyatira who lived in Philippi and responded to Paul's ministry. She and her household were baptized and she provided hospitality for Paul and his companions. Following their escape from prison, Paul and Silas went to her house, where believers had gathered.

📖 (16:14–15, 40)

Jason[1]
(met Paul c. AD 50)

Owner of a house in Thessalonica which was searched by those incensed by Paul and Silas's message that Jesus was the Messiah. When they did not find Paul and Silas there the crowd dragged Jason and other believers before the town officials, accusing them of harbouring troublemakers.

📖 (17:5–8)

Dionysius
(converted c. AD 50)

A member of the Areopagus in Athens. He was converted by Paul's ministry there.

📖 (17:34)

Damaris
(converted c. AD 50)

A woman converted by Paul's ministry at the Areopagus in Athens.

📖 (17:34)

Aquila, Priscilla
(associates of Paul AD 51–65)

Husband and wife who were close friends of Paul and who were also tentmakers. They gave Paul hospitality and hosted a house church. They had come to Corinth following an order from Claudius that Jews had to leave Rome. They accompanied Paul when he left Corinth and sailed to Syria.

📖 (18:1–3, 18–21, 26; Romans 16:3; 1 Corinthians 16:19)

Titius Justus
(met Paul AD 51)

A Gentile worshipper of God. Paul went to his house, next to a synagogue in Corinth, after he was opposed in the synagogue.

📖 (18:7)

Crispus
(converted AD 51)

The leader of a synagogue in Corinth. He and his household responded to Paul's teaching and believed in the Lord.

📖 (18:8)

Gallio
(proconsul AD 51–52)

Proconsul in the province of Achaia. Jews in Corinth brought Paul to Gallio, hoping he would condemn him. Gallio responded by saying that their accusation against Paul was a matter of Jewish law, not civil law and therefore not his responsibility.

He also chose not to intervene when the crowds turned on the synagogue leader Sosthenes.

📖 (18:12–17)

Sosthenes
(synagogue leader AD 52)

Leader of the synagogue in Corinth where Paul preached. The crowds beat him in front of Gallio when Gallio did not uphold the accusation against Paul.

📖 (18:17)

Apollos
(met Priscilla and Aquila AD 52)

A well-educated Jew from Alexandria who came to Ephesus when Priscilla and Aquila were there. Although he had a good knowledge of the Scriptures and spoke boldly about Jesus in the synagogue, he received further teaching from Aquila and Priscilla, who welcomed him into their home. With the encouragement of the believers in Ephesus he went to Achaia, where his ministry focused on using Scripture to show the Jews that Jesus was the Messiah. Paul explained to the church at Corinth that Apollos was a co-worker with him: there was to be no division in Corinth based on who they considered their human leader to be. Later, Paul had to persuade Apollos to return to Corinth.

📖 (18:24 – 19:1; 1 Corinthians 1:12; 3:4–6, 22; 4:6; 16:12; Titus 3:13)

Tyrannus
(?owner of hall AD 53–55)

A lecture hall in Ephesus was named after this man. Paul taught here for two years.

📖 (19:9)

Sceva
(mid C1st AD)

A Jewish high priest and father of seven sons.

📖 (19:14)

Erastus[1]
(associate of Paul AD 55)

Assistant of Paul, whom he sent with Timothy to Macedonia. Possibly to be identified with Erastus[2].

📖 (19:22)

Demetrius[1]
(silversmith AD 55)

A silversmith in Ephesus who feared that his business, making silver shrines for the god Artemis, would collapse following Paul's teaching about false gods. The resulting uproar saw Paul and his companions brought into the theatre but the city clerk defused the situation and dismissed the crowds.

📖 (19:24–28, 38)

Gaius[1]
(associate of Paul AD 53–55)

A travelling companion of Paul on his third mission trip. He was brought into the theatre at Ephesus with Paul following Demetrius[1]'s complaint.

📖 (19:29)

Aristarchus
(associate of Paul AD 53–65)

A Macedonian from Thessalonica who accompanied Paul on his third mission trip. With Paul he was brought into the theatre at Ephesus following Demetrius[1]'s complaint. He travelled with Paul through Macedonia to Greece. He sailed with Paul to his trial in Rome and was a fellow prisoner with him.

📖 (19:29; 20:4; 27:2; Colossians 4:10; Philemon 24)

Alexander[3]
(met Paul AD 55)

Appointed by Jews in Ephesus as their spokesperson in the uproar that followed Demetrius[1]'s complaint. However, he was shouted down by the crowd.

📖 (19:33–34)

Sopater
(associate of Paul AD 57)

Son of Pyrrhus, from Berea. He was one of Paul's companions when he left Greece and began his journey back through Macedonia to Troas. Probably to be identified with Sosipater.

📖 (20:4)

Pyrrhus
(early C1st AD)

Father of Sopater.

📖 (20:4)

Secundus
(associate of Paul AD 57)

From Thessalonica. One of Paul's companions when he left Greece and travelled back through Macedonia to Troas.

📖 (20:4)

Gaius[2]
(associate of Paul AD 57)

From Derbe. One of Paul's companions when he left Greece and travelled back through Macedonia to Troas.

📖 (20:4)

Tychicus
(associate of Paul AD 57–65)

From Asia. One of Paul's companions when he left Greece and travelled back through Macedonia to Troas. A trusted friend of Paul, he carried the letters to the Ephesians and, with Onesimus, to the Colossians. When Paul wanted Titus with him in Nicopolis, Paul decided that either Artemas or Tychicus would replace him in Crete.

📖 (20:4; Ephesians 6:21–22; Colossians 4:7–9; 2 Timothy 4:12; Titus 3:12)

Trophimus
(associate of Paul AD 57–65)

From Asia. One of Paul's companions when he left Greece and travelled back through Macedonia to Troas. He accompanied Paul to Jerusalem. After Paul's first period of imprisonment in Rome, Trophimus fell sick in Miletus and Paul left him there.

📖 (20:4; 21:29; 2 Timothy 4:20)

Eutychus
(met Paul AD 57)

A young man in Troas who fell asleep when he was listening to Paul in the early hours of the morning. He fell through a third-storey window and his dead body was recovered. However, Paul laid himself on the body and pronounced Eutychus alive.

📖 (20:9–12)

Mnason
(met Paul AD 57)

An early disciple from Cyprus. Paul and his companions stayed in his house on their way to Jerusalem.

📖 (21:16)

Ananias[3]
(high priest AD 47–59)

High priest presiding over the Sanhedrin in Jerusalem when Paul appeared before them. He gave the order that Paul should be struck on the mouth. Paul accused him of hypocrisy for his own violation of the law. It appears that Paul did not know that Ananias was the high priest. Ananias went with Tertullus to Caesarea to bring the case against Paul when he appeared before Felix. He had paid a large sum of money to acquire Roman citizenship.

📖 (23:2; 24:1)

Claudius[2] Lysias/Lysias
(commander AD 57)

The name of the commander (21:33; 22:24–30) who arranged for Paul to be sent from Jerusalem to Felix in Caesarea, having heeded the warning of Paul's nephew that the Jews planned to kill Paul the following day. He wrote a letter to Felix explaining the lack of evidence against Paul. He ordered Paul's accusers to appear before Felix with their evidence. Felix awaited his arrival in Caesarea before he would decide on the case against Paul.

📖 (23:17–30; 24:22)

Felix
(procurator c. AD 52–59)

Governor of Judea to whom Paul was sent by Claudius[2] Lysias. He was familiar with the early Christian movement and placed Paul under guard in Herod[1]'s palace until his accusers arrived. Having heard the case against Paul, he adjourned proceedings, kept Paul under guard but allowed him some freedom. He brought his wife to Paul to hear more about the Christian faith. When Porcius Festus succeeded him, Paul still remained in prison.

📖 (23:24, 26, 33–35; 24:2–27)

Tertullus
(met Paul AD 57)

A lawyer who brought the case against Paul on behalf of the Jewish authorities when Paul appeared before Felix in Caesarea.

📖 (24:1–8)

Drusilla
(c. AD 38–79)

Jewish wife of Felix. She accompanied her husband to listen to Paul speak about faith in Jesus.

📖 (24:24)

Porcius Festus/Festus
(procurator c. AD 59–62)

Succeeded Felix as governor of Judea. Paul argued that Festus should not hand him over to the Jews in Jerusalem but that he should be tried before Caesar in Rome. Festus elicited help from King Agrippa and, having heard Paul's testimony, they agreed together that Paul had done nothing worthy of imprisonment or death.

📖 (24:27; 25:1 – 26:32)

Agrippa[2]/Herod[4] (Agrippa II)
(AD 27–c.100)

Son of Herod[3]/Agrippa I. Ruled northern Palestine from AD 50 to 100. Brother of Bernice. He visited Festus in Caesarea and listened to Festus's dilemma about how to deal with Paul. He and his sister were treated with great honour when they came to hear Paul's passionate testimony, which was specifically focused on bringing Agrippa to faith. He agreed with Festus that Paul had done nothing worthy of imprisonment or death.

📖 (25:13 – 26:32)

Bernice
(born c. AD 28)

Sister of King Agrippa. She accompanied her brother on his visit to Festus in Caesarea and listened to Paul's testimony.

📖 (25:13, 23; 26:30)

Julius
(met Paul AD 59–60)

Roman centurion of the Imperial Regiment who accompanied Paul when he set out from Adramyttium for Rome, a journey which in the end took over three months. He was kind to Paul: when they stopped at Sidon he allowed Paul to be cared for by his friends. He was with Paul during the shipwreck and ordered the soldiers not to take Paul's life as they had planned.

📖 (27:1, 3, 6, 43)

Publius
(met Paul AD 59–60)

Chief official on the island of Malta. He offered generous hospitality to Paul and his companions for three days. When his father became sick Paul offered prayer and he was healed. This led to many more healings on the island.

📖 (28:7)

6 The Letters and Revelation

These books of the New Testament were written in the form of letters. They are addressed to churches or individuals and follow the normal conventions of first-century letter writing. They bring greetings and offer encouragement and instruction. They testify to the organization, worship and ministry in early Christian communities. Many of these letters were written by Paul and show his ongoing concern for churches he had established. The remaining letters were written by other leaders in the church. The final book of the Bible, Revelation, contains many visions and is full of imagery.

Romans

Paul
(wrote Romans c. AD 57)
See **Saul[2]/Paul** *in Acts, p. 236.*
📖 (1:1)

Phoebe
(mid C1st AD)

Female deacon in the church at Cenchraea whom Paul commended to the church at Rome. Paul asked the church to receive her and help her, just as she had helped Paul and others. She probably took Paul's letter to the Roman church.
📖 (16:1–2)

Epenetus
(mid C1st AD)

A close friend of Paul to whom he sent greetings. He was the first Christian convert in Asia.
📖 (16:5)

Mary[6]
(mid C1st AD)

She worked hard for the Roman church and Paul sent her his greetings.
📖 (16:6)

Andronicus, Junia (Junias)
(mid C1st AD)

Respected Jewish converts who had become Christians before Paul. They had been imprisoned with Paul and he sent them greetings. Probably husband and wife.
📖 (16:7)

Ampliatus
(mid C1st AD)

A close friend of Paul to whom he sent greetings.
📖 (16:8)

Urbanus
(mid C1st AD)

One of Paul's co-workers to whom he sent greetings.
📖 (16:9)

Stachys
(mid C1st AD)

A close friend of Paul to whom he sent greetings.

📖 (16:9)

Apelles
(mid C1st AD)

A faithful, tried-and-tested Christian greeted by Paul.

📖 (16:10)

Aristobulus
(mid C1st AD)

Head of a household to whom Paul sent greetings. Possibly the grandson of Herod[1] and brother of Herod[3]/ Agrippa I.

📖 (16:10)

Herodion
(mid C1st AD)

A Jew whom Paul greeted.

📖 (16:11)

Narcissus
(mid C1st AD)

A man in whose household the Christians were greeted by Paul.

📖 (16:11)

Tryphena, Tryphosa
(mid C1st AD)

Women, possibly sisters, whom Paul greeted. He respected their hard work in Christ.

📖 (16:12)

Persis
(mid C1st AD)

A close friend of Paul whom he greeted, remembering her hard work in Christ.

📖 (16:12)

Rufus[2]
(mid C1st AD)

Greeted by Paul, who also greeted Rufus's mother, who ministered as a mother to Paul. Possibly the same person as Rufus[1].

📖 (16:13)

Asyncritus, Phlegon, Hermes, Patrobas, Hermas, Philologus
(mid C1st AD)

Greeted by Paul.

📖 (16:14–15)

Julia
(mid C1st AD)

Greeted by Paul. Perhaps the wife or sister of Philologus.

📖 (16:15)

Nereus
(mid C1st AD)

Greeted, with his sister, by Paul.

📖 (16:15)

Olympas
(mid C1st AD)

Greeted by Paul.

📖 (16:15)

Timothy
(associate of Paul AD 50–65)

See **Timothy** *in 1 Timothy, p. 247.*

📖 (16:21)

Lucius[2]
(associate of Paul AD 57)

A Jew who sent greetings to the church at Rome.

📖 (16:21)

Jason[2]
(associate of Paul AD 57)

A Jew who sent greetings to the church at Rome. Possibly the same person as Jason[1].

📖 (16:21)

Sosipater
(associate of Paul AD 57)

A Jew who sent greetings to the church at Rome. Probably the same person as Sopater (Acts 20:4).

📖 (16:21)

Tertius
(associate of Paul AD 57)

Secretary of Paul who wrote down Paul's letter to the Romans. He added his own personal Christian greeting to the church at Rome.

📖 (16:22)

Gaius[3]
(associate of Paul AD 55–57)

Offered hospitality to Paul and others in the church, and sent his greetings to the church at Rome. He was baptized by Paul.

📖 (16:23; 1 Corinthians 1:14)

Erastus[2]
(associate of Paul AD 57)

A civil servant, Corinth's 'director of public works', who sent greetings to the church at Rome. A pavement that includes the Latin inscription of this name has been discovered in Corinth. Possibly the same person as Erastus[1].

📖 (16:23)

Quartus
(associate of Paul AD 57)

A Christian who sent his greetings to the church at Rome.

📖 (16:23)

1 Corinthians

Paul
(wrote 1 Corinthians c. AD 55)

See **Saul[2]/Paul** *in Acts, p. 236.*

📖 (1:1)

Chloe
(mid C1st AD)

Some members of her household told Paul about quarrels in the church at Corinth.

📖 (1:11)

Cephas
(died c. AD 65)

See **Simon[1]/Simon Peter/ Peter/Cephas** *in Matthew, p. 223.*

📖 (1:12)

Stephanas
(mid C1st AD)

His household were the first converts in Achaia and were baptized by Paul. They had served the church well at Corinth. Along with Fortunatus and Achaicus, he encouraged Paul and possibly delivered Paul's first letter to the Corinthian church.

📖 (1:16; 16:15–18)

Timothy
(associate of Paul AD 50–65)

See **Timothy** *in 1 Timothy, p. 247.*

📖 (16:10)

Fortunatus, Achaicus
(met Paul AD 55)

Along with Stephanas, these men encouraged Paul and possibly delivered Paul's first letter to the Corinthian church.

📖 (16:15–18)

2 Corinthians

Paul
(wrote 2 Corinthians c. AD 56)

See **Saul[2]/Paul** *in Acts, p. 236.*

📖 (1:1)

Timothy
(associate of Paul AD 50–65)

See **Timothy** *in 1 Timothy, p. 247.*

📖 (1:1)

Titus
(associate of Paul AD 48–65)

See **Titus** *in Titus, p. 249.*

📖 (2:13)

Aretas
(king of Nabateans 9 BC–AD 40)

King whose governor in Damascus tried to keep Paul in the city. Paul escaped by being lowered in a basket through a window in a wall. Aretas has been identified as the Nabatean King Aretas IV who was Herod[2] Antipas's father-in-law.

📖 (11:32–33)

Galatians

Paul
(wrote Galatians c. AD 49)

See **Saul[2]/Paul** in Acts, p. 236.

📖 (1:1)

Cephas
(died c. AD 65)

See **Simon[1]/Simon Peter/ Peter/Cephas** in Matthew, p. 223.

📖 (1:18; 2:9, 11, 14)

Ephesians

Paul
(wrote Ephesians c. AD 60)

See **Saul[2]/Paul** in Acts, p. 236.

📖 (1:1)

Tychicus
(associate of Paul AD 57–65)

See **Tychicus** in Acts, p. 240.

📖 (6:21)

Philippians

Paul
(wrote Philippians c. AD 54/62)

See **Saul[2]/Paul** in Acts, p. 236.

📖 (1:1)

Timothy
(associate of Paul AD 50–65)

See **Timothy** in 1 Timothy, p. 247.

📖 (1:1)

Epaphroditus
(mid C1st AD)

Close friend of Paul whom Paul respected as a 'brother, co-worker and fellow soldier' who was willing to risk his life in serving Christ. The church at Philippi sent him with a gift to Paul but he had become dangerously ill. When the church heard about his illness, they were very concerned, which caused Epaphroditus to worry. God restored Epaphroditus to health and Paul sent him back to Philippi, asking them to welcome him home with joy and honour.

📖 (2:25–30; 4:18)

Euodia, Syntyche
(mid C1st AD)

Two Christian women in the church at Philippi. They had worked well with Paul for the sake of the gospel but a disagreement had arisen between them. Paul pleaded with each of them to mend their differences and agree in the Lord.

📖 (4:2–3)

Clement
(mid C1st AD)

Christian in the church at Philippi who worked with Paul for the gospel.

📖 (4:3)

Colossians

Paul
(wrote Colossians c. AD 54/62)

See **Saul[2]/Paul** in Acts, p. 236.

📖 (1:1)

Timothy
(associate of Paul AD 50–65)

See **Timothy** in 1 Timothy, p. 247.

📖 (1:1)

Epaphras
(mid C1st AD)

Friend of Paul whom he described as a 'dear fellow servant' and his 'fellow prisoner in Christ'. He spread the gospel to the Colossians and was known for his hard work at Laodicea and Hierapolis and for his fervent prayer.

(1:7; 4:12; Philemon 23)

Tychicus
(associate of Paul AD 57–65)

See **Tychicus** in Acts, p. 240.

(4:7)

Onesimus
(met Paul c. AD 53/61)

See **Onesimus** in Philemon, p. 250.

(4:9)

Mark
(C1st AD)

See **John[5] Mark** in Acts, p. 237.

(4:10)

Jesus Justus
(associate of Paul AD 54/62)

A Jewish Christian who sent his greetings to the church at Colossae. He worked hard in God's service and comforted Paul.

(4:11)

Luke
(associate of Paul AD 57–65)

A doctor traditionally credited with the writing of the two-part history of the life of Jesus and the birth of the early church contained in Luke and Acts. He spent some time working with Paul.

(4:14; 2 Timothy 4:11; Philemon 24)

Demas
(associate of Paul AD 54/62)

Paul's travelling companion and fellow-worker who later abandoned Paul 'because he loved this world'.

(4:14; 2 Timothy 4:9–10; Philemon 24)

Nympha
(greeted by Paul AD 54/62)

Greeted by Paul, and hosted a church in her house.

(4:15)

Archippus
(mentioned by Paul AD 54/62)

Possibly the son of Philemon and Apphia. Paul encouraged him to fulfil the work he had received in the Lord.

(4:17; Philemon 2)

1, 2 Thessalonians

Paul
(wrote 1, 2 Thessalonians c. AD 51)

See **Saul[2]/Paul** in Acts, p. 236.

(1 Thessalonians 1:1; 2 Thessalonians 1:1)

Silas
(associate of Paul AD 49–65)

See **Silas/Silvanus** in Acts, p. 238.

(1 Thessalonians 1:1; 2 Thessalonians 1:1)

Timothy
(associate of Paul AD 50–65)

See **Timothy** in 1 Timothy, p. 247.

(1 Thessalonians 1:1; 2 Thessalonians 1:1)

1 Timothy

Paul
(wrote 1 Timothy c. AD 62)

See **Saul[2]/Paul** in Acts, p. 236.

(1:1)

Timothy
(associate of Paul AD 50–65)

Disciple from Lystra who became Paul's close friend and loyal assistant. His mother Eunice was a Jew and a believer who, together with his grandmother Lois, nurtured his faith and his knowledge of Scripture from an early age. His father was a Gentile, so Paul had Timothy circumcised to aid his usefulness in spreading the gospel among Jews. Timothy worked with Paul and Silas in sharing the gospel in Philippi, Thessalonica and Berea. His partnership with Paul is emphasized: his name is alongside Paul's at the opening of many letters. Paul described him as having 'proved himself . . . as a son with his father he has served with me in the work of the gospel' (Philippians 2:22). In writing his two letters to Timothy, Paul challenged Timothy to overcome his natural shyness, lack of self-confidence and physical illness so he could be strong in the spiritual battle, oppose false teachers, guard the truth and ensure he remain faithful in his personal life and in his Christian teaching and leadership.

📖 (1:1 – 6:21; Acts 16:1–3; 17:14–15; 18:5; 19:22; 20:4; 1 Corinthians 4:17; 2 Corinthians 1:1, 19; Philippians 1:1; 2:19–24; 2 Timothy 1:1 – 4:22)

Hymenaeus, Alexander[4]
(mid C1st AD)

False teachers who had wrecked their faith and the faith of others. They taught that the resurrection had already happened. Paul had disciplined them and expelled them from the church.

📖 (1:20; 2 Timothy 2:17–18)

2 Timothy

Paul
(wrote 2 Timothy c. AD 64)

See **Saul[2]/Paul** in Acts, p. 236.

📖 (1:1)

Timothy
(associate of Paul AD 50–65)

See **Timothy** in 1 Timothy, p. 247.

📖 (1:2)

Lois, Eunice
(Lois late C1st BC; Eunice early C1st AD)

Timothy's grandmother and mother respectively, who were Jewish

believers and who in his early years encouraged his faith and knowledge of the Scriptures.

📖 (1:5; 3:15; Acts 16:1)

Phygelus, Hermogenes
(mid C1st AD)

Two men in Asia who deserted Paul.

📖 (1:15)

Onesiphorus
(mid C1st AD)

Faithful friend of Paul. Onesiphorus helped Paul in Ephesus and made an effort to find Paul when he was imprisoned in Rome so he could refresh and encourage him. Paul asked for God's mercy on Onesiphorus and greeted his household.

📖 (1:16–18; 4:19)

Philetus
(mid C1st AD)

False teacher who, like Hymenaeus, had taught that the resurrection had already happened.

📖 (2:17)

Jannes, Jambres
(mid C15th BC)

Two men named by Paul as opponents of Moses. Jewish tradition identifies them as Egyptian magicians who tried to imitate the signs that Moses and Aaron performed. Their limited success led to Pharaoh hardening his heart (see Exodus 7:11–13, 22; 8:7).

📖 (3:8)

Crescens
(mid C1st AD)

Friend of Paul who went to Galatia, leaving Paul in Rome.

📖 (4:10)

Carpus
(met Paul c. AD 64)

Man with whom Paul had left his cloak in Troas. He asked Timothy to retrieve it.

📖 (4:13)

Alexander[5]
(met Paul c. AD 64)

Metalworker (coppersmith) in Rome who caused Paul harm by strongly opposing his message. Paul knew that God would judge Alexander for what he had done.

📖 (4:14–15)

Erastus[3]
(mid C1st AD)

An associate of Paul, whom he left in Corinth. Possibly the same person as Erastus[2] or, more likely, Erastus[1].

📖 (4:20)

Eubulus, Pudens, Linus, Claudia
(mid C1st AD)

Christians in Rome with Paul who sent greetings to Timothy.

📖 (4:21)

Titus

Paul
(wrote Titus c. AD 62)

See **Saul[2]/Paul** in Acts, p. 236.

📖 (1:1)

Titus
(associate of Paul AD 48–65)

Gentile converted through Paul's ministry who was not circumcised. He was Paul's 'partner and fellow worker', and proved himself personable, diplomatic and trustworthy. Titus accompanied Paul and Barnabas to Jerusalem. He helped heal the rift between Paul and the church at Corinth and organized a collection of money for the needy believers in Jerusalem. He accompanied Paul to Crete, where later Paul left him to consolidate the church. Paul wrote his letter to Titus, giving guidance on practical issues, including appointing elders, dealing with opposition, deciding what to teach and instructions about good living. Paul later sent Titus to Dalmatia.

📖 (1:1 – 3:15; 2 Corinthians 2:13; 7:6–7, 13–15; 8:6, 16–24; 12:18; Galatians 2:1–3; 2 Timothy 4:10)

Artemas
(mid C1st AD)

One of Paul's co-workers whom he considered sending to Crete to take Titus's place as leader of the church so Titus could spend the winter with Paul at Nicopolis.

📖 (3:12)

Zenas
(mid C1st AD)

Lawyer who travelled with Apollos to an unknown destination. Paul encouraged Titus to provide for their needs.

📖 (3:13)

Philemon

Paul
(wrote Philemon c. AD 54/62)

See **Saul[2]/Paul** in Acts, p. 236.

📖 (1)

Timothy
(associate of Paul AD 50–65)

See **Timothy** in 1 Timothy, p. 247.

📖 (1)

Philemon
(mid C1st AD)

Probably the husband of Apphia and the father of Archippus. He lived in Colossae and a church met in his home. Paul wrote a tactful letter to Philemon to appeal to him to be merciful in receiving 'as a brother' the runaway slave Onesimus, who was now repentant and returning to Philemon. Paul offered to pay personally any compensation that Philemon might require for the slave's absence.

📖 (1–25)

Apphia
(mid C1st AD)

Named in the opening greeting of Paul's letter to Philemon, she was probably Philemon's wife.

📖 (2)

Onesimus
(met Paul c. AD 53/61)

Slave who had run away from his master Philemon and had, it seems, stolen items from him. Encountering the ministry of Paul, Onesimus became a Christian and they became close friends. Paul would have liked to have kept Onesimus with him during his imprisonment because Onesimus (meaning 'useful') had become useful to him. However, Paul returned Onesimus to Philemon, trusting that Philemon would now receive Onesimus as a Christian brother; Paul offered to pay Philemon back for any debts that Onesimus owed his master. With Tychicus, Onesimus delivered Paul's letter to the Colossians.

📖 (10–21; Colossians 4:9)

Hebrews

The names mentioned in this book have already been listed under an earlier book.

James

James
(died AD 62)

See **James[3]** in *Matthew*, p. 225.

📖 (1:1)

1, 2 Peter

Peter
(died c. AD 65)

See **Simon[1]/Simon Peter/**
Peter/Cephas in *Matthew*, p. 223.

📖 (1 Peter 1:1; 2 Peter 1:1)

1, 2 John

John
(C1st AD)

See **John[2]/Joseph[7]/Joses** in *Matthew*, p. 224.

3 John

John
(C1st AD)

See **John[2]/Joseph[7]/Joses** in *Matthew*, p. 224.

Gaius[4]
(late C1st AD)

Close friend of John[2] to whom 3 John is addressed. John commended Gaius for his faithfulness and hospitality, and prayed for his health and welfare. He urged Gaius to follow God's good ways and expressed his eagerness to visit him soon.

📖 (1)

Diotrephes
(late C1st AD)

A selfish and ambitious man who had spread malicious gossip about John[2] and his associates. He had refused to welcome travelling Christians and had stopped others from welcoming them too. John promised to deal with him when he visited.

📖 (9–10)

Demetrius[2]
(late C1st AD)

A man known to Gaius[4] of whom John[2] and everyone else spoke well.

📖 (12)

Jude

Jude
(C1st AD)

Writer of the letter of Jude. He
identifies himself as 'a servant of
Jesus Christ and a brother of James'.
Probably the same person as **Judas[2]**
in Matthew, p. 225.

📖 (1)

Revelation

John
(C1st AD)

See **John[2]/Joseph[7]/Joses** *in
Matthew, p. 224.*

📖 (1:1, 4, 9; 22:8)

Satan

A personal spirit who opposes God in the spiritual and the earthly realms. His
overall aim is to undermine God's rule. He is especially associated with deceit,
temptation and testing, through which he tries to turn believers away from
obeying God. His name means 'accuser'. The death of Jesus Christ on the cross
was the significant moment of Satan's defeat and he will be finally defeated when
Jesus Christ returns.

Names, titles and descriptions of Satan

Abaddon, Apollyon (Destroyer)	Revelation 9:11
Adversary	Job 1:6
Angel of the Abyss	Revelation 9:11
Belial	2 Corinthians 6:15
Beelzebul, prince of demons	Matthew 12:24
Devil	John 8:44
Dragon	Revelation 12:9
Enemy	1 Peter 5:8
Evil one	Matthew 13:19
Father of lies	John 8:44
God of this age	2 Corinthians 4:4
Liar	John 8:44
Murderer from the beginning	John 8:44
Prince of this world	John 12:31
Ruler of the kingdom of the air	Ephesians 2:2
Satan	Revelation 12:9
Snake	Genesis 3:1
Tempter	Matthew 4:3

Antipas[2]
(late C1st AD)

A martyr mentioned in a letter to the church in Pergamum.

📖 (2:13)

Jezebel
See **Jezebel** *in 1 Kings, p. 101.*

📖 (2:20)

Abaddon/Apollyon (fallen angel)
Name of the angel who reigns over the world of the dead.

📖 (9:11)

Appendix: Selected entries from the Apocrypha

The Apocrypha is the name given to the collection of books recognized as deuterocanonical (being of secondary canonical rank) by the Roman Catholic and Orthodox churches, but excluded as apocryphal (outside the canon) by the Protestant churches. There are three categories:

- Books recognized by all Catholic and Orthodox churches (Tobit; Judith; Additions to Esther; Wisdom of Solomon; Sirach (Ecclesiasticus); Baruch; Letter of Jeremiah; Greek additions to Daniel: the Prayer of Azariah, Susanna, Bel and the Dragon; 1 and 2 Maccabees)

- Books recognized only by the Greek and Russian Orthodox churches (1 Esdras, Prayer of Manasseh, Psalm 151, 3 Maccabees)

- Other books: 2 Esdras (included in the Slavonic Bible); Book of Enoch (included in the Ethiopian Bible); Book of Jubilees (included in the Ethiopian Bible); Psalms of Solomon (included in some editions of the Septuagint); 4 Maccabees (included as an appendix in the Septuagint)

Tobit

Tobit
(set in C7th BC)

Son of Tobiel. Father of Tobias. Husband of Anna. He was a pious and charitable Jewish man from the tribe of Naphtali. He had helped many Jews during the time of the Assyrian oppression. However, he became very poor and had an accident, which caused him to go blind. In his desperation he prayed that God would let him die. But God restored his eyesight, his wealth and his reputation, and enabled him to find a wife for his son Tobias. He carefully instructed Tobias in the way he should live his life. He lived until he was 112 years old and was buried with honour in Nineveh.

📖 (1:1 – 14:15)

Tobias
(set in C7th BC)

Son of Tobit. Tobit sent Tobias away from the family home to secure some trust money from Gabael in Media. On the journey, Tobias met Raguel and married Raguel's daughter Sarah. Tobias returned to his father in Nineveh but when Tobit died, he and Sarah returned to Media, her family home. Tobias treated his father-in-law with great honour and inherited his wealth, along with that of his own father.

📖 (1:9, 20; 2:1–3; 3:17; 4:2 – 14:15)

Gabael

(set in C7th BC)

A man who lived in Rages in Media to whom Tobit sent Tobias in order to retrieve some money that he had placed in trust with Gabael.

📖 (1:14; 4:1–2, 20–21; 5:1–3, 6; 10:1–2)

Raguel

(set in C7th BC)

A relative of Tobit. Father of Sarah and husband of Edna. Raguel helped Tobias to find Gabael. He facilitated Tobias's marriage to his daughter and allowed them both to return to Tobit in Nineveh. After Tobit died, they returned to live with Raguel in Media. Raguel is treated with great honour by Tobias.

📖 (3:7–17; 6:11, 13; 7:1–16; 8:9–21; 10:7–13; 14:12–13)

Sarah

(set in C7th BC)

Daughter of Raguel and Edna. She had seven previous husbands (who had died on their wedding night) before she married Tobias.

📖 (3:7, 17; 6:11–12; 7:8–16; 10:10–12; 11:17; 12:12, 14)

Judith

Holofernes

(set in early C6th BC)

Chief General of Nebuchadnezzar's army, he led assaults against many nations before turning his brutal attention towards the Jews. Holofernes ignored Achior's warning that God would protect the Jews. He was killed by Judith.

📖 (2:4, 14–28; 3:5 – 4:2; 5:1–4; 5:22 – 6:10; 7:1, 6, 16, 26)

Achior

(set in early C6th BC)

Ammonite leader who testified to Holofernes about God's presence with the Jewish people throughout their history. Holofernes planned to kill him with the Israelites when he overthrew them but the Israelites honoured him for his service to them. He was circumcised and became a Jew.

📖 (5:5 – 6:21; 14:5–10)

Judith

(set in early C6th BC)

Daughter of Merari. The beautiful and courageous widow of Manasseh, from Bethulia. She encouraged the elders of her town to take a stand against the Assyrians. She prayed to God for help before gaining an audience with Holofernes, whom she enticed to trust her by means of her beauty and wise words. She stayed in the Assyrian camp for three days before taking up an invitation to wine and dine with Holofernes. In his drunken stupor, Judith killed him with a sword. The inhabitants of Bethulia attacked the Assyrians and took their camp. Judith offered a song of praise to the Lord. She was honoured and the Israelites were safe for the rest of her lifetime.

📖 (8:1 – 14:9; 15:8 – 16:25)

Sirach/Ecclesiasticus

Jesus ben Sirach

(early C2nd BC)

Writer of a selection of wisdom sayings translated by his grandson during the reign of Euergetes (c. 132 BC). Ben Sirach was a contemporary of the high priest Simon II, who died some time after 200 BC.

📖 (Prologue; 50:20, 27)

Baruch

Baruch

(late C7th BC)

See **Baruch[4]** in Jeremiah, p. 205.

📖 (1:1)

Susanna

Susanna
(set in C6th BC)

Beautiful daughter of Hilkiah. She lived in Babylon as the wife of Joakim and she feared the Lord. Two elders plotted against her when she refused to give in to their sexual demands. Condemned to death, she was saved at the last moment by the intervention of Daniel.

📖 (1–64)

Daniel
(c.620–after 537 BC)

A young man, led by the Holy Spirit, who intervened when Susanna was executed. He cross-examined the two elders who had brought the false charges against Susanna and exposed their lies.

📖 (44–64)

1–4 Maccabees

Antiochus IV Epiphanes
(215–164 BC; ruled 175–164 BC)

King of Syria and Asia Minor who sought the Hellenization of his kingdom, including Judea. In 170 BC he plundered the temple treasury and in 167 BC banned the practising of the Jewish faith. The temple sacrifices were replaced by sacrifices to idols, Scriptures were destroyed and it was forbidden to celebrate festivals, practise circumcision or keep food laws. This triggered the Maccabean uprising, which led to the purification of Jerusalem and the rededication of the temple in 164. When he heard his armies had experienced defeat in Judah, he became sick and died. His son Antiochus succeeded him.

📖 (1 Maccabees 1:10–64; 6:1–17;
     2 Maccabees 4:7; 5:15–26; 9:1–28)

Mattathias
(died c.166 BC)

Son of John. Father of Judas Maccabeus and four other sons. He had moved to Modein from Jerusalem following the desecration of the temple there. He led his family in mourning for Jerusalem and in taking a stand against the advancing Greek culture. He passed the leadership of resistance to his sons before he died at 146 years old. He was greatly mourned by the Israelites.

📖 (1 Maccabees 2:1–70)

John/Gaddi, Simon (Simeon)/ Thassi, Eleazar/Avaran, Jonathan/Apphus
(John/Gaddi died c.160 BC; Simon [Simeon]/ Thassi died 135 BC; Eleazar/Avaran died 162 BC; Jonathan/Apphus died 143 BC)

Four sons of Mattathias and brothers of Judas Maccabeus. They assisted Judas in his campaigns against the enemies of the Jews. When Judas died, Jonathan succeeded him and began to restore Jerusalem. He was assisted by Simon, who took up Jonathan's role and also was appointed high priest. Simon's son John succeeded him.

📖 (1 Maccabees 2:3–5, 14, 49–50, 65–69;
     3:2, 42; 5:24, 55, 63–65; 7:10; 9:19,
     28–49; 9:58 – 10:46, 59; 10:74 – 14:49;
     16:1–24)

Judas Maccabeus
(died 160 BC)

Son of Mattathias. With assistance from his brothers, he achieved liberation for the Jews by leading them in numerous battles. He also instigated a treaty of friendship with the Romans. He died in battle near Mount Azotus in a desperate fight against the army of Bacchides. He was buried in Modein, and Israel mourned for him for many days.

📖 (1 Maccabees 2:4, 14, 49–50, 66–69;
     3:1 – 9:31; 2 Maccabees 5:27; 8:1–7,
     12; 10:1, 21–35; 11:6–7; 12:5–9,
     11–12, 17–45; 14:1–2, 6, 11–14,
     17–26)

Alphabetical List of Names

Aaron	43
Abaddon	252
Abagtha	196
Abda	[1] 92; [2] 190
Abdeel	207
Abdi	[1] 137; [2] 164; [3] 178
Abdiel	133
Abdon	[1] 64; [2] 142; [3] 143; [4] 117, 166
Abednego	211
Abel	15
Abi-Albon	90
Abiasaph	45
Abiathar	76
Abida	27
Abidan	48
Abiel	[1] 70; [2] 90
Abiezer	[1] 53; [2] 90
Abigail	Nabal's wife [1] 76; [2] 87
Abihail	[1] 50; [2] 123; [3] 133; [4] 160; [5] 197
Abihu	45
Abihud	140
Abijah	[1] 69; [2] 97; Judah's king [3] 97; [4] 113; [5] 122; [6] 138; [7] 154; [8] 187
Abimael	20
Abimelech	*See* Abimelek
Abimelek	king of Gerar [1] 25; king of the Philistines [2] 28; son of Gideon [3] 62; [4] 200
Abinadab	[1] 69; [2] 73; [3] 78
Abinoam	61
Abiram	[1] 51; [2] 101
Abishag	91
Abishai	77
Abishalom	98
Abishua	[1] 133; [2] 141

Ananiah	183
Ananias	Sapphira's husband [1] 235; Christian in Damascus [2] 236; high priest [3] 241
Anath	60
Anathoth	[1] 138; [2] 187
Andrew	223
Andronicus	243
Aner	23
Angels	212
Aniam	139
Anna	229
Annas	229
Anthothijah	142
Antiochus IV Epiphanes	[Ap] 255
Antipas	Herod 2 [1] 225; [2] 252
Anub	128
Apelles	244
Aphiah	70
Apollos	239
Apollyon	252
Appaim	123
Apphia	250
Apphus	[Ap] 255
Aquila	239
Ara	141
Arad	142
Arah	[1] 141; [2] 168; [3] 184
Aram	[1] 19; [2] 25; [3] 141
Aran	36
Araunah	91
Arba	59
Archelaus	221
Archippus	247
Ard	40
Ardon	122
Areli	40
Aretas	246
Argob	110
Aridai	198
Aridatha	198
Arieh	110
Ariel	175

Azaliah	117
Azaniah	187
Azarel	[1] 151; [2] 155; [3] 159; [4] 178; [5] 190; [6] 195
Azariah	[1] 92; [2] 92; Judah's king: *see* Uzziah[1] [3] 108; [4] 122; [5] 124; [6] 134; [7] 134; [8] 134; [9] 136; [10] 145; Oded's son, prophet [11] 161; Jehoshaphat's son [12] 162; Jeroham's son, commander [13] 162; Obed's son, commander [14] 163; [15] 164; [16] 164; chief priest in Hezekiah's reign [17] 165; [18] 168; [19] 183; [20] 184; [21] 186; [22] 187; [23] 193; [24] 209; [25] 211
Azariahu	162
Azaz	132
Azaziah	[1] 152; [2] 158; [3] 165
Azbuk	182
Azel	143
Azgad	169
Aziel	152
Aziza	178
Azmaveth	[1] 90; [2] 143; [3] 150; [4] 159
Azor	220
Azriel	[1] 133; [2] 158; [3] 207
Azrikam	[1] 127; [2] 143; [3] 146; [4] 164
Azubah	[1] 104; [2] 122
Azzan	56
Azzur	[1] 187; [2] 204; [3] 210
Baal	[1] 132; [2] 143
Baal-Berith	112
Baal-Hanan	[1] 37; [2] 159
Baalis	209
Baana	[1] 92; [2] 92; [3] 168
Baanah	[1] 80; [2] 90; [3] 168; [4] 180
Baara	142
Baaseiah	137
Baasha	98
Bakbakkar	146
Bakbuk	171
Bakbukiah	[1] 190; [2] 193
Balaam	52
Baladan	114
Balak	52
Bani	[1] 138; [2] 144; [3] 169; [4] 182; [5] 185; [6] 186; [7] 186; [8] 191
Barabbas	226

Biztha	196
Blastus	237
Boanerges	227
Boaz	66
Bohan	59
Bokeru	143
Bukki	[1] 55; [2] 133
Bukkiah	155
Bunah	122
Bunni	[1] 186; [2] 187; [3] 190
Buz	[1] 25; [2] 133
Buzi	209
Caesars	228
Caiaphas	225
Cain	15
Cainan	231
Calcol	*See* Kalkol
Caleb	one of 12 who explored Canaan [1] 50; [2] 122
Canaan	18
Carcas	*See* Karkas
Carmi	*See* Karmi
Carpus	248
Carshena	*See* Karshena
Cephas	223
Chloe	245
Christ	*See* Jesus
Chuza	232
Claudia	249
Claudius	[1] 237; [2] 241
Clement	246
Cleopas	232
Clopas	233
Col-Hozeh	*See* Kol-Hozeh
Conaniah	*See* Konaniah
Cornelius	237
Cosam	230
Cozbi	*See* Kozbi
Crescens	248
Crispus	239
Cush	[1] 19; [2] 200
Cushan-Rishathaim	59

Eden	165
Eder	[1] 142; [2] 154
Edom	27
Eglah	80
Eglon	60
Egypt	19
Ehi	40
Ehud	left-handed man [1] 60; [2] 139
Eker	123
Ela	93
Elah	[1] 37; Israel's king [2] 99; [3] 110; [4] 129; [5] 145
Elam	[1] 19; [2] 142; [3] 156; [4] 168; [5] 170; [6] 195
Elasah	[1] 177; [2] 205
Eldaah	27
Eldad	50
Elead	140
Eleadah	140
Eleasah	[1] 124; [2] 143
Eleazar	Aaron's son [1] 45; [2] 69; [3] 89; [4] 154; [5] 175; [6] 177; [7] 195; [8] 220; [Ap] 255
Elhanan	[1] 89; [2] 89
Eli	68
Eliab	[1] 48; [2] 51; firstborn son of Jesse [3] 73; [4] 136; [5] 151; [6] 152
Eliada	[1] 82; [2] 94; [3] 161
Eliahba	90
Eliakim	palace administrator in Hezekiah's reign [1] 114; [2] 118; [3] 194; [4] 220; [5] 231
Eliam	[1] 85; [2] 91
Eliasaph	[1] 49; [2] 49
Eliashib	[1] 127; [2] 154; high priest in Nehemiah's time [3] 176; [4] 177; [5] 178; [6] 178
Eliathah	155
Elidad	55
Eliehoenai	[1] 156; [2] 173
Eliel	[1] 133; [2] 67, 136; [3] 142; [4] 142; [5] 149; [6] 150; [7] 151; [8] 151; [9] 165
Elienai	142
Eliezer	Abraham's servant [1] 24; Moses' son [2] 47; [3] 138; [4] 152; [5] 157; [6] 162; leader brought by Ezra [7] 172; [8] 177; [9] 177; [10] 178; [11] 230
Elihoreph	92
Elihu	[1] 67; [2] 151; [3] 156; [4] 158; Job's friend [5] 200
Elijah	prophet [1] 101; [2] 142; [3] 177; [4] 178

Gilead	[1] 53; Jephthah's father [2] 63; [3] 133
Ginath	100
Ginnethon	[1] 187; [2] 191
Gishpa	190
God	15
Gog	[1] 132; chief prince [2] 210
Goliath	74
Gomer	[1] 18; Hosea's wife [2] 213
Guni	[1] 41; [2] 133
Haahashtari	128
Habakkuk	215
Habazziniah	82
Hacaliah	*See* Hakaliah
Hacmoni	*See* Hakmoni
Hadad	[1] 27; [2] 36; [3] 37; Edomite [4] 93
Hadadezer	82
Hadassah	197
Hadlai	164
Hadoram	[1] 20; [2] 83
Hagab	171
Hagaba	171
Hagabah	171
Hagar	24
Haggadi	91
Haggai	217
Haggedolim	190
Haggi	40
Haggiah	136
Haggith	79
Hagri	91
Hakaliah	179
Hakkatan	174
Hakkoz	[1] 154; [2] 171; [3] 180
Hakmoni	160
Hakupha	171
Hallohesh	[1] 181; [2] 187
Ham	18
Haman	198
Hammath	126
Hammedatha	198
Hammoleketh	139

Hassenuah	[1] 144; [2] 189
Hasshub	[1] 146; [2] 181; [3] 183; [4] 187
Hassophereth	171
Hasupha	171
Hathach	*See* Hathak
Hathak	198
Hathath	129
Hatipha	171
Hatita	171
Hattil	171
Hattush	[1] 127; [2] 181; [3] 187
Havilah	[1] 19; [2] 20
Hazael	102
Hazaiah	188
Hazarmaveth	20
Haziel	153
Hazo	25
Hazzelelponi	127
Hazzobebah	128
Heber	[1] 40; Jael's husband [2] 61; [3] 129; [4] 142
Hebron	[1] 43; [2] 124
Hegai	197
Helah	128
Heldai	[1] 157; [2] 216
Heled	90
Helek	54
Helem	[1] 141; [2] 216
Helez	[1] 89; [2] 124
Heli	229
Helkai	192
Helon	48
Hemam	*See* Homam
Heman	wise [1] 93; temple musician [2] 136; [3] 152
Hemdan	36
Hen	216
Henadad	171
Hepher	[1] 54; [2] 128; [3] 148
Hephzibah	116
Heresh	146
Hermas	244
Hermes	244
Hermogenes	248

Herod	the Great [1] 221; Antipas [2] 225; Agrippa I [3] 237; Agrippa II [4] 242
Herodias	225
Herodion	244
Hezekiah	Judah's king [1] 111; [2] 170; [3] 215
Hezion	98
Hezir	[1] 154; [2] 187
Hezro	91
Hezron	[1] 39; [2] 39
Hiddai	90
Hiel	101
Hilkiah	[1] 114; found Book of Law [2] 117; [3] 138; [4] 145; [5] 156; [6] 185; [7] 189; [8] 191; [9] 204; [10] 205
Hillel	64
Hirah	37
Hiram	80
Hizki	142
Hizkiah	127
Hobab	50
Hobaiah	171
Hod	141
Hodaviah	[1] 127; [2] 133; [3] 144; [4] 170
Hodesh	142
Hodiah	[1] 130; [2] 186; [3] 187; [4] 187
Hoglah	54
Hoham	58
Holofernes	[Ap] 254
Holy Spirit	234
Homam	36
Hophni	68
Horam	58
Hori	[1] 36; [2] 50
Hosah	[1] 152; [2] 152
Hosea	212
Hoshaiah	[1] 193; [2] 209
Hoshama	126
Hoshea	[1] 46; Israel's king [2] 110; [3] 158; [4] 187
Hotham	[1] 140; [2] 149
Hothir	155
Hubbah	141
Hul	19
Huldah	117
Hupham	40

Isaac   24
Isaiah   115
Iscah   *See* Iskah
Iscariot   *See* Judas [1]
Ishbah   129
Ishbak   26
Ishbi-Benob   88
Ish-Bosheth   78
Ishhod   139
Ishi   [1] 123; [2] 130; [3] 131; [4] 133
Ishiah   [1] 138; [2] 151; [3] 154; [4] 155
Ishijah   178
Ishma   127
Ishmael   son of Abraham and Hagar [1] 24; killed Gedaliah [2] 120; [3] 143; [4] 162; [5] 163; [6] 177
Ishmaiah   [1] 150; [2] 158
Ishmerai   142
Ishpah   142
Ishpan   142
Ishvah   40
Ishvi   [1] 40; [2] 71
Iskah   22
Ismakiah   165
Israel   27
Issachar   Jacob's son [1] 33; [2] 156
Isshiah   *See* Ishiah
Ithai   90
Ithamar   45
Ithiel   [1] 189; [2] 200
Ithmah   150
Ithran   [1] 36; [2] 141
Ithream   80
Ittai   86
Izhar   43
Izliah   142
Izrahiah   138
Izri   155
Izziah   177

Jaakobah   131
Jaala   171
Jaare-Oregim   89
Jaareshiah   142

Jaasiel	[1] 150; [2] 159
Jaasu	178
Jaazaniah	[1] 121; Rekabite [2] 206; [3] 210; [4] 210
Jaaziah	155
Jaaziel	152
Jabal	17
Jabesh	109
Jabez	128
Jabin	[1] 59; [2] 60
Jacob	younger twin [1] 27; [2] 220
Jada	123
Jadah	143
Jaddai	179
Jaddua	[1] 187; [2] 191
Jadon	180
Jael	61
Jahath	[1] 127; [2] 134; [3] 137; [4] 153; [5] 154; [6] 166
Jahaziel	[1] 150; [2] 152; [3] 153; Spirit came on him [4] 162; [5] 173
Jahdai	125
Jahdiel	133
Jahdo	133
Jahleel	40
Jahmai	138
Jahzeel	41
Jahzeiah	176
Jahzerah	146
Jahziel	41
Jair	[1] 55; [2] 63; [3] 89; [4] 197
Jairus	227
Jakan	132
Jakeh	200
Jakim	[1] 142; [2] 154
Jakin	[1] 39; [2] 145; [3] 154; [4] 189
Jalam	35
Jalon	129
Jambres	248
James	Jesus' disciple, fisherman [1] 223; Jesus' disciple, Alphaeus's son [2] 224; Jesus' brother, author of letter [3] 225; Judas's father [4] 231
Jamin	[1] 39; [2] 123; [3] 186
Jamlech	131
Janai	132

Jehoiakim	118
Jehoiarib	[1] 145; [2] 154
Jehonadab	106
Jehonathan	[1] 161; [2] 192
Jehoram	king of Judah [1] 161; [2] 192
Jehoshaphat	[1] 82; [2] 92; king of Judah [3] 98; [4] 106
Jehosheba	106
Jehozabad	[1] 107; [2] 156; [3] 162
Jehozadak	134
Jehu	Hanani's son, prophet [1] 99; Israel's king [2] 102; [3] 124; [4] 131; [5] 150
Jehucal	*See* Jehukal
Jehudi	207
Jehukal	207
Jeiel	[1] 132; [2] 143; [3] 149; [4] 152; [5] 162; [6] 163; [7] 165; [8] 166; [9] 179
Jekameam	153
Jekamiah	[1] 124; [2] 126
Jekoliah	109
Jekuthiel	129
Jemimah	200
Jemuel	39, 53
Jephthah	63
Jephunneh	[1] 50; [2] 141
Jerah	20
Jerahmeel	[1] 122; [2] 155; [3] 207
Jered	129
Jeremai	178
Jeremiah	[1] 118; [2] 133; [3] 150; [4] 151; [5] 151; prophet [6] 167; [7] 187; [8] 193; [9] 206
Jeremoth	[1] 138; [2] 142; [3] 178; [4] 178; [5] 178
Jeriah	153
Jeribai	150
Jeriel	138
Jerimoth	[1] 138; [2] 150; [3] 154; [4] 155; [5] 158; [6] 160; [7] 165
Jerioth	122
Jeroboam	Jeroboam I [1] 98; Jeroboam II [2] 168
Jeroham	[1] 67; [2] 143; [3] 144; [4] 145; [5] 151; [6] 159; [7] 163
Jerub-Baal	61
Jerub-Besheth	61
Jerusha	110
Jesarelah	155
Jeshaiah	[1] 127; [2] 155; [3] 157; [4] 174; [5] 175; [6] 189

Joezer	151
Jogli	55
Joha	[1] 142; [2] 149
Johanan	tried to warn Gedaliah [1] 120; [2] 126; [3] 127; [4] 134; [5] 150; [6] 151; [7] 174; [8] 193
John	the Baptist [1] 222; Jesus' disciple, writer of Gospel and letters [2] 224; father of Simon Peter and Andrew [3] 225; [4] 235; John Mark, cousin of Barnabas [5] 237; [Ap] 255
John Mark	*See* John[5]
John the Baptist	*See* John[1]
Joiada	[1] 180; [2] 191
Joiakim	191
Joiarib	[1] 175; [2] 188; [3] 189
Jokim	130
Jokshan	26
Joktan	19
Jonadab	[1] 85; [2] 106
Jonah	the prophet [1] 214; [2] 225
Jonam	231
Jonathan	young Levite [1] 65; Saul's son [2] 71; Abiathar's son [3] 86; [4] 89; [5] 90; [6] 123; [7] 159; [8] 160; [9] 174; [10] 176; [11] 191; [12] 192; [13] 193; [14] 208; [15] 208; [Ap] 255
Jorah	170
Jorai	132
Joram	[1] 83; Israel's king [2] 105; [3] 157
Jorim	231
Jorkeam	123
Josek	230
Joseph	Jacob's son [1] 33; [2] 51; [3] 155; [4] 178; [5] 192; Mary's husband [6] 220; [7] 224; Jesus' brother [8] 225; of Arimathea [9] 226; [10] 229; [11] 231; [12] 234; Barnabas [13] 235
Joses	224
Joshah	131
Joshaphat	[1] 149; [2] 152
Joshaviah	150
Joshbekashah	155
Josheb-Basshebeth	89
Joshibiah	131
Joshua	Nun's son [1] 46; [2] 69; [3] 167; [4] 230
Josiah	Judah's king [1] 98; [2] 216
Josiphiah	174
Jotham	Gideon's son [1] 62; Judah's king [2] 109; [3] 125

Jozabad	[1] 107; [2] 150; [3] 151; [4] 151; [5] 165; [6] 167; [7] 175; [8] 177; [9] 177; [10] 186
Jozadak	134
Jubal	17
Judah	son of Jacob and Leah [1] 31; [2] 177; [3] 189; [4] 191; [5] 193; [6] 194; [7] 231
Judas	Iscariot [1] 225; Jesus' brother [2] 225; [3] 224; Galilean [4] 235; [5] 236; Judas Barsabbas [6] 238
Judas Maccabeus	[Ap] 255
Jude	251
Judith	28; [Ap] 254
Julia	244
Julius	242
Junia	243
Junias	*See* Junia
Jushab-Hesed	127
Justus	234
Kadmiel	[1] 170; [2] 187
Kalkol	93
Kallai	193
Karkas	196
Kareah	120
Karmi	[1] 39; [2] 58
Karshena	196
Kedar	27
Kedemah	27
Kedorlaomer	23
Keilah	130
Kelaiah	177
Kelal	178
Kelita	[1] 177; [2] 186
Kelub	[1] 128; [2] 159
Keluhi	178
Kemuel	[1] 25; [2] 55; [3] 158
Kenaanah	[1] 104; [2] 139
Kenan	17
Kenani	152
Kenaniah	[1] 152; [2] 157
Kenaz	[1] 35; [2] 37; [3] 59; [4] 129
Keran	36
Keren-Happuch	200
Keros	171

Mahseiah	206
Makbannai	151
Makbenah	125
Maki	51
Makir	Manasseh's son [1] 41; Ammiel's son [2] 84
Maknadebai	178
Malachi	216
Malchus	233
Malkam	142
Malkiel	40
Malkijah	[1] 137; [2] 145; [3] 154; [4] 177; [5] 177; [6] 178; [7] 182; [8] 184; [9] 185; [10] 187; [11] 195; [12] 208
Malkiram	126
Malki-Shua	71
Mallothi	155
Malluch	*See* Malluk
Malluk	[1] 138; [2] 178; [3] 178; [4] 187; [5] 187
Mamre	23
Manaen	238
Manahath	36
Manasseh	Joseph's son [1] 38; Judah's king [2] 116; [3] 178; [4] 178
Manoah	64
Maoch	*See* Maok
Maok	78
Maon	125
Marduk-Baladan	115
Mareshah	[1] 124; [2] 130
Mark	*See* John[5] Mark
Marsena	196
Martha	232
Mary	Jesus' mother [1] 221; Magdalene [2] 226; mother of James and John [3] 226; sister of Lazarus and Martha [4] 232; John Mark's mother [5] 237; [6] 243
Massa	27
Matred	37
Matri	71
Mattan	[1] 107; [2] 208
Mattaniah	Judah's last king [1] 119; Mika's son [2] 146; Heman's son [3] 155; [4] 162; Elam's descendant [5] 177; [6] 178; [7] 178; [8] 178; [9] 191; [10] 194; [11] 195
Mattatha	231
Mattathias	[1] 229; [2] 230; [Ap] 255
Mattattah	178

Mattenai	[1] 178; [2] 178; [3] 192
Matthan	220
Matthat	[1] 229; [2] 231
Matthew	224
Matthias	235
Mattithiah	[1] 147; [2] 152; [3] 155; [4] 179; [5] 185
Medad	50
Medan	26
Mehetabel	[1] 37; [2] 184
Mehida	171
Mehir	128
Mehujael	16
Mehuman	196
Melatiah	180
Melchizedek	24
Melea	231
Melek	117
Melki	[1] 229; [2] 230
Memucan	*See* Memukan
Memukan	196
Menahem	109
Menna	231
Meonothai	129
Mephibosheth	Jonathan's son [1] 80; Saul's son [2] 88
Merab	71
Meraiah	191
Meraioth	[1] 134; [2] 145
Merari	39
Mered	129
Meremoth	[1] 175; [2] 178; [3] 187
Meres	196
Merib-Baal	80
Merodach-Baladan	*See* Marduk-Baladan
Mesha	Moab's king [1] 105; [2] 124; [3] 142
Meshach	211
Meshech	*See* Meshek
Meshek	[1] 18; [2] 19
Meshelemiah	[1] 147; [2] 156
Meshezabel	[1] 180; [2] 187; [3] 191
Meshillemith	146
Meshillemoth	[1] 164; [2] 190
Meshobab	131

Meshullam	[1] 117; [2] 126; [3] 132; [4] 142; [5] 144; [6] 145; [7] 145; [8] 146; [9] 166; [10] 175; [11] 176; [12] 178; [13] 180; [14] 180; [15] 185; [16] 187; [17] 187; [18] 191; [19] 192; [20] 193; [21] 193
Meshullemeth	116
Methuselah	17
Methushael	16
Meunim	171
Me-Zahab	37
Mibhar	149
Mibsam	[1] 27; [2] 130
Mibzar	37
Mica	See Mika
Micah	from Ephraim [1] 65; [2] 84; [3] 132; [4] 154; prophet [5] 214; [6] 117
Micaiah	warned Ahab [1] 103; [2] 117; [3] 161; [4] 194; [5] 194; [6] 206
Michael	[1] 51; [2] 132; [3] 133; [4] 137; [5] 138; [6] 142; [7] 151; [8] 158; [9] 162; [10] 174; archangel [11] 212
Michal	71
Midian	26
Mijamin	[1] 154; [2] 177; [3] 187
Mika	[1] 84; [2] 146; [3] 187
Mikloth	[1] 143; [2] 157
Mikneiah	152
Mikri	145
Milalai	194
Milcah	See Milkah
Milkah	[1] 22; Zelophehad's daughter [2] 54
Miniamin	[1] 166; [2] 192; [3] 194
Miriam	Moses' sister [1] 46; [2] 129
Mirmah	142
Mishael	[1] 44; [2] 185; [3] 211
Misham	142
Mishma	[1] 27; [2] 131
Mishmannah	151
Mispar	168
Mispereth	168
Mithredath	Cyrus's treasurer [1] 167; [2] 172
Mizraim	See Egypt
Mizzah	35
Mnason	241
Moab	25
Moadiah	191

Parnach	*See* Parnak
Parnak	56
Parosh	168
Parshandatha	198
Paruah	92
Pasach	*See* Pasak
Pasak	140
Paseah	[1] 128; [2] 171; [3] 180
Pashhur	Malkijah's son in Jeremiah [1] 145; head of priestly family [2] 170; [3] 187; [4] 208
Patrobas	244
Paul	*See* Saul[2]/Paul
Pedahel	56
Pedahzur	48
Pedaiah	[1] 118; [2] 126; [3] 158; [4] 183; [5] 185; [6] 188; [7] 195
Pekah	110
Pekahiah	110
Pelaiah	[1] 127; [2] 186
Pelaliah	189
Pelatiah	[1] 127; [2] 131; [3] 187; [4] 210
Peleg	19
Pelet	[1] 125; [2] 150
Peleth	[1] 52; [2] 123
Peninnah	68
Penuel	[1] 127; [2] 142
Peresh	139
Perez	38
Perida	171
Persis	244
Peruda	171
Peter	223
Pethahiah	[1] 154; [2] 177; [3] 191
Pethuel	213
Peullethai	156
Phanuel	229
Pharaohs	23
Phicol	[1] 25; [2] 28
Philemon	249
Philetus	248
Philip	Jesus' disciple from Bethsaida [1] 224; Herodias's husband [2] 225; tetrarch [3] 229; evangelist [4] 235
Philologus	224
Phinehas	son of Eleazar the priest [1] 45; Eli's son [2] 68; [3] 175

Rufus	[1] 227; [2] 244
Ruth	66
Sabta	19
Sabtah	19
Sabteka	19
Sacar	*See* Sakar
Sakar	[1] 90; [2] 156
Sakia	142
Sallai	189
Sallu	[1] 144; [2] 191
Salma	126
Salmon	67
Salome	at Jesus' crucifixion [1] 227; Herodias's daughter [2] 222
Salu	53
Samlah	37
Samson	64
Samuel	68
Sanballat	179
Saph	88
Sapphira	235
Sarah	22; [Ap] 254
Sarai	22
Saraph	130
Sargon	202
Satan	251
Saul	Israel's king [1] 70; Paul [2] 236
Sceva	239
Seba	19
Secundus	240
Segub	[1] 101; [2] 122
Seir	36
Seled	123
Semakiah	156
Semein	230
Sennacherib	114
Seorim	154
Serah	40
Seraiah	[1] 83; [2] 120; [3] 120; [4] 128; [5] 131; [6] 168; [7] 187; [8] 189; [9] 207; read scroll in Jeremiah [10] 209
Sered	40
Sergius Paulus	238

Serug	20
Seth	17
Sethur	50
Shaaph	[1] 125; [2] 125
Shaashgaz	197
Shabbethai	[1] 177; [2] 186
Shadrach	211
Shagee	89
Shaharaim	142
Shallum	Israel's king [1] 109; [2] 117; Judah's king, Jehoahaz [3] 118; [4] 124; [5] 130; [6] 134; [7] 147; [8] 147; [9] 147; [10] 164; [11] 177; [12] 178; [13] 181; [14] 206
Shallun	182
Shalmai	171
Shalman	213
Shalmaneser	113
Shama	149
Shamgar	60
Shamhuth	157
Shamir	154
Shamma	141
Shammah	[1] 35; [2] 73; [3] 89; [4] 89
Shammai	[1] 123; [2] 125; [3] 129
Shammoth	89
Shammua	[1] 50; [2] 81; [3] 190; [4] 192
Shamsherai	142
Shapham	132
Shaphan	[1] 116; [2] 210
Shaphat	[1] 50; [2] 103; [3] 127; [4] 132; [5] 160
Sharai	178
Sharar	90
Sharezer	[1] 115; [2] 216
Shashai	178
Shashak	142
Shaul	[1] 37; [2] 39; [3] 135
Shavsha	83
Sheal	178
Shealtiel	126
Sheariah	143
Shear-Jashub	202
Sheba	[1] 19; [2] 20; [3] 26; [4] 88; [5] 132
Shebaniah	[1] 152; [2] 187; [3] 187; [4] 187
Sheber	125

Shebna	114
Shecaniah	*See* Shekaniah
Shechem	raped Dinah [1] 34; [2] 54; [3] 139
Shedeur	47
Sheerah	140
Shehariah	142
Shekaniah	[1] 127; [2] 154; [3] 166; [4] 173; [5] 173; [6] 176; [7] 183; [8] 184; [9] 191
Shelah	[1] 19; [2] 38
Shelemiah	[1] 156; [2] 178; [3] 178; [4] 183; [5] 195; [6] 207; [7] 207; [8] 207; [9] 208
Sheleph	20
Shelesh	141
Shelomi	56
Shelomith	[1] 47; [2] 126; [3] 153; [4] 157; [5] 160; [6] 174
Shelomoth	[1] 153; [2] 154
Shelumiel	48
Shem	18
Shema	[1] 125; [2] 132; [3] 142; [4] 185
Shemaah	150
Shemaiah	prophet to Rehoboam [1] 96; [2] 127; [3] 131; [4] 132; [5] 146; [6] 146; [7] 151; [8] 154; [9] 156; [10] 161; [11] 166; [12] 166; [13] 174; [14] 175; [15] 177; [16] 178; [17] 183; [18] 184; [19] 187; [20] 193; [21] 193; [22] 194; [23] 195; [24] 204; false prophet in Jeremiah [25] 205; [26] 206
Shemariah	[1] 150; [2] 160; [3] 178; [4] 178
Shemeber	23
Shemed	142
Shemer	[1] 100; [2] 138
Shemida	54
Shemiramoth	[1] 152; [2] 161
Shemuel	55
Shenazzar	126
Shephatiah	[1] 80; [2] 145; [3] 150; [4] 157; [5] 162; [6] 168; [7] 171; [8] 188; [9] 208
Shepho	36
Shephuphan	[1] 40; [2] 141
Sherebiah	[1] 175; [2] 185
Sheresh	139
Sheshai	51
Sheshan	123
Sheshbazzar	167
Shethar	196
Shethar-Bozenai	172

Shuham	40
Shuni	40
Shupham	54
Shuppim	156
Shuthelah	[1] 54; [2] 140
Sia	171
Siaha	171
Sibbecai	*See* Sibbekai
Sibbekai	88
Sidon	19
Sihon	52
Silas	238
Silvanus	238
Simeon	Jacob's son [1] 30; saw baby Jesus as Messiah [2] 229; [3] 231; Antioch prophet and teacher [4] 238; [Ap] 255
Simon	Simon Peter [1] 223; the Zealot [2] 224; [3] 225; Bethany leper [4] 226; of Cyrene [5] 226; Pharisee [6] 231; [7] 233; sorcerer [8] 236; tanner [9] 237; [Ap] 255
Simon Peter	*See* Simon[1]
Sippai	88
Sisera	army commander [1] 60; [2] 171
Sismai	124
Sithri	44
So	113
Soco	*See* Soko
Sodi	51
Soko	129
Solomon	81
Sopater	240
Sophereth	171
Sosipater	244
Sosthenes	239
Sotai	171
Stachys	244
Stephanas	245
Stephen	235
Suah	141
Susanna	232; [Ap] 255
Susi	51
Syntyche	246
Tabaliah	156
Tabbaoth	171

Timna	[1] 35; [2] 37
Timon	236
Timothy	247
Tiras	18
Tirhakah	115
Tirhanah	125
Tiria	129
Tirzah	54
Titius Justus	239
Titus	249
Toah	67
Tob-Adonijah	161
Tobiah	[1] 171; Ammonite official [2] 179
Tobias	[Ap] 253
Tobijah	[1] 161; [2] 216
Tobit	[Ap] 253
Togarmah	18
Tohu	67
Tokhath	117
Tola	[1] 40; [2] 63
Tou	83
Trophimus	240
Tryphena	244
Tryphosa	244
Tubal	18
Tubal-Cain	17
Tychicus	240
Tyrannus	239
Uel	178
Ulam	[1] 139; [2] 144
Ulla	141
Unni	[1] 152; [2] 191
Ur	148
Urbanus	243
Uri	[1] 47; [2] 93; [3] 177
Uriah	Hittite, Bathsheba's husband [1] 85; priest in Ahaz's reign [2] 111; [3] 175; [4] 185; prophet from Kiriath Jearim [5] 204
Uriel	[1] 135; [2] 151; [3] 161
Uthai	[1] 144; [2] 174
Uz	[1] 19; [2] 25; [3] 36
Uzai	183

Uzal	20
Uzza	[1] 116; [2] 141; [3] 171
Uzzah	touched the ark [1] 82; [2] 136
Uzzi	[1] 133; [2] 138; [3] 138; [4] 145; [5] 191; [6] 192; [7] 195
Uzzia	149
Uzziah	Judah's king [1] 108; [2] 135; [3] 159; [4] 177; [5] 188
Uzziel	Kohath's son [1] 44; [2] 131; [3] 138; [4] 155; [5] 165; [6] 181
Vaizatha	198
Vaniah	178
Vashti	195
Vophsi	51
Xerxes	Persian king [1] 171; Darius's father [2] 212
Zaavan	36
Zabad	*See* Jozabad[1]; [1] 107; [2] 123; [3] 140; [4] 149; [5] 178; [6] 178; [7] 179
Zabbai	[1] 178; [2] 182
Zabdi	[1] 142; [2] 159; [3] 190
Zabdiel	[1] 157; [2] 190
Zabud	92
Zaccai	*See* Zakkai
Zacchaeus	232
Zaccur	*See* Zakkur
Zadok	priest [1] 83; [2] 110; [3] 134; [4] 145; [5] 158; [6] 180; [7] 183; [8] 187; [9] 195; [10] 220
Zaham	160
Zakkai	169
Zakkur	[1] 50; [2] 131; [3] 155; [4] 155; [5] 174; [6] 180; [7] 187; [8] 195
Zalaph	183
Zalmon	90
Zalmunna	62
Zanoah	129
Zaphenath-Paneah	33
Zattu	168
Zaza	123
Zebadiah	[1] 142; [2] 142; [3] 151; [4] 156; [5] 157; [6] 161; Judah's leader [7] 162; [8] 174; [9] 177
Zebah	62
Zebedee	223

Alphabetical List of Names

Zebidah	118
Zebina	179
Zebul	63
Zebulun	33
Zechariah	Israel's king [1] 108; [2] 113; [3] 132; [4] 143; [5] 147; [6] 152; [7] 152; [8] 155; [9] 156; [10] 159; [11] 161; [12] 162; [13] 162; [14] 163; [15] 165; [16] 166; prophet after exile [17] 216; [18] 173; [19] 174; [20] 175; [21] 177; [22] 185; [23] 188; [24] 188; [25] 190; [26] 192; [27] 193; [28] 194; [29] 202; John the Baptist's father [30] 228
Zedekiah	prophet to Ahab and Jehoshaphat [1] 104; Judah's last king [2] 119; [3] 126; [4] 187; [5] 205; [6] 207
Zeeb	62
Zeker	143
Zelek	91
Zelophehad	54
Zemirah	138
Zenas	249
Zephaniah	[1] 120; [2] 137; [3] 204; prophet during Josiah's reign [4] 215; [5] 216
Zepho	35
Zephon	40
Zerah	[1] 35; [2] 36; brother of Perez [3] 38; [4] 135; [5] 137; [6] 161
Zerahiah	[1] 134; [2] 173
Zeresh	198
Zereth	128
Zeri	155
Zeror	70
Zeruah	96
Zerubbabel	126
Zeruiah	77
Zetham	153
Zethan	139
Zethar	196
Zia	132
Ziba	84
Zibeon	[1] 35; [2] 35
Zibia	142
Zibiah	107
Zicri	*See* Zikri
Ziha	[1] 171; [2] 190
Zikri	[1] 44; [2] 142; [3] 142; [4] 142; [5] 146; [6] 157; [7] 157; [8] 161; [9] 163; [10] 164; [11] 189; [12] 192

Zillah	17
Zillethai	[1] 142; [2] 151
Zilpah	30
Zimmah	[1] 134; [2] 137; [3] 165
Zimran	26
Zimri	killed by Phinehas [1] 53; [2] 58; Israel's king [3] 99; [4] 143
Ziph	[1] 124; [2] 129
Ziphah	129
Zippor	52
Zipporah	42
Ziza	[1] 131; [2] 153; [3] 160
Zohar	[1] 26; [2] 39; [3] 128
Zoheth	130
Zophah	141
Zophai	135
Zophar	199
Zuar	48
Zuph	67
Zur	[1] 53; [2] 143
Zuriel	49
Zurishaddai	48